An Introduction to World Cinema

SECOND EDITION

An Introduction to World Cinema

SECOND EDITION

ARISTIDES GAZETAS

McFarland & Company, Inc., Publishers
Jefferson, North Carolina, and London

All photographs provided by the Film Stills Archive
of the Museum of Modern Art, New York, N.Y.

LIBRARY OF CONGRESS CATALOGUING-IN-PUBLICATION DATA

Gazetas, Aristides, 1930–
An introduction to world cinema / Aristides Gazetas.— 2nd ed.
p.   cm.
Includes bibliographical references and index.

ISBN 978-0-7864-3907-2
softcover : 50# alkaline paper ∞

1. Motion pictures—History.   2. Motion pictures.   I. Title.
PN1993.5.A1G39   2008   791.4309 — dc22   2008009405

British Library cataloguing data are available

On the cover: Film stills (center) *À bout de souffle*, 1960;
(clockwise from top left) *Ladri di biciclette*, 1948; *Bronenosets Potyomkin*, 1925;
Shichinin no samurai 1954; *L'année dernière à Marienbad*, 1961;
Det sjunde inseglet, 1957; *Das Cabinet des Dr. Caligari*, 1920;
Die Blechtrommel, 1979; background ©2008 Creatas Images

Manufactured in the United States of America

McFarland & Company, Inc., Publishers
Box 611, Jefferson, North Carolina 28640
www.mcfarlandpub.com

To my children,
Michael, Sophie and Calliope,
for their continual sharing of
the wonderful world of motion pictures

Contents

Preface

The last century may be distinguished by the remarkable emergence of an industry based upon the invention of cinema. Using this invention, film became a kinetic art form following the unique abilities of the motion picture camera in effect to spatialize time, and dynamize space. The roots of motion pictures were formed in the popular culture of comic strips and dime-store novels. Film directors appropriated these popular cultural forms and reconstituted them into powerful narratives that still have the capacity to generate what we might call "lived experiences" for the viewer. By linking motion picture technology to serious narrative forms, entrepreneurs from different countries produced a variety of film narratives that included not only utopian dreams but disasters as well.

Early cinema developed into a global industry from the start of the 20th century with the exchange of short films between Europe and other countries of the world, thanks to the efforts of the Lumière brothers. Filmmakers were quick to exploit the socio-political context in narratives designed to move and thrill their audience, making film one of the most powerful ideological media of our times.

The power of films to inform and influence viewers is recognized today by the emergence of independent filmmakers who pursue the practices of Third Cinema. Using the new film technology, they depart from the earlier Hollywood studio system and its establishment of First Cinema and borrow techniques from the European tradition of auteurs and Second Cinema. Third Cinema filmmakers explore their own histories of colonialism and displacement, and the politics of representation as part of a postcolonial deconstruction. For these new filmmakers, the vital importance of their craft resides in film's ability to bring into the public sphere images that carry different voices in narratives, voices that were marginalized and hidden by the hegemony of First Cinema.

An Introduction to World Cinema starts from the time of the Impressionists—the time, too, when photography began to exert an influence upon the art world, forcing artists to view the world differently. Chapters move from country to country as they consider the development of different cinematic concepts in the making of a film narrative. Within each chapter these concepts are connected to short introductions of important philosophical and literary texts that interact with chosen film narratives at that particular time in history. Hence, film narratives cited in each chapter should be understood as an interpretation of a particular cultural construct or world view represented by the directors at that time.

Supplementary critical essays follow certain chapters. The essays provide different points of view on how particular directors understood and used the film medium. Further, the essays provide the reader with several theoretical frameworks for an understanding of the cinema since each essay examines the ways film narratives communicate values, beliefs and attitudes toward a resolution of a dramatic plot. Also, they explore certain unresolved conflicts relating to power, gender, and the social-political actions of groups that remain hidden within a narrative.

This book is intended as both a historical review of major films produced over the past hundred years and collection of cultural insights into film theory and practice. The aim is to unravel the ideological constructs woven into many action-adventures, comedies, westerns, romances, and other film genres. These films reflect a pattern of facts and events embedded within the context of a film narrative, revealing other texts and voices through the use of cinematic codes, special effects and subject positionings, which informs us to what we call "history."

The second edition of *An Introduction to World Cinema* is distinguished by the addition of two new chapters. Chapter 27 introduces the emergence of a group of young Canadian filmmakers, led by David Cronenberg, that follow a series of transgressive film narratives starting in the 1980s. The films emphasize an ability by such directors to dramatize the effects of changing sexual identities when caught in the light of the new social and political situations of today. Every transgressive film follows the ability of such directors to reconstitute the rise in changing sexual dynamics into violent conflicts that have the capacity to generate what we might call "lived experiences" for the viewer. By linking motion pictures to such serious narrative forms, Canadian film directors from different countries produce a variety of film narratives that include not only utopian dreams but political disasters as well. Such film narratives are reviewed, starting with Rozema's *I've Heard the Mermaids Singing* (1987) and conclude with *The History of Violence* (2005) by David Cronenberg.

A number of key films followed in the wake of Rozema's remarkable success with *Mermaids*—Egoyan's *Speaking Parts, The Adjuster* and *Exotica,* Bruce Macdonald's *Roadkill* and *Highway 61,* and John Greyson's *Zero Patience.*

The power of these films to inform and influence viewers is recognized today by the emergence of yearly film festivals where Canadian directors such as Atom Egoyan, Denys Arcand, David Cronenberg and a new group of independent filmmakers pursue the practices of Third Cinema.

In Chapter 28, the new final chapter, we discover the filmmakers who re-enter a film narrative to explore the spaces between reality and illusion, self and other.

The power of such films to inform and influence viewers concerning a generation of war strategies is recognized today by the emergence of independent filmmakers who pursue the practices of Third Cinema. Using new film technology, they transform each film into powerful motion pictures. Such dramatic films are melodramatic in their reconstruction and depiction of "actualities of lived experiences." Today new forms of terrorism located in various countries throughout the world continue to emerge following the patterns of war communicated to viewers challenging the master narratives in the exposure of such films to postmodern audiences today.

Thus, this second edition of *World Cinema* continues the study and analysis of narrative films as they emerge with emphasis on acts of terrorism as depicted in D.W. Griffith's *Birth of a Nation* (1915). This film displays acts of violence during the Civil War years and into the turbulent Reconstruction period and is followed by the new objectivity of G.W. Pabst as he explores the decadence and amorality that existed in the middle classes of Germany as found in his film *Pandora's Box* (1929).

In the 1930s, Eisenstein directed *Alexander Nevsky* (1938), which was filmed during the Stalinist period in Russia. This film warned the Soviet people of the oncoming German aggression leading to World War II. In France Jean Renoir's *The Crime of Monsieur Lange* (1935) displays a mise-en-scène that develops a social action towards a common goal for a group known as the Popular Front.

After the end of World War II a new political situation emerged in Germany where a number of young German filmmakers protested against the government and their strict reaction to terrorism and a police state. Thus the War Against Terrorism becomes a permanent struggle for such narrative films, one of which is entitled *Marianne and Juliane* (1981), where two sisters plan to take action against the state after learning about German violence and terror after World War II.

Today there are new shifts toward a cultural politics, one that becomes central to certain film narratives which re-enter the spaces between reality and illusion, self and other, fact and fiction in an imaginary play of power politics to reconsider acts of terrorism. Thus, by gaining an awareness of the cinematic genres used by most filmmakers viewers and readers alike gain a better understanding of several key concepts such as culture, ideology, ethics and aesthetics. They also can question why film directors choose particular myths and stories to contest "the already given" in a post-modern society where acts of terrorism are brought into play through such motion pictures.

This text was written mostly from lectures for my Film 330 course for the Department of Theatre and Film at the University of British Columbia. In 1993, the lectures became the basis for a course manual that complemented a 24-part film series produced by UBC Access in collaboration with the Open Learning Agency.

My debt of gratitude goes to Mark Bullen and Beth Hawkes of UBC Access for their editorial support and guidance. Also many thanks to John Wright, chairman of the Department of Theatre and Film, for directing each introductory segment of the program for television. Special mentions go to Joanne Gould and Sophie Peerless for their intelligent and careful readings of the text, and to Raul Inglis for his work on the second edition.

Introduction

Double Reflections: The Art and Politics of Motion Pictures

An understanding of film and its history depends upon the interplay of two significant characteristics. The first is an awareness of the structural design or form of the audio-visual elements employed by filmmakers and how they give these elements meaning and relative expressiveness. This may be called the aesthetic dimension. The second is a consideration of why people were depicted in the past in different situations and places in relation to the myths and ideologies that informed them about themselves and their contemporary world. This may be called the historic dimension. As historical perspectives shift from generation to generation, life experiences and beliefs embedded in these past periods will reveal familiar traits and actions that define the visual and aural spectacle as a mode of representation. These vary as to accuracy and verisimilitude as the filmmaker chooses definite images in this re-creation of past narratives for present-day audiences.

Thus, to interpret a particular film one must consider not only the artistic sensibilities and point of view of the director, but also the social and political character of the period under depiction. These two frames of reference unite the director's command of film techniques within a genre or constructual base with a personal or ideological narrative. Belief systems, found in any social, economic and political circumstance, are incorporated invisibly within every film narrative, exerting an influence on character motivations and personalities.

The industrial revolution in the 19th century opened new frontiers for the study of modern culture through the technology of photography and its development into motion pictures. With the birth of the cinema, early pioneers of motion pictures realized the power of this new technology. Film images not only gave spectators a subjective perceptual experience of viewing "reality" but it also provided a film experience whose uniqueness gave meaning and expression to new ways of seeing and interpreting any cultural event or discourse. When accompanied by written statements about historical and personalities, motion pictures, as an art form, recounted and reconstructed the "actualities of lived experience." Motion pictures became a commercial industry in the early 1900s as Edwin S. Porter and D.W. Griffith transformed them into dramatic film narratives. By 1915, after the nickelodeon age of experimentation, such dramatic narrative films like *The Birth of a Nation*, directed by D.W. Griffith, received public and critical acclaim for the narrative power of motion pictures. Although this powerful historic reconstruction of the American Civil War was brought to life by the technology of motion pictures, it also communicated a strong mythological discourse that posed challenges for a modern industrial society as to Griffith's interpretation of the significance of this historical age.

Griffith's melodramatic master narrative depicted the stress of war on human relationships torn apart by his reconstruction of the War Between the States. However, his version of the war aroused violent public reactions in Northern cities like New York and Boston. In fact, the Boston branch of the NAACP along with numerous public figures challenged Griffith's demeaning portrayal of African-Americans and his racist thoughts on the evils of miscegenation. They argued that the film presented the Ku Klux Klan as white emancipators of Southern honor; and that Griffith, as director, grounded his film with biblical messages advocating an evangelical mission. Civil action groups called for censorship of the film in every Northern city it was exhibited. A U.S. Supreme Court decision in 1916 responded to this controversy. The court ruled that motion pictures were industrial products outside the guarantees to freedom of speech. State censorship boards thus could prevent motion picture distribution and screenings (Mast 1981, p. 123).

Framework for the Text

What is at issue here? In any historical dramatization of the past, as in films like *Birth of a Nation*, do today's audiences question whether a film's narrative functions as propaganda within a cultural context? Do personal encounters with film narratives, whether at home or at the local cinema, appear to change a viewer's perception of the world and, more importantly, of themselves? How do such films appear to question or become "subversive of existing values, institutions, mores and taboos?" (Vogel 1974, p. 9). If the cinema, as Vogel argues, "is a place of magic where the psychological and environmental factors combine to create an openness to wonder and suggestion, then, how do they express values, beliefs and attitudes to influence viewer interaction emotionally with imagining selves and others?"

Some Characteristics of Film History

Motion pictures are one of the most important art forms, if not the most important, that developed in the 20th century, along with the psychological novel and the Theatre of the Absurd. In stating this position, we recognize the fact that motion pictures have revealed and reflected the joys and hopes of the modern in-dustrial society as well as the anguish, turmoil, and destructiveness created by different warring ideologies. In both instances, a history of film or motion pictures have shown a power and a pervasiveness to slowly influence and change our concepts of ourselves and others. For some countries, motion pictures have served as a cultural ambassador to bring about mutual understanding and respect. For other countries, they have become an ideological weapon to easily propagandize half-truths and deceptions.

From its beginning as a scientific instrument to make visual recordings as documents of life and to demonstrate animal and human behavior, motion pictures slowly advanced through various technological devices. These devices helped advance scientific knowledge and opened up many new possibilities for industrial progress during the 19th century. The developments achieved by the early cinematic cameras of Edison and Lumière could order or structure "reality" in manifold ways. The advent of cinema also coincided with revolutionary theories on time and space by Albert Einstein that shattered the world picture devised by Newtonian physics. Further, the advent of motion pictures paralleled the publication of Sigmund Freud's *The Interpretation of Dreams* (1900) and his inquiry into the power of the unconscious motives underlying cultural constructs of people's lives and indirectly influencing their beliefs and value systems.

An Introduction of World Cinema covers a broad survey of films and filmmakers, from the first exhibition in 1895 of a photographic technology that recorded moving images of actual events to the rapid commercial expansion and development into longer film narratives. At first, filmmakers borrowed stage practices from the melodramatic Victorian theatre before they found their own techniques of storytelling. By the 1920s, silent films developed into a major cultural product as innovations from the Modernist avant-garde movements were incorporated into new forms of cinematic structures by both American and European directors.

This book thus centers upon the important films and filmmakers of the past and present as they continue to influence one another by using various narrative techniques for filmmaking. Although there continues to be a diversity of approaches, a radical change has been made in the understanding and interpretation of motion pictures since May 1968. This moment in history openly challenged the accepted belief system of the Western powers, and other belief systems were advanced to redefine societal goals and relationships. Narrative films produced during this period were marked by radical changes from the classical Hollywood texts bringing to the fore a critique of modernism and a late modern period known as the "postmodern condition." This postmodern condition now advances critiques on Modernism, offering different definitions, standards and relationships between film and technology, film and ideology, and narrative film and its role as a shaper of contemporary society.

Through an understanding and interpretation of a number of key concepts such as culture, ideology, technology, aesthetics and others, narrative films are studied not as a direct reflection of "reality" but as a cinematic construct of a filmmaker who consciously shapes various film narratives into personalized texts. By gaining an awareness of the cinematic structures and forms used by filmmakers, this book strives for an understanding of how filmmakers represent people in their films and why they chose to recount particular myths or stories as they contest "the already given" and they interrogate the meta-narratives that stand as historical "truths." Thus while adhering to a chronology of time, today's postmodern films engage the viewer with a fusion of the past and present, reconstituting the ways memory and imagination validate their own narrative films. This revisioning of the past into the present becomes a significant strategy for today's filmmakers. Luis Buñuel, the Spanish surrealist director, states, "I strive for a cinema that will give me an integral vision of reality; it will increase my knowledge of things and beings, and will open to me the marvelous world of the unknown, which I can neither read about in the daily press nor find in the street" (Buñuel 1962).

The Crisis in Representation and the Politics of Difference

The narrative analysis and interpretation to be used in this text arises in response to the "crisis of representation" (Jameson 1984, p. vii). This crisis emerges from the challenge to the positivist paradigm by Jean-François Lyotard in his book, *The Postmodern Condition* (1984). Lyotard argues that science does not simply consist of a neutral body of knowledge claims about the world but rather "produces a discourse of legitimation with respect to its own status, a discourse called philosophy." Lyotard states that the postmodern involves "an incredulity toward metanarratives" (p. xxii–xxiv), and conceives of knowledge as paralogical; that is, as searching for and creating instabilities in the dominant perspectives of the world.

Narrative theory becomes a part of the postmodern voice that orientates itself through "little narratives" (*petit recits*) as an alternative way of making knowledge claims about the social world we live in. Accordingly, Lyotard conceives of "a postmodern sensibility" as one which continually critiques any foundational conception of knowledge. Therefore narrative theory recognizes the open-ended nature of knowledge claims. It examines the shifting terrain of meaning that makes up the social/political world and acknowledges the difficulty of making any universal claims concerning the nature of the human condition. It also acknowledges that as researchers and theorists we are never neutral observers of behavior because of the role we play in the construction of the social reality in any narrative, large or small (Mumby 1993, p. 5).

Within this formation of a "dialogical production of discourse" emerges a "politics of difference," where the post-colonial world attempts to break free of Western hegemony and boundries of race, class, and gender. It rises again as part of the postmodern discourse, and is located for Lyotard within local narratives. This discourse is concerned as much with process as with ends (Westwood 1991, p. 49). What is crucial is that these local narratives have core connections to global concerns.

In an interview with Jonathan Rutherford for an article called *The Third Space* (1990) Homi Bhabha stated his reasons for examining the politics of difference, hybridity and displacement:

> My purpose in talking about cultural difference rather than cultural diversity is to acknowledge that this kind of liberal relativist perspective is inadequate in itself and does not generally recognize the universalist and normative stance from which it constructs its cultural and political judgments. With the concept of difference, which has its theoretical history in post-structural thinking, psychoanalysis (where difference is very resonant), post–Althusserian Marxism, and the exemplary work of Fanon, what I was attempting to do was to begin to see how the notion of the West itself or Western culture, its liberalism and relativism — these very potent mythologies of "progress" — also contain a cutting edge, a limit. With the notion of cultural difference, I try to place myself in the position of liminality, in that productive space of the construction of culture as difference, in the spirit of alterity or otherness [Rutherford 1990, p. 209].

For readers of this text, an understanding of the nature of narrative films today are dependent on the interplay of two significant post-structural discourses or characteristics. First is an awareness of the structural design or form of the audio/visual elements in the narrative film where the concept of difference is multifaceted, interlaced with contradictions, yet raises important questions about the social relations and possibilities for social visions in a contemporary electronic world. The second is recognition and consideration of why people are or were depicted in the past in different situations and places in relation to the myths or ideologies that inform them about themselves and the history of the contemporary world. This may be called an historic perspective or an engagement of a history of film through a "politics of difference." As historical perspectives shift from generation to generation, it will be noted throughout the text why a multiplicity of intertexual strategies are used to promote a play of irony, multiple identities and contra-

dictions that undermine or "deconstruct" the possibility for any "always already given" interpretation of cultural identity.

Thus the goal of understanding any narrative film and its history will depend upon the consideration not only of the artistic sensibilities and point of view of the director, but also upon the social and political character of the period under depiction. Also as a contemporary history text the reader will explore reasons why a postmodern position, associated with Lacan, Foucault, and Derrida, et al. extends notions of cultural narratives which offers alternative models for understanding the legacy of the cinema today. These positions are, of necessity, grounded upon our understanding not only of the artistic sensibilities and point of view of the director, but also the social and political character of the period under depiction. These two frames of reference unite the director's use of film techniques within a genre or constructural base with a personal or ideological narrative.

The goal of this text will be to explore the cinematic possibilities of all film narratives within the "politics of representation." The task of the reader will be to seek out the implications of a critical analysis and interpretation of any film discourse as it discloses the problems created by the mythic structures hidden in an "informational" late capitalist society. The concept of a narrative discourse will be located on two levels:

> [1] as a communication phenomenon that culturally constructs human identities and role-playing and, [2] as a social phenomenon that reinforces or challenges social identity [Mumby 1993, p. 2].

The text concentrates upon an interplay between popular culture, symbolic representations and the aural/visual cinematic practices as part of a "culture of difference." The readings will provide strategies for the development of new forms of critical awareness that expands the cognitive capacities of learners in reading and understanding media images from film and television that now saturates our culture. This book, *An Introduction to World Cinema*, seeks out those images which communicate specific identities and power relations. Such images inform the spectator of the basic assumptions and ideologies of a given historical age.

The Cinematization of Contemporary Life

Today, we are surrounded by a wealth of images produced through film and television that inform and persuade us about our "imaginary" selves in multiple forms of representation. This new world of electronic image-transmission became directly linked to how motion pictures mediate information about the world while advancing discourses about American involvement in postwar political indoctrination. In relation to television broadcasts, every film narrative makes a connection between the "reality" of the image (mimesis) and the cultural constructs of our society. Therefore, each narrative (diegesis) contains within its illusionistic framework a convincing power to reconstitute reality based upon actual events. When asked why some people believe in the power of cinema, the producer in Peter Weir's film *The Truman Show* (1998) responded, "We accept the reality of the world as it is presented to us. It is as simple as that." The implication of this cinematic situation, one hopes, forces the viewer to realize that illusions are part of our reality. This becomes the political condition of our lives, as Bertolt Brecht, the German playwright and essayist, declared during the 1920s (Wright 1989, p. 21).

Before the 1960s, little was written about films that related motion pictures to broader cultural or historical contexts. Today, however, reconsideration of the medium as a valid and respectable subject for research has been confirmed by the sociological writings of Norman K. Denzin (1991). Denzin distinguishes three features of "the cinematization of contemporary life" upon which our visual culture is grounded:

1. "Reality" is now a staged, social production.
2. The "real" is now judged against its staged cinematic-video counterpart (Baudrillard 1983, p. 152).
3. The postmodern society thus "becomes a cinematic, dramaturgical production transformed by representations of the 'real' through the images and meanings that flow from the cinema and TV." Therefore, the metaphor of art as ideology not only mirrors life, it structures and reproduces it. Denzin concludes that "the postmodern society is a dramaturgical society" (Denzin 1991, p.23).

As part of any analysis or interpretation of film history, it is important to identify the social and political discourses that carry the formative ideological frameworks governing the communication and exchange of ideas depicted in film narratives. The reason for the unmasking of these ideas reflects the assumption that most cultural constructs operate in society as a way of assigning predetermined social discourses over time. As Bill Nichols states, "Ideology uses the fabrication of images and the processes of representation to persuade us that how things are is how they ought to be and that the place provided for us is the place we ought to have" (Nichols 1981, p. 1).

In the 1990s, Hollywood produced a number of film narratives that attempted to deconstruct the power of cinema to "construct reality" for viewers. First on the scene was Lawrence McTiernan's *Last Action Hero* (1993), starring Arnold Schwarzenegger who plays a superhero who deconstructs his own film persona. Then came James Cameron's *True Lies* (1994), also starring Schwarzenegger, in a Bond-like action-adventure that deconstructs the hero when the narrative doubles as a romantic comedy. Peter Weir's *The Truman Show* (1998) convinces us that a television show houses a real-life community. In *Pleasantville* (1999), directed by Gary Ross, we watch two teenagers leave the 1990s and enter the world of the 1950s through a TV situation comedy. Once there, they help the people in this small town discover the joys of living out their lives in full color instead of a strict black and white community. More intent on satirizing the power of television was Barry Livingson's *Wag the Dog* (1997), a timely comedy starring Robert DeNiro as a political consultant who creates (via television) an illusory war with Albania to divert media attention from a presidential indiscretion with a young woman.

Before these films of the 1990s, the constuction of reality by television was seen in Hal Ashby's film *Being There* (1979). Peter Sellers stars as Chance, an imaginary character who learns about the outside world and other people through watching television. His "real" world consists of tending to his employer's interior garden, and his actions are confined to his room and his job of nurturing the garden. The narrative is a satirical modern retelling of Plato's Myth of the Cave. Images projected by firelight onto a wall inside a darkened cave become the reality for prisoners trapped in this cave. Metaphorically, the retelling of this myth by Kosinski exchanges projected firelight images for the television screen. This screen becomes the reality of the Other for Chance.

The "cinematization of contemporary life," as Denzin states, occurs when Chance is forced to vacate the security of the house and its garden when his benefactor dies. As in the cave metaphor, Chance is "dazzled" by the sunlight as he walks into the outside world, but he is not completely blinded. As Kosinski (1971) states in his book, "So far, everything outside the gate resembled what he had seen on TV; the images were burned in his mind. He had the feeling that he had seen it all" (p. 24). In this way *Being There* becomes a modern allegory about the death of God, the imaginary self and the politics of representation as part of the

"necessary illusions" required by every narrative created for a social and political order.

References

Baudrillard, Jean. 1983. *Simulations.* Translated by Paul Foss, Paul Patton and Philip Beitchman. New York: Semiotext(e).

Buñuel, Luis. 1962. "Cinema: An Instrument of Poetry." *Theatre Arts,* 46 (July 1962): 18–19.

Denzin, Norman K. 1991. *Images of Postmodern Society: Social Theory and Contemporary Cinema.* London: Sage Publications.

Jameson, Frederic. 1984. *Postmodernism, or the Cultural Logic of Late Capitalism.* New Left Review.

Kosinski, Jerzy. 1971. *Being There.* New York: Harcourt Brace Jovanovich.

Lyotard, Jean-François. 1984. *The Postmodern Condition.* Minneapolis: University of Minnesota Press.

Mast, Gerald. 1981. *A Short History of the Movies,* 3rd Edition. Indianapolis: Bobbs-Merrill.

Mumby, Dennis K. 1993. *Narrative and Social Control.* Newbury Park, CA: Sage Publications Inc.

Nichols, Bill. 1981. *Ideology and the Image.* Bloomington: Indiana University Press.

Rutherford, Jonathan. 1990. *The Third Space.* London: Lawrence and Wishart.

Vogel, Amos. 1974. *Film as a Subversive Art.* New York: Random House.

Westwood, Sallie. 1991. *Radical Agendas? The Politics of Adult Education.* Leicester: National Institute of Adult Continuing Education.

Wright, Elizabeth. 1989. *Postmodern Brecht: A Representation.* New York: Routledge.

CHAPTER 1

The Invention of Motion Pictures: 1895–1910

Introduction

This chapter traces the pioneer work of Eadweard Muybridge and Etienne-Jules Marey and their scientific experiments with stop-action photography of animals and human beings in motion. These experiments followed the analytical paintings of Edgar Degas and Claude Monet and the school of French Impressionist painters of the 1870s. Breaking away from classical subjects, their paintings marked a careful color rendering of objects in changing patterns of reflected natural light. Like a camera snapshot, they attempted to capture the instantaneous moment of time. Muybridge's and Marey's projections of a series of stop-motion photographs led to the development of Edison's Kinetoscope and the invention of the Lumière Brothers' Cinématographe and the advent of motion pictures. The films of Louis Lumière were the inspiration for the "trick" films of Georges Méliès in 1896.

The Documentary Tradition and Impressionism

The invention of motion pictures is directly attributed to the photographic sequences of animals and human beings caught in motion by the multiple cameras of English photographer Eadweard Muybridge (1830–1904). Using a revolving disc that imitated the Zoetrope and other toys based upon the phi phenomenon or "persistence of vision," he was successful in simulated motion through the movement of a sequence of images. At a public exhibition in Paris in 1887, Muybridge combined over 20,000 stop-action photographs of animal locomotion, including men and women, into animated sequences. Using his own projection machine, the Zoopraxiscope, Muybridge achieved an authentic illusion of movement as these images of animals were projected in time and space on the screen. Striking similarities between the movement of animals and human beings became apparent in the process, seemingly to confirm Darwin's theory of evolution advanced in the 1860s.

In 1882, French scientist Etienne-Jules Marey (1830–1904) constructed a camera that contained a rotating disc, which when triggered was capable of "shooting" 12 frames per second. Marey wanted to analyze animals in motion; he was especially interested in the dynamics of birds in flight. His motive was to verify a body of knowledge through scientific research. Starting in 1888, the commercial exploitation of motion pictures required the technical know-how and business ingenuity of Thomas A. Edison (1847–1931) who, with his assistant, William K. L. Dickson (1860–1935), began the designs for a motion picture camera to complement his phonograph. After seeing Marey's use of roll film in his photographic gun, Edison changed his design from a disc to long strips of flexible roll film made by amateur photographer and inventor George Eastman in 1889. Dickson soon completed his design of an electrically controlled camera, the Kinetograph, and a peep-show machine called the Kinetoscope, giving viewers the thrill and novelty of perceiving life-like movements of vaudeville performers and boxing exhibitions.

Jules Marey (1830–1904) designed a rifle-camera, a *fusil photographique* that allowed him to "shoot" 12 small pictures a second in 1892. His interest was to document the sequential motion of a bird in flight using but one camera that could take multiple pictures per second.

Building upon the Kinetoscope, Louis Lumière (1864–1948) invented the Cinématographe, which combined moving images with front projection using intermittent movement. The portable, lightweight camera was hand-cranked and served as a printer and projector. The motion picture camera was now free of studio confinement for easy use outdoors as a cinematic recorder of any actual event. The first public exhibition of Lumière's new Cinématographe, featuring short, 50-second films, occurred in a small café in Paris in December, 1895. The subject of each film was the everyday activities of people and objects captured as *actualités* of Parisian life. The success of the exhibition was immediate, winning the enthusiastic support and wonder of the public, and constituting the official birth of the cinema as we know it today.

Precursors to Cinema — Impressionism and Kinetic Art

The French realist painters, beginning with Gustave Courbet in 1849, rejected the Classical and Romantic tenets of academic painting that proceeded from Greek and Roman mythology. Idealistic nudes and angels were part of this ideal world and, as concepts, unacceptable as part of the real world. Courbet refused to consider such idealistic images and recorded what was happening in the social life and times around him. Spurred on by the invention of photography and the Daguerreotype, Courbet and later Manet became observers of the city and landscape, capturing the events of the times aided by the camera.

By 1875, other artists in France and the United States followed their lead, using photography as a further step to revolutionize painting. They realized that every photographic print rendered an impressionistic interpretation of the world as mediated by the lens of the camera. The influence of photography in capturing and recording light in a moment of time created a new perception of figures in space, and this vision radically altered ways of painting from that moment on.

Claude Monet, Edgar Degas, Pierre-Auguste Renoir, Alfred Sisley, Camille Pisarro and Paul Cézanne used photographs to help them

Opposite, top: Sequential photographs of a galloping horse jumping over a hurdle. Using a Zoopraxiscope, Eadweard Muybridge projected these images onto a screen to demonstrate animal movement. His motion studies combined still photography with earlier picture toy devices to produce the illusion of movement. His techniques influenced Thomas Edison and the Lumière Brothers and the first motion picture devices. *Bottom:* Woman jumping off short riser. One of a wide range of photographic sequences of people and animals by Muybridge that appeared in his 1887 book, *Animal Locomotion.*

compose paintings that broke the established Academic traditions. Now their paintings displayed an analysis of objects in space as "impressions" created by the reflection of light and shadow. These impressionist paintings stripped the object of a painting from its heroic or anecdotal nature and thus broke away completely from the traditional models of visual representation.

In place of forms defined by linear and atmospheric perspective, framed within a homogenous space, these painters attempted to capture the fugitive atmospheric effects of light upon forms in a "painterly" manner without the use of chiaroscuro effects used to create illusions of three-dimensional space and plasticity in Renaissance perspectives. This painterly approach required an optical reading by the viewer to translate the parts into wholes as the artist strove to capture the changing relationship between reflected light and form in a moment in time. Although their technique was related to black and white photographic imagery, these painters worked in a chromatic color scale. Each painter thus registered all objects in colored reflected light patterns. In breaking the rules, these painters heeded the advice of art critic, journalist and poet Charles Baudelaire, who urged artists in 1861 to

> "be of their own time," to be modern by looking to transitoriness, the fugitive, the accidental as their subjects, as Manet and many of the Impressionists painted what they saw around them. At their disposal was a new tool, the photograph. Developed in the early 19th century, the photograph was particularly valued by some Impressionists as a means to judge reality, to capture unusual views, and to study figures in action. Photography aided them in their determination not merely to imitate nature but to capture some of its effects, such as light, motion or expression, in paint [Cole & Gealt 1989, p. 242].

These artists sought out spaces where sunlight brought about brilliant visual effects. A certain "element of lightheartedness and spontaneity" entered each painting as an emotional dynamism captured their "impressions" of the new urban life they witnessed. Monet's *The Seine at Vetheuil* (1880) displays bright sunlight reflected off water and colored foliage. Renoir captures sun and shadow in a holiday scene in *Dance at Moulin de la Galette* (1876). And Monet captures the light, air and atmosphere of the moving sky and wind in *Woman with a Parasol* (1875). Primarily, these painters revolted against the old rules because of their desire

> to record how the eye really sees, depicting figures cut off or caught in spontaneous movement and seen from unusual vantage points or perspectives. Above all, they wanted to paint in such a way that the brush marks captured not only the movement of light on the surface but also the constant motion of all life [*The New International Encyclopedia of Art* 1971, pp. 2276–2277].

Of all the Impressionist painters, Edgar Degas was a true precursor of the cinema. He goes further than the other French painters to capture the aesthetics of forms in motion. His favorite outdoor site was the racetrack, and indoors he studied the opera or rehearsals of the ballet. From 1866 to 1881, Degas used photographs to give immediacy and authenticity to his paintings of race horses or ballerinas. He combined a new kind of multi-dimensional perspective borrowed from Japanese prints which we now associate with cinema through the oblique camera viewpoint. In *Steeplechase — The Fallen Jockey* (1866) he captures the full flight of horses' hoofs off the ground. The camera helped him arrest the theatrical effects of young ballet dancers in *The Rehearsal of the Ballet Onstage* (1874). In his *Young Dancer* (1880), his nude sketches for the sculpture show three poses, front, side and back, of the female form, paralleling Eadweard Muybridge's studies in stop-motion photography of similar studies (Cohen 1979, pp. 13–38).

It is not surprising that many inventors aspired to make a motion-picture device that would take advantage of this artistic departure in painting, to capture, through individual frames of stop-action photographs, the impressions of this changing, moving environment of forms arrested in a play of reflected light and shadow. For scientific reasons these kinetic-

Thomas Edison with his new Kinetoscope machine, holding a perforated celluloid film strip made by Eastman Kodak.

cinematic representations of life forms would supplant and test the nature of theoretical knowledge with that of direct optical experience. Hence Edison and others pursued their own interests in developing a motion picture camera from the serial stop-action photographs of Muybridge and Marey not just as a primary means of studying human beings and animals in motion but for entertainment values as well.

The Artistic Traditions of Edison, Lumière and Méliès

When Thomas A. Edison grasped the commercial potential in Eadweard Muybridge's serial photographs, he engaged his assistant, W. K. L. Dickson, to invent a device that could "do for the eye what the phonograph does for the ear." At first, Dickson attempted but failed to reconstruct these photographic single-framed images onto a film strip that was attached to a light-sensitive drum akin to the phonograph. He then discovered George Eastman's new flexible camera film designed in 1889 to replace glass photographic plates. Since it was a roll film, Dickson divided it in half and punched perforations on the side to help pass it through the camera he had built, advancing the film with an electric motor. At the International Exposition of 1893 in Paris, Edison displayed the two devices perfected by Dickson as the Kinetoscope and Kinetograph. They were conceived as peep-show machines that gave single viewers the novelty and thrill of perceiving vaudeville performers engaged in life-like actions. Inventors and businessmen alike saw the potential for profit from this essentially amusement device, but they also saw its limitations and set out to find ways to incorporate a magic lantern to project these images onto large screens in front of a theatre audience.

In December, 1895, the Lumière Brothers held an exhibition in Paris using their motion picture projector that offered audiences simple photographic "actualities" of life. By 1896, Robert Paul demonstrated a similar projection device in London. Edison bought Thomas Armat's device and displayed this camera-projector as his new Vitascope-Vitagraph in April of that year at Koster and Bial's vaudeville theatre in New York City.

The early films made by Dickson for Edison's company were based upon cinematic recordings of typical vaudeville acts of jugglers, dancers and simple stage chase sequences. More notable were the recordings of the Rice-Irwin Kiss and Fred Ott's sneeze. These performances caught the imagination of the audiences of that day. Edison's Kinetograph was a large and cumbersome machine due to an electric motor used to operate the camera. Filming took place in the Black Maria, a large barn-like shed built on railway tracks in order to rotate to catch sunlight during each part of the day. The large camera was fixed indoors and focused on a specified stage area. Here the performers were filmed. The material ranged from a restaging of the Corbett-Courtney fight, round by round, to other vaudeville acts. These short films became a chief attraction for Edison's Kinetoscope parlors that rose in popularity as they exploited these films as peep shows. These films lacked a sense of real time or place.

In contrast to the early Edison films, the films of Louis and Auguste Lumière were shot out-of-doors in direct sunlight with their light-weight Cinématographe. Freed from studio restrictions, these films documented live-action events such as *Workers Leaving the Factory, Arrival of a Train, Feeding the Baby, Watering the Gardener* and others, all made in 1895. These filmed events had a depth of field that contributed to the realism of the single long take representation of life within the town or city. As impressions of real time and space, these motion pictures gave spectators the phenomena of life as a process of movement and change. However, the position of the camera and the framing of the scene imposed traditional pictorial relationships. Each Lumière film is carefully composed to balance the left and right objects in motion within the frame. There is also an interplay of foreground and deep space using diagonal perspectives of painting and still photography to achieve the illusion of three-dimensional space in the framing of the image. Action is sustained by having people or vehicles move forward toward the camera. Only in recordings of boats or swimmers at the seashore does the action move away from the camera. The exception is a recording of the movement of ocean waves.

When theatrical producer and director Georges Méliès (1861–1938), attended the first public screening of Lumière's short films on December 28, 1895, at the Grand Café in Paris, he quickly understood how he could combine theatrical tricks within the optical illusionism of motion pictures. For him, the magic of the theatre could find its realization in motion pictures,

The John C. Rice/May Irwin Kiss (1896), shot by W. K. L. Dickson for Edison's Kinetoscope, brought a theatrical kiss from the stage version of *The Widow Jones* to the screen for music hall patrons to enjoy.

granting him a far better impression of actual movement than earlier animated optical devices such as Emile Reynaud's Praxinoscope.

When the Lumière Brothers refused to sell him one of their cameras, Méliès went to England and purchased a similar camera from R. W. Paul. From that machine he devised his own camera-projector. At first he sought out films made by the Edison company, then formed his own Star-Film company. By April, 1896, he began to produce, direct and photograph his own theatrical one-shot films. Over the next ten years, Méliès produced, directed and distributed over 500 short films of fantasy and wonder that attracted large urban audiences. These short films ran into multiple scenes and lasted up to 15 minutes. Méliès fixed his camera in the center of the orchestra at a distance to frame the proscenium arch. Then he staged the action using a one-scene, one-take strategy. His direction gave each film a linear development that utilized stage mechanics to produce various effects. In place of a curtain, he devised ways of fading in and fading out of the action for each scene. These dissolves gave spectators the sense of seeing tableaux vivants come to life through his recording on film. Many of these staged fantasies were translations of stories from Grimm's fairy tales, Jules

Verne's science-fiction stories and contemporary newspaper articles that he dramatized.

His most popular "trick" films were staged and photographed in this manner. They included *Cendrillon / Cinderella* (1899), *Le Voyage dans la lune / A Trip to the Moon* (1902), *Le Mélomane / The Melomaniac* (1903), *Voyage à travers l'impossible / The Impossible Voyage* (1904), and *A la conquête du pole / The Conquest of the Pole* (1912). Each film demonstrated his use of time-lapse photography to produce visual spectacles not achievable in the theatre. These "special effects" were deemed "magical" and amazed the spectators. As spectacles, they were achieved using double exposures, dissolves, and disappearing acts of actors and objects. The resulting transformations manipulated the action in time and space, thus exhibiting Méliès' skill as a magician. In producing a series of "trick" films Méliès is credited with creating a "cinema of attractions" which recently has become part of the special effects for blockbuster films today, whose digital computer animation provides spectacular illusions for today's filmmakers.

With these developments in early film, the first critic to analyze the cinema from this viewpoint was Dr. Hugo Munsterberg (1863–1916). In 1916 he wrote *The Photoplay: A Psy-*

Lumière Brothers — *Feeding the Baby* (1895).

chological Study. As chairman of the philosophy department at Harvard, he focused his treatise on the narrative film and its psychological effects upon the mental processes of the viewer. For Munsterberg, the art of the cinema is "the art of the mind" insofar as movies are capable of transforming reality into an object of imagination that completely isolates the viewer from the real world. Munsterberg claims that it is the mind that actualizes these images of light and shadow projected onto the screen. The mind adjusts to these images of the outer world of time, space and causality and replaces them through attention to the forms of the inner world made up of memory, imagination and emotion. The unity of the plot with its film

representations complete the power of the mind to internalize these visual experiences of the outer world. Finally, Munsterberg claims: "To picture emotions must be the central aim of the photoplay" (p. 48). On Munsterberg's theory of film Dudley Andrew (1975) writes:

> The primitive illusion of movement given to us by the mind's operation on intermittent photographs is supplemented by select attention attained via angle, composition, image size, and lighting. Corresponding to memory and imagination are the natural resources of editing which compress or expand time, create rhythms, and render flashbacks and dream scenes [p. 19].

Opposite, top: The first Lumière poster to advertise the Cinématographe Lumière (1896) using a sketch from a comic episode of a playful boy stepping on the garden hose, thus in turn, watering the gardener. *Bottom:* Lumière Brothers' *Watering the Gardener* (1895). Despite the poor quality of this rare still, it is obvious that the scene is the same as the one depicted in the poster above.

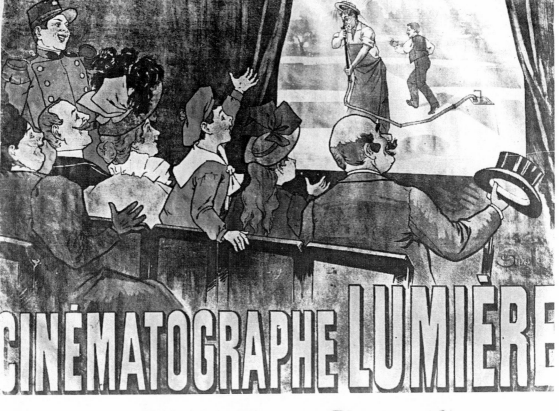

The history of film, then, for Munsterberg, functions through various forms of cinema containing narratives or stories formulated primarily to activate the minds of spectators as earlier forms of visual non-kinetic art do for our contemporary culture.

References

Andrew, Dudley J. 1975. *The Major Film Theories: An Introduction.* New York: Oxford International Press.

Cohen, Keith. 1979. *Film and Fiction: The Dynamics of Change.* New Haven: Yale University Press.

Cole, Bruce, and Adelheid Gealt. 1989. *Art of the Western World.* New York: Summit Press.

Mast, Gerald (ed.). 1982. *The Movies in Our Midst: Documents in the Cultural History of Film in America.* Chicago: The University of Chicago Press.

Munsterberg, Hugo. 1916. *The Film: A Psychological Study; The Silent Photoplay in 1916.* Reprint, New York: Dover Publications, 1970.

The New International Encyclopedia of Art. 1971. New York: Greystone Press.

Zuffi, Stefano, and Francesca Castria. 1998. *Modern Painting: The Impressionists and the Avant Garde of the Twentieth Century.* Translated by Christopher H. Evans. New York: Barron's Educational Series.

CHAPTER 2

Early Narratives and the Nickelodeons

Introduction

A series of important commercial and artistic factors affected the early development of motion pictures as an industry. Thomas Alva Edison was one of the pivotal figures between 1895 and 1905. He clearly envisioned how one could make profits from the invention of motion pictures. His French competitors, the Lumière Brothers, had taken the lead due to their ability to project motion pictures in front of an audience. Georges Méliès, a Parisian director of Theatre Robert-Houdin, took advantage of Lumière's invention and began making one-reel films based upon fantasies and fairy tales. Edison soon had his own machine, the Vitascope, capable of film projection. After his assistant, W. K. L. Dickson, left to form his own company, American Biograph, Edison hired Edwin S. Porter as projectionist and director of the Edison company. Porter imitated the work of Méliès and directed two important films, *The Life of an American Fireman* (1902) and *The Great Train Robbery* (1903), that revolutionized the narrative structure of motion pictures. *The Great Train Robbery* was such a success with urban audiences that a movie craze was started.

New storefront theatres called nickelodeons flourished throughout the country to profit from film exhibition. By 1908 Edison realized that the growth of nickelodeons using pirated films resulted in a large loss of revenue. Edison formed the Motion Picture Patents Company (MPPC) with nine other producers to control film production and distribution in the United States. Independents challenged this monop-

oly and a patents war ensued. Quickly the independents decided to import their own films from Europe as Adolph Zukor and many other producers did. Others traveled to Hollywood to make their own films while other producers in New York faced the hired guns of the MPPC. American Biograph hired D. W. Griffith, who, with Billy Bitzer as cameraman, directed hundreds of one-reel melodramas over a five year span for this studio. Other directors such as Mack Sennett and Charlie Chaplin came to prominence as their comic routines became box-office successes.

The Early History and Commercialization of Motion Pictures

Once the technological advancements in the camera and projector became a reality in the late 1890s, the commercial exploitation of this new marvel posed a serious dilemma for those inventors who desired to profit from the invention. Where could the exhibition of motion pictures prove profitable? Where could these short films be shown to a paying public? Furthermore what kinds of motion pictures would draw an audience?

When we look back to the early history of motion pictures in America between 1895 and 1905, and prior to the nickelodeon boom, one inventor and entrepreneur led the way. Thomas Alva Edison became the first major American investor to envision how to profit from the invention of motion pictures. At first, he did not seek to project his films, for he was more interested in selling the "machine in a box" — the Kinetoscope — and providing the "software" or film strips that would give viewers a "peep show." Using the film technology developed by W. K. L. Dickson, the Edison Manufacturing Company produced a steady production of short 50-foot films required by these machines. By 1895, Kinetoscope parlors, designated as "penny arcades," opened in large cities throughout the country. In 1896, with the development and acquisition of the Vitascope, Edison, with Edwin S. Porter's assistance, successfully projected motion pictures in vaudeville theatres as part of the bill of performances. But the novelty of these short films soon wore off in comparison to actual live vaudeville acts. His programs from *Sea Waves* to the *Bar Room* soon became repetitive to the audiences and made them "chasers" that cleared the theatre before the next performance. But Edison wanted to expand the possible outlets for films knowing that Lumière's public projection of their "*actualités*" in small cinemas in Paris was steadily growing into a successful financial enterprise, one that Edison wanted to duplicate in America.

We can make a useful comparison between Edison's commercial ventures into motion pictures with the Lumière Brothers and why both Edison and the Lumières wanted to develop their inventions into a commercial reality and an industry. First, it is easy to recognize that Lumière's camera, the Cinématographe, had a decisive advantage over Edison's Kinetograph. The Frenchman's camera was lightweight and portable, while Edison's was bulky and large. Thus, the Cinématographe enabled cameramen to move freely about outdoors to record, in documentary fashion, newsworthy films of actual events. The camera was handcranked, and not dependent on electricity as was the Kinetograph. Further, unlike Edison's Black Maria studio, the camera offered its operators few indoor lighting problems, and like the TV camera today, used natural daylight to their advantage to photograph important events as they happened anywhere in the world.

With this knowledge at hand, the Lumière Brothers decided from the start to manufacture their invention at home and to seek markets worldwide for their camera. Their camera could be easily changed into a projector and also into a printing machine. These technical features allowed a trained operator to travel with this equipment to any foreign city or country, shoot events by day, develop them at night in a hotel room, and give a screening the same night. Leaders throughout the world purchased the camera and were trained how to operate it. The buyers were the elite class, heads of government, kings, kaisers, emperors and maharajahs, who sought the instrument to document their own royal festivals and performances. Even an American president, Teddy Roosevelt, allowed a few cameramen to photograph him in striking poses as he marched up San Juan Hill during the Spanish-American War of 1898. After the worldwide marketing demonstrations, the Lumière Brothers took orders to sell the equipment to anyone who wished to buy it. The company then concentrated on the manufacture and sale of their Cinématographe and the documentary films they had made on their travels for their customers.

To compete with the Cinématographe, Edison obtained the rights to Thomas Armat's projector in 1895. This machine incorporated the Latham Loop, a device to prevent the film strip from breaking. Edison called the new machine the Vitascope, and gave the first showing at Koster and Bial's Music Hall in 1896. He also realized at this time that other entrepreneurial businessmen were interested in making profits from producing, distributing and exhibiting their own motion pictures. They were hiring cameramen and setting up rooftop studios in New York and Fort Lee, New Jersey, to capitalize on the growing public demand for motion pictures. Even Edison's chief assistant, W. K. L. Dickson, left his employ in 1895 to form the American Biograph studios. There Dickson constructed a new motion picture camera, the Mutoscope, which avoided Edison's own patents. Other ambitious film exhibitors followed suit. They leased the rights to Edison's film cameras and projectors and copied or pirated foreign European films and short one-reelers to make

Scene from Georges Méliès' *The Kingdom of the Fairies,* **one of a number of theatrical tableaux that Méliès combined with his special "magical" effects created only by the motion picture camera.**

a profit wherever they could. By the end of 1905, rival companies in America and France surpassed both Edison and the Lumière Brothers in the film business.

Two contrasting and important cinematic practices flourished at this early stage of film history. Films shot in documentary style from 1895 to 1905 were not edited. Like the Lumière films, they "rendered the world as it is" in their presentation of news stories of the day. Meanwhile, the development of fantasy films by Georges Méliès, with "in-film," stop-motion editing, enabled some directors to create a "magic realism" for their fictional narratives. These films recreated the world according to the filmmaker's imagination. Both tendencies influenced other directors in film production as the demand to tell simple narratives held the interest of the audience and helped them iden-

tify with characters in the filmed events. Footage then would be restaged and shot in studios to augment genuine footage shot in the field, allowing those producers who had the means to dramatize events as docudramas, turning them into a new form of visual propaganda.

Two Important Films of Edwin S. Porter

In *Before the Nickelodeon* (1991), Charles Musser documents the formative years of film production in the United States between 1896 and 1908. Musser's book and later film center on Porter's early work with the Edison Company, where film production evolved from one-shot documentaries into a story-telling

Stills from Edwin S. Porter's *The Life of an American Fireman*. A variety of close-ups of a "thought balloon" conveying the mental visions of a character to the audience, a fire alarm, and the interior and exterior scenes of a building on fire. The film marked the beginnings of montage editing.

medium. Musser recalls when Edison hired Edwin S. Porter as a cameraman, electrician and projectionist in 1896 to demonstrate his new Vitascope at Koster and Bial's Music Hall before a full house. Part of this inaugural exhibition of front-projected motion pictures was a short excerpt from a stage play known as the Rice-Irwin Kiss. According to a newspaper reviewer attending this memorable event, "The whole scene lit up with the bioscopic present-ment of the kiss. Their smiles and glances and expressive gestures—the joyous osculations were repeated again and again as the audiences shrieked and howled approval."

In 1897, Porter and crew traveled the countryside to demonstrate the Vitascope while gathering documentary footage of their travels, sometimes photographing from a moving train. These travelogues became a staple feature of film exhibitions that included slides of historical scenes and world travels. Like the IMAX theatres of today, these films attracted 5,000 people a day who came to the Eden Musée in New York City to be informed and entertained by motion pictures. With the outbreak of war between Cuba and the United States in 1898, documentary footage taken by other cinematographers was sent back to Porter in New York. Acting as a film editor and director, Porter combined this footage with filmed reenactments of naval battles to give the public a dramatic visual account of the war (Musser 1991, pp. 126–137).

By 1900, Edison had built a new studio in New York and hired Porter as his chief film producer and director. Porter continued to respond to audiences who desired cinematic accounts of news events happening within the country, from the assassination of President McKinley and the escapades of Teddy Roosevelt to the exploits of the fire department and the capture of various armed bandits. Building his short film narratives from the sensational stories carried by daily newspapers such as Hearst's *New York American* and Pulitzer's *New York World,* Porter playfully reconstructed these stories into one-shot films showing one continuous action from beginning to end staged without a moving camera. Films like *Capture of the Biddle Brothers* (1902) and *Fun in a Bakery Shop* (1902) reveal the skill in reconstituting the actions of protagonists. There is also a sense of parody in some of Porter's filmmaking when he used political cartoons to capture the deeds of public figures of the day. Such is the result of *Terrible Teddy, the Grizzly King* (1901). Other films show an understanding of the secret time-lapse photography used by Méliès and his "trick" films which follow the linear narrative generally found in fairy tales and comic strips. By making *Jack and the Beanstalk* (1902), Porter imitated the structure of theatrical story-telling Méliès had perfected. Yet Porter's experience with documentary footage allowed him to experiment and capitalize on the vital connection between documentary films shot in real time and studio scenes shot within a theatrical space. Thus Porter was able to expand the linear narrative used by Méliès with the introduction of simultaneous actions through cross-cutting one scene with a different one. This juxtaposition of original filmed footage with staged reenactments allowed Porter to cut back and forth from one to another, thereby developing tension or suspense within the narrative.

In Porter's *The Life of an American Fireman,* this editing technique was employed to heighten the dramatic effect of the last-minute rescue. At the start of the film, the first shots show the thoughts of a fireman through a "balloon," borrowed from comic strips. The fireman envisages his wife and daughter in a fire; the film then cuts to a close-up of a fire alarm and a hand pulling the alarm. Documentary footage follows of fire fighters answering the

alarm. Porter then combines these scenes with staged events of firemen entering the building by ladder and parallel shots of the dramatic rescue of the woman and child trapped inside the burning building. In some versions of the film the editing of the rescue scenes shows intercutting from the exterior arrival of the firemen at the building to the interior room where firemen break down the door, creating a new narrative dimension. Though there is serious debate raised by Musser on the date of this innovation, Porter's film easily demonstrates how he integrated factual footage within a fictional tale. He also altered the one-shot scene into a series of shots. As Mast and Kawin (1996) state: "We make sense of a narrative, a story, not merely on the basis of the action as presented but on the interplay between those events and our mental ability to connect them into a meaningful chronological sequence" (p. 41).

Porter's *The Great Train Robbery* was shot in 1903. Like his earlier chase films, it is a story of a train hold-up, a chase sequence, before the climactic shootout with the bandits. The intercutting is clearly shown between each filmed event in which the audience follows the narrative. Jumps in time and place, called *ellipses,* connect different scenes to the over-all story. Further, Porter realized that he did not have to play the scene out to its conclusion but could cut from one scene to another within the logic of the story. Porter also integrates outdoor scenes with indoor scenes photographed as staged actions. However, it was the dramatic continuity of the story, realistically depicting the armed hold-up by the bandits and their casual killing of a train passenger, that fascinated contemporary audiences.

Its successful exhibition throughout the country brought crowds to storefront theatres and started a public craze for motion pictures. With *The Great Train Robbery,* Porter's editing strategies were a turning point in the art of film narration, completely altering the power motion pictures would have in contemporary society. Today, this short film is part of *The Grey Fox* (1983), a turn-of-the-century Western directed by Phillip Borsos about a famous Canadian bank robber affectionately known as the "gentleman bandit."

Edwin S. Porter — *The Great Train Robbery* (1903) — an exterior shot showing two armed men transferring the train engineer to a locked mail car. Though rather badly deteriorated, the shot still displays a visual depth-of-field perspective obtained by the camera lens.

The Birth of the Nickelodeons

The Great Train Robbery became the catalyst in the growth of storefront theatres renamed nickelodeons. At last, entrepreneurs such as Adolph Zukor, later president of Paramount Pictures, and Carl Laemmle, of Universal, saw the tremendous profits to be made in films. When Zukor decided to screen Porter's classic in 1903, he made so much money that he converted his store into a proper theatre. Other exhibitors like William Fox and Marcus Loew found that *The Great Train Robbery* increased their profits miraculously.

In 1904, John P. Harris and Harry Davis also converted a storefront theatre into a lavishly decorated cinema house in Pittsburgh. They were the first of thousands of exhibitors in the United States who opened their doors each day to paying customers. These theatres were tiny with under 200 seats, but allowed 12 to 18 performances a day, seven days a week. They operated under an amusement license. The majority of patrons were young men and women, mostly new immigrants to America, who had settled in the large cities as the primary labor force for the industrial centers. Most of these newcomers spoke little or no English. But the universal language and power of the silent film narratives and travelogues could be enjoyed by all.

The Motion Picture Patents Company

By 1909, close to 8,000 nickelodeons had opened throughout the country. Nickelodeons required a large number of films each week:

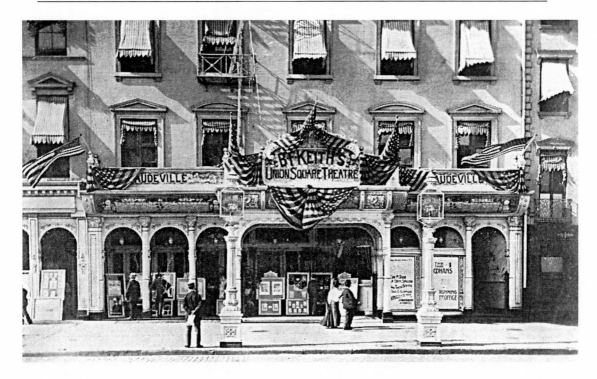

B. F. Keith's Union Square Theatre, New York; facade of storefront theatre. By 1908 there were over 5,000 nickelodeons in the United States, named as such because customers paid a nickel for each showing.

About six one-reelers made up a single program. Programs sometimes changed several times each week, requiring additional films. Now a middleman was needed who could provide the producer with a certain amount of sales and distribution while lowering the costs paid out by the exhibitor. Thus the three-part structure in the film industry emerged involving, as it does today, the producer, the distributor and the exhibitor of motion pictures.

To maximize control over this new economic structure, Edison merged his company with nine other producers into a combine or trust company called the Motion Picture Patents Company. Its distributing arm was the General Film Company. General Film would grade all theatres showing films according to quality, fix a standard rental fee, determine both the release dates and programs, and force each exhibitor to pay a weekly license fee of two dollars.

Although Edison thought this would bring order and profits into the film industry from the staggering success of the new nickelodeons, three important factors came into play to ha-

rass the trust. First was a public outcry about the moral content of films and a demand for local censorship. The advocates and politicians who sought "clean" and morally uplifting films forced the trust to establish its own censorship board in 1908 to control film content. By 1915 this board became the National Board of Review. The second factor was the desire of exhibitors to avoid license fees and to continue their "duping" practices to reduce film costs. The third factor centered on films which featured "star attractions" that would draw repeat customers to the theatre. This also meant they wanted to exhibit foreign films made in France, England or Italy not under the control of the censors or the trust.

A number of independent producers, namely Carl Laemmle, William Fox and Adolph Zukor, openingly challenged the monopoly of the trust. Their suits brought about legal and illegal battles for the next six years in what was called the Patents War, in which the trust hired gunmen to seek out the independent producers and try to put them out of business. Some independents sought better locations for all-year shooting

In 1912 Adolph Zukor formed Famous Players to bring filmed versions of famous plays to New York audiences, following the French model called Film d'Art. Sarah Bernhardt is seen here in *Queen Elizabeth*, which reproduced 19th century theatrical conventions in a style dubbed "canned theatre."

and settled in a remote town in California called Hollywood. There, in the sunny, warm weather, they built outdoor sets and historical locales to meet the growing demand for films created by the nickelodeon boom.

Film d'Art and Famous Players Film Company

The rebellion of the independent producers was partly in response to their interest in importing multi-reel French and Italian feature-length films based upon noted stage plays and novels featuring famous actors and actresses. Again, the pivotal figure in the United States for advancement of this aesthetic international movement was Edwin S. Porter. After he left Edison in 1912, he persuaded his friend, Adolph

Zukor, to invest in presenting Sarah Bernhardt, starring in her filmed version of *La Reine Elisabeth / Queen Elizabeth* (1912). A new company was formed called Famous Players, headed by Porter as Director-General. Zukor brought in Daniel Frohman to help assist with leasing a New York theatre. With a successful engagement and financial returns on his investment, Zukor then engaged Porter to direct *The Count of Monte Cristo* (1913) and *The Prisoner of Zenda* (1913), both of them filmed versions of stage plays. Porter filmed these plays in a predictable theatrical manner, with actors performing for the camera as they would on stage. Both productions drew large urban audiences to the theatres and were popular hits of the day. In fact, these films helped give the cinema some prestige as an art form but they did nothing to advance the ways narrative films would tell a

Blanche Sweet as a typical D. W. Griffith heroine using telegraphy to call for help in *The Lonedale Operator* (1911). In creating melodramatic situations, Griffith employed cross-cutting between parallel story lines to create suspense for his traditional last-minute rescues.

story cinematically. That accomplishment awaited the films of D. W. Griffith.

The more spectacular and persuasive multi-reel films were made by Italian directors in the Film d'Art style. First was Enrico Guazzoni's *Quo Vadis?* (1912), based on an historical novel about Nero and Christian persecution. This silent film had lavish settings, a musical score and special effects that enthralled the viewing audiences. It was followed by another Italian epic drama, Giovanni Pastrone's *Cabiria* (1914), which, more than any other historical drama, proved that multi-reel productions of this kind were hugely profitable. These epics inspired the work of D. W. Griffith, who created his own epic narratives based upon his interpretation of American history. When he felt ready to direct

such an epic, Griffith used all his knowledge gained as a film director at Biograph Studios over the previous five years to demonstrate how stories can be told cinematically (Robinson 1986, p. 18).

D. W. Griffith and Biograph Studios

After his introduction into film techniques by Porter at the Edison studios, Griffith later found employment at Biograph as an actor and writer of melodramas. By 1908, with the great demand for one-reelers by the nickelodeons, Griffith was asked to direct a film. His own attitude toward melodrama was implemented by the film knowledge of the Biograph camera-man, Billy Bitzer. For this first film, *Adventures of Dolly* (1908), Bitzer wrote down the outline of the shot sequences for Griffith to follow. From then on, the two men became the industry's most innovative and productive partnership. Griffith learned film language from Bitzer, from the establishing and panorama shot to the close-up where the placement of the camera depended upon the content of the shot. He complemented these shots with cross-cutting or parallel editing to function as relational devices for tension and suspense. Griffith made a most important discovery: "Films could recreate the activities of the mind: the focusing of attention on one object or another (by means of a close-up), the recalling memories or projecting of imaginings (by flashback, flashforward or mindscreen), the interplay between events (by means of cross-cutting)" (Mast and Kawin 1996, p. 58). These cinematic elements, detailed by film theorist Hugo Munsterberg, are all brought together in the final chase scenes of every Griffith film.

Besides Griffith, Mack Sennett (1880–1960) also directed for Biograph, where he learned many lessons in shooting and editing from Griffith. Sennett's forte was slapstick comedy or farce which he borrowed from French filmmakers. He set out two strict rules for his comic chases: Either the plot involved mistaken identity or the central character suffered from a swelled-up ego waiting for the fall. He enjoyed taking the most apparent melodramatic situation to set these two gags in motion using stereotypical characters who brought about an anarchic world through their own obsessions. With a stable of stars including Charlie Chaplin, Gloria Swanson, Mabel Normand, Harold Lloyd and the Keystone Kops, his simple plots set in motion different people and objects in various comedies of collusion resulting, through many improbable ways, in law and order coming back together. Some of his plots parodied Griffith's last-minute rescues, using cross-cutting at a furious pace. A fine example of Sennett's slapstick comedy is *Teddy at the Throttle* (1917). In this film, Sennett has the heroine chained to the railroad tracks while Teddy, the heroic dog, attempts to rescue her during a rain storm. One can compare this film with Griffith's earlier thriller, *The Lonedale Operator* (1911). Whatever the source, Sennett relished his ability to churn out many short comic films that formed the basis of screen comedy in Hollywood.

References

Mast, Gerald, and Bruce F. Kawin. 1996. *A Short History of the Movies.* 6th Ed. Boston and London: Allyn and Bacon.

Musser, Charles. 1991. *Before the Nickelodeon: Edwin S. Porter and the Edison Manufacturing Company.* Berkeley: University of California Press.

Robinson, David. 1986. *The Illustrated History of the Cinema.* New York: Macmillan.

CHAPTER 3

D. W. Griffith and Cinematic Language: 1910–1919

Introduction

D. W. Griffith became the first American director to establish the cultural significance of motion pictures. He discovered the expressive power of montage editing in his epic melodramas, *The Birth of a Nation* (1915) and *Intolerance* (1916), which became the "grammar and rhetoric" for feature-length films. Griffith was responsible for breaking down a scene into a series of cinematic units called shots. These cinematic units related to a series of shifting "beats" that carried the significant emotional change in character and produced a force to advance the narrative. Griffith's use of framing shots together with his editing skills in using cross-cutting or the "switchback" enabled him to manipulate time and space, and to increase audience tension and suspense in his last-minute rescues. With his cameraman, Billy Bitzer, he introduced naturalistic effects in tonal lighting and three dimensional interiors. After leaving Biograph, he produced and directed *Birth of a Nation*, which brought him both fame and fortune. Due to the film's deplorable depiction of blacks, and its support for the vigilantism of the Ku Klux Klan, Griffith was charged with racism and his film faced nationwide censorship. Griffith's films are full of allegorical images which illuminate his own evangelical vision of Good and Evil, and his own sense of Victorian sentimentality. As a director and propagandist, his second epic, *Intolerance*, dealt with our inhumanity to one another in hopes of quieting the racial controversy over *The Birth of a Nation*. Yet the strength of his own pacifism could not overcome the late entry of the United States into World War I in 1917. After the box-office failure of *Intolerance*, Griffith never recovered his independence as a producer-director, nor could he ignore the censorship battles emerging from the ideological and moral issues arising from his films. Yet, the power of his cinematic achievements remain today. They have influenced many directors worldwide, giving motion pictures credibility in their use of history in narrative films and "history on film."

D. W. Griffith — Historical Spectacle and Family Melodrama

David Wark Griffith was known as the father of the American film. He was born in Kentucky in 1875, a decade after the American Civil War ended. He died in Hollywood, a forgotten and lonely man, in 1948. Griffith started out as a poet and playwright, but Edwin S. Porter signed him on as an actor in 1907. He began directing one-reel melodramas and adventure films for the Biograph Company to meet the demands of the nickelodeon programs for ten-minute, one-reel films.

Over the next five years, from 1908 to 1913, Griffith produced and directed over 400 one-reel and two-reel films for Biograph Studios in New York. These early films displayed his interest in headline stories about the courage of single, young women caught in the dynamics of

Lillian (left) and Dorothy Gish, as part of D. W. Griffith's company, represent single, working women walking past each other in a crowded urban scene from *The Musketeers of Pig Alley* (1912).

city life and a world of street crime and corruption. Many of these films highlighted themes relating to an assault on values and moral wisdom. Sharp contrasts in these melodramatic adventures are the primary focus of Griffith's early films, from *A Corner in Wheat* (1909), *The Lonedale Operator* (1911), to *The Musketeers of Pig Alley* (1912) and including his biblical drama *Judith of Bethulia* (1913).

It was during this period that Griffith developed a film language to help him tell his narratives cinematically. The major film techniques he created to manipulate screen times and space included innovative camera placement and movement, dramatic interior lighting, and parallel or cross-cutting that enhanced the dramatic tensions within the scene.

Griffith's cinematic practices influenced all future filmmaking and directly revolutionized the impact of motion pictures upon audiences to become the foremost cultural art form of the 20th century.

Griffith's filmmaking apprenticeship began at Biograph Studios under the tutelage of Billy Bitzer, where he perfected his gift for transforming sentimental melodramas into exciting, suspenseful film narratives. As a director, he found that the Biograph owners allowed him time to experiment with developing actors to play before the cameras in a more realistic manner. Griffith also sought new ways to create film continuity by cutting on the action and by careful placement of the camera. Following the literary models of Dickens and other 19th century writers, Griffith adopted an editing style that visualized the dramatic conflicts of melodrama. He then showed the audience what it needed to know without confusing close-ups or jump-cuts.

In fact, Griffith credited himself with "founding the modern techniques of (film) art" that had "revolutionized motion picture drama." With an intuitive understanding of how to frame the camera image, he declared publicly that he was the first to use the long shot and the close-up, the flashback (or, as he termed it, the "switchback"), the fade-in and the fade-out, the iris lens to pick out details, the concept of editing for parallel action, the atmospheric use of lighting, and "naturalistic" acting methods in motion pictures (Griffith, quoted by Geduld 1971, p. 6). For Griffith, montage editing consisted of an effective breakdown of an action into a sequence of shots. He controlled the narrative by cross-cutting between simultaneous actions with rhythmic editing, and produced visual symbolism and poetic details with close-ups and medium shots to engage the emotional intimacy of the audience. However, the reader must remember that Griffith also delegated responsibility for capturing the staged action to his resourceful and skillful cameraman, Billy Bitzer.

Griffith's melodramatic vision was drawn from the theatre. Stage techniques allowed him to introduce new subtleties to the plot and use existing cinematic devices to create dramatic and emotional expressiveness. Griffith understood that in filming stage melodramas, the director must develop a psychological relationship with the audience. Intuitively, he knew that the art of the film was to address the mind of the viewer. Thus, Griffith strove to capture the viewer's attention by presenting his heroine in some crisis situation. By skillfully editing expressive parts of the body, such as hands or faces, he could reveal the state of mind of the character. This would activate the imagination of the viewer and generate dramatic tension in Griffith's films. To do this Griffith depended upon camera angle, image size, tonal lighting and over-all composition as key ingredients to capture the emotions of the viewer. By developing faster cutting techniques, he could then alternate the flow of images with inter-cutting and parallel editing to compress or expand time, creating the desired rhythmic tensions for the narrative. Dream sequences and flashbacks then could easily enter the plot as part of the melodramatic elements in the narrative. Such actions were supplemented by a musical score.

For Griffith, the main objective of the photoplay was to engage the viewer through the projection of mental states of fear and anxiety in the major events in the narrative. His training in the melodramatic traditions of 19th century theatre helped him explore the turmoil and inner life of his characters, especially young lovers who are separated from each other through accident, authority, politics or vice. Being a man of romantic sentiment, Griffith would script his melodramas so that these lovers would conquer temptations and dangers of one kind or another and become reunited. In doing so, the lovers were able to overcome and destroy the pervasive and destructive evil forces they faced, usually embodied in the stereotypical villain, who, as a stage character, was depicted as a person motivated by greed, lust or revenge.

Using this melodramatic formula in all his films, Griffith was one of the first film directors to make suspense thrillers, gangster stories, social-realism dramas and romantic melodramas. He adapted the best of the romantic plays and novels of the day, works from de Maupassant to Dickens. His war films, adventure stories and costume dramas are comparable to the soap operas of today's television, which use the same melodramatic formulas and stereotypes.

It was the large-scale epic religious melodramas, such as *Quo Vadis,* imported from Italy, that prompted Griffith to envisage creating multi-reel films of his own. He wanted his films to draw the critical acclaim and the attention of middle-class audiences in New York. However, Griffith was restrained by his own company, which did not want to make feature-length films. In 1913, he decided to break with Biograph's restrictions on multi-reel films to experiment with the elasticity of the feature-length film. He secretly moved his film crew to Southern California and began filming his four-reel biblical epic, *Judith of Bethulia.* In trying to match the Italian spectacle, he built a walled city with opulent settings and filled it with crowds of people. For the first time, he realized that a new form of cinema was necessary to help him visually describe the assault and defense of the city. He explored different forms of montage and *mise-en-scène* to capture the emotional tensions of battle. His extravagant means included hiring hundreds of extras for the crowd scenes. When Biograph heard of the thematic treatment, it refused to release the film. Griffith decided to become an independent, and joined Harry E. Aiken of Reliance-Majestic, whose distribution company, Mutual, would help finance his own film about the American Civil War in return for four two-reelers that Griffith agreed to produce. Realizing that audiences might never see his own *Judith of Bethulia,* Griffith envisaged a scenario that would allow him to reconstruct the spectacular battles of the Great War as well as exploit themes on the conflict between Good and Evil through the sentiment of family melodrama. The result of Griffith's creative efforts was the making of *The Birth of a Nation.* He defended this film on a world view he believed he shared with other Christians and their sense of retribution that was grounded in 19th century Victorian morality.

The Evangelical Vision

A film historian does not only equate Griffith's mastery of cinematic techniques with his uses of montage editing in the development of film narratives. His historical importance grows out of his proficiency in using melodramatic constructions derived from the theatre to advance an ideological position and to reveal to the audience a moral universe in operation. Each film he made underscores a Manichean world of Good and Evil, and showed how Evil, personified in the selfish or greedy or lustful villain, must fall to the moral imperative of Good. To aid him in this conflict he called upon the heroines of his melodramas, played with delicacy and force by such actresses as Lillian and Dorothy Gish, Mae Marsh and Blanche Sweet, to provide audiences with a sensitive evocation of women in danger.

Griffith was brought up with these messages by an evangelical Methodist mother, after his father died when Griffith was only ten. His father was a Confederate cavalry officer during the American Civil War. Both parents influenced their son on the importance of the Bible as a revealed text and the vitality of the Christian spirit in the family.

Many Christian families joined the Evangelical Protestant movement during the 1880s and 1890s and proclaimed as their goal the achieving of a Kingdom of God on Earth. After the war, followers formed an Evangelical Alliance, headed by Josiah Strong, whose agenda was "to save our American civilization and thoroughly season it with the salt of Christianity giving a Christian civilization to the world." For Strong, the moral, social and intellectual aspirations of Americans was a Protestant paideia, a religious education which incorporated what Strong referred to as "God's charge to his chosen people and the nation's responsibility to God." As such, it fulfilled part of the ideals of the Progessive movement in education that saw families, churches, and civic institutions training individuals to thrive in an urban, industrial society (Cremin 1961).

The Birth of a Nation

Thomas Dixon's novel and stage play *The Clansman* gave Griffith the material he needed to connect his own ideological message with an epic film narrative, *The Birth of a Nation.* He believed the impact of this film would "reform the world," especially the sin-ridden urban world, by returning its people to the values Griffith learned from the evangelical missionaries and his own parents. In an interview, Lillian Gish said that when she worked with Griffith he "told us we were something new in the world, a great power that had been predicted in the Bible as the universal language. And it was going to end wars and bring about the Millennium. Films, for Griffith, were going to bring understanding among men — and bring peace to the world" (Gish 1969, p. 128).

In **Birth of a Nation** (1915), D. W. Griffith based his version of the American Civil War upon Thomas Dixon's novel **The Clansman.** The film covers the war years and the turbulent Reconstruction period. The film brought to the screen the actions of a racist organization known as the White Knights, or Ku Klux Klan. The revival of the Klan as vigilantes brought about protests and calls for censorship from the NAACP and other Northern civil rights groups.

In the second part of *The Birth of a Nation,* Griffith deals with the terror and fear caused by the newly emancipated black soldiers and the carpetbaggers of the North who began their exploitation of the South. In the film's view, the struggle to rid the South of the evils of these scalawags and their domination over Southern women led to the formation of the Ku Klux Klan (as the unification of the whites against the emancipated blacks) and an attack on the folly of miscegenation. The recovery of moral law and order follows with the appearance of the Christ figure to herald the restoration of peace and harmony, and the beginning of the Millennium in America. Unification of the families during the Reconstruction period also continues the melodramatic closing.

The message Griffith brought to his audience was clear. The world is corrupt, Evil exists in the Manichean mode, and Good has the moral imperative to destroy this Evil. This black and white polarity of issues depicted by terrifying images of war and violence, such as white women being attacked and threatened with rape by blacks or lecherous "half-breeds," exerted a powerful influence over the audiences. Still, the realistic reconstruction of the Great Civil War in America by Griffith became a sensational box-office smash hit despite public outrage and calls for censorship.

Press coverage of the day focused on the racial controversy awakened by the film and proved that every spectator did not view *Birth of a Nation* in the way Griffith had hoped. Griffith faced public outrage from liberal and black American organizations such as the National Association for the Advancement of Colored People (NAACP), which published in 1915 an article deploring these racial slurs and racist portrayals: "Fighting a Vicious Film" called them "aggressively vicious and defamatory. It is spiritual assassination. It degrades the censors that passed it and the white race that endures it." The issue of "hate literature" became a *cause célèbre* for film censorship. The NAACP article attacked the advertisements in local Hearst newspapers asserting that the purpose of the film was "to resort to the meanest vilification of the Negro race." Several state censorship boards in the North attempted to cut out scenes of misrepresentation in the film. Ohio's censorship boards refused to permit its exhibition and banned the film in many urban centers with large black populations for fear of race riots.

In his defense, Griffith published a pamphlet in 1916, *The Rise and Fall of Free Speech in America*, in which he argues that his critics misunderstood the Messianic message in his film. According to Griffith, censorship of free speech seemed to be the issue, but for the liberal critics it was a question of the power of motion pictures to distort history about American life and values. Not only did this film misinform audiences but it tended to indoctrinate them toward certain values and attitudes under the guise of entertainment. As a political weapon, *The Birth of a Nation* propagated a racist ideology within the melodramatic narrative of the film itself. Thus, the call for national censorship of motion pictures became a prominent issue in the history of film. In 1915, the Supreme Court decision *Mutual v. Ohio* upheld the right of the state of Ohio to ban *The Birth of a Nation* on the grounds that free speech was not the issue, that motion pictures were a business, and as such were not entitled to First Amendment protection.

In the NAACP attack on *The Birth of a Nation*, Northern liberals were outraged at these simplistic depictions and the blatant historical and racial distortions that emerged from Griffith's film. Jane Addams condemned the film outright. She called it "pernicious caricature of the Negro race." Further she added in a later interview: "You can use history to demonstrate anything when you take certain of its facts and emphasize them to the exclusion of the rest" (Schickel 1984, p. 283). However, Hearst's newspapers gave the film a review which declared that "Children must be sent to see this masterpiece. Any parent who neglects this advice is committing an educational offense." Within the American debate, Griffith achieved his goal. He brought the power of films to the middle class, and persuaded them that movies could not only appeal to the emotions of a wider audience, but that films also could reconstruct and reinforce certain cultural values and beliefs of that audience (NAACP, quoted in Mast 1982, p. 123).

Film as History — Intolerance (1916)

By rewriting history according to his own biases, Griffith clearly could demonstrate that history can be interpreted as a series of events in which bigotry and racism always exist. He decided to produce a film of epic scope to strike back and overwhelm his critics. In his conception of *Intolerance,* Griffith chose three basic stories with a fourth derived from the story of Christ. Each story illustrated a given situation in which humanity repeats the same acts of bigotry and destruction outside of any moral order. In this manner, Griffith reinterprets history with his own reconstruction of historical events.

Griffith envisioned *Intolerance* as a film that could easily exploit the way 19th century artists illustrated Bible stories. Miriam Hansen (1991) states that Griffith took advantage of "the connotations attached to specific traditions of representations, whether popular or scholarly, thus acknowledging — in order to manipulate — the iconographic conventions associated with the respective historical periods" (p. 175). By retaining these accepted historical renditions of time and place, Griffith's epic drama could "anchor the truth in a historical tableau" rather

Lillian Gish in a cameo role as the eternal mother in "The Hand That Rocks the Cradle" from Griffith's *Intolerance*. This transitional visual device tried to unify the various narratives.

than in a depiction of an objective view of history (p. 175). Therefore, thematically, the film narrative was designed to produce a particular emotional and intellectual effect to convince the audience of the authenticity of the historical incident. Further, Griffith placed intertitle cards to remind the spectator that the tableaux vivants depicted in the film were a faithful reconstruction of an historical event.

Griffith selected these stories to describe the ways love and charity attempt to overcome hatred and intolerance. Using a familiar melodramatic situation in all four stories, he then demonstrates the confrontation between the power of Desire and the power of the Law. In each episode, the Spirit of Justice attempts to come to rescue the female subject, when her redemption follows a "moral imperative" toward equal opportunities in life experiences of marriage and motherhood.

According to Hansen, Griffith's film characters address the heterosexual women in the audience. He carefully presents each heroine, such as The Dear One, in "The Mother and the Law" section of *Intolerance*, facing one sexual crisis after another, usually caused by the threat of male sexuality. Many women spectators easily identify with the woman in danger depicted on the screen, as the melodrama heightens the emotional reactions and reinforces an internal

The Babylonian sequence in *Intolerance*. The auctioning off of the Mountain Girl in the marriage market. She is saved by the appearance of Belshazzar, her beloved, who suspends the law of the market. Her identity is given free play within his bisexual realm.

psychological state of the character. By capturing the attention of this particular spectator, and addressing her as the subject of the film, Griffith then can pose the moral dilemma faced by the single, unwed woman. Hansen, commenting on the various depictions of women in *Intolerance,* makes a strong argument that Griffith expresses some of the most radical social views of women of that era, making some scenes in the film precursors of the "Roaring Twenties" and the coming of the Jazz Age.

These romantic views revive some of the essential ideas of Romanticism summarized by Malcolm Cowley in his study *Exile's Return* (1976). They include the ideas of salvation, paganism, liberty, equality, and the idea that the ritual of love should not be controlled by moral prescriptions. In the "Fall of Babylon" section

of *Intolerance*, scenes of sexual activity, for pleasure alone, are not regarded as sinful. On the contrary, the downfall is caused by the betrayal of jealous priests who wish to destroy Belshazzar and his worship of the Goddess Ishtar and her Temple of Love and Pleasure so they can return to power with their own paternalistic God Bel. Throughout the film, Griffith's message is that the single woman must be protected during times of social change and sexual crisis.

Griffith's crusade for a moral order to end the chaos and crises of modern life suffered the same fate as the evangelical movement after World War I when the influence of Protestantism rapidly declined. By the 1920s the romantic view of the world was contrasted to the spectacular growth of capitalism and industry.

In "The Modern Story" in *Intolerance* (1916), the husband returns home. One of four interlocking narratives that carries Griffith's theme, with cross-cutting between historical periods to create dramatic tensions.

Secularism entered into a more ethical rather than religious phase. Yet Griffith's film innovations influenced different filmmakers in Europe and the Soviet Union. After they saw *Intolerance*, these directors began to experiment with a new and revolutionary form of film narration.

Griffith After Intolerance

The influence of *Intolerance* after the end of World War I is readily apparent in the films of Sergei Eisenstein, Vsevolod Pudovkin, Fritz Lang and Carl Dreyer as well as in the work of Erich von Stroheim. Griffith moved away from Hollywood and returned to New York to direct a number of feature films from 1919 to 1931. Five of them received critical acclaim when Griffith

was rediscovered by film critics of the 1960s. *Broken Blossoms* (1919), *Way Down East* (1920), *Orphans of the Storm* (1921), *The White Rose* (1923) and *Isn't Life Wonderful* (1924) thematically attempt to depict their heroines overcoming the ordeals of racial intolerance and strife in one form or another and to triumph over the shortcomings of life itself. Yet Griffith framed each film within his older melodramas, offering the audience a "shallow sentimentality" that was deemed by critics as "old-fashioned and biased." However, with *Isn't Life Wonderful*, Griffith shot the film in Germany during the hectic days of the Weimar Republic using "actualities" or found locations for most of the documentary filming. At the end of the silent period in 1927, Griffith's artistic methods were considered too extravagant for financial backing. He attempted two sound films,

The St. Bartholomew's Day Massacre in France. The final scene of militia killing innocent people, including Dark Eyes, in Griffith's *Intolerance.*

Abraham Lincoln (1930) and *The Struggle* (1931). Each film was found wanting an audience, but *The Struggle* appeared to be more than a fictional story since it conveyed Griffith's own battle with the demons of alcohol.

References

Cowley, Malcolm. 1951. *Exile's Return.* Reprint, New York: Dover Publications, 1976.

Cremin, Lawrence T. 1961. *The Transformation of the School: Progressivism in American Education, 1876–1956.* New York: Teachers College–Columbia University Press.

Geduld, Harry M. 1971. *Focus on D. W. Griffith.* Englewood Cliffs, N.J.: Prentice Hall.

Gish, Lillian, and Ann Pinchot. 1969. *The Movies, Mr. Griffith, and Me.* Englewood Cliffs, N.J.: Prentice Hall.

Griffith, D. W. 1916. "The Rise and Fall of Free Speech in America." In *The Movies in Our Midst: Documents in the Cultural History of Film in America.* Edited by Gerald Mast. Chicago: The University of Chicago Press, 1982.

Hansen, Miriam. 1991. *Babel and Babylon: Spectatorship in American Silent Film.* Cambridge, Mass.: Harvard University Press.

National Association for the Advancement of Colored People. 1915. "Fighting a Vicious Film: Protest Against *The Birth of a Nation.*" In *Movies in Our Midst.* Edited by Gerald Mast. Chicago: The University of Chicago Press, 1982.

Schickel, Richard. 1984. *D. W. Griffith: An American Life.* New York: Simon & Schuster.

CHAPTER 4

UFA and the German Studio System: 1919–1925

Introduction

The development of the film industry in Germany occurred after the state secretly obtained ownership through the merger of various German film companies in 1917, under the leadership of General Erich Ludendorff. He ordered the creation of the Universum Film Aktien-gesellschaft, or UFA, as a means to produce German propaganda films to support the war. Large movie studios were built outside of Berlin in Neu-Babelsburg for this purpose. After the war, the new Weimar Republic took over the management of UFA and encouraged the film community to develop its own talent and foster new ideas that would further advance the greatness of German culture.

During the formation of the German studio system, a cinema was developed upon the ways cinematic images could evoke psychological states of being. The German quest for a new visual means to objectify these inner states of consciousness matched the efforts of Swedish and Danish filmmakers who employed the symbolist theory of correspondences. These early German filmmakers merged settings and lighting to emphasize different moods and feelings that would project an emotion or "soul state." Robert Wiene's *The Cabinet of Dr. Caligari* (1919) employed Expressionism and its graphic distortions of space and shadows that stylized physical reality and presented a subjective view of the protagonist. With F. W. Murnau, cinematographic special effects replaced such theatrical representations to project these mysterious states of mind. The use of Roman-

tic Expressionism was contested by G. W. Pabst and adherents of the New Objectivity (*Neue Sachlichkeit*), whose films explored the decadence and amorality of the middle classes. The form-consciousness of these German directors reached spectacular heights in the work of Fritz Lang, who included expressionistic architecture in *Metropolis* (1927) to evoke a totalitarian society trapped by its own fantasies.

In the Tradition of the Symbolists

The German film industry followed the tradition developed by the earlier silent films directed and produced in Sweden by Victor Sjöström (Seastrom) and Mauritz Stiller before 1914 and World War I. These Swedish films adopted the Romantic style of the symbolist poets and painters of the 19th century, led by Stéphane Mallarmé (1842–1898), whose Romantic theories of art provided the artistic inspiration for these directors.

Mallarmé believed that all art, including poetry and drama, is an expression of an "inner condition" of human beings rather than the "false sensibility" or "objective description" of an external action of social conditioning in middle-class environments. This premise changed the goals of the artist from the obligation to "represent" the visible, natural world to a subjective rendering and exploration of people caught in the space between each world. Thus, these artists and painters discarded the theories of the realists and impressionists that

In *The Cabinet of Dr. Caligari* (1919), Dr. Caligari (Werner Krauss) stands outside a carnival tent on the fair grounds inviting a woman (Lil Dagovar) to attend the show. Both actors perform in expressionistic make-up and costumes to emphasize intense emotional feelings in an environment of dread and doom.

prevailed at that time, 1885–1900, so they could develop a new range of images that would "clothe the idea in a perceptible form" and convey the more intangible qualities of mood and atmosphere derived from natural forms and colors.

Often they adapted the novels of Selma Lagerlöf, who employed traditional legends and myths of the past to express the "soul state" of those caught in a psychological conflict between internal desires and outward social conventions. The dramas were enacted in natural environments such as dark forests, sunlit meadows and towering mountains that became symbols of hidden forces controlling people's fortunes and ruling their futures.

These formal characteristics emerged from

the artists' study of Shakespeare's *Hamlet*, whose chief character's introspection and melancholy became an example of a world haunted by lust and murder. From this dramatic and poetic model, the Symbolist poets stated that imagination and fantasy were the key elements necessary to release the inner realities of their heroes. Visions and hallucinations as well as other psychic phenomena were pursued in the cultivation of the poet's own subjective states of being. In the drama, *The Outlaw and His Wife* (1918), Swedish director Victor Sjöström uses natural imagery to reflect the passion of two lovers seeking refuge in the mountains after they are exiled by their society. Sjöström made other film adaptations of Lagerlöf novels, notably *Thy Soul Shall Bear*

Witness (1920) for the Svensk Filmindustri. In other film adaptations from Lagerlöf novels, Mauritz Stiller, a colleague of Sjöström, evoked ghosts and medieval witchcraft to represent the metaphysical forces overcoming human passions. These stunning visual settings are characteristic of *Sir Arne's Treasure* (1919), *Gunnar Hede's Saga* (1922) and *The Atonement of Gosta Berling* (1924), featuring Greta Garbo.

The themes and styles of the Symbolist poets also were visualized by painters as in the expressionist work of Edvard Munch (1863–1944) and James Ensor (1860–1949). Their paintings influenced the early work of *Die Brücke* (The Bridge), a German group of expressionist artists, from 1910 onward. After the First World War, Expressionism became the most influential artistic and cultural movement in Europe, flourishing in Norway, Denmark, Germany and France, not only in the visual arts but also in the theatre and the cinema.

Germany's defeat in World War I concluded with the Treaty of Versailles in 1919. The effects of this treaty caused the new leaders of the country to focus on regaining some prestige through Germany's own artistic and cultural efforts. Before the war's end, the German Reich, headed by General Ludendorff, ordered the merger of the main German production companies and built a large complex of studios outside Berlin in 1917, Universum Film Aktiengesellschaft (UFA). This merger was to propagate German ideas, talent and culture. It would also prepare films as anti-propaganda to offset the vicious Allied propaganda campaign mounted against the Germans.

The new Weimar Republic replaced the ruling Bismarck monarchy overthrown by the Allied victory. Max Weber, one of the leading German sociologists, helped write a new constitution, preparing the way for a democratic and anti–Marxist government. However, within the fabric of the defeated nation, many oppositional political forces struggled for control as the urban population faced growing unemployment, inflation and a crippled economy. Rather than enjoying the prosperity Americans knew during the 1920s, the German people faced severe hardships resulting in an economic cut-throat policy. Most commercial operations became decadent and amoral. Bertolt Brecht's satirical play, *The Threepenny Opera*, featuring "Mack the Knife," critically revealed the flagrant corruption of the free-enterprise system.

Between 1919 and the coming to power of Hitler in 1933, the growth and success of all the German arts, from architecture to filmmaking, was remarkable. This outcome depended upon an organizational concept derived from the theatrical imagination of 19th century German opera composer Richard Wagner, who desired to unify all production elements in his operas or music-dramas to properly render German myth and folklore. This theory of integration of all aspects of artistic creation is called *Weltanschauung*, a total work of art. The idea redefined the stagecraft of director Max Reinhardt, who incorporated the theory into innovative staging of contemporary expressionistic plays of Franz Wedekind and George Kaiser as well as classical plays of Friedrich Schiller and Shakespeare. From the theatre troupe of Max Reinhardt, the German film industry drew most of its directors, designers and actors, including directors William Dieterle, Ernst Lubitsch, and F. W. Murnau along with actors Elisabeth Bergner, Marlene Dietrich, Emil Jannings and Conrad Veidt. Under the reign of producer Erich Pommer, all film production at UFA integrated the work of these artists in the creation of the symbolic moods and characters for their expressionistic films.

The Cabinet of Dr. Caligari

A Czech poet, Hans Janowitz, and the young Austrian artist Carl Mayer shared revolutionary views on the role of identity and authority in the post–World War I Berlin and the new Weimar Republic. Their collaboration in 1918 on a script idea by Janowitz led to the first and most influential German Expressionist art film ever made, one that became the forerunner of almost every film noir and horror film that followed it.

Das Kabinett des Dr. Caligari / *The Cabinet of Dr. Caligari* is based upon Mayer's individual experiences of psychic phenomena while

Interior shot of Caligari's trailer with Cesare (Conrad Veidt) being fed by Dr. Caligari (Werner Krauss) as he rests in a coffin-shaped bed. The setting displays the black and white painted lights and shadows suggestive to the viewer of a personal world deliberately distorted and unbalanced.

under hypnotic treatment, and a bizarre sex-slaying in Hamburg witnessed by Janowitz. Mayer contributed his mental duels with German army psychologists. The two were able to fuse their own experiences and integrate the elements into the original Caligari story when they witnessed a strongman's act at a fair; the strongman achieved feats of strength in a hypnotized state. He then accompanied his feats with statements about future events, full of appalling dangers and disasters for members of the audience.

Using the fairground as their setting, Janowitz and Mayer depict Dr. Caligari as a circus magician traveling with Cesare, a somnambulist who can read the future. This ominous sideshow attracts the attention of our hero, Francis, after we learn a serial killer is loose

committing brutal and unmotivated murders. Francis attends the show with his friend Alan and a woman, Jane, the romantic interest of both men. She is the same woman seen in the opening framing scene as a "vision" by our storyteller.

Cesare is played by Conrad Veidt, who emerges from an upright coffin-like box during the act. Dr. Caligari, the mad magician, is played by Werner Krauss. Both actors employ distorted, angular gestures to complement their costumes and make-up in a proper expressionist manner. The doctor tells the audience that Cesare will answer questions about the future. Alan, in a state of excitement, asks how long he has to live. Cesare's answer: until dawn. This sets the turning point of the narrative, leaving the audience in that space of

In Wiene's *The Cabinet of Dr. Caligari* (1919), Dr. Caligari (Werner Krauss), a hypnotist, awakens his sleepwalker, Cesare (Conrad Veidt) to perform his act of predicting the future, all within an expressionistic setting.

tension and suspense awaiting to see how this prediction will be carried out.

Why would this film be considered revolutionary in its time? According to film theorist and sociologist Siegfried Kracauer (1889–1966) in *From Caligari to Hitler,* this tale of horror reflected the fatal tendencies inherent in the German system of adoration and idolization of unlimited authority, and the demand for domination over individuals. This unyielding authority is presented in the story as the character Caligari, who ruthlessly violates all human rights and values. Cesare, as representative of the common person, is not only a sleepwalker, but also the instrument of monstrous evil, one who blindly carries out Caligari's wishes.

Kracauer affirms that Janowitz and Mayer designed Cesare as a representative of the unthinking German male, one who succumbs to compulsory military service for the state, drilled to kill or be killed. In the original story, Caligari escapes a manhunt and seeks refuge in a lunatic asylum. Here the authors reveal that the director of the asylum and Caligari are one and the same person. Confronted by Francis about Cesare and the murders, Caligari is put into a straitjacket, thus demonstrating symbolically how insane authority is abolished, and that reason can conquer irrational fears.

But the story does not reach the screen in this way. Robert Wiene, chosen by UFA production boss Erich Pommer to direct the film, switched one key sequence in the film and transformed the body of the original script into a play within a play. By adding a framing story Wiene basically reversed the original intent of Janowitz and Mayer. If the original exposed the madness and ruthlessness of authority, then

Nosferatu 33. Prana-Film.

In F. W. Murnau's *Nosferatu* (1922), Max Schreck plays the Count who has left his castle and arrives in Bremen, bringing with him the plague. As the vampire, Dracula, his ghost-like figure emerges from below deck.

Wiene's Caligari supports authority and convicts its antagonist of madness. Thus a production decision altered a subversive story and turned it into a conformist one. Yet Kracauer claims that the film also reflects a "double aspect of German life by coupling a reality in which Caligari triumphs with a dream fantasy in which the same authority is overthrown" (Kracauer 1947, p. 67). So *The Cabinet of Dr. Caligari* proceeds from an antiestablishment filmscript into an expressionist film narrative that recounts the paranoid delusions of a representative of the German people.

This film also introduced scenic devices developed on the stage by the symbolist and expressionist designers to visually express interior states of being, the moods and atmospheres of a subjective nature. The film's innovations in this regard were created by the painted sets and decor designed by expressionist artists Hermann Warm, Walter Röhrig and Walter Reimann. Their work was not "impressionistic" reflections created anamorphically by concave and convex mirrors but by graphically created distortions of light and shadow in which the actor performed.

For the French film critic André Bazin, these expressionistic devices substituted staged illusions for a camera's ability to give the spectator an unstaged portrayal of reality. As such, they may be classified as works of art but they can be confusing to the spectator by avoiding a basic cinematic concern of rendering the phenomenal world. Yet for *The Cabinet of Dr. Caligari*, the graphic distortions in perspective and the contrasting black and white oblique forms support the states of anxiety and terror depicted in the film narrative. This "spiritual unrest" seems to obsess the psyche in all German writings and films, according to Lotte Eisner in *The Haunted Screen.* She claims that the expressionists were solely interested in images that conveyed a subjective state emanating from one's mind. With this kind of stylization of environments, the furnishings and acting adapted to it to achieve a dynamic synthesis. The lead actors, Werner Krauss as Dr. Caligari and Conrad Veidt as Cesare, achieved an acting style of believable gestures and facial expressions to complement the idea. In contrast to them, the other actors were locked into a romantic-realistic style with old-fashioned cloaks, top hats and morning coats that signified a normal perspective outside the dream or fantasy.

Considering early film narratives, *The Cabinet of Dr. Caligari* is extremely conservative in experiments with camera movement or placement. The director, Robert Wiene, had little knowledge of Griffith's contributions to film language. The film continuity of *Caligari* is essentially that of artificially arranged scenes similar to the stagecraft Georges Méliès constructed using a stationary camera. The director relied upon visual effects rather than montage editing and camera angles. Yet regarding set design, psychological probing and thematic ambiguity, and its attempts to project internal and subjective thoughts through the external and objective world, *Caligari* had immense influence on the expressionistic style of German silent films that followed it.

The Count in *Nosferatu* as he appears in his castle to welcome Jonathan, who is unaware of the supernatural powers of the vampire. Soon the Count will visit Jonathan in his quarters after dinner. The poor quality of this original reflects the deteriorated state of most films from the silent era, but the image of the Count remains horrific.

F. W. Murnau *and* Nosferatu

F. W. Murnau (1889–1931) trained as an art historian before directing films at UFA. Previously he apprenticed as a stage director with Max Reinhardt's company. According to Lotte

Eisner, Murnau's early films explored the melodramatic traumas suffered by a man under the spell of forbidden erotic pleasures. After some success with these films, he selected the legendary vampire story, *Dracula*, published in 1897 by Bram Stoker, and loosely adapted it into *Nosferatu, the Vampire* (1922). The original novel involved a man's quest to overcome the repressed desires of his own sexuality trapped within a Victorian society. Murnau decided to employ a realistic style that carried the symbolist message as declared by the great German poet, Heine, who called Germany "a country which relishes the horrors of delirium, the dreams of old witches and is the kingdom of ghosts."

In seeking hidden malevolent forces within natural images, Murnau filmed on location, an exception to UFA's studio-controlled methods, and sought out dark skies, stormy seas and empty mountains to foretell the approach of the vampire. By staying within the realistic tendency of photographic imagery, Murnau's cinematic work shows a distinct influence of the symbolist filmmaking of the Swedish directors, Sjöström and Stiller. His work also suggests the mystery of the expressionist vision in cinematic terms, relying on negative, ghost-like images, double exposures and shadowy lighting effects that supplanted *Caligari*-like production design.

The screen's first vampire was Max Schreck, whose rat-like face, sharpened teeth and cadaverous eyes created an absolutely terrorizing image. In his haunted castle, Nosferatu is frequently photographed from an extremely low angle to represent him as a gigantic and sinister figure on the screen. His shadow is cast across objects and walls in a distorted and angular way. This spider-like vision arrives in Bremen, a coastal sea town, in a rat-infested death ship carrying his coffin under one arm as he steps on shore. Murnau uses stop-motion photography to indicate the actual motion of inanimate objects to accompany the vampire's arrival. His use of *mise-en-scène* shows a directorial skill with in-depth photography that helps eliminate many inter-title messages. Together with low-key, high contrast expressionistic lighting to generate mood and atmosphere, Murnau achieves an effective integration of character within various landscapes and interior settings through his filming on location.

The Last Laugh *and the Subjective Camera*

The final silent film Murnau directed in Germany that brought him to Hollywood in 1926 was his classic *Der letzte Mann / The Last Laugh* (1924). This film followed Max Reinhardt's other theatrical tradition of small scale productions called the *Kammerspiel*. Murnau fully exploited the possibilities of camera movement and camera placement as a narrative tool. The camera techniques were developed by Karl Freund, who complemented the *mise-en-scène* with lighting that emphasized the ghost-ridden atmosphere similar to that of his vampire film. Murnau carefully directed this account of the everyday life of a hotel doorman, from his proud position at an elegant Berlin hotel, demonstrated by his magnificent uniform, to his dismissal and subsequent lowly status as a washroom attendant causing him personal ridicule and rejection. To capture and reflect to the audience the emotional turmoil and suffering of this character, Murnau utilized a moving camera, giving us a subjective state-of-mind of the character. The first subjective state occurs after he is demoted and returns home to face his daughter's wedding. He drinks heavily and we see his drunken state as the camera moves freely to record his disjointed reactions and movements. The subjective camera shot also manipulates a number of dream states that we witness as the doorman undergoes attempts to regain his position of power after his fall from stature.

The realism achieved by Murnau in this film followed a new trend toward filmmaking that projected the cynicism and disillusionment felt in Berlin by the middle of the decade. The realities of cut-throat living and prostitution were compared to food shortages and poverty. Filmmakers such as G. W. Pabst decided to deromanticize their films and record the appalling economic and political condition around them. This new style of production was

G.W. Pabst's *Pandora's Box* (1929) is known as a masterpiece of cinematic social realism. This film concerns the financial and spiritual disillusionment of the middle class who struggle to maintain their lives in postwar Vienna during the twenties.

called the *Neue Sachlichkeit,* or New Objectivity.

    In fact, prior to Pabst, the German cinema had evolved through its various phases as essentially a cinema of mise-en-scène rather than of montage, since it had developed in isolation from Griffith and his Russian successors. Pabst's own contribution to film technique was the discovery that the perceptual fragmentation created by editing within scenes could be effectively concealed for the purpose of narration by cutting a shot in the midst of a motion which is completed in the next shot. This kind of cutting or continuity editing became fundamental to his classical sound film [Cook, p. 135].

    In 1925, Pabst directed *Die Freudlose Gasse / Joyless Street,* starring Greta Garbo and Asta Nielsen as women who are caught in the throes of poverty and economic chaos. In his departure from dream images or hallucinations, Pabst's street films become intimate portraits of bread lines and bourgeois decadence. His later film, *Pandora's Box* (1929), starring Louise Brooks, goes deeply into the decadence and amorality of the upper middle classes caught in excesses of extramarital relationships. Pabst also directed Brecht's *Threepenny Opera,* following the same directorial style, much to the chagrin of Brecht, who fought to have the film destroyed since Pabst cut out all references to the causes of political turmoil.

Fritz Lang and Mythmaking

A third major filmmaker who established a solid career in Hollywood is perhaps the most versatile of the German directors, Fritz Lang (1890–1976). He is noted not only for his psychological melodramas and thrillers, but also for his romantic and symbolic productions based upon historical myths and legends. Yet his work is unlike Griffith's or that of the later Soviet film directors, since he reconstructed history and the legends of the past through the development of heroic fantasy figures who controlled the destinies of humanity.

Lang, who was a particularly resourceful director, was able to make films in virtually any genre. In the 1920s his films—big-budget, large-scale epics made for mass audiences—stretched the limits of the silent-film era. "With the best special effects available at the time, Lang's world ... was peopled by spies, dragons, legendary heroes, dictators, master criminals and futuristic demagogues" (White 2000).

Lang's first critical success was the allegorical film *Destiny* (1921), which depicted the symbolic struggle between Love and Death among colossal settings similar to the stage designs of Adolphe Appia and Gordon Craig. Throughout his films, his heroes and heroines exist in another world, dominated by some arch villain who is ready to destroy them. When Lang decided to project his mythic visions of the past into the future, he engineered his most spectacular film, *Metropolis*. In a modernistic urban center, the struggle of Love is played against the designs of a villain and his Death machine. In this film, Lang incorporated an expressionistic style to great effect to indicate a totalitarian society presided over by an electrical dynamo, Moloch. Although the staging of the crowd scenes is most spectacular, the creation of an androgynous android, one of the first replicants in the history of cinema, becomes a turning point in the film. Yet the film succumbs to melodrama, retreats into the sanctuary of the Gothic church, and the mythic implications of this new technological marvel are easily destroyed, as are the schemes of the arch-villain creator. However, the idea of a totalitarian dictator was a fiction that soon became a German reality.

References

Cook, David. 1990. *A History Of Narrative Film 2nd Edition*. New York: W.W. Norton & Company

Eisner, Lotte H. 1969. *The Haunted Screen: Expressionism in the German Cinema and the Influence of Max Reinhardt*. Berkeley: University of California Press.

Kracauer, Siegfried. 1947. *From Caligari to Hitler: A Psychological History of the German Film*. Princeton: Princeton University Press.

Vogel, Amos. 1974. *Film as a Subversive Art*. New York: Random House.

White, Rob. 2000. "The Permanent Magic of Fritz Lang." www.bfi.org.uk

CRITICAL ESSAY

"Caligari"

by Siegfried Kracauer

The Czech Hans Janowitz, one of the two authors of the film *Das Kabinett des Dr. Caligari* (*The Cabinet of Dr. Caligari*), was brought up in Prague — that city where reality fuses with dreams, and dreams turn into visions of horror.[1] One evening in October 1913 this young poet was strolling through a fair at Hamburg, trying to find a girl whose beauty and manner had attracted him. The tents of the fair covered the Reeperbahn, known to any sailor as one of the world's chief pleasure spots. Nearby, on the Holstenwall, Lederer's gigantic Bismarck monument stood sentinel over the ships in the harbor. In search of the girl, Janowitz followed the fragile trail of a laugh which he thought hers into a dim park bordering the Holstenwall. The laugh, which apparently served to lure a young man, vanished somewhere in the shrubbery. When, a short time later, the young man departed, another shadow, hidden until then in the bushes, suddenly emerged and moved along — as if on the scent of that laugh. Passing this uncanny shadow, Janowitz caught a glimpse of him: he looked like an average bourgeois. Darkness reabsorbed the man, and made further pursuit impossible. The following day big headlines in the local press announced: "Horrible sex crime on the Holstenwall! Young Gertrude ... murdered." An obscure feeling that Gertrude might have been the girl of the fair impelled Janowitz to attend the victim's fu-

neral. During the ceremony he suddenly had the sensation of discovering the murderer, who had not yet been captured. The man he suspected seemed to recognize him, too. It was the bourgeois — the shadow in the bushes.

Carl Mayer, co-author with Janowitz of *Caligari*, was born in the Austrian provincial capital of Graz, where his father, a wealthy businessman, would have prospered had he not been obsessed by the idea of becoming a "scientific" gambler. In the prime of his life he sold his property, went, armed with an infallible "system," to Monte Carlo, and reappeared a few months later in Graz, broke. Under the stress of this catastrophe, the monomaniac father turned the sixteen-year-old Carl and his three younger brothers out into the street and finally committed suicide. A mere boy, Carl Mayer was responsible for the three children. While he toured through Austria, peddling barometers, singing in choirs and playing extras in peasant theatres, he became increasingly interested in the stage. There was no branch of theatrical production which he did not explore during those years of nomadic life — years full of experiences that were to be of immense use in this future career as a film poet. At the beginning of the war, the adolescent made his living by sketching Hindenburg portraits on postcards in Munich cafés. Later in the war, Janowitz reports, he had to undergo repeated examinations of his mental condition. Mayer seems to have been very embittered against the high-ranking military psychiatrist in charge of his case.

The war was over. Janowitz, who from its outbreak had been an officer in an infantry regiment, returned as a convinced pacifist, animated by hatred of an authority which had sent millions of men to death. He felt that absolute authority was bad in itself. He settled in Berlin, met Carl Mayer there, and soon found out that this eccentric young man, who had never before written a line, shared his revolutionary moods and views. Why not express them on the screen? Intoxicated with Wegener's films, Janowitz believed that this new medium might lend itself to powerful poetic revelations. As youth will, the two friends embarked on endless discussions that hovered around Janowitz' Holstenwall adventure as well as Mayer's mental duel with the psychiatrist. These stories seemed to evoke and supplement each other. After such discussions the pair would stroll through the night, irresistibly attracted by a dazzling and clamorous fair on Kantstrasse. It was a bright jungle, more hell than paradise, but a paradise to those who had exchanged the horror of war for the terror of want. One evening, Mayer dragged his companion to a sideshow by which he had been impressed. Under the title "Man or Machine" it presented a strong man who achieved miracles of strength in an apparent stupor. He acted as if he were hypnotized. The strangest thing was that he accompanied his feats with utterances which affected the spellbound spectators as pregnant forebodings.

Any creative process approaches a moment when only one additional experience is needed to integrate all elements into a whole. The mysterious figure of the strong man supplied such an experience. On the night of this show the friends first visualized the original story of *Caligari*. They wrote the manuscript in the following six weeks. Defining the part each took in the work, Janowitz calls himself "the father who planted the seed, and Mayer the mother who conceived and ripened it." At the end, one small problem arose: the authors were at a loss as to what to christen their main character, a

psychiatrist shaped after Mayer's archenemy during the war. A rare volume, *Unknown Letters of Stendhal,* offered the solution. While Janowitz was skimming through this find of his, he happened to notice that Stendhal, just come from the battlefield, met at La Scala in Milan an officer named Caligari. The name clicked with both authors.

Their story is located in a fictitious North German town near the Dutch border, significantly called Holstenwall. One day a fair moves into the town, with merry-go-rounds and sideshows—among the latter that of Dr. Caligari, a weird, bespectacled man advertising the somnambulist Cesare. To procure a license, Caligari goes to the town hall, where he is treated haughtily by an arrogant official. The following morning this official is found murdered in his room, which does not prevent the townspeople from enjoying the fair's pleasures. Along with numerous onlookers, Francis and Alan—two students in love with Jane, a medical man's daughter—enter the tent of Dr. Caligari, and watch Cesare slowly stepping out of an upright, coffinlike box. Caligari tells the thrilled audience that the somnambulist will answer questions about the future. Alan, in an excited state, asks how long he has to live. Cesare opens his mouth; he seems to be dominated by a terrific, hypnotic power emanating from his master. "Until dawn," he answers. At dawn Francis learns that his friend has been stabbed in exactly the same manner as the official. The student, suspicious of Caligari, persuades Jane's father to assist him in an investigation. With a search warrant the two force their way into the showman's wagon, and demand that he end the trance of his medium. However, at this very moment they are called away to the police station to attend the examination of a criminal who has been caught in the act of killing a woman, and who now frantically denies that he is the pursued serial murderer.

Francis continues spying on Caligari, and, after nightfall, secretly peers through a window of the wagon. But while he imagines he sees Cesare lying in his box, Cesare in reality breaks into Jane's bedroom, lifts a dagger to pierce the sleeping girl, gazes at her, puts the dagger away and flees, with the screaming Jane in his arms, over roofs and roads. Chased by her father, he drops the girl, who is then escorted home, whereas the lonely kidnaper dies of exhaustion. As Jane, in flagrant contradiction of what Francis believes to be the truth, insists on having recognized Cesare, Francis approaches Caligari a second time to solve the torturing riddle. The two policemen in his company seize the coffinlike box, and Francis draws out of it — a dummy representing the somnambulist. Profiting by the investigators' carelessness, Caligari himself manages to escape. He seeks shelter in a lunatic asylum. The student follows him, calls on the director of the asylum to inquire about the fugitive, and recoils horror-struck: the director and Caligari are one and the same person.

The following night — the director has fallen asleep — Francis and three members of the medical staff whom he has initiated into the case search the director's office and discover material fully establishing the guilt of this authority in psychiatric matters. Among a pile of books they find an old volume about a showman named Caligari who, in the eighteenth century, traveled through North Italy, hypnotized his medium Cesare into murdering sundry people, and, during Cesare's absence, substituted a wax figure to deceive the police. The main exhibit is the director's clinical records; they evidence that he desired to verify the account of Caligari's hypnotic faculties, that his desire grew into an obsession, and that, when a somnambulist was entrusted to his care, he could not resist the temptation of repeating with him those terrible games. He had adopted the identity of Caligari. To make him admit his crimes, Francis confronts the director with the corpse of his tool, the somnambulist. No sooner does the monster realize Cesare is dead than he begins to rave. Trained attendants put him into a straitjacket.

This horror tale in the spirit of E. T. A. Hoffmann was an outspoken revolutionary story. In it, as Janowitz indicates, he and Carl Mayer half-intentionally stigmatized the omnipotence of a state authority manifesting itself in universal conscription and declarations of war. The German war government seemed to the authors the prototype of such voracious au-

thority. Subjects of the Austro-Hungarian monarchy, they were in a better position than most citizens of the Reich to penetrate the fatal tendencies inherent in the German system. The character of Caligari embodies these tendencies; he stands for an unlimited authority that idolizes power as such, and, to satisfy its lust for domination, ruthlessly violates all human rights and values. Functioning as a mere instrument, Cesare is not so much a guilty murderer as Caligari's innocent victim. This is how the authors themselves understood him. According to the pacifist-minded Janowitz, they had created Cesare with the dim design of portraying the common man who, under the pressure of compulsory military service, is drilled to kill and to be killed. The revolutionary meaning of the story reveals itself unmistakably at the end, with the disclosure of the psychiatrist as Caligari: reason overpowers unreasonable power, insane authority is symbolically abolished. Similar ideas were also being expressed on the contemporary stage, but the authors of *Caligari* transferred them to the screen without including any of those eulogies of the authority-freed "New Man" in which many expressionist plays indulged.

A miracle occurred: Erich Pommer, chief executive of Decla-Bioscop, accepted this unusual, if not subversive, script. Was it a miracle? Since in those early postwar days the conviction prevailed that foreign markets could only be conquered by artistic achievements, the German film industry was of course anxious to experiment in the field of aesthetically qualified entertainment.[2] Art assured export, and export meant salvation. An ardent partisan of this doctrine, Pommer had moreover an incomparable flair for cinematic significance of the strange story Mayer and Janowitz submitted to him, he certainly sensed its timely atmosphere and interesting scenic potentialities. He was a born promoter who handled screen and business affairs with equal facility, and, above all, excelled in stimulating the creative energies of directors and players. In 1923, Ufa was to make him chief of its entire production.[3] His behind-the-scenes activities were to leave their imprint on the pre–Hitler screen.

Pommer assigned Fritz Lang to direct *Cali-*

gari, but in the middle of the preliminary discussions Lang was ordered to finish his serial *The Spiders*; the distributors of this film urged its completion.[4] Lang's successor was Dr. Robert Wiene. Since his father, a once-famous Dresden actor, had become slightly insane toward the end of his life, Wiene was not entirely unprepared to tackle the case of Dr. Caligari. He suggested, in complete harmony with what Lang had planned, an essential change of the original story—a change against which the two authors violently protested. But no one heeded them.[5]

The original story was an account of real horrors; Wiene's version transforms that account into a chimera concocted and narrated by the mentally deranged Francis. To effect this transformation the body of the original story is put into a framing story which introduces Francis as a madman. The film *Caligari* opens with the first of the two episodes composing the frame. Francis is shown sitting on a bench in the park of the lunatic asylum, listening to the confused babble of a fellow sufferer. Moving slowly, like an apparition, a female inmate of the asylum passes by: it is Jane. Francis says to his companion: "What I have experienced with her is still stranger than what you have encountered. I will tell it to you."[6] Fade-out. Then a view of Holstenwall fades in, and the original story unfolds, ending, as has been seen, with the identification of Caligari. After a new fade-out the second and final episode of the framing story begins. Francis, having finished the narration, follows his companion back to the asylum, where he mingles with a crowd of sad figures—among them Cesare, who absent-mindedly caresses a little flower. The director of the asylum, a mild and understanding-looking person, joins the crowd. Lost in the maze of his hallucinations, Francis takes the director for the nightmarish character he himself has created, and accuses this imaginary fiend of being a dangerous madman. He screams, he fights the attendants in a frenzy. The scene is switched over to a sickroom, with the director putting on horn-rimmed spectacles which immediately change his appearance: it seems to be Caligari who examines the exhausted Francis. After this he removes his spectacles and, all mildness, tells his assistants that Francis believes him to be Caligari. Now that he understands the case of his patient, the director concludes, he will be able to heal him. With this cheerful message the audience is dismissed.

Janowitz and Mayer knew why they raged against the framing story: it perverted, if not reversed, their intrinsic intentions. While the original story exposed the madness inherent in authority, Wiene's Caligari glorified authority and convicted its antagonist of madness. A revolutionary film was thus turned into a conformist one—following the much-used pattern of declaring some normal but troublesome individual insane and sending him to a lunatic asylum. This change undoubtedly resulted not so much from Wiene's personal predilections as from his instinctive submission to the necessities of the screen; films, at least commercial films, are forced to answer to mass desires. In its changed form *Caligari* was no longer a product expressing, at best, sentiments characteristic of the intelligentsia, but a film supposed equally to be in harmony with what the less educated felt and liked.

If it holds true that during the postwar years most Germans eagerly tended to withdraw from a harsh outer world into the intangible realm of the soul, Wiene's version was certainly more consistent with their attitude than the original story; for, by putting the original into a box, this version faithfully mirrored the general retreat into a shell. In *Caligari* (and several other films of the time) the device of a framing story was not only an aesthetic form, but also had symbolic content. Significantly, Wiene avoided mutilating the original story itself. Even though *Caligari* had become a conformist film, it preserved and emphasized this revolutionary story—as a madman's fantasy. Caligari's defeat now belonged among psychological experiences. In this way Wiene's film does suggest that during their retreat into themselves the Germans were stirred to reconsider their traditional belief in authority. Down to the bulk of social democratic workers they refrained from revolutionary action; yet at the same time a psychological revolution seems to have prepared itself in the depths of the collective soul. The film reflects this double aspect of German life by coupling a reality in which Caligari's authority triumphs with a hallucination in which the same authority is overthrown. There could be no better configuration of symbols for that uprising against the authoritarian dispositions which apparently occurred under the cover of a behavior rejecting uprising.

Janowitz suggested that the settings for Caligari be designed by the painter and illustrator Alfred Kubin, who, a forerunner of the surrealists, made eerie phantoms invade harmless scenery and visions of torture emerge from the subconscious. Wiene took to the idea of painted canvases, but preferred to Kubin three expressionist artists: Hermann Warm, Walter Röhrig and Walter Reimann. They were affiliated with the Berlin Sturm group, which, through Herwarth Walden's magazine *Sturm*, promoted expressionism in every field of art.[7]

Although expressionist painting and literature had evolved years before the war, they acquired a public only after 1918. In this respect the case of Germany somewhat resembled that of Soviet Russia where, during the short period of war communism, diverse currents of abstract art enjoyed a veritable heyday.[8] To a revolutionized people expressionism seemed to combine the denial of bourgeois traditions with faith in man's power freely to shape society and nature. On account of such virtues it may have cast a spell over many Germans upset by the breakdown of their universe.[9]

"Films must be drawings brought to life": this was Hermann Warm's formula at the time that he and his two fellow designers were constructing the Caligari world.[10] In accordance with his beliefs, the canvases and draperies of *Caligari* abounded in complexes of jagged, sharp-pointed forms strongly reminiscent of gothic patterns. Products of a style which by then had become almost a mannerism, these complexes suggested houses, walls, landscapes. Except for a few slips or concessions— some backgrounds opposed the pictorial convention in too direct a manner, while others all but preserved them — the settings amounted to a perfect transformation of material objects into emotional ornaments. With its oblique chimneys on pell-mell roofs, its windows in the form of arrows or kites and its treelike

arabesques that were threats rather than trees, Holstenwall resembled those visions of unheard-of cities which the painter Lyonel Feininger evoked through his edgy, crystalline compositions.[11] In addition, the ornamental system in *Caligari* expanded through space, annulling its conventional aspect by means of painted shadows in disharmony with the lighting effects, and zigzag delineations designed to efface all rules of perspective. Space now dwindled to a flat plane, now augmented its dimensions to become what one writer called a "stereoscopic universe."[12]

Lettering was introduced as an essential element of the settings— appropriately enough, considering the close relationship between lettering and drawing. In one scene the mad psychiatrist's desire to imitate Caligari materializes in jittery characters composing the words "I must become Caligari"— words that loom before his eyes on the road, in the clouds, in the treetops. The incorporation of human beings and their movements into the texture of these surroundings was tremendously difficult. Of all the players only the two protagonists seemed actually to be created by a draftman's imagination. Werner Krauss as Caligari had the appearance of a phantom magician himself weaving the lines and shades through which he paced, and when Conrad Veidt's Cesare prowled along a wall, it was as if the wall had exuded him. The figure of an old dwarf and the crowd's antiquated costumes helped to remove the throng on the fair's tent-street from reality and make it share the bizarre life of abstract forms.

If Decla had chosen to leave the original story of Mayer and Janowitz as it was, these "drawings brought to life" would have told it perfectly. As expressionist abstractions they were animated by the same revolutionary spirit that impelled the two scriptwriters to accuse authority — the kind of authority revered in Germany — of inhuman excesses. However, Wiene's version disavowed this revolutionary meaning of expressionist staging, or, at least, put it, like the original story itself, in brackets. In the film *Caligari* expressionism seems to be nothing more than the adequate translation of a madman's fantasy into pictorial terms. This was how many contemporary German reviewers understood, and relished, the settings and gestures. One of the critics stated with self-assured ignorance: "The idea of rendering the notions of sick brains ... through expressionist pictures is not only well conceived but also well realized. Here this style has a right to exist, proves an outcome of solid logic."[13]

In their triumph the philistines overlooked one significant fact: even though *Caligari* stigmatized the oblique chimneys as crazy, it never restored the perpendicular ones as the normal. Expressionist ornaments also overrun the film's concluding episode, in which, from the philistines' viewpoint, perpendiculars should have been expected to characterize the revival of conventional reality. In consequence, the *Caligari* style was as far from depicting madness as it was from transmitting revolutionary messages. What function did it really assume?

During the postwar years expressionism was frequently considered a shaping of primitive sensations and experiences. Gerhart Hauptmann's brother Carl — a distinguished writer and poet with expressionist inclinations — adopted this definition, and then asked how the spontaneous manifestations of a profoundly agitated soul might best be formulated. While modern language, he contended, is too perfected to serve this purpose, the film — or the bioscop, as he termed it — offers a unique opportunity to externalize the fermentation of inner life. Of course, he said, the bioscop must feature only those gestures of things and of human beings which are truly soulful.[14]

Carl Hauptmann's views elucidate the expressionist style of Caligari. It had the function of characterizing the phenomena on the screen as phenomena of the soul — a function which overshadowed its revolutionary meaning. By making the film an outward projection of psychological events, expressionist staging symbolized — much more strikingly than did the device of a framing story — that general retreat into a shell which occurred in postwar Germany. It is not accidental that, as long as this collective process was effective, odd gestures and settings in an expressionist or similar style marked many a conspicuous film. *Variety*, of 1925, showed the final traces of them.[15] Owing to their stereotyped character, these settings

and gestures were like some familiar street sign — "Men at Work," for instance. Only here the lettering was different. The sign read: "Soul at Work."

After a thorough propaganda campaign culminating in the puzzling poster "You must become Caligari," Decla released the film in February 1920 in the Berlin Marmorhaus.[16] Among the press reviews — they were unanimous in praising Caligari as the first work of art on the screen — that of *Vorwärts*, the leading Social Democratic Party organ, distinguished itself by utter absurdity. It commented upon the film's final scene, in which the director of the asylum promises to heal Francis, with the words: "This film is also morally invulnerable inasmuch as it evokes sympathy for the mentally diseased, and comprehension for the self-sacrificing activity of the psychiatrists and attendants."[17] Instead of recognizing that Francis' attack against an odious authority harmonized with the Party's own antiauthoritarian doctrine, *Vorwärts* preferred to pass off authority itself as a paragon of progressive virtues. It was always the same psychological mechanism: the rationalized middle-class propensities of the Social Democrats interfering with their rational socialist designs. While the Germans were too close to Caligari to appraise its symptomatic value, the French realized that this film was more than just an exceptional film. They coined the term "*Caligarisme*" and applied it to a postwar world seemingly all upside down; which, at any rate, proves that they sensed the film's bearing on the structure of society. The New York première of *Caligari*, in April 1921, firmly established its world fame. But apart from giving rise to stray imitations and serving as a yardstick for artistic endeavors, this "most widely discussed film of the time" never seriously influenced the course of the American or French cinema.[18] It stood out lonely like a monolith.

Caligari shows the "Soul at Work." On what adventures does the revolutionized soul embark? The narrative and pictorial elements of the film gravitate toward two opposite poles. One can be labeled "Authority," or, more explicitly, "Tyranny." The theme of tyranny, with which the authors were obsessed, pervades the screen from beginning to end. Swivel-chairs of enormous height symbolize the superiority of the city officials turning on them, and, similarly, the gigantic back of the chair in Alan's attic testifies to the invisible presence of powers that have their grip on him. Staircases reinforce the effect of the furniture: numerous steps ascend to police headquarters, and in the lunatic asylum itself no less than three parallel flights of stairs are called upon to mark Dr. Caligari's position at the top of the hierarchy. That the film succeeds in picturing him as a tyrant figure of the stamp of Homunculus and Lubitsch's Henry VIII is substantiated by a most illuminating statement in Joseph Freeman's novel, *Never Call Retreat*. Its hero, a Viennese professor of history, tells of his life in a German concentration camp where, after being tortured, he is thrown into a cell: "Lying alone in that cell, I thought of Dr. Caligari; then, without transition, of the Emperor Valentinian, master of the Roman world, who took great delight in imposing the death sentence for slight or imaginary offenses. This Caesar's favorite expressions were: 'Strike off his head!'—'Burn him alive!'—'Let him be beaten with clubs till he expires!' I thought what a genuine twentieth century ruler the emperor was, and promptly fell asleep."[19] This dreamlike reasoning penetrates Dr. Caligari to the core by conceiving him as a counterpart of Valentinian and a premonition of Hitler. Caligari is a very specific premonition in the sense that he uses hypnotic power to force his will upon his tool—a technique foreshadowing, in content and purpose, that manipulation of the soul which Hitler was the first to practice on a gigantic scale. Even though, at the time of *Caligari*, the motif of the masterful hypnotizer was not unknown on the screen—it played a prominent role in the American film *Trilby*, shown in Berlin during the war—nothing in their environment invited the two authors to feature it.[20] They must have been driven by one of those dark impulses which, stemming from the slowly moving foundations of a people's life, sometimes engender true visions.

One should expect the pole opposing that of tyranny to be the pole of freedom; for it was doubtless their love of freedom which made Janowitz and Mayer disclose the nature of tyranny. Now this counterpole is the rallying-point of elements pertaining to the fair—the fair with its rows of tents, its confused crowds besieging them, and its diversity of thrilling amusements. Here Francis and Alan happily join the swarm of onlookers; here, on the scene of his triumphs, Dr. Caligari is finally trapped. In their attempts to define the character of a fair, literary sources repeatedly evoke the memory of Babel and Babylon alike. A seventeenth century pamphlet describes the noise typical of a fair as "such a distracted noise that you would think Babel not comparable to it," and, almost two hundred years later, a young English poet feels enthusiastic about "that Babylon of booths— The Fair."[21] The manner in which such Biblical images insert themselves unmistakably characterizes the fair as an enclave of anarchy in the sphere of entertainment. This accounts for its eternal attractiveness. People of all classes and ages enjoy losing themselves in a wilderness of glaring colors and shrill sounds, which is populated with monsters and abounding in bodily sensations—from violent shocks to tastes of incredible sweetness. For adults it is a regression into childhood days, in which games and serious affairs are identical, real and imagined things mingle, and anarchical desires aimlessly test infinite possibilities. By means of this regression the adult escapes a civilization which tends to overgrow and starve out the chaos of instincts—escapes it to restore that chaos upon which civilization nevertheless rests. The fair is not freedom, but anarchy entailing chaos.

Significantly, most fair scenes in Caligari open with a small iris-in exhibiting an organ-grinder whose arm constantly rotates, and, behind him, the top of a merry-go-round which never ceases its circular movement.[22] The circle here becomes a symbol of chaos. While freedom resembles a river, chaos resembles a whirlpool. Forgetful of self, one may plunge into chaos; one cannot move on in it. That the two authors selected a fair with its liberties as contrast to the oppressions of Caligari betrays the flaw in their revolutionary aspirations. Much as they longed for freedom, they were apparently incapable of imagining its contours.

There is something Bohemian in their conception; it seems the product of naïve idealism rather than true insight. But it might be said that the fair faithfully reflected the chaotic condition of postwar Germany.

Whether intentionally or not, *Caligari* exposes the soul wavering between tyranny and chaos, and facing a desperate situation: any escape from tyranny seems to throw it into a state of utter confusion. Quite logically, the film spreads an all-pervading atmosphere of horror. Like the Nazi world, that of *Caligari* overflows with sinister portents, acts of terror and outbursts of panic. The equation of horror and hopelessness comes to a climax in the final episode which pretends to re-establish normal life. Except for the ambiguous figure of the director and the shadowy members of his staff, normality realizes itself through the crowd of insane moving in their bizarre surroundings. The normal as a madhouse: frustration could not be pictured more finally. And in this film, as well as in *Homunculus*, is unleashed a strong sadism and an appetite for destruction.[23] The reappearance of these traits on the screen once more testifies to their prominence in the German collective soul.

Technical peculiarities betray peculiarities of meaning. In Caligari methods begin to assert themselves which belong among the special properties of German film technique. Caligari initiates a long procession of 100 percent studio-made films. Whereas, for instance, the Swedes at that time went to great pains to capture the actual appearance of a snowstorm or a wood, the German directors, at least until 1924, were so infatuated with indoor effects that they built up whole landscapes within the studio walls. They preferred the command of an artificial universe to dependence upon a haphazard outer world. Their withdrawal into the studio was part of the general retreat into a shell. Once the Germans had determined to seek shelter within the soul, they could not well allow the screen to explore that very reality which they abandoned. This explains the conspicuous role of architecture after *Caligari*—a role that has struck many an observer. "It is of the utmost importance," Paul Rotha remarks in a survey of the postwar period, "to grasp the significant part played by the architect in the development of the German cinema."[24] How could it be otherwise? The architect's façades and rooms were not merely backgrounds, but hieroglyphs. They expressed the structure of the soul in terms of space.

Caligari also mobilizes light. It is a lighting device which enables the spectators to watch the murder of Alan without seeing it; what they see, on the wall of the student's attic, is the shadow of Cesare stabbing that of Alan. Such devices developed into a specialty of the German studios. Jean Cassou credits the Germans with having invented a "laboratory-made fairy illumination,"[25] and Harry Alan Potamkin considers the handling of the light in the German film its "major contribution to the cinema."[26] This emphasis upon light can be traced to an experiment Max Reinhardt made on the stage shortly before *Caligari*. In his *mise-en-scène* of Sorge's prewar drama *The Beggar* (*Der Bettler*)—one of the earliest and most vigorous manifestations of expressionism—he substituted for normal settings imaginary ones created by means of lighting effects.[27] Reinhardt doubtless introduced these effects to be true to the drama's style. The analogy to the films of the postwar period is obvious: it was their expressionist nature which impelled many a German director of photography to breed shadows as rampant as weeds and associate ethereal phantoms with strangely lit arabesques or faces. These efforts were designed to bathe all scenery in an unearly illumination marking it as scenery of the soul. "Light has breathed soul into the expressionist films," Rudolph Kurtz states in his book on the expressionist cinema.[28] Exactly the reverse holds true: in those films the soul was the virtual source of the light. The task of switching on this inner illumination was somewhat facilitated by powerful romantic traditions.

The attempt made in *Caligari* to co-ordinate settings, players, lighting and action is symptomatic of the sense of structural organization which, from this film on, manifests itself on the German screen. Rotha coins the term "studio constructivism" to characterize "that curious air of completeness, of finality, that surrounds each product of the German studios."[29] But organizational completeness can be achieved only if the material to be organized does not object to it. (The ability of the Germans to organize themselves owes much to their longing for submission.) Since reality is essentially incalculable and therefore demands to be observed rather than commanded, realism on the screen and total organization exclude each other. Through their "studio constructivism" no less than their lighting the German films revealed that they dealt with unreal events displayed in a sphere basically controllable.[30]

In the course of a visit to Paris about six years after the première of *Caligari*, Janowitz called on Count Etienne de Beaumont in his old city residence, where he lived among Louis Seize furniture and Picassos. The Count voiced his admiration of *Caligari*, terming it "as fascinating and abstruse as the German soul." He continued: "Now the time has come for the German soul to speak, Monsieur. The French soul spoke more than a century ago, in the Revolution, and you have been mute.... Now we are waiting for what you have to impart to us, to the world."[31]

The Count did not have long to wait.

Notes

1. The following episode, along with other data appearing in my pages on *Caligari*, is drawn from an interesting manuscript Mr. Hans Janowitz has written about the genesis of this film. I feel greatly indebted to him for having put his material at my disposal. I am thus in a position to base my interpretation of Caligari on the true inside story, up to now unknown.

2. Vincent, *Histoire de l'Art Cinématographique*, p. 140.

3. *Jahrbuch der Filmindustrie*, 1922/3, pp. 35, 46. For an appraisal of Pommer, see Lejeune, *Cinema*, pp. 125–31.

4. Information offered by Mr. Lang, Cf. p. 56.

5. Extracted from Mr. Janowitz's manuscript. See also Vincent, *Histoire de l'Art Cinématographique*, pp. 140, 143–44.

6. Film license, issued by Board of Censors, Berlin, 1921 and 1925 (Museum of Modern Art Library, clipping files); *Film Society Programme*, March 14, 1926.

7. Mr. Janowitz's manuscript; Vincent, *Histoire de l'Art Cinématographique*, p. 144; Rotha, *Film Till Now*, p. 43.

8. Kurtz, *Expressionismus*, p. 61.

9. In Berlin, immediately after the war, Karl Heinz Martin staged two little dramas by Ernst Toller and Walter Hasenclever within expressionist settings. Cf. Kurtz, *ibid.*, p. 43; Vincent, *Histoire de l'Art Cinématographique*, pp. 142–43; Schapiro, "Nature of Abstract Art," *Marxist Quarterly*, Jan.–March 1937, p. 97.

10. Quotation from Kurtz, *Expressionismus*, p. 66. Warm's views, which implied a verdict on films as photographed reality, harmonized with those of Viking Eggeling, an abstract Swedish painter living in Germany. Having eliminated all objects from his canvases, Eggeling deemed it logical to involve the surviving geometrical compositions in rhythmic movements. He and his painter friend Hans Richter submitted this idea to Ufa, and Ufa, guided as ever by the maxim that art is good business or, at least, good propaganda, enabled the two artists to go ahead with their experiments. The first abstract films appeared in 1921. While Eggeling — he died in 1925 — orchestrated spiral lines and comblike figures in a short he called *Diagonal Symphony*, Richter composed his *Rhythm 21* of squares in black, gray and white. One year later, Walter Ruttmann, also a painter, joined in the trend with *Opus I*, which was a dynamic display of spots vaguely recalling X-ray photographs. As the titles reveal, the authors themselves considered their products a sort of optical music. It was a music that, whatever else it tried to impart, marked an utter withdrawal from the outer world. This esoteric *avant garde* movement soon spread over other countries. From about 1924, such advanced French artists as Fernand Léger and René Clair made films which, less abstract than the German ones, showed an affinity for the formal beauty of machine parts, and molded all kinds of objects and motions into surrealistic dreams.— I feel indebted to Mr. Hans Richter for having permitted me to use his unpublished manuscript, "Avantgarde, History and Dates of the Only Independent Artistic Film Movement, 1921–1931." See also *Film Society Programme*, Oct. 16, 1927; Kurtz, *Expressionismus*, pp. 86, 94; Vincent, *Histoire de l'Art Cinématographique*, pp. 159–61; Man Ray, "Answer to a Questionnaire," Film Art, no. 7, 1936, p. 9; Kraszna-Krausz, "Exhibition in Stuttgart, June 1929, and Its Effects," *Close Up*, Dec. 1929, pp. 461–62.

11. Mr. Feininger wrote to me about his relation to *Caligari* on Sept. 13, 1944: "Thank you for

your ... letter of Sept. 8. But if there has been any-thing I never had a part in nor the slightest knowledge of at the time, it is the film *Caligari*. I have never even seen the film.... I never met nor know the artists you name [Warm, Röhrig and Reimann] who devised the settings. Some time about 1911 I made, for my own edification, a series of drawings which I entitled: 'Die Stadt am Ende der Welt.' Some of these drawings were printed, some were exhibited. Later, after the birth of *Caligari*, I was frequently asked whether I had had a hand in its devising. This is all I can tell you...."

12. Cited by Carter, *The New Spirit*, p. 250, from H. G. Scheffauer, *The New Spirit in the German Arts.*— For the *Caligari* décor, see also Kurtz, *Expressionismus*, p. 66; Rotha, *Film Till Now*, p. 46; Jahier, "42 Ans de Cinéma," *Le Rôle Intellectuel du Cinéma*, pp. 60–61; "The Cabinet of Dr. Caligari," *Exceptional Photoplays*, March 1921, p. 4; Amiguet, *Cinéma! Cinéma!*, p. 50. For the beginnings of Werner Krauss and Conrad Veidt, see Kalbus, *Deutsche Filmkunst*, I, 28, 30, and Veidt, "Mein Leben," *Ufa-Magazin*, Jan. 14–20, 1927.

13. Review in *8 Uhr Abendblatt*, cited in *Caligari-Heft*, p. 8.

14. Carl Hauptmann, "Film und Theater," *Der Film von Morgen*, p. 20. See also Alten, "Die Kunst in Deutschland," *Ganymed*, 1920, p. 146; Kurtz, *Expressionismus*, p. 14.

15. Cf. p. 127.

16. *Jahrbuch der Filmindustrie*, 1922/3, p. 81.

17. Quoted from *Caligari-Heft*, p. 23.

18. Quotation from Jacobs, *American Film*, p. 303; see also pp. 304–5.

19. Freeman, *Never Call Retreat*, p. 528.

20. Kalbus, *Deutsche Filmkunst*, I, 95.

21. McKechnie, *Popular Entertainments*, pp. 33, 47.

22. Rotha, *Film Till Now*, p. 285. For the role of fairs in films, see E. W. And M. M. Robson, *The Film Answers Back*, pp. 196–97.— An iris-in is a technical term for opening up the scene from a small circle of light in a dark screen until the whole frame is revealed.

23. Cf. p. 33.

24. Rotha, *Film Till Now*, p. 180. Cf. Potamkin, "Kino and Lichtspiel," *Close Up*, Nov. 1929, p. 387.

25. Cited in Leprohon, "Le Cinéma Allemand," *Le Rouge et le Noir*, July 1928, p. 135.

26. Potamkin, "The Rise and Fall of the German Film," *Cinema*, April 1930, p. 24.

27. Kurtz, *Expressionismus*, p. 59.

28. *Ibid.*, p. 60.

29. Rotha, *Film Till Now*, pp. 107–8. Cf. Potamkin, "Kino and Lichtspiel," *Close Up*, Nov. 1929, p. 388, and "The Rise and Fall of the German Film," *Cinema*, April 1930, p. 24.

30. Film connoisseurs have repeatedly criticized *Caligari* for being a stage imitation. This aspect of the film partly results from its genuinely theatrical action. It is action of a well-constructed dramatic conflict in stationary surroundings— action which does not depend upon screen representation for significance. Like *Caligari*, all "indoor" films of the postwar period showed affinity for the stage in that they favored inner-life dramas at the expense of conflicts involving outer reality. However, this did not necessarily prevent them from growing into true films. When, in the wake of *Caligari*, film technique steadily progressed, the psychological screen dramas increasingly exhibited an imagery that elaborated the significance of their action. *Caligari*'s theatrical affinity was also due to technical backwardness. An immovable camera focused upon the painted decor; no cutting device added meaning of its own to that of the pictures. One should, of course, not forget the reciprocal influence *Caligari* and kindred films exerted, for their part, on the German stage. Stimulated by the use they made of the iris-in, stage lighting took to singling out a lone player, or some important sector of the scene. Cf. Barry, *Program Notes*, Series III, program 1; Gregor, *Zeitalter des Films*, pp. 134, 144–45; Rotha, *Film Till Now*, p. 275; Vincent, *Histoire de l'Art Cinématographique*, p. 139.

31. From Janowitz's manuscript.

References

Amiguet, Fréd.-Ph. *Cinéma, Cinéma!* Lausanne and Genève, 1923

Barry, Iris. *Program Notes.* Museum of Modern Art Film Library. [Reviews of and commentary on films.]

Caligari-Heft. Was Destuche Zeitungen über den Film Berichten. Berlin. [A publicity pamphlet issued by Decla-Bioscop Konzern.]

Carter, Huntly. *The New Spirit in the Cinema.* London, 1930.

Freeman, Joseph. *Never Call Retreat.* New York, 1943. [A novel.]

Gregor, Joseph. *Das Zeitalter des Films.* 3rd ed. Wien, 1932.

Jacobs, Lewis. *The Rise of the American Film: A Critical History.* New York, 1939. [2nd ed. Teachers College Press, 1968.]

Jahrbuch der Filmindustrie (Berlin, 1923). 1. Jahrgang: 1922/3.

Kalbus, Oskar. *Vom Werden Deutscher Filmkunst* (Altona-Behrenfeld, Germany, 1935). I: Der stumme Film; II. Der Tonfilm.

Kurtz, Rudolf. *Expressionismus und Film.* Berlin, 1926.

McKechnie, Samuel. *Popular Entertainments Through the Ages.* London, 1931.

Pabst, G. W., "Servitude et Grandeur d'Hollywood," *Le Rôle Intellectuel du Cinéma.* Société des Nations, Cahier 3 (Paris, 1937), pp. 251–55.

Robson, E. W., and M. M. Robson. *The Film Answers Back.* London, 1939.

Rotha, Paul. *The Film Till Now.* London, 1930. [Rev. ed. Boston: Twayne, 1960].

Vincent, Carl. *Histoire de l'Art Cinématographique.* Bruxelles, 1939.

CHAPTER 5

The Impact of D. W. Griffith on Soviet Montage: 1919–1925

Introduction

Soviet filmmakers used a variety of methods to exploit the power of film as an ideological tool to influence and proselytize the audience toward the goals and values of the new communist state. At first, the ideas of the new communist regime were incorporated into newsreels designed to indoctrinate the people. After the Civil War in Russia, the cinema was given greater importance by the new Soviet leaders, especially Lenin, who envisioned the social and political possibilities of film to educate the masses about the new Soviet society. The most influential theorists, such as Lev Kuleshov and Vsevolod Meyerhold, were employed in Moscow's new Film School to teach a handful of talented young filmmakers the art of editing using the work of D. W. Griffith as their model.

By 1925, the Soviets fully launched their exhibition program of propaganda films. These films were made by four major filmmakers: Dziga Vertov, Sergei Eisenstein, Vsevolod Pudovkin and Alexander Dovzhenko, in various film centers in the Soviet Union. Established upon the ideological framework of Marxism, these feature films implemented the words of Lenin "to transform Socialism from a Utopia into a Science in a class struggle to seize political power and to organize a Socialist state." The Soviet filmmakers adopted the machine aesthetic of the constructivist and futurist manifesto whereby a "pictorial realism" presented the dynamics and forces of modern science and technology that would reshape the postwar world of the 1920s and the future of humankind.

For these film artists, modern art was not only scientific but an art form using technology in the service of a new revolutionary state. Experimental at first, its chief task was a "dynamic transformation of society" featuring a logic of structure, a logic of invention and a formative principle, to interpret the actual world through the Hegelian-Marxist dialectic of conflict and resolution of opposites. The theatrical work of Meyerhold and Eisenstein visualized constructivist dynamics of space-time kinetics to reconstitute older art forms into cinematic forces toward a new social and political entity.

The Kuleshov Workshop demonstrated that real time and space were subordinate to the process of editing. Griffith's great epics, *The Birth of a Nation* and *Intolerance*, became models for learning new techniques of montage editing for both Eisenstein and Pudovkin. Vertov's film magazine *Kino-Pravda* found his *agit-prop* techniques able to capture the dynamics of "life caught unawares" in his documentary films. Dovzhenko applied the ideas of "creative geography" to create a "poetic cinema" through the use of metaphors and elliptical editing. Out of this creative experimentation, formalist filmmaking learned to manipulate any socio-political happening into a dynamic narrative through the power of the film image. These innovations in film form brought excitement to the world. Today their rediscovery has energized a new film generation.

Constructivism

Before the Great War (1914–1918) and the Bolshevik Revolution of 1917, modernist attacks upon traditional European painting and sculpture had produced work from the Expressionists like James Ensor and Edvard Munch and the cubists like Picasso and Georges Braque. They, in turn, influenced the Italian Futurists, especially Filippo Marinetti and Umberto Boccioni. These visual artists proclaimed in their manifestos that the new realities of the industrial revolution brought a modern age into existence. They acknowledged the powers of planes, automobiles and locomotives, of dynamic machines, to transform time and space. The futurists actively sought the destruction of the museum, of history, and of past traditions with the establishment of an "ideal order" situated upon the expression of speed, force and violence. These machines and their dynamism would lead modern humankind into a "new reality" created by art, science and technology. The transformations would be exposed through cinematic forms.

These cubo-futurist ideas were reconstructed by Russian artists, such as Vladimir Tatlin, Alexander Rodchenko and El Lissitzky into a post-revolutionary Marxist movement, Constructivism. The major theme behind this artistic movement was the socialization of art to meet the material needs and aspirations of the revolutionary proletariat class. As argued by Naum Gabo in his *Realist Manifesto of 1920*, Constructivism would achieve its goals through the combination of science, technology and art by creating a new vision and synthesis for a new society.

> The realization of our perceptions of the world in forms and images of time and space is the only aim of our pictorial and plastic art. We construct our work as the universe constructs its own, as an engineer constructs bridges ... In creating things (objects) we take away all accidental and local features leaving only the constant rhythm of the forces in them [Gabo, quoted in Chipp 1968, p. 328].

By merging the forms of this new non-objective art with the needs of the formation of a new society, the Soviet leaders decided to develop and train artist-engineers to produce work illustrative of the relevance and power of modern technology and the new communist state. Their employment of constructivist principles and ideas met the needs of the revolutionary Soviet forces and became the dominant influence in Soviet theories of filmmaking, especially in the documentary work of Dziga Vertov and Sergei Eisenstein, and in the thematic content of Alexander Dovzhenko. Both Vertov and Eisenstein advanced theories on the nature of cinematic language and the relationship between film and reality that continues to influence filmmakers today.

As had the German film industry, the Soviets nationalized film production in 1919 through the creation of a new Ministry of Education and Propaganda headed by Lenin's wife, Nadezhda. Under the Cinema committee, this film school, the All Union State Institute of Cinematography, was located in Moscow and known by its initials as the VGIK. Its prime purpose was to train actors and technicians in the art of *Agitki*, political propaganda newsreels edited for the purpose of agitation and propaganda, thus called "*agit-prop*." These newsreels traveled to large urban centers throughout the vast Soviet Union after the Civil War (1917–1921) using "Agit-trains" and boats as mobile propaganda centers. Vertov directed *The Agit-Train VTSIK* (1921) and a 13-reel *History of the Civil War* (1922) using documentary footage. The propaganda campaigns highlighted posters, cartoons and theatrical sketches as well as film newsreels to disseminate news of Red victories and White defeats and to inform and win over the mostly illiterate population on the benefits of the new Soviet state and its policies. (An exciting film reconstruction of the Russian Civil War featuring these agit-prop trains can be viewed in the 1981 film *Reds*, directed by Warren Beatty.)

Dziga Vertov and Kino-Pravda

A young man in his twenties named Dziga Vertov, born Denis Kaufman (1896–1954), became the Moscow editor of agit-prop newsreels for the Cinema committee. His intent was to put together the latest documentary footage on the progress of the war and the success of the Red Army, in a fashion similar to today's television newscasts. Film truth, or *Kino-Pravda* as Vertov saw it, was a documentation of socialist reality. His theory of documentary filmmaking was based upon the truth of "fragments of reality." When assembled together as an art form, the rhetoric of these war images carried to the people the impact of a highly emotional ideological vision of a Marxist society. With his notion of the objective camera or *Kino-Eye,* Vertov stressed that bits of truth on the screen must be organized thematically so that the whole film appears to convey a cultural truth. However, he knowingly implanted cinematic techniques of a formalist nature such as split screens, superimpositions and bizarre camera angles with camera tricks of stop-motion, pixilation and rapid montage to reenforce the magic of the cinema and its visual impact.

When Stalin replaced Lenin in 1928, Vertov's documentary ideas collided with a new production style called "social realism," as decreed by the All-Party Congress on Film Questions. This new Soviet film strategy aimed to organize fictional film content within the range of political goals of the party. The Congress also ruled that Soviet directors should avoid formalist methods in film production, a directive aimed both at Vertov and Eisenstein. Yet Vertov asked, quite rightly, how could a documentary filmmaker predict or guarantee what "truths" he would find when he recorded on film the changing world of daily life? Frustrated by these regulations, he left Moscow when his concept for a "city symphony" was accepted by Soviet authorities at a film studio in Kiev. This film project would document the daily life of people living and working within the new urban centers of the Soviet Union, although Vertov carefully withheld specifying shots or sequences. With his brother Mikhail Kaufman as cinematographer, he created an epic film on the reflexive role of cinema in modern life. *Man with a Movie Camera* (1929) presents on one level a kaleidoscopic vision of urban existence in the Soviet Union, organized according to the rituals of life from early dawn to dusk.

At the same time, the spectator is engaged with a discourse on filmmaking through actual images of the man making the film, while simultaneously recording these actions of people awaking, going to work, and at play. Hence, a spectator sees both the film techniques involved in making a film and witnesses at the same time the footage of the film being made. By making the audience consciously aware of how a film mediates physical reality, Vertov constantly reminds the viewers of the many film tricks and contrivances that can deliberately alter the human perception of these "images of reality." Vertov's own delight and playfulness as a director of self-reflective cinema strongly influenced the work of Chris Marker, Jean-Luc Godard and Jean Rouch when the French New Wave came into prominence in the 1950s.

The Kuleshov Workshop

Vertov's theories augmented the theories of Lev Kuleshov (1899–1970), co-founder of the Soviet silent cinema. Like Vertov, Kuleshov was a cinematographer during the Civil War. He also was a competent director. At the age of 20, he was given permission to found his own workshop for research into film techniques outside the formal structure of the VGIK.

The Kuleshov Workshop devoted itself almost exclusively to experiments in montage editing, since raw film stock was scarce. Joining the group were students like Pudovkin, who concerned themselves with a study of Griffith's epic *Intolerance* and, later, when the foreign blockade was lifted in 1920, a print of Griffith's *The Birth of a Nation.* As indicated in Chapter 3, *Intolerance* was based upon four different stories that were unified into an epic spectacle through extensive intercutting. Though the stories occurred in different times and places, Griffith illustrated thematically how intolerance was still practiced from biblical times to the present. While Griffith used parallel editing, intertext titles and close-ups, Kuleshov and his students examined the editing techniques of cross-cutting and contrast cutting to engage the sympathy of the audience as they also advanced the narrative in each episode. They also matched Griffith's use of rapid and rhythmic editing to generate emotional tension and suspense during his famous last-minute rescues in both films. From these studies, Kuleshov and his students concluded that the three basic functions of montage editing are as follows:

1. A *narrative* function through cross-cutting from one action to another and through flashbacks.

2. An *intellectual* function through metaphorical or metonymical cuts between images or by parallel cutting between similar actions. Meaning is generated thus by contrast, correspondence or a signifying chain of connections among those images,

3. An *emotional* or psychological function based upon setting tempo through rapid montage or the content of the shot. Rhythmical editing could increase narrative tensions while tonal or formal cuts could increase emotional suspense (Kawin and Mast 1996, pp. 177–78).

Kuleshov's goal was to discover the ways in which film editing or montage communicated meaning to an audience on all three levels simultaneously. As recounted in Vsevolod Pudovkin's book *Film Technique and Film Acting*, Kuleshov displayed his knowledge of the impact of montage through the "Kuleshov effect" in which the image in a shot has two distinct values as a cinematic sign. One value is what the image possesses in itself as a photographic image of reality, and the second is what it acquires when placed in a metonymic relationship or connection to other images in a different shot. Kuleshov concluded that meaning in cinema is a function of editing and not of different shots of the photographed reality; meaning arises from the sequential arrangements of these shots in relationship to each other. Further experiments revealed to Kuleshov that film was able to create the impression or illusion of spatial and temporal unity by editing together shots taken in different places at different times, then logically weaving them into the narrative. The creation of "artificial landscapes" was called creative geography. Thus the "dynamatization of space" and the "spatialization of time" is controlled by the narrative in the process of montage editing.

A Dialectical Approach to Film Form

Sergei Eisenstein (1898–1948) placed special emphasis on the art and theory of editing images in a film. His theory of editing conforms to his understanding of the laws of change. When these laws of change are applied to art forms they take on the dynamics of a dialectic of opposites to create new concepts. He stated that "dialectical montage is an idea that arises from the collision of independent shots—shots even opposite to one another" (Eisenstein 1969, p. 49). As a filmmaker, he shared this belief with his Russian colleagues, Kuleshov and Pudovkin, that editing or montage was the foundation of film form. When Eisenstein applied dialectical montage to editing his films, he strove to capture a visual counterpoint of opposing images that would mentally combine in the spectator's mind into a new abstract idea. Eisenstein found various ways to juxtapose shots, from countering different movements in shots to varying the temporal dimensions of the shots. (One may note these montage effects in the *Battleship Potemkin*'s Odessa Steps sequence.) He explained how other techniques produce conflict by juxtaposing different shots of contrasting size, shape, volume, direction and lighting. Further examples of conflict can be obtained through change of camera position and through varying the length of shots. The result is to continually create dynamic tensions and rhythms between the collision of different independent images that force the spectator into an intellectual exploration of ideas through the dialectical structure.

One can understand how the impact of editing techniques first used by Griffith in *Intolerance*, primarily for representational and narrative reasons that involved the audiences in 19th century melodramas, was advanced by the Soviet filmmakers into a new method. For these directors like Eisenstein, Vertov and Pudovkin, editing served mainly to create expressive or symbolic meanings using dissimilar images linked synthetically to produce particular metaphoric and metonymic relationships. In *Battleship Potemkin* (1925), Eisenstein based his editing on psychological stimulation of the audience rather than the narrative logic of the story. Film viewers may have become accustomed to this editing strategy from Alfred Hitchcock mystery thrillers later on. Soviet montage was developed to mold and reinforce the values and ideology of the new Soviet state. Soviet silent films emphasized the revolution and the coming of a new age and a new government. They propagandized the efforts of the proletariat and the coming of the machine to bring new life to the country. Compared to expressionistic techniques used by German directors, Soviet constructivism concentrated on a documentary form of realism. Where the German directors created the mood of the internal world through expressionistic film noir lighting, the Soviet directors placed greater value on montage editing, in accordance with the constructivist credo and its emphasis on movement in space-time and multiple views of an action through cinematic abstractions of life by the *Kino-Eye*.

The Films of Sergei Eisenstein

The most influential of these directors was Sergei Eisenstein, who, under the tutelage of Meyerhold, designed a formalist approach to film form in the juxtaposition of film images as seen in his great epic *Battleship Potemkin* (1925). Eisenstein's early theatre work incorporated these constructivist ideas. For Shaw's play, *Heartbreak House*, Eisenstein designed an old wooden sailing ship in the form of a modern steamship, and then abstracted the elements of the ship into a kinetic sculpture according to constructivist aims. On an angular-space stage he placed spiraling ramps, open staircases, and other machine elements that were suspended by cables. Many of these elements were used in his earlier films when he abstracted similar features on board the battleship *Potemkin*.

Eisenstein's formalist montage techniques differed considerably from Pudovkin's. Pudovkin strove to maintain a relational "link-age" of images that connected them to emotional responses akin to Griffith, but Eisenstein wanted to create a new dialectical meaning through the "collision of images." He was knowledgeable of the cubist collages of Picasso and Tatlin, and decided to use a newsreel look in his cinematographic experiments. Using the principles of collages, in which real materials are combined with painted or illusionistic renderings, he incorporated an actual fragment or document of reality directly into his films, thus breaking completely away from the static illusionism of traditional art. When projected, these cinematic images of reality transferred the objects themselves onto the screen. As separate images they gained new meaning when reassembled and juxtaposed to other images in his film. Eisenstein's montage constructed meaning metonymically, according to the power images as signifiers have to make connections to other signifiers, assuring an impact upon the spectator in a calculated and predetermined manner. Thus, Eisenstein, like the artist-engineer he was, employed the effects of cinematic perception and its powers of attraction to "produce an image embodying the content of the theme with utmost vividness" (Eisenstein 1970, p. 65).

Eisenstein was greatly influenced by Griffith's way of reconstructing and recreating a storyline. Like Griffith, once the theme of the film was agreed on from the Soviet perspective, Eisenstein strove to make the spectacle appear to be as intensely real on the screen as if the action were actually taking place before our eyes. With this objective in mind, his strategy in filmmaking was four-fold. First, the spectacle on the screen must be created from actual elements of physical reality. When this environment is photographed in unstaged newsreel or documentary style, it will appear to be intensely realistic. This historical accuracy creates the visual texture within the film. Second, Eisenstein decided to use non-actors or very few trained actors in the leads, instead he cast the roles with people whose faces and bodies told us what we needed to know about their character. This use by Eisenstein of stereotypes, as revealed in his films, is designated as "typage." Third, the use of actual locations inhabited by

A scene from the Odessa Steps sequence in Sergei M. Eisenstein's *Battleship Potemkin* (1925). The mother and child fall under the volleys of Czarist soldiers.

real people and not actors could easily be controlled by the director through careful camera placement, lighting and camera angles. When this technique was combined with various editing strategies, Eisenstein knew he could produce the intellectual, narrative and emotional results he wanted. Fourth, thematic or ideological considerations are always dominant over the narrative elements. Eisenstein wanted each sequence to reenforce and reconstitute the basic discourse of the film. His films lack a linear plot; rather, they follow a narrative of collective action by people who unite to overthrow the inhumanity of despots who cause injury and death. He follows this basic scenario in all his films, starting from his first major film *Strike* (1924). In this film Eisenstein utilizes documentary footage to illustrate how men and machinery can take up collective action

against evil and unjust tyrants. *Battleship Potemkin* develops from this same overriding moral concern.

The Odessa Steps Sequence

This famous film sequence from Eisenstein's *Battleship Potemkin* illustrates some of the "oppositions" he employs to create emotional and intellectual tensions. He describes how the dialectical theory of montage and the "collision of forces" occurs in this sequence after the title card "Suddenly" appears.

> A tight shot of a row of jackbooted feet step in unison onto the first flight of stone stairs. Then there are *close-ups* of people rushing chaotically. Then, *long shots* of the same scene. The chaotic movement is fol-

Reverse angle of mother and child as they appear to the soldiers firing at them. Eisenstein's montage editing in *Battleship Potemkin* intercut various shots to demonstrate his theory of collision, one which captures the fear, horror and confusion of the dramatic sequence.

lowed by shots showing the feet of soldiers as they march *rhythmically* down the steps. Tempo increases. Rhythm accelerates. When the downward movement of the people reaches the bottom, a solitary figure of a mother carrying her dead son, slowly goes up the stairs. Further rushing away from the soldiers while the mother cries out, "My child is hurt."

Close-ups give place to *long shots*. The *chaotic* rush of people is contrasted to the *rhythmic* march of the soldiers firing on the crowd. One aspect of movement gives way to another, the descent of the perambulator. *Descent* give place to *ascent*. The many volleys of the rifles give over to one shot of the battleship's guns. At each step there is a leap from one dimension to an-

other, from one quality to another" [Eisenstein 1968, p. 14].

The acclaim garnered by the exhibition of *Battleship Potemkin* throughout the world gave credence to the goals of the Soviet Revolution and brought fame to Eisenstein. Yet, when Stalin replaced Lenin in 1927, Eisenstein's film career took a decisive turnaround and he left Moscow to entertain ideas of making films in Hollywood. His political beliefs were shunned by the movie magnates and only the sponsorship of the Socialist writer Upton Sinclair helped him develop the film project *Que Viva Mexico* (1932). Financial pressures and arguments over the script caused Sinclair to cancel the project and sell the filmed footage to a

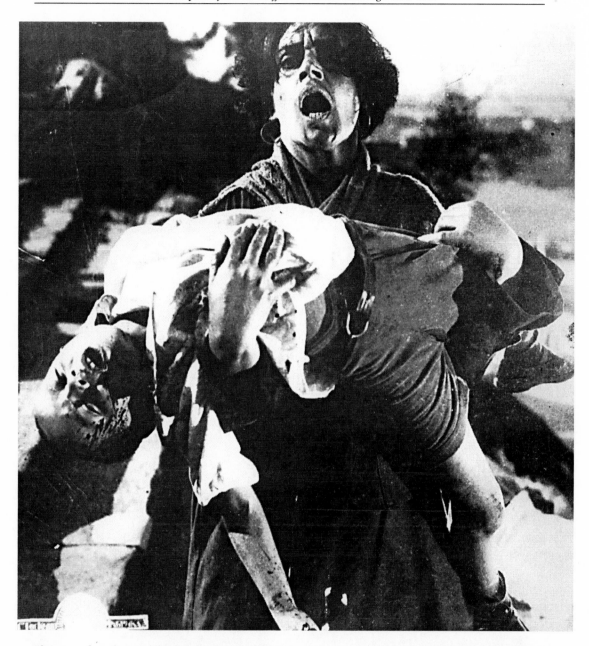

Close-up of mother and dead child as part of the Odessa Steps sequence before the bombardment from the battleship *Potemkin* starts the Revolution of 1905. Taken from the 1976 restored version, this still reveals details difficult to see in the previous photos, which come from the deteriorated original.

lesser Hollywood producer, who edited the film and released it in 1933 as the melodrama *Thunder over Mexico*.

On the eve of a Nazi invasion, Eisenstein was asked to make a film about Prince Alexander Nevski of Novgorod, the great Slavic hero who rallied the Russians to fight invading Teutonic Knights in the 13th century. The film was clearly meant to serve as a rallying cry against the Nazis, who were gaining power in Eastern Europe. This would be Eisenstein's first sound film, and according to George Sadoul, Eisenstein conceived the project as "an opera in which Sergei Prokofiev's brilliant score would alternately complement and conflict with the film's visual rhythms" (Cook 1990, p. 372). The film's sound score accomplished the realization of Eisenstein's theories of contrapuntal sound.

"Every shot in *Alexander Nevski* is painstakingly composed in terms of the plastic arrangement of space, mass, and light within the frame" (Cook 1990, p. 372). The invaders, for instance, were always shown in geometric formation, while the Russians were depicted asymmetrically, suggesting a comparison of the rigid Germans with the disorganized, but forceful, Russians. One of the most arresting impressions of the film was perhaps influenced by the costuming of Ku Klux Klan members in *The Birth of a Nation*. Eisenstein dressed his German invaders in menacing helmets with only tiny slits for the eyes, so their faces, unlike the Russians,' were never visible. Also, the military symbols on the knights' uniforms were clearly designed to resemble the German swastika, and the atrocities committed to the people of Pskov by the Teutonic Knights serve to remind viewers of the violence of the Nazis.

"The film's most impressive sequence is the famous Battle of the Ice on frozen Lake Peipus in northwest Russia, actually shot in the outskirts of Moscow in midsummer with artificial snow and ice. Here the decisive battle between the Teutons and the Russian defenders is rendered in a spectacular audiovisual montage complete with swish pans and a jolting, rough-and-tumble camera style that would not be seen again until the early days of the French New Wave" (Cook 1990, pp. 372–373).

The Films of Vsevolod Pudovkin and Alexander Dovzhenko

Vsevolod Pudovkin (1893–1953) and Alexander Dovzhenko (1894–1956) are the other dominant Soviet filmmakers of this silent era. Both contributed major films concerning the heroic

With the use of operatic music to rally the Russian people against German forces led by 13th-century Teutonic Knights, Eisenstein's *Alexander Nevsky* (1938) revives the battle between the Russians and the Germans in an impressive sequence known as the Battle on the Ice.

Storming the gates of the prison in Vsevolod I. Pudovkin's *Mother* (1926).

men and women who made the Revolution a reality. Pudovkin was a disciple of Lev Kuleshov. His first film, *Mechanics of the Brain* (1926), is based upon Pavlovian theories of reflex conditioning. His attraction to behaviorist methods followed his editing experiences with the psychological consistency he found in working with montage sequences from D. W. Griffith's *Intolerance* at the Kuleshov Workshop. Pudovkin's methods of editing stressed those elements that controlled the "psychological guidance" of the spectator through relational editing. This practice imitated D. W. Griffith's work directly by the use of cross-cutting to depict simultaneous actions, the use of symbolism and the use of *Leitmotifs* that emphasized the basic theme of the melodrama. Of more importance is his concept of "plastic materials," in which close-ups of objects could reveal the inner feel-

ings of a character. His notable films of the silent period were *Mother* (1926), *The End of St. Petersburg* (1927) and *Storm over Asia* (1928). These films demonstrate Pudovkin's interest in a central character who unwittingly is forced to act on the behalf of the public good rather than on his or her personal interests.

Pudovkin adapted Maxim Gorki's short novel, *Mother*, as a film experiment to awaken revolutionary passions for the new Soviet cause. This message becomes the central theme of the film. The narrative relies upon strong personal appeal through "building forces" that overcome the Czarist attacks and their injustices. Pudovkin stresses this political reawakening through the central character during an absurd mock trial that sends her son to prison. In retaliation against the court, she takes up the subversive political cause of her son and helps

Planning the escape with other prisoners in *Mother*. The emphasis is on capturing the solidarity of the revolutionaries.

The son is captured by Cossack soldiers as his mother watches the revolutionaries being slaughtered in Pudovkin's *Mother*.

him escape from prison. The two meet again in a May Day demonstration that coincides with a prison break of other political prisoners. During this final sequence Pudovkin introduces images of the break-up of the ice on the river, with cross-cuts of the son's escape and the formation of the May Day demonstration and conflict against mounted Cossack soldiers. This emotional climax is modeled directly on Griffith's *Way Down East.* The montage effects of the massacre overwhelm the viewer and raise the pathos of the film into a powerful emotional experience leading to political awareness.

Alexander Dovzhenko directed two major film poems, *Arsenal* (1929) and *Earth* (1930). These films employ the kind of editing created by painterly impressions of his beloved Ukrainian landscape. Unfamiliar with rapid montage editing used by Eisenstein or Pudovkin, with shots governed by compositional, graphic or tonal content or by rhythm and movement within the frame, Dovzhenko structures his film with visual metaphors that enrich a common event. He then enlarges the thematic content within the action by referring the primary images to other images with related meanings and associations. This poetic process allows the director to introduce elliptical jumps in time and space that integrate the central character's action while changing the mood and place of the action. His assemblage of shots corresponds with the notion of "creative geography" exploited in films by Lev Kuleshov. When imaginatively structured by Dovzhenko, this alternative method of film montage focuses upon dream symbolism and folklore.

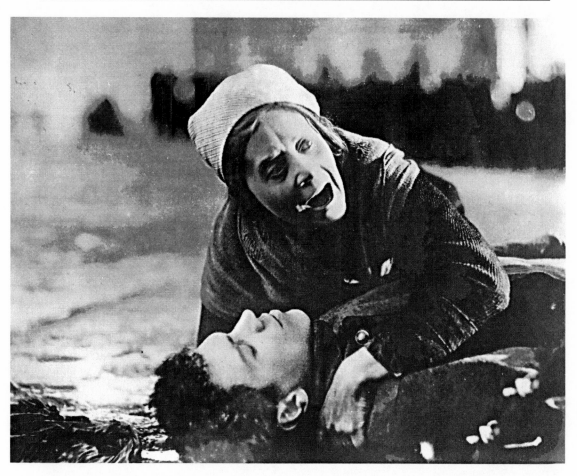

The mother realizes what is happening too late and cries out after her son is struck down. From this moment she becomes the flag carrier for the revolutionaries and joins the attack against their enemies in *Mother*.

Although Dovzhenko's films are framed within the dynamic conflicts arising from the transformation of the older agrarian communities to the newer collective farming systems of the Soviet state, themes of innocence, nostalgia and patriotism are metaphorically mixed with the new social reality of the modern totalitarian state. The conflicts that are fought lose all moral integrity, and the spectacle of death occupies a major portion of his films. The "machine aesthetic," embraced by the futurists and constructivists, takes on a cruel and sinister representation. It is symbolized by the modern farm tractor, which evokes a Frankensteinian image, destroying the spirit of the people who become victimized by the effects of its all-encompassing power.

Dovzhenko's childlike naiveté and inno-cence were paramount in his desire to work as a film artist. His "poetic cinema" takes its place during the 1920s as a full-fledged art form. Thus, his poetic strategies celebrate "the simple working man, the creator of earthly fruits. [It] is a primary feature of Dovzhenko's philosophy. The passion of his films and writings is always intended to further the revolutionary reconstruction of the world — and of man first of all" (Carynnyk 1973, p. xli). The montage editing of Dovzhenko is comparable to collages of Picasso and Braque in that they make the viewer more aware of the process of cinematic realities. Like Robert Rauschenberg's new combine paintings, poetic cinema attempts to narrow the gap between art and life by deconstructing the illusions created by any traditional work of art.

References

Carynnyk, Marco. 1973. "Introduction" in Alexander Dovzhenko. 1973. *Alexander Dovzhenko: The Poet as Filmmaker.* Translated by Marco Carynnyk. Cambridge, Mass.: MIT Press.

Chipp, Herschel B. 1968. *Theories of Modern Art: A Source Book by Artists and Critics.* Berkeley: University of California Press.

Cook, David A. 1990. *A History of Narrative Film 2nd Ed.* New York: W.W. Norton.

Eisenstein, Sergei. 1968. *The Battleship Potemkin.* Translated by Gillon R. Aiken. London: Lorrimer Publishing Co.

_____. 1969. *The Film Sense* (rev. ed.). Edited and translated by Jay Leyda. New York: Harcourt Brace Jovanovich.

_____. 1970. *Notes of a Film Director* (rev. ed.). Translated by X. Danko. New York: Dover Publications.

Kuleshov, Lev. 1974. *Kuleshov on Film.* Translated by Ronald Levaco. Berkeley and Los Angeles: University of California Press.

Mast, Gerald, and Bruce F. Kawin. 1996. *A Short History of the Movies.* 6th ed. Boston and London: Allyn and Bacon.

Pudovkin, V. I. 1959. *Film Technique and Film Acting.* London: Vision Press.

CHAPTER 6

The French Avant-Garde Tradition and Surrealism

Introduction

In Paris of the 1920s, the French avant-garde filmmakers joined forces with the cubist, Dadaist and surrealist painters to create experimental films that conjured up a cinematic dreamscape, a fantasy world in motion. For the Dadaists, this contradictory relationship of subjective and objective states of mind was a deliberate attack against the materialistic tastes of the bourgeoisie. They were led by Marcel Duchamp, Francis Picabia and Man Ray, who "liberated" machine-made forms through their nonsensical displacements. The Surrealist movement then advocated the idea of "pure psychic automatism" in the creation of art works. Within this surreal mode of expression, documentary or objective reality is displaced by an inner world of dreams where strange and unpredictable happenings create a multiplicity of viewpoints. The absence of linear narratives in the non-objective or abstract films gave impetus to the development of new methods in cinematographic imagery using camera tricks similar to those favored by Méliès. In rejecting traditional models of film form based upon 19th century literature and drama, these artists advanced ideas from other media and disciplines. As experimental filmmakers, they stressed alternative ways for cinematic expression to interpret the ambiguities and absurdities of the modern world.

For Buñuel and Dalí, desire creates an irrational state of being, one that ignores logic and rationality as depicted in their film *Un Chien andalou* (1928). Other French Impressionist film directors like Marcel L'Herbier and Jean Epstein followed the concepts of the Italian playwright, Luigi Pirandello, who advanced the notion that illusion and reality are interchangeable. Using this concept, they created moody surreal dramas through camera effects. From this group of filmmakers emerged two dominant French directors, Jean Vigo and Jean Renoir, who carried these avant-garde ideas into the sound films of the 1930s.

The Impact of Dada and Surrealism on Motion Pictures

While the artists in the Soviet Union used motion pictures to advance their cause for a new world and a new economy based upon the positive virtues of technology, the French and German artists who returned to Paris during the 1920s explored the potential of the cinema as a new art form. From Marey's chronophotographs of people and animals at the turn of the century, painters like Marcel Duchamp pursued the dynamism of kinetic actions and multiple viewpoints in the style of Cubism. They were influenced by the French philosopher Henri Bergson (1859–1941), who in his 1911 book *Creative Evolution* (1998) theorized upon time, motion and change. He employed the cinema as a paradigm to explain that "reality" is, in actuality, the changing perception of a form that can be caught in time and space by an instantaneous snapshot (p. 317). Knowledge, in the modern mind, then becomes a form of thinking related to the process of filming. For humanity, the conscious act of thinking processes the memories of a past with a comprehension of the present for an expectation of future possibilities. Thus Bergson concludes, the *"mechanism of our ordinary knowledge is of a cinematographical kind"* (p. 306).

The Italian Futurists also took up the philosophy of Bergson as the authority for their emphasis on the process of filming as a "kinetic dynamism" for synthesizing memories and sense perceptions into a coherent presentation of "simultaneity." In their 1916 manifesto, *The Futurist Cinema,* they attacked the established bourgeois culture and its "misuse" and contamination of cinema. They declared that:

> The Cinema is an autonomous art. The cinema must therefore never copy the stage. The cinema, being essentially visual, must above all fulfil the evolution of painting, detach itself from reality, from photography, from the graceful and solemn. It must become anti-graceful, deforming, impressionistic, synthetic, dynamic, free-wording [Apollonio, quoted in Le Grice 1977, p. 10].

Much of the bravado of the futurist artists remains in their manifestoes as they lost their leadership with the deaths of Umberto Boccioni and Antonio Sant'Elia in the war. In Italy under a new postwar political regime, their ideas were turned into propaganda for the rise of fascism under the dictatorship of Mussolini.

Other European artists were fascinated by the novelty of motion pictures, especially the "trick" films of Méliès, who, as a magician, conjured dreamscapes in his films that appeared to exist simultaneously within a "real" world. For avant-garde artists and poets, the world of dreams and fantasy could combine with the realm of the "marvelous," and through the free play of imagination they envisioned new and revolutionary happenings through the new medium of motion pictures. Yet before attempts to revolutionize art took place, the Dada movement arose and revolted against the art world in protest for horrors incurred by the First World War. Their nonsense activities subverted the logic, rationalism and rhetoric that

justified the killings of millions of people. Satire and parody were their major weapons to challenge the dominance of bourgeois art. Their work also critiqued the "fixed" viewpoints of Renaissance art while playfully experimenting with new forms of perception related to the cinema. They used this new technology in an ironic manner to deconstruct the ideological worldview brought into being by European imperialism.

The "gratuitous act," an act that breaks the chain of causality, reveals the paradoxical gesture of Dada. Dada was an indictment of the petit bourgeois society and its faith in modern industrialization. Its manifestoes claimed that this society was directly responsible for feelings of hysteria and shock created by the Great World War. Dadaists produced ironic parodies as artists creatively trapped by this same bourgeois society, and they displayed their anger and frustration as artists and poets in two primary ways. First, some presented a violent and nihilistic attack on reason and rationality that supported this society that they claimed was degenerate. This attack deliberately employed nonsense and antisense as it fought against the propaganda that supported the madness of war. Second, the Dadaists took to performance art using improvisational methods, games, masks and buffoonery to emphasize the absurdity of their situation. Picabia, Duchamp and Man Ray led this attack by taking machine-made products and constructed absurdist art forms to illustrate their uselessness. This nihilistic movement originated in Zurich in 1916 during the final days of World War I, and was led by a Swiss visual artist, Hans Arp, a German theatre director, Hugo Ball, and a French-Romanian poet, Tristan Tzara.

Dada is related in many ways to the theatrical notion of farce, discussed in the next chapter on silent comedy. The main contention of farce is that the artist and poet can retaliate against the logic and reason of their opponent through unrelated and unexpected improvisations and unrehearsed happenings. As a parodic device, the play ironically inverts the situation for comedic effects. The production of anti-art material led by such artists as Picabia and Duchamp became a concerted movement in the early 1920s that frequently outraged bourgeois sensibilities and scandalized the traditional concepts of beauty and art. The most notorious artist who publicly challenged the established art world with his wit and humor may have been Marcel Duchamp. Today, Neo-Dada has reappeared in the work of Andy Warhol, Jim Dine, Roy Lichtenstein, and other Pop Artists to again attack the bourgeois notions of Art.

Thus Dada's central force was a kind of mad humor derived from a cacophony of noise machines, free word associations, nonsense lectures and chance happenings uncontrolled by logic or reason. Dada's intent was the direct inverse of the futurists and constructivists whose artists extolled technology and who believed in mechanization, revolution and war, and the rational and logical means, however brutal, to provide a solution to human problems in an industrial, capitalist world. When Duchamp selected material for his sculptures from ordinary mass-produced objects after the scandal over his painting *Nude Descending a Staircase, No. 2* at the Armory Show of 1913 in New York, he deliberately chose them with indifference to their visual appeal or aesthetic values. His first "readymades" were dislocations and displacements that shifted the object out of its normal contexts. A bicycle wheel was mounted on a stool, a urinal was mounted on a wall, signed as A. Mutt, and labeled *Fountain*, and a hat rack was suspended from the ceiling. In each instance, Duchamp intervened in the "normal" aesthetic perception of these objects, in which their renaming suggested that "new identities and relationships" be established to break out of traditional bourgeois habits. These simple dichotomies become the foundation of René Clair's *Entr'acte* (1924) featuring Duchamp and Man Ray.

Later, sculptures based upon machine imagery became kinetic art when mechanized by Duchamp. This interaction displayed some form of sexual energy that displaced the mechanical energy usually derived from modern technology. These satiric combinations of sculpture and paintings destroyed the logic of machines and reinstated the mysterious internal forces of the human libido into the frame-

work. The work of Duchamp culminates in the most deliberately obscure painting of the 1920s, *The Bride Stripped Bare by Her Bachelors, Even*, executed on glass. This complex metaphor of a "love machine" is full of implicit sexual overtones as Duchamp brings his Dadaesque attack into the world of dreams and the Freudian concept of the unconscious. Here the artistic world of Surrealism was born, giving primary significance to the marvelous, the irrational and the accidental or chance coupling of man and woman or machine with machine.

The experimental phase of avant-garde cinema of the 1920s grew out of Cubism, as developed by Picasso and Braque before World War I. Like futurist paintings and sculptures, it explored ways artists could visualize a change of forms in sequential actions similar to motion pictures. Early "abstract" films of this kind were created by Hans Richter and Viking Eggeling, working together in Berlin after the war. Following the Dada experiments of Marcel Duchamp, these filmmakers utilized his idea of the readymade and the concept of displacement. Richter's first film, *Rhythmus 21* (1921), employs the rectangular movie screen as a two dimensional white surface where different rectangular planes of white, grey and black interact kinetically within the screen space. Richter's filmmaking process "liberates" the image or form from its fixed or preconceived physical context and allows for constantly changing relationships following a rhythmical "contrast-analogy," thus providing ambiguous readings. In doing this, Richter redirects the viewer to new visual perceptions and sensations of the image and object. A release of the image and object into new possibilities allows the filmmaker to challenge the preconceived notions held by the viewer as well as assist in locating hidden meanings through displacement. Richter's *Ghosts before Breakfast* (1927) continues his work in the Dadaist mode using various forms of trick photography to capture the escapades of a flight of hats in a dream-like sequence comparable to a René Magritte painting. However, Victor Eggeling's short film, *Diagonal Symphony* (1925), dismisses any presence of Dada. His film depends upon the transformation of basic forms designed to achieve an illusion of movement with a sense of a musical structure and logical precision.

Films and the Irrational Play of Forms in Space and Time

Duchamp, Man Ray, Fernand Léger, René Clair and other Dadaists introduced the concept of film as a form of thinking. They demonstrated as part of the Surrealist movement a seriousness of purpose in search of a new vision for art beyond their desire to outrage their enemies. They intended to critically reexamine the premises, rules, logical bases and traditions which dominated the rational concepts and aesthetic notions of artworks. In 1922 Man Ray moved from New York to Paris with Duchamp to continue his experimental work in photography and film. As a Dadaist, he was seeking new plastic possibilities for art forms created from cinematic abstraction. In *Retour à la Raison* (1923) Man Ray first used various camera angles and close-ups of moving objects framed in a variety of lighting patterns to disengage the forms from their original setting to create an ambiguous identity. Ray then edited the sequences of shots based upon a kinetic relationship, not a symbolic one, hence emphasizing the continuity of kinetic patterns. He also advanced the use of lensless photography with his rayogram technique, drawing attention to the materiality of film and the photochemical transformation of images by light. His short films of the period are truly collages of filmic material in which chance occurrences of images produce shock and novelty in a Dadaist manner. In *Anemic Cinéma* (1927), Duchamp plays in a Dadaist fashion with the sensation of optical perception using two revolving discs made of white circles on a black field that rotate in opposite directions. While the discs rotate, Duchamp adds written material to comment upon the nonsensical action taking place as his phrases mirror the actions of the revolving circles.

In René Clair's first feature film, *Paris qui dort / The Crazy Ray* (1923), he displays his own fascination with the absurd realities created by the world of cinema. In constructing this motion picture, Clair incorporates cinematic techniques created by stop-motion photography to convert the "real" world into a surreal fantasy. His central character is Dr. Craze, who employs a science-fiction raygun to paralyze people caught in everyday social activities. Luckily, a group of people atop the Eiffel Tower escape the effects of the raygun and descend to the ground to investigate the situation. Here they find people caught in compromising positions, frozen in acts of robbery or illicit romantic trysts. In some ways the film can be read as a parable attacking the French class system, its artificial social conventions and the desire for wealth at all costs. When the group finally locates the mad scientist, Dr. Craze, they persuade him to turn off the paralyzing raygun. Then Clair has fun bringing everyone back to life, exposing their actions through special cinematic effects.

By 1924, Breton and the Surrealist movement incorporated Dada into its manifestoes, influencing visual artists like Picabia and Salvador Dalí, who acted as collaborators with Clair and Buñuel. Not only did they play with visual forms juxtaposed in a space-time interval, but they visualized surreal dreamscapes of the mind as cinematic possibilities.

Surrealism, as a 1920s art movement, developed in artworks, literature and film in association with the Freudian notion of the Unconscious. The art forms emphasized expressions of dream-like images and free association of visionary subjects that the artist's imagination projected as an interior state of mind. This development of thought processes, as the real function of the mind, was centered around André Breton, a Marxist writer and editor of the Parisian review *Literature* (1919–1924). Breton defined the nature of Surrealism in his *First Manifesto* of 1924 as "pure psychic automatism by which it is intended to express, either verbally or in writing, the true function of thought. Thought dictated in the absence of all control exerted by reason and outside all aesthetic or moral preoccupation" (Breton, quoted in Chipp 1968, p. 412).

The central principle operating in surrealism, as applied to the film medium, was its recourse to "chance occurrences" created through

The fantasy begins in René Clair's *Paris qui dort* (1925) when Dr. Craze uses a paralyzing ray machine to stop time. A few people escape the rays and decide to meet on the Eiffel Tower.

the use of "pure psychic automatism." In paintings the images more often were of a personal nature but carried certain psychological constants. Whatever the abstract nature of a "surreal" image of an object within a motion picture, it always contained illogical juxtapositions to other images to demonstrate a magical, irrational, hallucinatory, dream-like quality in the free association of forms. The surrealist approach to filmmaking was designed to shock the viewer by this visual displacement rather than to establish any logical or plausible explanation of the actions within the context of the scene.

In the film *Entr'acte*, (1924) René Clair, in collaboration with Francis Picabia, offers a succession of apparently unrelated images in an attempt to display the most scandalous and grotesque humor arising from a simple ritual that becomes a prolonged chase sequence. Clair also plays with the notion of chance encounters

in the opening sequences as he juxtaposes images with events to subvert our expectations of traditional rituals. He shows us a chess game being played by Marcel Duchamp and Man Ray but outdoors on a roof of a building, a cannon being set off by Erik Satie and Francis Picabia, a bearded man in a ballerina outfit, and a sniper aiming at a moving target similar to Duchamp's rotating discs. The second half is a chase sequence that exposes a crowd of mourners pursuing a runaway hearse through the streets of Paris. Clair uses a number of different camera angles and slow-motion effects to create a dream-like dance from the otherwise pedestrian forms of pursuit. Further, Clair deliberately assaults the audience with transformations of objects and activities as people simply disappear by the wave of a magic wand, in a manner similar to what occurs in Méliès' trick films. Most of these filmic effects are achieved simply by changing the point-of-view of the image-object or by the use of double exposure, mirror reflections, stop-motion photography and camera speeds.

Entr'acte demonstrates that when a film work deviates from the conventional expectations of its audiences, it rises above its mimetic capacity to explore new directions in human interactions. Picabia's surrealist scenario called upon Clair's knowledge of film techniques to create a world that would simply transform images from an objective reality into a hyper– or sur-reality.

After *Entr'acte,* Clair directed three silent fantasies combining the cinematic tricks of Méliès with the slapstick style of a Mack Sennett farce. Again he used farce as an ideological weapon to attack the dead social conventions that confined a person's own liberty and freedom as in *Le Voyage imaginaire* (1925) and *Le Fantôme du Moulin-Rouge* (1925). His more farcical attack on dehumanizing social conventions is presented in his social satire *Un Chapeau de paille d'Italie / The Italian Straw Hat* (1927), in which a young lady loses her hat while engaging in an extramarital affair. The film becomes an extended chase sequence of her efforts to recover the hat, thereby allaying her husband's suspicions of infidelity. With the coming of sound, Clair directed two satires in which he demonstrated his ability to merge musical sounds and noises to augment his farcical sequences, *Le Million* (1931) and *À Nous la Liberté* (1932). In the mid–1930s, Hollywood engaged Clair to direct a number of comic fantasies, notably *The Ghost Goes West* (1936) and *The Flame of New Orleans* (1941) with Marlene Dietrich.

Another non-narrative experimental film that contains absurd humor and surreal displacements is *Ballet Mécanique* (1924). This experimental film was designed and directed by Fernand Léger to demonstrate his fascination

Rare René Clair's **Entr'acte** (1924) is a short film filled with editing sequences that serve Dada's goals of breaking away from "logic." In this sequence a ballerina is revealed to be a bearded man dancing in a tutu.

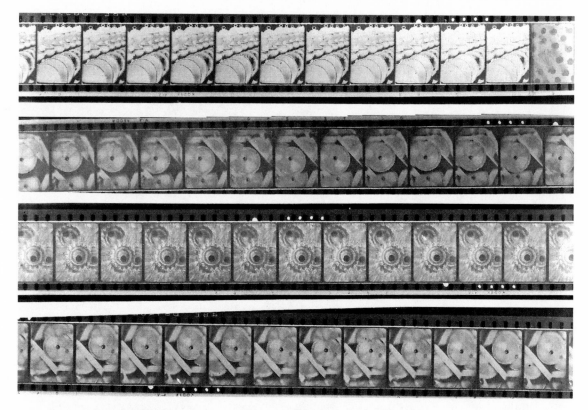

Fernand Léger's **Ballet Mécanique** (1924) is an experimental film that transposes paintings into moving abstract forms, stressing the mechanical nature of filmmaking. In part, it takes a cubist view of objects, presenting them from multiple viewpoints without subjective or emotional values.

with the spirited interplay of industrial forms and urban life. Most images are typical of analytical cubism rather than surreal; they capture the activities of people caught unawares of the machine-made world by the expressive force of the camera. Léger's point-of-view reveals "a new process of vision ... using a subject matter devoid of emotional or intellectually associative values" (Lawder 1975, p. 67). Léger juxtaposes the aesthetic forms of the new material world with humorous analogies of humankind fragmented into simple geometric shapes. Although the film is rhythmically structured by a musical score, the lighting and framing reveal objects in space isolated from their contexts. By changing rhythms and point-of-view, Léger displaces real action by multiple repetitions of triangles, circles and squares that verge on the absurd in his cinematic world. Hence, inanimate objects are given life through cinematic movement and human beings appear overtly mechanical, caught in the repeti-

tion of work as in the Greek myth about the chores of Sisyphus.

Films and the Creation of Surreal Fantasies of the Mind

The most famous collaboration of surreal artist and film director was the team of Salvador Dalí and Luis Buñuel. In 1928, they created the surreal fantasy *Un Chien andalou / An Andalusian Dog*. With the approval of Breton, the film was shown at Studio 28, which specialized in avant-garde films. The film explores how certain visual stimuli dislocate and disorient a person from his or her natural surroundings and transfer the viewer into a dream-like state of being. In this film, one moves from a waking state into a dream state where time and space are illogically displaced within the scenario. The characters are caught in a pantomime of passion that involves the

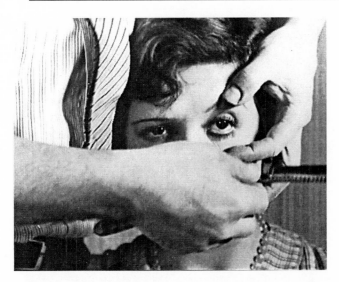

In the opening dream sequence of Luis Buñuel's *Un Chien andalou / An Andalusian Dog* (1928), a cloud passing by the moon, followed by the image of a man using a straight razor to slice a woman's eye, startles the audience with the shock of such an act.

transformation of commonplace objects into repulsive symbols. The film is a pure fantasy. From the opening shock of a sliced eyeball, a comment on the blindness of perceptions, Buñuel creates a surreal-symbolic universe in realistic images, but one that is both puzzling and shocking. Every image and action undermines viewers' abilities to interpret the images and the attending responses. The result is a film in which appearances are associated with a world of dreams, one that defies the capacity of the spectator to translate the narrative into a rational whole.

Dalí and Buñuel were able to capture the magical, hallucinatory yet enigmatic quality of dream imagery in this film. The film also enjoys an incomparable facility for passing over

Another surrealist image from *Un Chien andalou* that expresses the repression of desires controlled by the forces of culture and religion. Buñuel juxtaposes unrelated objects, a priest pulling two pianos that reveal two dead donkeys lying inside them.

the bridge of reality in both directions. It accomplishes this first by objectifying most convincingly the mental images of the mind; second, by making exterior reality submit to our own subjective perceptions. In this manner, *Un Chien andalou* facilitates the kind of release from the mundane events of everyday life that the surrealists sought.

Buñuel, like René Clair, was a social satirist who engaged surrealist techniques to a fuller extent as a weapon in his rebellion against bourgeois culture and the Catholic Church. He rejected camera tricks in favor of actual dramatic content photographed in a neorealistic manner. In his next film, *L'Âge d'or* (1930), his surreal images and actions shocked the audience as his depiction of erotic encounters disrupts and overturn social conventions. Set up as visual gags, his *l'amour fou* provoked the censure of church and state dignitaries against the dream-like sexual assaults and their repressions depicted in an openly de Sadean manner.

Films and the Poetic Release of Human Passions and Desires

Although Buñuel was involved with themes of sexual desires and social inhibitions, the major concern of the impressionist filmmakers was to use more consistent plot developments and still express the inner anxieties and states of mind of the central character. More influential on their mode of filmmaking was Henri Bergson's notion of duration or time, in which cinema is the mechanism to incorporate the state of time in space. Here the camera can capture dream-like environments through its ability to distort and manipulate real time and space. These film directors would capture a surreal but natural setting through the use of slow-motion effects, double exposures, and moody contrasts in lighting to capture atmospheric "impressions of forms" emerging and dissolving into space. The *mise-en-scène* was constructed to emphasize the ambiguity of the images captured in a time-space construct by the scenario. These visual impressions thus mysteriously liken such images and their symbolic depictions to a surreal yet subjective dreamspace.

Louis Delluc (1890–1924), a French film critic, came under the influence of American films directed by DeMille, Thomas Ince and Chaplin. As the leader of this impressionist group of filmmakers, he advocated a French cinema based upon the Symbolist poets such as Mallarmé and Baudelaire. Filmmaking to him would develop from a feeling or sentiment in correspondence with an object of desire. Usually the story found its dramatic unfolding in a fatalistic erotic relationship. His use of atmospheric settings and photogenic images are seen in *Fièvre / Fever* (1921), *La Femme de nulle part / The Woman from Nowhere* (1922) and *L'Inondation* (1922). Here he displayed a visual style in which he projected images as symbols of desire, using selective fragments to represent reality. Careful cinematic dissolves blurred temporal relationships between different events making them puzzling and enigmatic for the spectator. The most prominent directors in this style were Germaine Dulac (1882–1942), one of cinema's first female directors, Marcel L'Herbier (1888–1979), a Symbolist poet who was concerned with the use of Pirandellian effects to create alternate levels of illusion and reality, and Jean Epstein (1897–1953). This style reappeared within The French New Wave with Alain Resnais' *L'Année dernière à Marienbad / Last Year at Marienbad* (1961). Dulac employed a more expressionist style in rendering a psychological study of a failed marriage in *La Souriante Madame Beudet / The Smiling Madame Beudet* (1923). In *Feu Mathias Pascal / The Late Matthew Pascal* (1925), L'Herbier includes surreal elements of chance, accidental encounters and coincidence causing the main characters to attain outcomes contradictory to those that they desired. Jean Epstein directed *La Chute de la maison Usher / The Fall of the House of Usher* (1928) which he adapted from the Edgar Allan Poe story. He employed strong contrasts of light and dark and soft-focus photography to establish a surreal dream-like visual effect. Another impressionist filmmaker who was more commercial within this mode was Abel Gance (1889–1981). In *La Roue* (1922) he applied Dulac's notion of filming a "symphonic poem based upon images" with surreal techniques of transformational and accelerated montage. His most notable contribution to film history was his six-hour historical drama *Napoléon* (1927), which incorporated a triptych screen process called Polyvision, which enabled simultaneous actions to take place. As was the practice in Cinerama, Gance used three separate screens to carry contrasting and complementary images which could be extended into one panoramic image for the spectacular war scenes.

Cinematography: The Creative Use of Reality

Maya Deren was one of the leading American avant-garde filmmakers of the 1940s. Her experimental films alter the inherent reality of the cinematic image by deliberately distorting spatio-temporal relationships in ways similar to the methods used by Marcel L'Herbier and other French avant-garde filmmakers. Her methods include the use of slow motion, reverse motion and freeze frames that break the domination of the space-time continuum. Deren's essay, "Cinematography: The Creative Use of Reality," explains how the film medium can filter a spectator's perception of reality through a combination of selection, expansion and manipulation of the moving image. Thus, an artist can use the authority of the photographic image as a creative art form in filmmaking, one that gains expressiveness through editing and special effects. In this way, the artist can create new associations and meanings that transfigure space, time and causality.

References

Apollonio, Umbro (ed.). 1970. *Futurist Manifestos.* London: Thames & Hudson. Reprint, 1973.

Armes, Roy. 1985. *French Cinema.* London: Secker & Warburg.

Bergson, Henri. 1911. *Creative Evolution.* New York: Henry Holt. Reprint, New York: Dover Publications, 1998.

Buñuel, Luis. 1983. *My Last Sigh.* Translated by Abigail Israel. New York: Alfred A. Knopf, Inc.

Chipp, Herschel B. 1968. *Theories of Modern Art: A Source Book by Artists and Critics.* Berkeley: University of California Press.

De La Colina, José and Tomás Pérez Turrent. 1992. *Objects of Desire: Conversations with Luis Buñuel.* Edited and translated by Paul Lenti. New York: Marsilio Publishers.

Deren, Maya. 1960. "Cinematography, The Creative Use of Reality." *Daedalus* 89, no. 1 (Winter 1960). In *Film Theory and Criticism.* Edited by Gerald Mast, Marshall Cohen and Leo Braudy. New York and London: Oxford University, 1992.

Lawder, Standish D. 1975. *The Cubist Cinema.* New York: New York University Press.

Le Grice, Malcolm. 1977. *Abstract Film and Beyond.* Cambridge, Mass.: MIT Press.

Richter, Hans. 1970. *Dada: Art and Anti-Art.* London: Thames and Hudson.

CHAPTER 7

Hollywood Silent Films in the Jazz Age: 1919–1929

Introduction

Between 1919 and 1929, the American film industry grew and prospered in Hollywood, where the major movie studios were located. The "Big Three" were Paramount, Metro-Goldwyn-Mayer and First National. Smaller studios such as Warner Bros., Fox and Universal also produced Hollywood feature films to meet the demands of the new urban middle-class customers. These studios promoted the mystique of the silent screen stars, such as Greta Garbo and Rudolph Valentino, in a variety of romantic melodramas. Directors such as Cecil B. DeMille, Erich von Stroheim and Ernst Lubitsch were also headlined by Paramount as they made social satires on the open sexuality in the Jazz Age. Charlie Chaplin and Buster Keaton led the comics with farces and slapstick comedies that also drew millions of fans to the box office.

The Hollywood studio system standardized the production of motion pictures during this decade. A division of labor, introduced by Thomas H. Ince, organized and diversified the making of films, from the writing of detailed shooting scripts to the shooting schedule, editing and final marketing of the film. All in all, Hollywood films were mass-produced as popular entertainment to appeal to the public taste for sentiment, slapstick humor, mild erotica, and a sense of justice and retribution, with a taste for the depiction of bloodshed and violence. As the decade progressed, a new code on moral issues was introduced to limit the depicted adultery, divorce, drinking and drug-taking, forcing Hollywood film producers to create the Hays Office.

Popular Genres and the Folk Art Tradition

Although the marketing of glamorous stars was one of the major drawing cards of the major studios to bring audiences to the motion picture "palaces," the real reasons for the success of motion pictures during the silent period were the popular genre films, from the western to the family melodrama and the comedies of Chaplin and Keaton. As described by art historian Erwin Panofsky (1947), the American genre films of the 1920s were perceived as shapers of public opinion, tastes and attitudes. He suggests that motion pictures or "the movies," as a popular narrative form, emerged from an ancestry of popular romances and melodramas, sometimes called *kitsch* (meaning inferior and pretentious) entertainment, as derived from popular songs, romantic dime store novels and pulp magazines. The appeal of motion pictures was largely due to their status as affordable family entertainment, easily accessible to a thriving urban audience. As part of the popular culture, motion pictures transported the spectator along with their stars and adventures into a romantic world, seemingly able to overlook the social and political problems of the day. Accordingly, Panofsky claims that genre films operate on a folk art level characterized by five features. Movies appeal to our "primitive sense of justice" following the Protestant work ethic that rewards virtue and punishes vice. Movies also appeal to our feelings of empathy and our sentimental responses to "acts of fate." Third, an innate desire to witness "bloodshed and cruelty" is satisfied by the spectacle of conflict and violence in movies. Fourth, our taste and pleasure in voyeurism is satisfied through acts of sensuality discreetly observed and enacted. Finally, our enjoyment of films derives from our witnessing forms of crude physical humor or slapstick that satisfy primitive social impulses.

Later social critics of motion pictures, such as Robin Wood, Robert Sklar, John Cawelti and others challenge these five characteristic features of genre films as categorized by Panofsky. They perceive motion pictures as powerful and pervasive communicators of cultural myths that propagate and reinforce the sociopolitical system. These critics also claim that such films support the dominant ideological values of a conservative middle class.

Although most popular genre films contain combinations of these melodramatic features, D. W. Griffith and other film directors produced several realistic social problem films for the nickelodeons. However, the frankness and realism in the depiction of a social system at work caused the "progressive reformers" to call for film censorship. As Robert Sklar (1975) commented in *Movie-Made America,* these "guardians of traditional culture" wanted to control the access to information so that the new immigrant classes would remain ignorant of the social system in which they lived. According to Sklar, "The struggle over movies, in short, was an aspect of the struggle between classes. Taking place, as it did, in the realm of leisure and amusements, and in a society where to speak of class conflict was a breach of good taste, it was always invariably masked" (p. 123).

By the early 1920s, "progressive" reformers threatened to boycott the movies or pass censorship laws. This forced the film industry to rethink its scenarios and to withdraw any socially subversive film narratives. New film scenarios that mirrored or reflected the values of the middle class and a more restrained, well-to-do citizenry came into existence as light comedy romances, adventure thrillers, domestic melodramas, westerns, social satires or slapstick comedies. They incorporated the basic genre elements of success or retribution, sentiment, sensation, pornography and crude humor found in typical film scenarios. Within this popular framework, film narratives addressed a younger generation of audiences from the social and moral viewpoint of the dominant society. Movies, as a form of popular culture, thus avoided direct confrontation with the social problems of the era, while a social and moral stance was implicitly stated in the film narrative. A majority of silent films thus became escapist entertainment involved in romantic themes from medieval romances, fantasies and legends that grew into a powerful industry in a few years' time.

Motion Picture Industry and Big Business

After the Treaty of Versailles was signed in 1919, formally ending World War I, the American motion picture industry permanently relocated its production headquarters to Hollywood. However, the financial reins that capitalized investment in motion pictures were maintained in New York. The independent producers were headed by Adolph Zukor of Paramount/Famous Players, William Fox of Fox Productions and Carl Laemmle of Universal. They had fought and defeated the Motion Picture Patents Company and its distribution arm, General Trust. As vertically integrated monopolies in their turn, they controlled the distribution and exhibition of their own motion pictures.

In 1924, the Big Three studios, Paramount, First National and MGM, consolidated their film production and distribution companies by acquiring their own theatre chains. Zukor's Paramount Pictures absorbed a number of smaller companies while Louis B. Mayer and Sam Goldwyn created MGM, as the production arm for Loew's theatre chain. First National depended upon independent producers to supply films to its movie houses. The overall expansionist development of the film industry followed the capitalist tendencies of industrialized nations. Filmmaking practices were standardized to increase large-scale production of movie spectacles. Hollywood studios used mass-marketing campaigns for their films, fully exploiting the new communications media as newspapers, magazines and radio advertisements captured the attention of a growing urban audience in the major cities. Exotic motion picture theatres were built to house this audience during the 1920s in cities such as New York, Chicago, Boston, Philadelphia, Baltimore, Los Angeles and many smaller ones. By 1927, it is estimated that nearly 450 to 500 films were being produced yearly in Hollywood for nearly 20,000 theatres in the United States, which drew approximately 80 million spectators each week.

A New Morality and the Hays Office

A new morality emerged during the Jazz Age of the 1920s. It grew out of a new, resurging romantic discourse in an affluent capitalist society. This new morality challenged a Victorian conformity imposed by "guardians" of the state. As a way of life, it emphasized sensation and sexual license. It was a revolt by the "lost" generation against the strict morality and rationalism of the past. This new morality encouraged different forms of personal liberation, following the writings of such 19th century writers and Romantic poets as Henry Thoreau and Walt Whitman. Romantic philosophy believed in a return to Nature and the innate goodness of human beings. People would trust their instincts and emotions over reason and intellect. Many of its preoccupations and ideas disposed an individual toward Gothic, Faustian or Promethean myths. In these myths, the individual is seen at the very center of all life experiences; thus Romanticism allows for the expression of one's own unique feelings and an interpretation of life. Romantic feelings are still central to contemporary film narratives exploring theories on the childlike, the psychological, the revolutionary and the organic relationships of human beings and their nature.

Hollywood promoted this Romantic image through high-powered packaging and marketing of glamorous and sultry stars on the silent screen, creating a culture shock for middle-class audiences. As they do today, many stars set the norms for fashion or incited sensational news items based upon their wealth or sexual indiscretions. Female "sirens" like Theda Bara, Alla Nazimova, Clara Bow, Lupe Velez, Pola Negri, Gloria Swanson and Greta Garbo became romantically charged screen personalities who made Hollywood a romantic legend. Male stars were also packaged as upright and virtuous "good guys" such as William S. Hart, or as exotic romantic "Latin lovers" like Rudolph Valentino and Ramon Novarro. Valentino's audience appeal was phenomenal. His screen performances depicted him as charming, fascinating, dangerous and romantically irresistible. His film adventures allowed him to pursue desirable women and to engage in other seductive acts that some Americans considered taboo or forbidden.

In the 1920s, with the introduction of the production heads and the studio system, a number of American directors expanded the range of genre films that emerged during this period. King Vidor, James Cruze, John Ford and Raoul Walsh directed epic sagas such as Cruze's *The Covered Wagon* (1923) and Ford's *The Iron Horse* (1924), while Walsh directed Douglas Fairbanks in *The Thief of Bagdad* (1924) and Vidor created the romantic war story, *The Big Parade* (1925). Other American directors, like Cecil B. DeMille, directed situation comedies as their films attempted to address the problems of modern marriage and its impact upon the new postwar generation. Three films directed by DeMille at the beginning of the decade satirized extramarital relationships among the new middle classes. In his own fashion, DeMille flirted with titillating disrobing scenes that gave audiences a taste of mild pornography as "modern" marriages strained under the pressures of adultery in the Jazz Age. The titles of these films, beginning with *Male and Female* (1919), *Why Change Your Wife?* (1920) and *Forbidden Fruit* (1921), indicate an obvious production strategy based upon romantic love that sought to liberate the average man and woman from the strict codes of the traditional morality. In these orgiastic fantasies, DeMille's films depict how his female characters achieve temporary reconciliation with their mates after overcoming temptation and sin.

The romantic appeal of the new morality in the early 1920s was a radical shift from the Victorian moral codes of good and evil. After the Spanish Flu epidemic of 1918–1919, the new morality broke away from the disillusionment and cynicism of the postwar period. It encouraged to a large degree feminist groups after women won the right to vote in 1920. However, many religious and reformist groups took political action against the content of feature films that exploited sexual promiscuity, wealth or the use of drugs, or those that encouraged adultery, divorce or reckless living. Matters in Hollywood became scandalous when a small brochure spread rumors on "the sins of Hollywood" that included allegations of depravity, sexual license and amorality among Hollywood stars. The national press picked up the details after the Fatty Arbuckle case of alleged rape and murder became headlines. After the 1921 Arbuckle trial, daily newspapers covered the sensational murder of William Desmond Taylor, a leading director for Paramount in 1922. Moral outrage was inflamed by these Hollywood incidents. An indignant public protest threatened to boycott all "sex pictures" at the new theatres.

The leading film producers, fearing huge economic losses and afraid of state and federal censorship legislation, decided to form their own self-regulating production organization "to establish and maintain the highest possible moral and artistic standards" in motion picture production. In 1922, Hollywood created the Motion Picture Producers and Distributors of America (MPPDA) and hired Will Hays, a right-wing conservative, as president to serve as the official spokesperson for the film industry. MPPDA became known as the Hays Office after Hays wrote up a list of *Don'ts* and *Be Carefuls* to guide producers and directors on the ethical content of film narratives. Hays then acted as a press agent to protect the image of the film industry from bad publicity (Hays 1923, pp. 205–212).

In the 1920s, Cecil B. DeMille formed his own repertory group of stars and created a million-dollar spectacle based upon biblical stories of adultery and redemption. Using a pseudo-religious setting comparable to Griffith's Babylon production, he directed *The Ten Commandments* in 1923, with sexual license and violence predominant. But DeMille adhered to the Hays code known as "compensating values," in which practitioners of illicit sex would be punished and virtue rewarded according to DeMille's own interpretation of moral conduct. He became famous with movie audiences by providing voyeuristic sex scenes just short of pornography. DeMille produced and directed *King of Kings* in 1927. This reconstruction of the life of Christ adhered to the moral codes of righteousness for all to witness.

Two notable directors from Germany, Ernst Lubitsch, born in Berlin in 1892, and Erich von Stroheim, born in Vienna in 1885, established themselves in Hollywood as masters of the silent screen with a number of feature films also dealing with sex, violence and retribution, but in different ways. Lubitsch was a master of an aristocratic style and grace that has been called "the Lubitsch touch." His sophisticated silent comedies were made at Paramount studios, but unlike DeMille, Lubitsch incorporated a sense of European elegance and charm that was indicated in the rich costumes and decor of his films. In Europe, he had established himself as a master of bedroom farce, a mixture of sexual intrigues that befell kings and nobles. Lubitsch was able to transplant these sexual fantasies onto the screen in Hollywood. His first American film was *Rosita* (1923) followed by *The Marriage Circle* (1924) and *Forbidden Paradise* (1924). Each film depicts upper class socialites caught in an absurd situation generally related to some extramarital affair that one or the other partner is trying to conceal. These farcical situations depend upon nuance and inference in the acting with some visual indication to physical objects located in the *mise-en-scène*.

Erich von Stroheim pursued a different world than Lubitsch, a world where sexual desires coupled with the need for power and wealth became the driving obsessions of his central characters. His films are naturalistic melodramas that primarily exemplify the powerful element of retribution and justice. Moral codes are broken for psycho-sexual reasons. As they are revealed in dreams, von Stroheim dares to show the power unleashed by repressed desires. In each of his silent films, from *Blind Husbands* (1919), *Foolish Wives* (1922), *The Merry Widow* (1925) and *Greed* (1925), von Stroheim concentrates on carefully planned long shots and long takes to create a unified *mise-en-scène* where the actions unfold. These carefully planned and executed shots help present a consistent realistic environment in which human degradation abounds clearly as a result of "lustful" activities. The films of von Stroheim are black comedies on adultery that delve into the emotional havoc created by unhinged sexual passions ultimately leading to the death and destruction of the central characters.

A third European director, also from Vienna, was Josef von Sternberg (1894–1969). His first successful film, *The Salvation Hunters* (1925), was made in Hollywood. The director is noted for directing and producing *Underworld* (1927) and *The Docks of New York* (1928), the latter the first talking picture made for Paramount studios. In 1930 he returned to Germany to direct the film version of Heinrich Mann's novel, *Der Blaue Engel / The Blue Angel* (1930), starring Marlene Dietrich and Emil Jannings. By rerecording the film in German and English, von Sternberg helped it become an international hit. Returning to Hollywood, he brought Dietrich back with him to star in *Morocco* (1930), featuring Gary Cooper. Then von Sternberg cast Dietrich as Shanghai Lili, a glamorous yet mysterious woman who finds herself reunited with her ex-lover, Clive Brooks, on a train traveling from Peking to Shanghai. In *Shanghai Express* (1932) von Sternberg called upon his lighting skills as a cinematographer to create a series of exotic tableaux that emotionally evoked scenes of sensual pleasure and deception within a tragic farce of sexual desire.

The Concept of Farce in Motion Pictures

To properly understand the prominent silent film directors of the 1920s, like Chaplin, Keaton, von Stroheim, Lubitsch, DeMille or von Sternberg, one must comprehend the concept of farce. Farce, as defined in *The Oxford Companion to the Theater,*

> is an extreme form of comedy in which laughter is raised at the expense of probability — particularly by horseplay and bodily assault. It must, however, retain its hold on humanity, even if only in depicting the grosser faults of mankind; otherwise it degenerates into travesty and burlesque. In modern usage, the word farce is applied to a full-length play dealing with some absurd situation hinging generally on extra-marital relations— hence the term "bedroom farce" [Hartnoll 1983, p. 272].

The absurdity in farce expresses the real absurdity of life. If Art imitates Life, as Eric Bentley claims, a mimetic art such as film and photography will only imitate the surfaces of reality. For this reason, directors like von Stroheim and Chaplin must find external representations that act as symbols for what is developed in film as a social reality. Therefore, in any film narrative, the primacy of the plot or the unfolding action in the story must work upon the mind of the protagonist symbolically. Like Freud's study of the interpretation of dreams, farce indicates to an audience the disguised fulfillment of repressed sexual drives and wishes. An analysis of the plot used by von Stroheim in *Greed* exposes the symbolic nature of the conflict in the opening sequence. Then we follow the protagonist as his sought-after dream becomes a reality. However, elements of farce continually enter into the situation to advance the action. As conflicts arise, the protagonist aggravates the situation, when the real motives of other characters are revealed. The previous normal situations become more unreal and absurd until the conflict becomes so aggravated, the characters enter into a nightmare. In the end they all perish, unable to differentiate between their own dreams and the harsh reality that punishes them. This is the tragic farce endured by Emil Jannings as the professor in von Sternberg's *The Blue Angel*, as he howls on stage as the clown who realizes he has lost his dream world with Lola Lola.

Farce, as used by Chaplin, Keaton, and von Stroheim makes this comparison between

In von Sternberg's *Shanghai Express* (1932), strong black and white shadows capture Marlene Dietrich and Clive Brooks in a moment of dramatic tension as they travel by train toward Shanghai.

dreams and farce not just as an analogy but as a force directed toward achieving identity and status. In Chaplin's *The Kid* (1921) and *The Gold Rush* (1925), surreal dreams are activated in the film narrative to help Charlie achieve his own desires, be it food or the woman he adores. The comedy is achieved when he returns to reality and things are different. In Keaton's *The Navigator* (1924), the same comedy situation prevails. After the hero gets married, his honeymoon becomes a nightmarish dream when he and his bride mistakenly board an abandoned ship that carries the lovers off into unknown waters.

To rescue oneself from the dilemmas of life, certain cultural constructs are created that enforce principles upon one's behavior. This concept of ethical behavior is central for farce to exist since farce attacks the notion that human nature should be constrained by cultural norms, especially regarding the marriage game and sexual proclivities. In Jean Renoir's social satires of the 1930s, from *La Chienne* (1931) to the classic *Le Règle du jeu / The Rules of the Game* (1939), he demonstrates how unnatural these norms are. Farce is evident as his characters contrast the various ways they, as adults,

Mack Sennett's *Keystone Kops* (1912). Sennett's comedies displayed slapdash physical action without realistic violence and bloodshed. His short films were hilarious sight gags featuring Charlie Chaplin, Mabel Normand, Fatty Arbuckle and Ben Turpin.

attempt to avoid and circumvent such social constructs in different extramarital affairs. All cultures survive by accepting certain principles of human behavior in the celebration of life; thus, the marriage joke exists because people within a culture know that these societal norms exist.

The Films of Charlie Chaplin

Comic farces were happily suited to the silent screen, and used successfully by Mack Sennett and his clowns in the zany behavior that broke all rules, natural and societal, in every Keystone comedy chase that concluded his films. Sennett was the person who discovered Charlie Chaplin (1889–1977), recognizing that Chaplin's pantomimes were based essentially on farcical situations. Chaplin is known as a *farceur,* an actor who without sound or speech concentrates on body movements. His earlier silent comedies for Sennett developed his cinematic awareness of depicting farce for the screen.

Chaplin laced his farce within melodramatic

In Charlie Chaplin's **The Cure** (1917), Chaplin revolves himself in and out of a sanitarium in pursuit of Edna Purviance while trying to overcome bouts with alcohol, the masseur and Eric Campbell, the over-matched villain.

situations, but where melodrama affords a healthy release over our fears and our impulse to flee from danger and death, farce depends on the impulse to attack and wage battle with whatever weapon is at hand. Chaplin usually presents the audience with a melodramatic situation as in his early two-reelers, then uses farcical elements to escape. Farce seems simple to Chaplin. You go right at the problem and attack it before it attacks you. It is simple for Chaplin because he tends to accept appearances directly as his own reality.

Chaplin was a protégé of Mack Sennett, whose zany direction of knockabout farces for Keystone Films helped Charlie develop the character of the Little Tramp, a sad-faced clown who took on the world at a moment's notice. At Mutual, Chaplin directed and starred in 12 two-reel comedies such as *The Rink, The Cure,*

The Immigrant and *The Pawnshop* that made him the most popular silent film star in America by 1916. *The Cure* (1917) is a situational comedy in which Charlie finds himself in a health spa recovering from a bout of drunkenness. The film is full of Chaplin's zany antics, including a classical sequence in which his over-indulgence leads into an encounter with a masseur who threatens his life and limb.

The Pawnshop (1916) is typical of all Chaplin's early comedies, with his theatrical gifts for pantomime mixed with his mischievous ability to cause havoc for his customers. Charlie's famous scene is the careful and deliberate destruction of an alarm clock, under the doubtful eye of a client. The picture also depicts the squalor of slum life in the crowded city, where Charlie's survival tactics enable him to beat-

A publicity photo of Charlie Chaplin signing papers forming the new production company, United Artists, in 1919 with D. W. Griffith and Mary Pickford.

up on, cheat or humiliate anyone less nimble or inventive than himself. The people he encounters in his filmic environment are not exaggerations like the bully in *Easy Street* (1917), but Chaplin could combine farce with sentimentality and slapstick in most of his films because, as the Little Fellow, he always retaliates against life-threatening situations and authority groups such as revivalist religion and policemen.

In 1921, Chaplin created his first feature film, *The Kid*, featuring Jackie Coogan. This autobiographical comedy-drama concerns the Tramp's encounter with poverty, hunger and unemployment while raising an orphaned boy in the London slums. The film is a loosely structured story in which Chaplin attacks figures of authority who attempt to place the child in an orphanage. Chaplin's assault upon representatives of law and order allows the action to be motivated by his character. His satiric efforts reveal certain social ills, mainly caused by life in the slums and welfare, that have bred human breakdowns.

The Pilgrim (1923), *A Woman of Paris* (1923) and *The Gold Rush* (1925) were feature-length films that continued Chaplin's satirical attacks on human hardships and his attempts to overcome them. After the conversion to sound in 1927, Chaplin took a defiant stand to continue his work as a mime artist and integrated musical scores with his first two sound films, *City Lights* (1931) and *Modern Times* (1936). Both films are social commentary upon economic inequalities facing the "common man" during the Depression Era.

In Charlie Chaplin's *The Kid* (1921), Chaplin plays the Tramp in his first feature film, co-starring Jackie Coogan as the castaway foundling he takes into custody. The sentiment for Chaplin rises as he outwits the police, the doctors and the orphanage workers before the child's real parents appear.

Buster Keaton is up in the rigging in his 1924 film *The Navigator*, looking for land as he finds himself caught in a surrealist wedding cruise traveling on an abandoned ocean freighter heading nowhere.

In Buster Keaton's *The General* (1927), against the background of the American Civil War, cavalrymen watch a Northern supply train crash into a creek as part of an absurd battle between the States.

The Films of Buster Keaton

The silent films of Buster Keaton (1895–1966) are structured closely to action-adventure genres and contain many melodramatic elements. But Keaton is a romantic man of action. In *The Navigator* (1924)and *The General* (1927), we sense that Keaton pays strict attention to the dramatic logic of the plot even if it is absurd to do so. The farcical element of absurdity plays throughout all of Keaton's films. Each film presents a situation in which Keaton chooses to control his fate, rather than have it decided for him. He undertakes tasks with a singleness of purpose that forces him to risk his life, but in doing so he overcomes the odds. His opponents, both natural and man-made, would overwhelm most heroes, but Keaton is not phased by the challenge. With a skillful tenacity in using mechanical devices, be they huge ocean liners or powerful locomotives, he achieves his goal by using the very same powerful objects as forces to win the day as well as the hand of his sweetheart.

Keaton was far more interested in ways to use the camera to create cinematic realities than was Chaplin, who was satisfied just to record his mimes. Keaton's greatest cinematic *tour de force* occurs in *Sherlock, Jr.* (1924), when Keaton, as the motion-picture projectionist, desires to physically join the action on the screen. He falls asleep and steps out of his own body, and into the screen, becoming part of the screen world of time and space. While he maintains his own spatial continuity, the film process of montage and superimposition manipulates his screen persona. This is refreshingly restaged by Woody Allen in *The Purple Rose of Cairo* (1985), when a matinee idol steps off the screen into the life of an adoring fan played by Mia Farrow.

The films of Chaplin and Keaton relate to

Buster Keaton's *The General* (1927) stars the stone-faced Keaton as Johnny Grey, a Southern railroad engineer chasing Northern spies who have hijacked his steam engine. The suspenseful comedy romance is played out with improvised sight gags flawlessly executed by Keaton himself.

Freud's theory of repression and wish fulfillment in their social satires and farces. Their narratives become a complex set of interrelationships that lead the protagonist into a set of paradoxes or absurdities. These paradoxes are the cause of dream symbolism. Dream symbols are elaborate and picturesque fantasies that arise without one's knowledge or consent and even against one's intentions. But as dreams they help one investigate the unconscious aspect of conscious psychic acts.

Keaton and Chaplin explore the surreal aspects of wish fulfillment in some of their films, notably in *The Navigator* and *The Kid*. *The Navigator* is an anxiety journey into the world of matrimony for Keaton. When the ocean liner is set adrift Keaton has to learn how to accept responsibility for steering the ship. When he learns that the ship is abandoned, it becomes

a complex labyrinth where strange passageways and chambers leave Keaton open to possible dangers. Naturally, all this occurs during the night. The actions within this narrative thus symbolize the unconscious state of a dreamer. After various adventures in the South Seas, where cannibals capture the couple, Keaton and his mate escape and are finally rescued when a submarine surfaces to take them back to safety.

References

Brownlow, Kevin, and John Kobal. 1979. *Hollywood: The Pioneers*. New York: Alfred A. Knopf.

Hartnoll, Phyllis (ed.). 1983. *The Oxford Companion to the Theatre*. 4th ed. New York: Oxford University Press.

Hays, Will H. 1923. "The Motion Picture Industry." In *The Movies in Our Midst.* Edited by Gerald Mast. Chicago: The University of Chicago Press, 1982.

Panofsky, Erwin. 1947. "Style and Medium in Motion Pictures." In *Film Theory and Criti-cism.* Edited by Gerald Mast, Marshall Cohen and Leo Braudy. 4th ed. New York and London: Oxford University Press, 1992.

Sklar, Robert. 1975. *Movie-Made America: A Cultural History of American Movies.* New York: Random House.

CHAPTER 8

Hollywood and the Sound Films of the 1930s

Introduction

The introduction of a soundtrack in 1926 to complement the film image was accomplished by the development of Vitaphone's sound-on-disc by Warner Bros. This technological innovation followed Harry Warner's decision to provide an orchestral sound track to attract audiences to movie houses outside the larger urban centers. With the release of *The Jazz Singer* in 1927, Warner Bros. created a tremendous audience response to this film. Rival major studios, realizing the financial gains for sound on their own feature films, decided to invest in another sound system to take advantage of the new sound technology. By 1929, Fox's Movietone sound-on-film system had become the choice for the film industry in America.

There were many technical problems associated with the integration of sound with image that required innovative solutions: a means was needed to provide for camera mobility; some device was required to help record moving actors; and a new camera was necessary for on-location shooting. It took more than five years before the industry learned to combine sounds from all sources and link movement and dialogue successfully in feature films. The technical requirements of sound for feature films also brought Wall Street financiers into the motion picture industry to help pay the costs of sound conversion in thousands of movie palaces throughout the country. Five major studios emerged, each with its own creative team of producers, directors and stars. There was also another new element required, a screenwriter, who joined the Hollywood studios. This gifted person was someone who knew how to write dialogue for actors in films. Prominent writers and journalists from New York were hired at high salaries to supply this need. One of the most successful writers was Ben Hecht, who wrote the screenplay for *Scarface* (1932). He based his scenario on the life of Al Capone, a Chicago gangster who rose to wealth and power through a series of gangland slayings during Prohibition. Howard Hawks directed this melodrama using various sound effects to heighten the realism of the action.

Sound-on-Disc and Sound-on-Film: 1926–1932

The development of sound recording systems for films follows the evolution of the motion pictures since the time when Thomas A. Edison originally commissioned the invention of the Kinetograph in 1889. Edison's notion was to provide a visual accompaniment to his own newly invented phonograph. At the Paris World Exposition of 1900, various inventors from the United States, Germany and France exhibited different systems to synchronize sound recordings with motion pictures. Their inventions were unsuccessful for two reasons: Their machines were unable to synchronize the sound-on-disc or wax cylinder with the visual movements recorded on film, and these inventors had no technical solution on how to amplify the sound for wider presentation in a large theatre space.

When silent film directors like D. W. Griffith and Abel Gance perfected the techniques of film editing to tell a story with moving images, using longer, two-reel films, further experiments to perfect phono-film sound systems died out. By 1910, most storefront theatres and nickelodeons employed pianists who could improvise musical scores to accompany the shorts. Meanwhile, in first-run theatres, musicians were hired to provide orchestral background music for longer film narratives that ran to six reels.

With the building boom of the early 1920s, movie palaces were constructed to hold large orchestras and huge Wurlitzer organs to simulate the orchestral effects necessary for many silent films. Hollywood studios followed the example set by D. W. Griffith, who introduced musical scoring for both his *The Birth of a Nation* and *Intolerance*. Other European directors commissioned serious composers, including Erik Satie, Jean Sibelius, Paul Hindemith and Dmitri Shostakovich, to write original music for their respective European feature films. Hollywood followed this tradition for its prestige feature films of the 1920s. It is thus not too surprising that Harry Warner went all out to combine background sound with silent moving pictures in hopes of increasing the audience's enjoyment of the film experience in 1925, especially when smaller theatres could not include orchestras. He also knew full well that only first-run theatres in large cities could afford full-scale orchestras or Wurlitzer organs to accompany their prestige feature films.

The search for an effective yet inexpensive technology to integrate recorded sound with films began when Vitagraph offered the larger Hollywood studios, like Paramount and MGM, rights to use its system. Wall Street financial houses also were looking for new investment opportunities in motion pictures at the same time. Although the Big Three decided to hold off conversion to sound-on-disc for economic reasons, Jack Warner decided to take advantage of the situation at hand. Gambling on the tremendous growth potential for his studio, he made a firm commitment to Western Electric's offer and set out to produce new films using sound production to capture the market. He secured the services of Waddill Catchings, a financial strategist from the investment firm of Goldman Sachs, and with the infusion of new capital, Warner Bros. began its experiments with the new Vitaphone system to make its studio more competitive with the Big Three.

In the fall of 1926, Warners released its first sound feature, *Don Juan,* a costume romance starring John Barrymore. By this time Vitaphone had successfully synchronized a sound-on-disc recording mechanically with the film projector. The sound track was only a musical score with a dramatic sound-effects track and not a "talkie," but it gave the select movie houses the equivalent of a full orchestral score performed by the New York Philharmonic Orchestra for their out-of-town exhibitions. The grand opening of this film also featured a brief filmed speech by Will Hays, the new head of the Motion Picture Producers and Distributors of America, and some sound shorts featuring musicians and opera stars from the Metropolitan Opera Company of New York. Despite a poor reaction to the program, Warners launched a promotional campaign for its sound system, with Hays predicting that feature films with recorded sound would be the future for new Hollywood productions.

Warner Bros.' commitment to this new technology was not shaken, although 1926 was an unprofitable year for this studio. Its investment in movie house conversions and in building four new sound stages in Hollywood did not diminish the production schedule set by Darryl Zanuck and Jack Warner. They did have limited success with the first Vitaphone program for *Don Juan* as it proved to be a box-office hit, enjoying record-breaking runs in New York, Chicago and other large American cities.

Paramount, MGM and First National were hopeful that this new sound phenomenon would not become too successful at the start, since they had just begun their own aggressive approach to sound conversion. But each large studio had a number of good economic reasons not to plunge into sound films. With the number of screens they had in their respective theatre chains, the expense to convert equipment and facilities for both production and projection would be very costly. These studios also wanted to avoid paying royalties to either Warners for the use of Vitaphone or to William Fox, who was developing his own sound-on-film system. Sound recording in the studios was an unknown factor that could easily alter production techniques, and as yet no one was trained to make the transition to sound features. Additionally, despite the tremendous growth and prosperity of these large integrated studios, a boom in sound features would make the current production of silent films obsolete. If the "talkies" did catch on now, what would happen to those foreign stars in Hollywood who could not speak English? Finally, the entire world market for silent films could change overnight when sound films and spoken English became an important element for audiences to understand the film narrative.

The threat to the Big Three was significant. Warner Bros. had taken the lead and Paramount, MGM and First National convened a "council of war" to decide upon a strategy to hold off these impending economic changes. They agreed upon a development of a rival sound-on-film system that would eventually triumph over Warners' Vitaphone sound-on-disc system. But Jack Warner already knew he could succeed with his sound system. He announced in 1927 that all Warner Bros. silent films would be produced with a good synchronous musical sound track. Further, he would invest heavily in a solid Broadway musical play, *The Jazz Singer*, in which seven popular songs would augment the synchronized orchestral score and some Jewish cantorial music. With vaudeville star Al Jolson cast in the lead, the work was conceived as a silent film using pantomime and excessive gestures, with the dialogue carried by intertitles. However, the improvised introductions to the songs ad-libbed by Jolson proved captivating to audiences, adding a new dramatic dimension to this feature film. As a result, *The Jazz Singer*, using the dynamic singing style of Al Jolson and the sound-on-disc synchronized musical score, became a huge financial success. In one calcu-

lated gamble, Jack Warner revolutionized the movie industry.

By the fall of 1928, when Warner Bros. completed its soundstages in Hollywood, it made the first all-talking feature, *The Lights of New York*, and released a second Jolson film, *The Singing Fool* (1928), an "all-talking, all-singing, all-dancing" musical feature film that also was a box-office hit. The public demand for sound pictures gave this studio the jump in developing new technologies related to the production of sound pictures or "talkies." With this solid advantage over its competitors, Warner Bros. increased its holdings with First International, a fully integrated company with an extensive distribution system and a studio facility in Burbank. Warner Bros. also bought up a large number of theatres from the Stanley Corporation that solidified its theatre chains and completed its expansion into a major studio in Hollywood.

Paramount and MGM, realizing the tremendous gains acquired by Warners, began to quickly convert their studios to soundstages. In 1929, both studios entered the sound era on solid financial footing, but both still had to withstand an attempted takeover by William Fox, who decided to expand his theatre holdings at the expense of MGM. Fox also had developed a sound-on-film system that could easily compete with the Vitaphone system. However, two major events occurred that William Fox did not anticipate. An antitrust suit launched by Louis B. Mayer to check the takeover of Loew's theatres prevented Fox from closing the deal. Then, Fox found himself in the hospital, seriously injured in auto accident that killed his chauffeur. Suddenly, the October stock market crash of 1929 struck and Fox, who had overextended himself financially, lost his entire paper fortune of stocks and bonds. Warner Bros. was able to buy up the remaining shares in First National while other creditors took control of its remaining assets, thereby removing Fox from the motion picture business.

Before the October 1929 crash, Warner Bros. fortunately had raised a loan through Catchings to cover the cost of the new sound conversions for its theatre holdings. By early 1929,

Jack Warner was able to pay off those loans and purchase other theatre facilities. Paramount and MGM had to join forces with other Wall Street financiers to purchase William Fox's sound-on-film system, Movietone, a system easier to install in their movie theatres. Two sound companies, Western Electric, a subsidiary of American Telephone and Telegraph, controlled by J. P. Morgan, and RCA Photophone, part of the Chase Manhattan Bank under the Rockefellers, became interested in taking over the film industry. The struggle between Western Electric and RCA carried over from radio to film. Radio Corporation of America joined forces with Joseph P. Kennedy to form a new film company, RKO (Radio-Keith-Orpheum). Western Electric then became an affiliate of Paramount and MGM. These industrial maneuverings gave the financial control of the motion picture over to the Wall Street financiers which, in turn, lead directly to a new conservatism in feature film production that was to lessen the sensationalism of its sexual content.

The new source of financial control of the major movie studios was only part of the overall changes occurring in the motion picture industry with the introduction of sound technology. Warners' Vitaphone system of sound-on-disc soon gave way to the superior sound-on-film system devised by Fox Movietone and RCA. This Photophone system optically recorded sound patterns on the film strip as variations of light. When the film strip was projected, light patterns were converted into sounds and provided a more reliable synchronization with the projected image. However, recording sound in the major studios created serious production problems for the film industry.

The earliest talkies became motionless as actors and directors dealt with hidden microphones placed in hand props or as parts of the setting. Not only did microphones inhibit actors' movements, but they also inhibited fluid film editing, especially Griffithuse of montage and crosscutting between scenes or actors. As a result, early sound recording forced movies to become virtually static as producers recorded live stage performances on film, resulting in cries by movie critics of "canned theatre."

In the earliest talkies, sound recordings further required the camera to become fixed, encased in a sound-proof booth to eliminate the noise of the motor. To regain camera mobility, a metal cover or "blimp" was added to the camera body. Now, heavier cameras could move freely on dollies for tracking shots or on cranes as they did during the silent days. A second problem arose from the necessity to free the actors' movements while speaking and remove them from the planted, stationary microphones. This problem was solved by the invention of the microphone extended on a long pole held above the heads of the actors. This directional microphone was then capable of recording the spoken dialogue while remaining out of the frame.

Some film critics saw the integration of synchronous sound, especially spoken dialogue, with the moving image as the collapse of cinema as a creative art form. In his book *Film as Art* (1932), Rudolf Arnheim claimed that such sound effects would corrupt the visual aesthetics of silent film. Yet two Soviet directors, Eisenstein and Pudovkin, recognized the potential for sound because they believed it added another dimension to motion pictures. They recommended using sound as a counterpoint to visual montage. Other European directors like René Clair believed that silent films provided an international language available to all. At first, Clair opposed all-talking feature films and was concerned about the language barriers that would have to be overcome to permit films to enter international markets. Now motion pictures needed to invent a new branch of dubbing and subtitling to allow sound films into foreign markets. With this problem in mind, Paramount and MGM experimented with multilingual feature films. Both Josef von Sternberg's *The Blue Angel* with Marlene Dietrich, and Clarence Brown's *Anna Christie* (1930) starring Greta Garbo, were made in English and German versions. Yet these film productions were a costly solution.

Instead, Hollywood invested in musicals; they were new and very popular, and would help bridge the language gap while retaining

Ernst Lubitsch's *The Love Parade* (1929). This early experimental sound film featured musical numbers dubbed in to capture the light-hearted love songs sung in a prototype fashion as romantic Parisian operettas.

their dominance in the European film market. Leading this new genre was Ernst Lubitsch (1892–1947), a German director who came to Hollywood in 1921 on the strength of a series of exotic costume dramas featuring Pola Negri. With the advent of sound, as producer-director for Paramount he restyled light operetta plots into fashionable bedroom farces for his singing stars Maurice Chevalier and Jeanette MacDonald or Claudette Colbert, as in *The Love Parade* (1929), *The Smiling Lieutenant* (1931) and *The Merry Widow* (1934). The "Lubitsch touch" also found its reputation in sophisticated comedies starring Greta Garbo and Marlene Dietrich, in *Trouble in Paradise* (1932) and *Design for Living* (1933).

Warner Bros. experimented with the revue format, borrowing heavily from Broadway hits that featured musical song and dance acts. *Gold Diggers of Broadway* (1929) followed Warners' success with Jolson in Lloyd Bacon's *The Singing Fool*. Most musical numbers were staged within the film narrative as if they were part of a performance before an audience. This convention allowed for various cinematic montages while adhering to the demands of each production number. Mervyn LeRoy directed both *Gold Diggers* narrative sequences while Busby Berkeley used kaleidoscopic patterns of chorus girls in his choreography. In Bacon's *42nd Street* (1933), the production number "Shuffle Off to Buffalo" is presented as a real stage presentation, while Fox's *Sunny Side Up* (1929), directed by David Butler, demonstrates

Paul Muni as Tony Camonte in *Scarface* (1932) fights with his sister, Ann Dvorak, in a climactic scene after revealing a secret incest theme between the two. Howard Hawks directed this early gangster film.

a typical full chorus number from a Broadway musical. When the talented Fred Astaire danced with Ginger Rogers in *Flying Down to Rio* (1933) for RKO Pictures, musicals became identified as youth-oriented romances that celebrated lovers' unions through a number of song-and-dance routines.

Walt Disney was the most adventuresome filmmaker who recognized the artistic possibilities of orchestrating animated action with musical rhythms in his first cartoons, *Skeleton Dance* (1928), *Steamboat Willie* (1929) featuring Mickey Mouse, and using color as in *The Three Little Pigs* (1933). But it was no surprise that filmmakers such as Charlie Chaplin resisted the use of dialogue. Chaplin's two features of the 1930s, *City Lights* (1931) and *Modern Times*, both used a synchronized musical soundtrack and special effects but were shot to

enhance the pantomimes of the Little Tramp. Chaplin composed the scores for these films and because he had complete artistic and financial control over his work, he was able to make these films without dialogue.

Chaplin did not use dialogue until 1940, when he satirized Hitler in *The Great Dictator* with Jack Oakie as Mussolini. Other silent film comedians such as Buster Keaton and Harold Lloyd slowly went into decline as they lost their ability to improvise sight gags and slapstick comedy within the new studio system geared to sound.

Musical scores now served as an integral part of a film narrative to provide a showcase for other cabaret singers such as Fanny Brice, Sophie Tucker and Helen Morgan. With the perfection of sound recording, zany comics such as the Marx Brothers also entered film

Paul Muni as Tony Camonte, a Capone-styled mobster, poses for a publicity shot with his "boys" before he starts a gangland war to eliminate his rivals in *Scarface.*

history when they transferred their theatrical hits, *The Cocoanuts* (1929) and *Animal Crackers* (1930), into comic film farces whose surreal antics, wisecracks and *double entendres* brought new life to film comedies. Verbal jokes and sound effects also aided the appearances of two other stage comedians, W. C. Fields and Mae West. The screen persona of Fields depended upon his one-liners about his love of alcohol, his hatred of babies, animals, and authority figures. In his Mack Sennett farce, *Tillie's Punctured Romance* (1928), we see him in action, with a raspy gin-soaked voice, issuing caustic advice and criticism. Mae West's special appeal was her playful satire of a vamp, coupled with delightful one-line delivery of sexual innuendoes in her hearty talks with her male associates. In *My Little Chickadee* (1940), Fields and West teamed together as a happy wedded couple hoping to achieve marital bliss.

While recorded music and dialogue enhanced the appeal of the musical comedy genre, the audience also accepted the highlife attitudes as escapist fare for a society caught in the Great Depression of the 1930s. The gangster genre emerged as another narrative form that gathered force because of the impact of sound effects. These early gangster films, Mervyn LeRoy's *Little Caesar* (1930), starring Edward G. Robinson, William Wellman's *The Public Enemy* (1931) with James Cagney, and Howard Hawks' *Scarface* (1932), starring Paul Muni, all focused on arch criminals who set out to gain wealth and power through a deliberate "war" with their enemies. With screenplays more in keeping with the tragic hubris of Greek legends, the deaths of these men owe more to flaws in character than to a conflict between good and evil. Dialogue and street jargon play important roles in establishing this character-

Paul Muni plays Tony Camonte caught in a shootout with the police using his newly acquired tommy gun in this scene from *Scarface*.

ization, as does the use of multiple sound effects of the city.

Scarface is Howard Hawks' rendition of Ben Hecht's version of the Al Capone story. As an example of a classical Prohibition-era gangster film of the early 1930s, Hawks infused this drama with the excitement of a realistic sound track punctuated by loud machine gun fire,

honky-tonk music from speakeasies and furious car chases with screeching auto tires and more gunfire. The leading role starred Paul Muni as Tony Camonte, the famed cynical mobster who rises to wealth and power in a large Midwestern metropolis through a series of fanatical gangland slayings. The brutal depiction of violence and the realistic glorification of this mobster caused a furor among movie audiences and censors alike because of an absence of law and order in the film narrative to control mobsters like Camonte. Two years of wrangling with the Hays Office forced Hawks to subtitle the film *Scarface: The Shame of the Nation* and to introduce a new scene in which civic groups denounce the criminal and called for justice. The final shootout between the mobster and the police has been retained, revealing the famous electric sign flashing the "World is Yours," an ironic comment on the life and death of Tony Camonte.

By 1935, most mature feature sound films were supported by another audio innovation. It was employed by Raoul Walsh (1887–1980), who decided to continue making outdoor action adventures, especially westerns. He directed shooting on location as he did with silent films, then returned with the footage to the studio and added sound that was recorded at a later time. With more advanced sound equipment, Walsh perfected a system that enabled him to dub the sounds precisely synchronized with the visual actions recorded on film. In France, Jean Renoir and René Clair were able to incorporate sounds from all sources for their

social satires that linked narrative action through the presence of telephones and radios within the narrative. Renoir also used the moving camera to capture the flow of the action toward a new "poetic realism." From *La Chienne* (1931) to *La Règle du jeu / The Rules of the Game* (1939), Renoir's film narratives easily blended sound with moving image.

References

Gomery, Douglas. "Writing the History of the American Film Industry: Warner Brothers and Sound." *Screen 17,* no. 1 (Spring 1976). In *Movies and Methods: An Anthology.* Vol. II. Edited by Bill Nichols. Berkeley: University of California Press, 1985.

Jacobs, Lewis. 1968. *The Rise of the American Film: A Critical History.* 2nd ed. New York: Teachers College Press.

Lawson, John Howard. 1967. *Film: The Creative Process.* 2nd ed. New York: Hill and Wang.

Mast, Gerald, and Bruce F. Kawin. 1996. *A Short History of the Movies.* 6th ed. Boston and London: Allyn and Bacon.

Nowell-Smith, Geoffrey (ed.). 1996. *The Oxford History of World Cinema.* New York: Oxford University Press.

French Cinema of the 1930s

Introduction

During the 1930s, the French film industry responded quickly to the advent of sound technology and drew directly from the theatrical and literary sources familiar to the world. The well-known 19th century French novels by Balzac, Flaubert, Zola and de Maupassant were adapted to the screen, staying within the French literary tradition. These stories of crime and violence displayed passions of love rather than greed. As French films, the scenarios acknowledged the robust sexuality and earthiness in human relationships that many American films lacked. The film translations teamed talented actresses with the prominent leading men of the day, creating a demand for these romantic French "art films" in the American marketplace.

Jean Renoir uses theatrical metaphors in *La Grande Illusion / The Grand Illusion* (1937) and *La Règle du jeu / The Rules of the Game* (1939) to reflect upon the dissolution of the social and political aristocracy during a period of crisis brought on by the Great Depression, the threat of Fascism and another world war. Marcel Carné's two major films, *Quai des brumes / Port of Shadows* (1938) and *Le Jour se lève / Daybreak* (1939), identify the romantic fatalism that awaits his heroes who decide to self-destruct. Both directors invite the film audience into this disquieting, cynical world to depict how men and women are controlled and destroyed by the conventions of the ruling elite. In this artificial world "the rules of the game" always depend upon the play of actors adjusting to certain roles and accepting the social contract.

French Cinema During the 1930s

The introduction of sound technology to the French film industry coupled with the worldwide economic crisis brought about the collapse of the two largest film studios, Gaumont and Pathé, by 1935. Further production difficulties arose due to the practice of multi-language shooting until suitable subtitling and dubbing became economically viable. The high costs of sound-film production also saw the end of private patronage to finance independent productions, especially those involved in avant-garde movements related to surrealism. Fortunately, Luis Buñuel was able to complete his indictment of French capitalist society with his *L'Âge d'or / The Golden Age* in 1930, only to have the government ban the film after André Breton called it the first authentic surrealist sound film. Meanwhile, Jean Cocteau completed his controversial film *Le Sang d'un poète / The Blood of a Poet*, also in 1930. This reworking by Cocteau of the Pygmalion myth uses voice-over narration and subtitles. It is often mistaken for a surrealist fantasy, as Cocteau uses painted images within a staged setting in attempts to bring a sculpture to life, but it is a carefully constructed symbolic film.

Much more influential in the exploration of surrealist themes in film was Jean Vigo (1905–1934), who mounted a successful surrealist attack on French authority and social conventions. Vigo was able to produce two short documentaries and two longer fictional films before his death at the age of 29. His early sound film, *Zéro de Conduite / Zero for Conduct* (1933), photographed by cinematographer Boris Kaufmann, portrays a student revolt by

Jean Vigo's *Zéro de Conduite* (1933) captures the anarchic child's world inside a French boarding school. It is highlighted by a rebellious pillow fight scene shot in slow-motion to give the film a surreal sense of free-floating images in contrast to the formal, repressive authoritarian world of teachers and adults. Though of poor quality, this photo manages to convey the dreamlike atmosphere of the scene.

a group of young boys at a boarding school in France. The film tells the story from the point-of-view of four young anarchists. Their quest for freedom from the petty regimentation by deranged school teachers in the classroom takes on farcical dimensions. Vigo employs slow-motion effects to create a surreal world made up of dream images that transcend time and space in a dormitory in which the rebellion begins. The following morning the boys initiate a rooftop attack on school dignitaries during an outdoor school assembly. Because of the subversive stance taken by Vigo toward authority, the French government withheld the film from distribution until 1945. When shown in England during the 1960s, this film influenced English director Lindsey Anderson (b. 1923) who wrote and directed *If ...* (1968), in which

he depicts the devastating attack on school officials by a similar group of revolutionary students.

In Vigo's next narrative film *L'Atalante* (1934), he merged the naturalist tendencies in the American silent cinema of Griffith with the formal expressiveness of the French avant-garde to depict a tender yet haunted love story. Vigo demonstrated his skill as a filmmaker by poetically contrasting the life of young newly-weds both onboard and off a barge traveling down the Seine on their honeymoon. He also integrated sound effects to support the rich visual imagery that follows a story of separation and reunion as his characters move from fantasy into their own reality as it is transformed in a dream-like surreal fashion, a "poetic realism."

The major influence for the development of sound film in France came directly from theatrical and literary sources. Novels from the 19th century by Stendhal, Balzac, Flaubert, Zola and de Maupassant provided film directors and their scenarists with excellent stories to adapt into films. The scenarios were written primarily in the literary tradition by Jacques Feyder, Marcel Pagnol, Marcel Carné and Charles Spaak. The scripts excelled in their depth of characterization. When these scripts were translated into films, the directors had the skills of accomplished actresses such as Arletty, Michele Morgan, Françoise Rosay and Simone Simone to add important psychological nuances to the dramas. They were joined by such prominent actors as Jean-Louis Barrault, Louis Jouvet, Jean Gabin, Harry Baur and Raimu. The result of this filmic collaboration was the growth of French language films that found a secure market in North America. Small "art cinemas" in New York, Chicago and San Francisco gave these feature films long runs. It came as no surprise that the first five annual New York Film Critics' Awards went to French films and directors. *La Kermesse héroique / Carnival in Flanders* (1935), directed by Jacques Feyder won in 1936, followed by Anatole Litvak's *Mayerling* (1936) in 1937, Renoir's *The Grand Illusion* won in 1938, *Regain / Harvest* (1937), directed by Marcel Pagnol in 1939 and Pagnol's *La Femme du boulanger / The Baker's Wife* (1938) in 1940.

Oddly enough, Pagnol started directing adaptations of his own famous Marseilles trilogy about César and Fanny as a means to record the stage version of the novels. Although these films were called "canned theatre," they were instrumental in popularizing the use of sound in the French film industry. The successes of these filmed narratives also led Pagnol to build his own studio and begin adaptations of other novels by Jean Giono, a playwright who shared his respect for traditional folktales depicting innocent yet sensuous characters. These stories required on-location shooting to establish the authentic details for the "slice of life" reality of the story. Because of this trend, Pagnol's direction of these comedies of rural life is simple and direct. *The Baker's Wife* featured Raimu, as a disgruntled baker, who cannot bake bread for the village after he discovers his wife has eloped with a stupid but handsome shepherd boy. To restore order, the villagers organize to bring her back. Raimu's acting and the story achieved wide applause even though it was noted that the direction and editing was less than "cinematic." In 1986, Pagnol's short stories, *Jean de Florette* and *Manon des Sources* resurfaced in fine cinematic renditions by director Claude Berri (b. 1934), in color, with a tragic lyricism and power that gave authority to the cultural heritage of these characters.

The Films of Jean Renoir

Jean Renoir (1894–1979) is considered by film critics as the most exceptional French filmmaker of the 1930s. He made some 15 films during this period, working with scripts that covered many genres in his own individualistic style. His cinematic work is indebted to the French farces of Eugene Scribe, Georges Feydeau and Pierre Beaumarchais, but basically they are akin to Molière and the tradition of the Italian *commedia dell'arte* of the 17th century. Like Molière's theatre pieces, Renoir's films are social satires wherein theatrical farce becomes the major strategy used by the directors working within the realism of the 19th century novel. Renoir is able to use farce both as a means to criticize the decaying social and political structures of his country and to recognize some of the historical problems French citizens must come to grips with during the 1930s. In all his films, he acknowledges the aristocratic class structure that automatically imposed a chivalric tradition upon a changing political world.

The nature of farce interested Renoir because he could illustrate a set of paradoxes about human relationships that indirectly led to a series of absurdities. In his first sound film, *La Chienne / The Bitch* (1931), starring Michel Simon, he cleverly demonstrates this in a story of a bank clerk and Sunday painter who seeks out a prostitute for love and affection. When he discovers his mistress is exploiting him, he chokes her to death, then allows her pimp to be executed for the murder. This turn of events is unexpected, but farce is absurd and this film illustrates how farce creates a structure of absurdities, many of which are simply paradoxical. But then, farce also incorporates a series of coincidences that Renoir plays upon in which random chance seems to operate. Thus, the conflict of values that causes the tragic ending becomes an outcome of misrule or mischief or play that dictates an ending; one that is fortunate for one but fatal for the other. Renoir plays with these irrational forces and absurd coincidences to create the surprises in a simple farcical plot about desire and the law. The satiric fantasies and their outcomes are what audiences come to expect with Renoir. In *La Chienne,* the painter says goodbye to painting and welcomes the absurdities of bohemian day-to-day existence. Renoir's *mise-en-scène* developed an extensive use of a moving camera to take advance of natural sync-sound recordings when filming in actual locations. This strategy reduced the need for montage and added a three-dimensional depth-of-field to his sequences, one that André Bazin found praiseworthy in his essay on the evolution of the cinema.

In Renoir's next film, *Boudu sauvé des eaux / Boudu Saved from Drowning* (1932), also starring Michel Simon as a tramp, he pursues this farcical sense of anarchy further. In this film, a tramp is saved from drowning only to face the superficial conventions of bourgeois life. In response, he seduces the wife of his rescuer as well as the man's mistress, then escapes the tyranny of these conventions by faking his own drowning, only to resurface again to relish his newly won freedom. This film was remade in Hollywood by Paul Mazursky as *Down and Out in Beverly Hills* (1986), starring Nick Nolte and Bette Midler.

Renoir teamed with screenwriter Jacques Prevert to direct *Le Crime de Monsieur Lange / The Crime of Monsieur Lange* (1935). The film is based on Renoir's political commitment to a group known as the Popular Front, a coalition of Socialists, Communists and other left-wing parties. The Popular Front won the 1936 election and Leon Blum became Prime Minister.

However, one year later in 1937, the front was defeated and the French right wing returned to power. Renoir develops his political parable by comparing a socialist cooperative of employees with an unsavory and exploitative capitalist proprietor, Batala, who owns a publishing house. As an unscrupulous businessman, Batala buys the rights to a series of Western stories written by one of his employees, Monsieur Lange, but denies him royalties. Creditors force Batala to flee, and presumably he is killed in a train crash. Monsieur Lange then persuades other employees to run the business as a cooperative. The venture proves successful due to the popularity of Lange's cowboy hero, "Arizona Jim." However, the owner Batala reappears. He survived the crash and now seeks to reclaim the prosperous business. But Monsieur Lange decides to murder "the dead man," then flee the country with his love, Valentine. At the border, Valentine recounts the story to some workmen who, acting like a jury, acquit them of the crime and agree to help the couple escape to freedom.

Renoir's masterful *mise-en-scène* visualized the concept of social action toward a common cause by placing the action within a single-set tenement and courtyard. Here, in the respective print shop and laundry, all the communal action and dialogue between the owner and employees takes place. Within this identifiable space, Renoir uses a mobile camera and in-depth photography that links separate scenes as part of a continuous world. There are few static shots; instead Renoir's camera carries the spectator into and out of scenes by panning and traveling shots that reframe the action. Group shots are favored as Renoir transfers attention from one character to another, allowing the spectator to participate in the unfolding action. Renoir's covert endorsement of the solidarity of the workers in this film reflects his commitment to the Popular Front and their efforts for social and economic control over the lives of workers. The tragic irony is that violence apparently becomes a necessary measure to ensure the success of the cooperative.

"*The Crime of Monsieur Lange* may not be the most famous film made by Renoir, but it's a film that seems to be well-loved by those who know it. It crested a wave of popular French sentiment before the onslaught of European fascism. The moment was almost too utopian" (Campbell 2005).

After making an explicit film for the Popular Front in 1936, Renoir decided to make an anti-war film that enlarged upon the themes about men being trapped and conditioned by the social conventions of their times. In 1937, he made *La Grande Illusion*, starring Erich von Stroheim and Pierre Fresnay as the aristocratic officers who are linked by their heritage as professional soldiers. The plot is less important than the interaction of these major characters carrying out their roles and the different ways war prisoners try to escape from acting as physical and mental hostages to the artificial social conventions or "the rules of the game." The film is set during World War I, but Renoir declines to depict men in combat. Patriotic fer-

vor is displayed by men only in song and dance in the support of their war effort. Renoir is more interested in exploring what happens to men who become prisoners to conventions that contravene community, friendship and love. These conventions reveal the social and political relationships that identify one's nationality, class, rank and religious prejudice. In revealing these biases, Renoir skillfully integrates a sound track within several scenes contrasting two songs, one French, the other German, to establish identifying *Leitmotifs* throughout the film.

Renoir borrowed the basic plot for *The Rules of the Game* from Musset's comedy of manners, *Les Caprices de Marianne*, which, in turn, derives from the Italian *commedia dell'arte*. This popular, actor-centered form of comedy was imported into France in the 17th century by Molière. The scenario or script was improvised

A young aviator hero in Jean Renoir's *The Rules of the Game* (1939) meets his alluring Marquise (Nora Gregor) at a house party through the help of his friend, Octave, a societal gamester played by Jean Renoir himself. Octave organizes the social revels, then finds himself paying the price.

The Marquis de la Chesnaye (Marcel Dario) salutes his aviator rival in a playful mood as the romantic comedy of *The Rules of the Game* gets underway, only to move to farce as Renoir captures the escapades of an outdated aristocracy observing petty class distinctions.

according to the actions of a set of stock characters who represented stereotypes of the society. The stock characters were divided into three groups. First were the professional types consisting of Pantalone, the father-figure and lecher; El Dottore, the learned pedant; and El Capitano, as the cowardly warrior. Second were the pairs of lovers, young and attractive, who dressed fashionably and moved elegantly. The major action of the plot centered around their love-making strategies. They were aided or hindered by the third group, the servants or comic types.

Renoir uses all these characters for his *Rules of the Game* to explore a past social world where each character plays an assigned role. Then, as director, he allows the actors playing these characters to improvise their lines and actions according to the way they interpret the roles. Into this social world, Renoir introduces the modern hero, an aviator, ignorant of the rules and the part he must play, but motivated by an ardent desire for the mistress of the house. His arrival precipitates the action of the comedy, as Renoir, charmingly playing Octave, the go-between, sets the stage before confusion arises between the personal objectives and the societal rules and goals.

Renoir purposely chose an aristocratic château to accommodate an expired society and its characters. The château is carefully maintained by the master of the house, Robert de la Chesnaye, a lover of mechanical toys. In this cloistered world, Renoir develops a double

The Marquise and her maid, Lisette, share intimacies about their respective husbands and lovers in this scene from *The Rules of the Game*.

plot involving masters, lovers and servants. Renoir directs the attention of the viewer of this satire toward the follies and deficiencies of the stock authority figures who are more concerned with the manners and rules of the game than with outsiders who cannot conform or play within the conventions set by society. Renoir focuses our attention upon the humor that arises from the horseplay, contradictions and coincidences that support this social construct. Treating it as a sometimes elaborate bedroom farce, he contrasts the natural attractions of lovers to each other with the social forms of behavior required by the ruling class. The film also becomes a serious investigation into themes of individual freedom and social commitment. In comparing two pairs of lovers, Renoir entertains various possibilities in showing that people don't want fences to restrict their behavior, but on the other hand, the film reveals a need for collective organization. As Octave realizes, once he has triggered the action, "there is one thing that is terrible, and that is everyone has his reasons." Thus this great French film moves quickly from slapstick comedy and chase sequences into an older social world already embracing a theatrical dance with death.

The double plot of *Rules of the Game* is motivated by two servants, one a fool, the gamesman Schumacher, and the other a knave, Octave. Octave is a rough but kindly social parasite, the promoter for one of the lovers, who yet carries with him the spirit of mischief. It is Octave who brings the main lovers together at the château, and it is Octave, as the knave, who sets off the fool, Schumacher, who is jealous of Octave when he catches him flirting with his wife, Lisette. The major battle concerns Octave and Schumacher, one that brings out the farcical elements in this social satire. Paradoxically, Octave becomes an unwitting fool by his attempts to move between the worlds of masters and servants. Unintentionally, his actions precipitate the final catastrophe.

Renoir invites the audience into this delightful yet disquieting comedy of manners to display how men and women can be controlled or destroyed by the social conventions of the ruling elite. These rules of the game are never permanently fixed, but depend upon transformations by individuals who revise them when the social constructs no longer concede to a person's freedom.

When life offers no escape from the rules of society, a person enters into a fatalistic film noir vision as visualized by Marcel Carné and Jacques Prévert. Carné directed two films, *Quai de brumes / Port of Shadows* and *Le Jour se lève / Daybreak*, both romantic crime thrillers starring Jean Gabin. In *Port of Shadows*, Gabin portrays an army deserter trapped in a seedy waterfront bar. He attempts to protect his lover, Michele Morgan, while he waits for two criminals intent on seeking revenge. In *Daybreak*, Gabin is cornered by the police in an attic after committing a crime of passion. In each film, criminal elements apparently act as agents of an avenging fate that has doomed Gabin's character and his hopes of escape. The predestined outcomes found in these dramas are precursors to the stage plays of Beckett and Ionesco in the Theatre of the Absurd and the bleak American film noir thrillers that emerged after World War II. *Daybreak* was remade in Hollywood as a noir vehicle for Henry Fonda in 1947 as *The Long Night,* directed by Anatole Litvak.

The imprecise term "poetic realism" is used to characterize the films of Vigo, Carné and Renoir because these filmmakers were able to blend an artful lyricism with realistic renditions of life. Seeking to unite "poetic realism" politically with the Popular Front movement, the French Socialists under the Leon Blum government of 1936 encouraged Renoir to make a number of films depicting the history of the Socialist movement, such as *La Vie est à nous / People of France* (1936) and *La Marseillaise* (1937). In these romantic interpretations of events that set off the French Revolution, Renoir analyzes the problems faced by the proletariat as they attempted to break free of the aristocracy and the coming of the capitalist ideology.

References

Bazin, André, 1973. *Jean Renoir.* Edited by François Truffaut. New York: Simon & Schuster.

Campbell, Zach, 2005. "*The Crime of Monsieur Lange.*" www.SlantMagazine.com

Mast, Gerald. 1973. *Filmguide to Rules of the Game.* Bloomington: Indiana University Press.

Renoir, Jean. 1974. *My Life and My Films.* New York: Atheneum.

Thiher, Allen. 1979. *The Cinematic Muse: Critical Studies in the History of French Cinema.* Columbia and London: University of Missouri Press.

"The Evolution of the Language of Cinema"

by André Bazin

By 1928 the silent film had reached its artistic peak. The despair of its elite as they witnessed the dismantling of this ideal city, while it may not have been justified, is at least understandable. As they followed their chosen aesthetic path it seemed to them that the cinema had developed into an art most perfectly accommodated to the "exquisite embarrassment" of silence and that the realism that sound would bring could only mean a surrender to chaos.

In point of fact, now that sound has given proof that it came not to destroy but to fulfill the Old Testament of the cinema, we may most properly ask if the technical revolution created by the sound track was in any sense an aesthetic revolution. In other words, did the years from 1928 to 1930 actually witness the birth of a new cinema? Certainly, as regards editing, history does not actually show as wide a breach as might be expected between the silent and the sound film. On the contrary there is discernible evidence of a close relationship between certain directors of 1925 and 1935 and especially of the 1940s through the 1950s. Compare for example Erich von Stroheim and Jean Renoir or Orson Welles, or again Carl Theodore Dreyer and Robert Bresson. These more or less clear-cut affinities demonstrate first of all that the gap separating the 1920s and the 1930s can be bridged, and secondly that certain cinematic values actually carry over from the silent to the sound film and, above all, that it is less a matter of setting silence over against sound than of contrasting certain families of styles, certain basically different concepts of cinematographic expression.

Aware as I am that the limitations imposed on this study restrict me to a simplified and to that extent enfeebled presentation of my argument, and holding it to be less an objective statement than a working hypothesis, I will distinguish, in the cinema between 1920 and 1940, between two broad and opposing trends: those directors who put their faith in the image and those who put their faith in reality. By "image" I here mean, very broadly speaking, everything that the representation on the screen adds to the object there represented. This is a complex inheritance but it can be reduced essentially to two categories: those that relate to the plastics of the image and those that relate to the resources of montage, which, after all, is simply the ordering of images in time.

Under the heading "plastics" must be included the style of the sets, of the make-up, and, up to a point, even of the performance, to which we naturally add the lighting and, finally, the framing of the shot which gives us its composition. As regards montage, derived initially as we all know from the masterpieces of Griffith, we have the statement of Malraux in his *Psychologie du Cinéma* that it was montage that gave birth to film as an art, setting it apart from mere animated photography, in short, creating a language.

The use of montage can be "invisible" and this was generally the case in the prewar classics of the American screen. Scenes were broken down just for one purpose, namely, to analyze an episode according to the material or dramatic logic of the scene. It is this logic which conceals the fact of the analysis, the mind of the spectator quite naturally accepting the view-points of the director which are justified by the geography of the action or the shifting emphasis of dramatic interest.

But the neutral quality of this "invisible" editing fails to make use of the full potential of montage. On the other hand these potentialities are clearly evident from the three processes generally known as parallel montage, accelerated montage, montage by attraction. In creating parallel montage, Griffith succeeded in conveying a sense of the simultaneity of two actions taking place at a geographical distance by means of alternating shots from each. In *La Roue* Abel Gance created the illusion of the steadily increasing speed of a locomotive without actually using any images of speed (indeed the wheel could have been turning on one spot) simply by a multiplicity of shots of ever-decreasing length.

Finally there is "montage by attraction," the creation of S. M. Eisenstein, and not so easily described as the others, but which may be roughly defined as the reinforcing of the meaning of one image by association with another image not necessarily part of the same episode — for example the fireworks display in *The General Line* following the image of the bull. In this extreme form, montage by attraction was rarely

used even by its creator but one may consider as very near to it in principle the more commonly used ellipsis, comparison, or metaphor, examples of which are the throwing of stockings onto a chair at the foot of a bed, or the mild overflowing in H. G. Clouzot's *Quai des orfèvres*. There are of course a variety of possible combinations of these three processes.

Whatever these may be, one can say that they share that trait in common which constitutes the very definition of montage, namely, the creation of a sense or meaning not proper to the images themselves but derived exclusively from their juxtaposition. The well-known experiment of Kuleshov with the shot of Mozhukhin in which a smile was seen to change its significance according to the image that preceded it, sums up perfectly the properties of montage.

Montage as used by Kuleshov, Eisenstein, or Gance did not give us the event; it alluded to it. Undoubtedly they derived at least the greater part of the constituent elements from the reality they were describing but the final significance of the film was found to reside in the ordering of these elements much more than in their objective content.

The matter under recital, whatever the realism of the individual image, is born essentially from these relationships — Mozhukhin plus dead child equal pity — that is to say an abstract result, none of the concrete elements of which are to be found in the premises; maidens plus apple trees in bloom equal hope. The combinations are infinite. But the only thing they have in common is the fact that they suggest an idea by means of a metaphor or by an association of ideas. Thus between the scenario properly so-called, the ultimate object of the recital, and the image pure and simple, there is a relay station, a sort of aesthetic "transformer." The meaning is not in the image, it is in the shadow of the image projected by montage onto the field of consciousness of the spectator.

Let us sum up. Through the contents of the image and the resources of montage, the cinema has at its disposal a whole arsenal of means whereby to impose its interpretation of an event on the spectator. By the end of the silent film we can consider this arsenal to have been full. On the one side the Soviet cinema carried to its ultimate consequences the theory and practice of montage while the German school did every kind of violence to the plastics of the image by way of sets and lighting. Other cinemas count too besides the Russian and German, but whether in France or Sweden or the United States, it does not appear that the language of cinema was at a loss for ways of saying what it wanted to say.

If the art of cinema consists in everything that plastics and montage can add to a given reality, the silent film was an art on its own. Sound could only play at best a subordinate and supplementary role: a counterpoint to the visual image. But this possible enhancement — at best only a minor one — is likely not to weigh much in comparison with the additional bargain-rate reality introduced at the same time by sound.

Thus far we have put forward the view that expressionism of montage and image constitute the essence of cinema. And it is precisely on this generally accepted notion that directors from silent days, but as Erich von Stroheim, F. W. Murnau, and Robert Flaherty, have by implication cast a doubt. In their films, montage plays no part, unless it be the negative one of inevitable elimination where reality superabounds. The camera cannot see everything at once but makes sure not to lose any part of what it chooses to see. What matters to Flaherty, confronted with Nanook hunting the seal, is the relation between Nanook and the animal; the actual length of the waiting period. Montage could suggest the time involved. Flaherty however confines himself to showing the actual waiting period; the length of the hunt is the very substance of the image, its true object. Thus in the film this episode requires one setup. Will anyone deny that it is thereby much more moving than a montage by attraction?

Murnau is interested not so much in time as in the reality of dramatic space. Montage plays no more of a decisive part in *Nosferatu* than in *Sunrise*. One might be inclined to think that the plastics of his image are impressionistic. But this would be a superficial view. The composition of his image is in no sense pictorial. It adds nothing to the reality, it does not deform

it, it forces it to reveal its structural depth, to bring out the preexisting relations which become constitutive of the drama. For example, in *Tabu*, the arrival of a ship from left screen gives an immediate sense of destiny at work so that Murnau has no need to cheat in any way on the uncompromising realism of a film whose settings are completely natural.

But it is most of all Stroheim who rejects photographic expressionism and the tricks of montage. In his films reality lays itself bare like a suspect confessing under the relentless examination of the commissioner of police. He has one simple rule for direction. Take a close look at the world, keep on doing so, and in the end it will lay bare for you all its cruelty and its ugliness. One could easily imagine as a matter of fact a film by Stroheim composed of a single shot as long-lasting and as close-up as you like. These three directors do not exhaust the possibilities. We would undoubtedly find scattered among the works of others elements of nonexpressionistic cinema in which montage plays no part — even including Griffith. But these examples suffice to reveal, at the very heart of the silent film, a cinematographic art the very opposite of that which has been identified as "*cinéma par excellence*," a language the semantic and syntactical unit of which is in no sense the Shot; in which the image is evaluated not according to what it adds to reality but what it reveals of it. In the latter art the silence of the screen was a drawback, that is to say, it deprived reality of one of its elements. *Greed*, like Dreyer's *Jeanne d'Arc*, is already virtually a talking film. The moment that you cease to maintain that montage and the plastic composition of the image are the very essence of the language of cinema, sound is no longer the aesthetic crevasse dividing two radically different aspects of the seventh art. The cinema that is believed to have died of the soundtrack is in no sense "*the* cinema." The real dividing line is elsewhere. It was operative in the past and continues to be through thirty-five years of the history of the language of the film.

Having challenged the aesthetic unity of the silent film and divided it off into two opposing tendencies, now let us take a look at the history of the last twenty years.

From 1930 to 1940 there seems to have grown up in the world, originating largely in the United States, a common form of cinematic language. It was the triumph in Hollywood, during that time, of five or six major kinds of film that gave it its overwhelming superiority: (1) American comedy (*Mr. Smith Goes to Washington*, 1936); (2) The burlesque film (The Marx Brothers); (3) The dance and vaudeville film (Fred Astaire and Ginger Rogers and the Ziegfeld Follies); (4) The crime and gangster film (*Scarface, I Am a Fugitive from a Chain Gang, The Informer*); (5) Psychological and social dramas (*Back Street, Jezebel*); (6) Horror or fantasy films (*Dr. Jekyll and Mr. Hyde, The Invisible Man, Frankenstein*); (7) The western (*Stagecoach*, 1939). During that time the French cinema undoubtedly ranked next. Its superiority was gradually manifested by way of a trend towards what might be roughly called stark somber realism, or poetic realism, in which four names stand out: Jacques Feyder, Jean Renoir, Marcel Carné, and Julien Duvivier. My intention not being to draw up a list of prize-winners, there is little use in dwelling on the Soviet, British, German, or Italian films for which these years were less significant than the ten that were to follow. In any case, American and French production sufficiently clearly indicate that the sound film, prior to World War II, had reached a well-balanced stage of maturity.

First as to content. Major varieties with clearly defined rules capable of pleasing a worldwide public, as well as a cultured elite, provided it was not inherently hostile to the cinema.

Secondly as to form: well-defined styles of photography and editing perfectly adapted to their subject matter; a complete harmony of image and sound. In seeing again today such films as *Jezebel* by William Wyler, *Stagecoach* by John Ford, or *Le Jour se lève* by Marcel Carné, one has the feeling that in them an art has found its perfect balance, its ideal form of expression, and reciprocally one admires them for dramatic and moral themes to which the cinema, while it may not have created them, has given a grandeur, an artistic effectiveness, that they would not otherwise have had. In

short, here are all the characteristics of the ripeness of a classical art.

I am quite aware that one can justifiably argue that the originality of the postwar cinema as compared with that of 1938 derives from the growth of certain national schools, in particular the dazzling display of the Italian cinema and of a native English cinema freed from the influence of Hollywood. From this one might conclude that the really important phenomenon of the years 1940–1950 is the introduction of new blood, of hitherto unexplored themes. That is to say, the real revolution took place more on the level of subject matter than of style. Is not neorealism primarily a kind of humanism and only secondarily a style of filmmaking? Then as to the style itself, is it not essentially a form of self-effacement before reality?

Our intention is certainly not to preach the glory of form over content. Art for art's sake is just as heretical in cinema as elsewhere, probably more so. On the other hand, a new subject matter demands new form, and as good a way as any towards understanding what a film is trying to say to us is to know how it is saying it.

Thus by 1938 or 1939 the talking film, particularly in France and in the United States, had reached a level of classical perfection as a result, on the one hand, of the maturing of different kinds of drama developed in part over the past ten years and in part inherited from the silent film, and, on the other, of the stabilization of technical progress. The 1930s were the years, at once, of sound and of panchromatic film. Undoubtedly studio equipment had continued to improve but only in matters of detail, none of them opening up new, radical possibilities for direction. The only changes in this situation since 1940 have been in photography, thanks to the increased sensitivity of the film stock. Panchromatic stock turned visual values upside down, ultrasensitive emulsions have made a modification in their structure possible. Free to shoot in the studio with a much smaller aperture, the operator could, when necessary, eliminate the soft-focus background once considered essential. Still there are a number of examples of the prior use of deep focus, for example in the work of Jean Renoir. This had always been possible on exteriors, and given a measure of skill, even in the studios. Anyone could do it who really wanted to. So that it is less a question basically of a technical problem, the solution of which has admittedly been made easier, than of a search after a style — a point to which we will come back. In short, with panchromatic stock in common use, with an understanding of the potentials of the microphone, and with the crane as standard studio equipment, one can really say that since 1930 all the technical requirements for the art of cinema have been available.

Since the determining technical factors were practically eliminated, we must look elsewhere for the signs and principles of the evolution of film language, that is to say by challenging the subject matter and as a consequence the styles necessary for its expression.

By 1939 the cinema had arrived at what geographers call the equilibrium-profile of a river. By this is meant that ideal mathematical curve which results from the requisite amount of erosion. Having reached this equilibrium-profile, the river flows effortlessly from its source to its mouth without further deepening of its bed. But if any geological movement occurs which raises the erosion level and modifies the height of the source, the water sets to work again, seeps into the surrounding land, goes deeper, burrowing and digging. Sometimes when it is a chalk bed, a new pattern is dug across the plain, almost invisible but found to be complex and winding, if one follows the flow of the water.

The Evolution of Editing Since the Advent of Sound

In 1938 there was an almost universal standard pattern of editing. If, somewhat conventionally, we call the kind of silent films based on the plastics of the image and the artifices of montage, "expressionist" or "symbolistic," we can describe the new form of story-telling "analytic" and "dramatic." Let us suppose, by way of reviewing one of the elements of the experiment of Kuleshov, that we have a table covered with food and a hungry tramp. One can imagine that in 1936 it would have been edited as follows:

(1) Full shot of the actor and the table.

(2) Camera moves forward to a close-up of a face expressing a mixture of amazement and longing.

(3) Series of close-ups of food.

(4) Back to full shot of person who starts slowly towards the camera.

(5) Camera pulls slowly back to a three-quarter shot of the actor seizing a chicken wing.

Whatever variants one could think of for this scene, they would all have certain points in common:

(1) The verisimilitude of space in which the position of the actor is always determined, even when a close-up eliminates the decor.

(2) The purpose and the effects of the cutting are exclusively dramatic or psychological.

In other words, if the scene were played on a stage and seen from a seat in the orchestra, it would have the same meaning, the episode would continue to exist objectively. The changes of point of view provided by the camera would add nothing. They would present the reality a little more forcefully, first by allowing a better view and then by putting the emphasis where it belongs.

It is true that the stage director like the film director has at his disposal a margin within which he is free to vary the interpretation of the action but it is only a margin and allows for no modification of the inner logic of the event. Now, by way of contrast, let us take the montage of the stone lions in *The End of St. Petersburg*. By skillful juxtapositioning a group of sculptured lions are made to look like a single lion getting to its feet, a symbol of the aroused masses. This clever device would be unthinkable in any film after 1932. As late as 1935 Fritz Lang, in *Fury*, followed a series of shots of women dancing the can-can with shots of clucking chickens in a farmyard. This relic of associative montage came as a shock even at the time, and today seems entirely out of keeping with the rest of the film. However decisive the art of Marcel Carné, for example, in our estimate of the respective values of *Quai des brumes* or of *Le Jour se léve* his editing remains on the level of the reality he is analyzing. There is only one proper way of looking at it. That is why we are witnessing the almost complete disappearance of optical effects such as superimpositions, and even, especially in the United States, of the close-up, the too violent impact of which would make the audience conscious of the cutting. In the typical American comedy the director returns as often as he can to a shot of the characters from the knees up, which is said to be best suited to catch the spontaneous attention of the viewer — the natural point of balance of his mental adjustment.

Actually this use of montage originated with the silent movies. This is more or less the part it plays in Griffith's films, for example in *Broken Blossoms*, because with *Intolerance* he had already introduced that synthetic concept of montage which the Soviet cinema was to carry to its ultimate conclusion and which is to be found again, although less exclusively, at the end of the silent era. It is understandable, as a matter of fact, that the sound image, far less flexible than the visual image, would carry montage in the direction of realism, increasingly eliminating both plastic impressionism and the symbolic relation between images.

Thus around 1938 films were edited, almost without exception, according to the same principle. The story was unfolded in a series of setups numbering as a rule about 600. The characteristic procedure was by shot-reverse-shot, that is to say, in a dialogue scene, the camera followed the order of the text, alternating the character shown with each speech.

It was this fashion of editing, so admirably suitable for the best films made between 1930 and 1939, that was challenged by the shot in depth introduced by Orson Welles and William Wyler. *Citizen Kane* can never be too highly praised. Thanks to the depth of field, whole scenes are covered in one take, the camera remaining motionless. Dramatic effects for which we had formerly relied on montage were created out of the movements of the actors within a fixed framework. Of course Welles did not invent the in-depth shot any more than Griffith invented the close-up. All the pioneers used it and for a very good reason. Soft focus only ap-

peared with montage. It was not only a technical must consequent upon the use of images in juxtaposition, it was a logical consequence of montage, its plastic equivalent. If at a given moment in the action the director, as in the scene imagined above, goes to a close-up of a bowl of fruit, it follows naturally that he also isolates it in space through the focusing of the lens. The soft focus of the background confirms therefore the effect of montage, that is to say, while it is of the essence of the story-telling, it is only an accessory of the style of the photography. Jean Renoir had already clearly understood this, as we see from a statement of his made in 1938 just after he had made *La Bête humaine* and *La Grande Illusion* and just prior to *La Règle du jeu*: "The more I learn about my trade the most I incline to direction in depth relative to the screen. The better it works, the less I use the kind of set-up that shows two actors facing the camera, like two well-behaved subjects posing for a still portrait." The truth of the matter is, that if you are looking for the precursor of Orson Welles, it is not Louis Lumière or Zecca, but rather Jean Renoir. In his films, the search after composition in depth is, in effect, a partial replacement of montage by frequent panning shots and entrances. It is based on a respect for the continuity of dramatic space and, of course, of its duration.

To anybody with eyes in his head, it is quite evident that the sequence of shots used by Welles in *The Magnificent Ambersons* is in no sense the purely passive recording of an action shot within the same framing. On the contrary, his refusal to break up the action, to analyze the dramatic field in time, is a positive action the results of which are far superior to anything that could be achieved by the classical "cut."

All you need to do is compare two frames shot in depth, one from 1910, the other from a film by Wyler or Welles, to understand just by looking at the image, even apart from the context of the film, how different their functions are. The framing in the 1910 film is intended, to all intents and purposes, as a substitute for the missing fourth wall of the theatrical stage, or at least in exterior shots, for the best vantage point to view the action, whereas in the second case the setting, the lighting, and the camera angles give an entirely different reading. Between them, director and cameraman have converted the screen into a dramatic checkerboard, planned down to the last detail. The clearest if not the most original example of this are to be found in *The Little Foxes* where the *mise-en-scène* takes on the severity of a working drawing. Welles' pictures are more difficult to analyze because of his over-fondness for the baroque. Objects and characters are related in such a fashion that it is impossible for the spectator to miss the significance of the scene. To get the same results by way of montage would have necessitated a detailed succession of shots.

What we are saying then is that the sequence of shots "in depth" of the contemporary director does not exclude the use of montage — how could he, without reverting to a primitive babbling? — he makes it an integral part of his "plastic." The story-telling of Welles or Wyler is not less explicit than John Ford's but theirs has the advantage over his that it does not sacrifice the specific effects that can be derived from unity of image in space and time. Whether an episode is analyzed bit by bit or presented in its physical entirety cannot surely remain a matter of indifference, at least in a work with some pretensions to style. It would obviously be absurd to deny that montage has added considerably to the progress of film language, but this has happened at the cost of other values, no less definitely cinematic.

This is why depth of field is not just a stock in trade of the cameraman like the use of a series of filters or of such-and-such a style of lighting, it is a capital gain in the field of direction — a dialectical step forward in the history of film language.

Nor is it just a formal step forward. Well used, shooting in depth is not just a more economical, a simpler, and at the same time a more subtle way of getting the most out of a scene. In addition to affecting the structure of film language, it also affects the relationships of the minds of the spectators to the image, and in consequence it influences the interpretation of the spectacle.

It would lie outside the scope of this article to analyze the psychological modalities of these relations, as also their aesthetic consequences,

but it might be enough here to note, in general terms:

(1) That depth of focus brings the spectator into a relation with the image closer to that which he enjoys with reality. Therefore it is correct to say that, independently of the contents of the image, its structure is more realistic;

(2) That it implies, consequently, both a more active mental attitude on the part of the spectator and a more positive contribution on his part to the action in progress. While analytical montage only calls for him to follow his guide, to let his attention follow along smoothly with that of the director who will choose what he should see, here he is called upon to exercise at least a minimum of personal choice. It is from his attention and his will that the meaning of the image in part derives.

(3) From the two preceding propositions, which belong to the realm of psychology, there follows a third which may be described as metaphysical. In analyzing reality, montage presupposes of its very nature the unity of meaning of the dramatic event. Some other form of analysis is undoubtedly possible but then it would be another film. In short, montage by its very nature rules out ambiguity of expression. Kuleshov's experiment proves this *per absurdum* in giving on each occasion a precise meaning to the expression on a face, the ambiguity of which alone makes the three-successively exclusive expressions possible.

On the other hand, depth of focus reintroduced ambiguity into the structure of the image if not of necessity — Wyler's films are never ambiguous — at least as a possibility. Hence it is no exaggeration to say that *Citizen Kane* is unthinkable shot in any other way but in depth. The uncertainty in which we find ourselves as to the spiritual key or the interpretation we should put on the film is built into the very design of the image.

It is not that Welles denies himself any recourse whatsoever to the expressionistic procedures of montage, but just that their use from time to time in between sequences of shots in depth gives them a new meaning. Formerly montage was the very stuff of cinema, the texture of the scenario. In *Citizen Kane* a series of superimpositions is contrasted with a scene presented in a single take, constituting another and deliberately abstract mode of story-telling. Accelerated montage played tricks with time and space while that of Welles, on the other hand, is not trying to deceive us; it offers us a contrast, condensing time, and hence is the equivalent for example of the French imperfect or the English frequentative tense. Like accelerated montage and montage of attractions these superimpositions, which the talking film had not used for ten years, rediscovered a possible use related to temporal realism in a film without montage.

If we have dwelt at some length on Orson Welles it is because the date of his appearances in the filmic firmament (1941) makes more or less the beginning of a new period and also because his case is the most spectacular and, by virtue of his very excesses, the most significant.

Yet Citizen Kane is part of a general movement, of a vast stirring of the geological bed of cinema, confirming that everywhere up to a point there had been a revolution in the language of the screen.

I could show the same to be true, although by different methods, of the Italian cinema. In Roberto Rossellini's *Paisà* and *Allemania anno zero* and Vittorio De Sica's *Ladri di biciclette*, Italian neorealism contrasts with previous forms of film realism in its stripping away of all expressionism and in particular in the total absence of the effects of montage. As in the films of Welles and in spite of conflicts of style, neorealism tends to give back to the cinema a sense of the ambiguity of reality. The preoccupation of Rossellini when dealing with the face of the child in *Allemania anno zero* is the exact opposite of that of Kuleshov with the close-up of Mozhukhin. Rossellini is concerned to preserve its mystery. We should not be misled by the fact that the evolution of neorealism is not manifest, as in the United States, in any form of revolution in editing. They are both aiming at the same results by different methods. The means used by Rossellini and de Sica are less spectacular but they are no less determined to do away with montage and to transfer to the screen the *continuum* of reality. The dream of Zavattini is just to make a ninety-minute film of the life of a man to whom nothing ever happens. The most "aesthetic" of the neorealists, Luchino Visconti, gives just as clear a picture as Welles of the basic aim of his directorial art in *La terra trema*, a film almost entirely composed of one-shot sequences, thus clearly showing his concern to cover the entire action in interminable deep-focus panning shots.

However we cannot pass in review all the films that have shared in this revolution in film language since 1940. Now is the moment to attempt a synthesis of our reflections on the subject.

It seems to us that the decade from 1940 to 1950 marks a decisive step forward in the development of the language of the film. If we have appeared since 1930 to have lost sight of the trend of the silent film as illustrated particularly by Stroheim, F. W. Murnau, Robert Flaherty, and Dreyer, it is for a purpose. It is not that this trend seems to us to have been halted by the talking film. On the contrary, we believe that it represented the richest vein of the so-called silent film and, precisely because it was not aesthetically tied to montage, but was indeed the only tendency that looked to the realism of sound as a natural development. On the other hand it is a fact that the talking film between 1930 and 1940 owes it virtually nothing save for the glorious and retrospectively prophetic exception of Jean Renoir. He alone in his searchings as a director prior to *La Règle du jeu* forced himself to look back beyond the resources provided by montage and so uncovered the secret of a film form that would permit everything to be said without chopping the world up into little fragments, that would reveal the hidden meanings in people and things without disturbing the unity natural to them.

It is not a question of thereby belittling the films of 1930 to 1940, a criticism that would not stand up in the face of the number of masterpieces, it is simply an attempt to establish the notion of a dialectic progress, the highest expression of which was found in the films of the 1940s. Undoubtedly, the talkie sounded the knell of a certain aesthetic of the language of film, but only wherever it had turned its back on its vocation in the service of realism. The sound film nevertheless did preserve the essentials of montage, namely discontinuous description and the dramatic analysis of action. What it turned its back on was metaphor and symbol in exchange for the illusion of objective presentation. The expressionism of montage has virtually disappeared but the relative realism of the kind of cutting that flourished around 1937 implied a congenital limitation which escaped us so long as it was perfectly suited to its subject matter. Thus American comedy reached its peak within the framework of a form of editing in which the realism of the time played no part. Dependent on logic for its effects, like vaudeville and plays on words, entirely conventional in its moral and sociological content, American comedy had everything to gain, in strict line-by-line progression, from the rhythmic resources of classical editing.

Undoubtedly it is primarily with the Stroheim-Murnau trend — almost totally eclipsed from 1930 to 1940 — that the cinema has more or less consciously linked up once more over the last ten years. But it has no intention of limiting itself simply to keeping this trend alive. It draws from it the secret of the regeneration of realism in story-telling and thus of becoming capable once more of brining together real time, in which things exist, along with the duration of the action, for which classical editing had insidiously substituted mental and abstract time. On the other hand, so far from wiping out once and for all the conquests of montage, this reborn realism gives them a body of reference and a meaning. It is only an increased realism of the image that can support the abstraction of montage. The stylistic repertory of a director such as Hitchcock, for example, ranged from the power inherent in the basic document as such, to superimpositions, to large close-ups. But the close-ups of Hitchcock are not the same as those of C. B. DeMille in *The Cheat* (1915). They are just one type of figure, among others, of his style. In other words, in the silent days, montage evoked what the director wanted to say; in the editing of 1938, it described it. Today we can say that at last the director writes in film. The image — its plastic composition and the way it is set in time, because it is founded on a much higher degree of realism — has at its disposal more means of manipulating reality and of modifying it from within. The filmmaker is no longer the competitor of the painter and the playwright, he is, at last, the equal of the novelist.

CHAPTER 10

The Hollywood Golden Years: 1930–1945

Introduction

The emergence of the sound era in Hollywood at the end of the 1920s and the consolidation of the major studios was instrumental in shaping American cultural life during the Depression and the Second World War. This was the age of the great movie stars such as Marlene Dietrich, Greta Garbo, Katharine Hepburn, Bette Davis, Judy Garland, Mickey Rooney, Cary Grant, Gary Cooper, Clark Gable, James Stewart and James Cagney. Their star power drew huge audiences to the movies week after week. The major studios, MGM, Paramount, Warner Bros., Twentieth Century–Fox, and RKO, Columbia and Universal produced hundreds of great genre movies from the new musicals of Broadway to western and gangster sagas. The coming of sound brought excitement to motion pictures, not only through the introduction of spoken dialogue, or sounds of music to underscore the drama, but also as actual sound effects of urban violence to shock and terrify the audience. Adult dialogue also brought with it a sense of sexual play with language in double entendres and innuendoes. Thus the early sound era found sexual display and violence rampant in a series of gangster films, *Little Caesar, The Public Enemy* and *Scarface,* and melodramas like *Anna Christie, Hell's Angels* and *Blond Venus.* Hollywood also produced New York stage shows that featured the comic sexual subversions of the Marx Brothers in *Monkey Business, Horse Feathers* and *Duck Soup,* and Mae West in *She Done Him Wrong.* Sexual frankness also flourished in musical dramas such as *Gold Diggers of 1933,* and operettas set in Paris, Vienna or Berlin like *The Merry Widow* and *Naughty Marietta.*

The novelty of actors talking or singing in motion pictures that helped make motion pictures a powerful mass medium also brought strong religious reactions to keep sex and crime films within moral bounds. The Legion of Decency's threats of boycotts forced the movie industry to live up to the moral standards of its Production Code. The new Breen Office devised a formula of "compensating moral value" to balance the "good" from "evil" in a narrative film. As a result, motion picture producers such as David O. Selznick and Darryl F. Zanuck began a new strategy of filmmaking that promoted traditional middle-class morality and became a significant cultural force in American life. Although the commercial aspects of this industry masked its ideological content, motion pictures directly influenced public opinions, beliefs and values that characterized the American way of life.

Hollywood's Production Code of the 1930s

In 1930, Father Daniel Lord, S.J., and Martin Quigley, a prominent Catholic layman and publisher of the *Motion Picture Herald,* drafted a production code for Hollywood that clearly outlined in 12 major headings what could not be included in motion pictures. Among the totally forbidden subjects for films were depictions of any kind of sexual promiscuity, or sexual perversion, "white slavery," drug trafficking and nudity. Adultery, seduction, rape and crimes against the law could not be explicitly treated or justified. They may enter into the plots of film stories but justice and the law must prevail. Scenes of passion had to be treated with an honest acknowledgment of the relationship and criminals were not to be made into heroes.

Further, vulgarity, and obscenity "in spoken word, gesture, episode or plot is against divine and human law and hence altogether outside the range of subject matter." The depiction of sex and violence in Howard Hawks' *Scarface* (1932) and the growing moral permissiveness in other feature films caused Lord and Quigley to form the National Legion of Decency. With the possible threat of economic sanctions not only by the Catholic Church but also by state censor boards, the major studios for the MPPDA hired Joseph Breen, another Catholic layman, to head the Hays Office and administer the Production Code. From 1934 to 1954, Breen held power as administrator of the code through the awarding of a seal of approval to all Hollywood films that observed the production code of 1930. Since all studio heads were members of the MPPDA, they adhered to the code and its moral decisions on what could be depicted in motion pictures. The Legion of Decency had other reasons to impose its code of censorship on films. Some historians perceived the Legion taking it upon itself to eliminate political dissent when films would "portray, approvingly, concepts rooted in philosophies attacking the Christian moral order." In 1938, the Legion stated that "it views with grave apprehension those efforts now being made to utilize the cinema to spread ideas antagonistic, not only to Christian morality but to all religions."

Hollywood producers also used the code to keep politically minded writers in place. The 1930s saw a nascent "moral majority" politicizing their opinions in a similar manner concerning social issues of abortion and child welfare. As citizens, they endorsed the same moral system espoused by the production code and, like the Legion, also kept political dissent and diversity of opinions down. In 1934, Louis de Rochemont adapted the radio broadcasts of the "March of Time" into a short documentary film newsreel. The original radio format dramatized the news using stage actors from Broadway, especially members of the Mercury Theatre Company including Orson Welles, Agnes Moorehead and Ray Collins. Rochemont took a definitive yet biased opinion on the news, gave it a story line and attuned the nation to the political urgencies of the decade. The newsreels followed the exploits of the leading politicians in the world including Hitler, Chamberlain and Mussolini. Rochemont used investigative reporting techniques to film subversive activities such as Nazi rallies orchestrated by Gerald L. K. Smith in America. This interaction between stage performers and newsreel films brought Orson Welles to the attention of RKO management. Welles directed portions of *Citizen Kane* (1941) using a *News on the March* format. This introduced a series of overlapping flashbacks connected to the voice-over commentary that provided a montage composite of the life of an historic but fictional personality named Charles Foster Kane.

Today, *Citizen Kane* is considered the most innovative and outstanding film of this sound period. Welles effectively combined dialogue with images and action cinematically so that they reinforced one another. The sound effects helped reveal characters through flashbacks, dream sequences, and other cinematic techniques that dramatized the film noir style and mood of the film. The story is fashioned like a mystery-thriller in search of the identity of a dead person. The film presents various perspectives of Kane's life as viewers discover how effective he is in controlling the fates of others; yet Kane exhibits existentialist beliefs that are contradictory to the American way of life. His goals at first are to acquire wealth and power and use it for a good cause. His Declaration of Principles espouses faith in the capitalist system, in loyalty, affection and honest work. Later, we realize that Citizen Kane is as ruthless a crime boss as are Little Caesar or Al Capone. As a publisher of a chain of newspapers, Kane boasted that he could "dictate to the people what to think." Political beliefs and alliances with other political figures are impor-

The young Charles Foster Kane is out in the snow with his sled, while his foster parents arrange his inheritance with a financier from New York in this scene from *Citizen Kane*, directed by Orson Welles in 1941.

tant features in *Citizen Kane*, since assumptions are made by the press on the moral aspects of conducting business. Kane states: "You don't want to make promises you don't want to keep," which he constantly does in the film. Ironically, with all his wealth, he never could "buy" the one thing he desired most.

Welles, in focusing upon the Kane "mystery," infuses the story with film noir characteristics that visualize the settings as ominous and mysterious environments, trapping and engulfing their victims. In other ways, the film describes the memories of Kanecolleagues as shadows, and shows how other people's perceptions of Kane had a direct effect upon the way the public understood this man as a newspaper tycoon.

The Hollywood Studios and Genre Films

Hollywood emerged from the silent films to become a giant entertainment industry. There were five powerful studios under the creative control of a few producers like Irving Thalberg, Hal Wallis, Darryl F. Zanuck, David O. Selznick and Budd Schulberg. They administered the production of 50 or more major feature films each year for their respective studios. As Thomas Schatz notes in his book, *Hollywood Genres* (1981), "In the gradual development of the business of movie production, experimentation gave way to a standardization as a matter of fundamental economics" (p. 4). Thus each of these major studios refined the art of making motion pictures with the introduction of assembly-line methods to economize feature-length narrative production.

Genre films developed during the silent period as certain stories became popular and profitable for the film industry. With the introduction of sound, new genres emerged to take advantage of spoken dialogue and sound effects, such as Broadway musicals, fast-action gangster films, witty screwball comedy and horror films. Each genre was distinguished by a fixed formula and contained predictable actions of a protagonist in conflict with certain cultural myths. These conflicts were resolved by strong moral forces strengthening the collective values and expectations of the audience.

Each Hollywood studio specialized in its own unique production style to carry these genre formulas to the general audiences. The films also featured the right packaging of "glamorous stars" as box office attractions that audiences would recognize. Paramount and MGM were the most competitive of the big studios. Paramount displayed an ornate romantic style to complement its directors' skill in European high society drama, social satires and DeMille's historic sexual fantasies. Metro-Goldwyn-Mayer emulated a youthful Hollywood fashion style for its American-based musicals, melodramas and romantic action-adventures adapted from popular novels like Frank Lloyd's *Mutiny on the Bounty* (1935). Warner Bros. produced back-stage musicals, gangster and detective thrillers and working-class stories for mass audiences. In the 1940s, Warners teamed Humphrey Bogart with Lauren Bacall in romantic thrillers and made action-adventures with Errol Flynn and Olivia de Havilland, while Twentieth Century–Fox produced lavish historical dramas on the evolution of the United States featuring Tyrone Power and Linda Christian. John Ford, in particular, specialized in historical reconstructions of America's past in *Stagecoach* (1939), *Young Mr. Lincoln* (1939) and *The Grapes of Wrath* (1940). RKO Radio Pictures was a newcomer to the Hollywood scene. The studio's interest in sound reproduction led to a notable series of musical fantasies for the dancing team of Fred Astaire and Ginger Rogers. The studio also produced Howard Hawks "screwball" comedies, Merian C. Cooper's *King Kong* (1933), science-fiction adventures, and brought Orson

Welles to Hollywood where he directed and starred in *Citizen Kane*. Universal Studios acted as distributors for David O. Selznick, who produced films directed by Alfred Hitchcock and historical sagas, notably *Gone with the Wind* (1939). Universal also specialized in creating horror films such as *Dracula* (1931), directed by Tod Browning, and *Frankenstein* (1931), directed by James Whale.

During this 15-year period, Hollywood productions gained worldwide dominance. The major studios distributed and exhibited their productions in their chains of motion picture theatres and overseas markets. Over this period, a set of expectations and attitudes grew between the audience and the studios in relationship to these popular stories and their heroes and heroines. The basic ideological constructs hidden within these formula-driven stories appeared to justify some particular interests or sustain a value system through a particular way of depicting social relationships. By 1935, it is estimated that close to 80 million viewers faithfully attended the movies each week. Some were escaping the hardships caused by unemployment and the Great Depression. What they viewed were film narratives depicting human beings triumphing over adversity, whatever the moral, economic or political causes. Mast and Kawin (1996) contend that this optimism, propagated by Hollywood genre films, strengthened the resolve of the audience and reinforced their belief that "good" people can improve their situation despite the poor economic and political climate (p. 253).

For cultural historian Robert Sklar (1975), Hollywood genre films became a persuasive form of political influence over the audiences during this Golden Age. "A new generation of studio managers and producers was coming to power" (p. 175). In turn, each Hollywood studio hired screenwriters and journalists, such as Ben Hecht (*Scarface*) and Dudley Nicols (*Stagecoach*), who artfully developed the formulas of certain genre films. Each film they scripted presented a distinct problem-solving strategy that affected the reception of the film by the general audience. The various resolutions at the ends of the films influenced the opinions of the audience and reinforced certain

John Ford's *Stagecoach* (1939), a landmark western shot in Monument Valley, introduced John Wayne as the Ringo Kid. Just freed from prison, the Kid desires to exact revenge in a nearby town, the end of the stagecoach ride. Ford studies contrasting moral values with a motley group of travelers. This interior scene explores why Wayne sides with the social outcast, Claire Trevor, as other members of the stagecoach decide to exclude her from their conversation.

cultural constructs and ideologies of the society. As basic allegories of human relationships, these film narratives can be understood as a conscious struggle of the protagonist between good and evil without any question of ambiguity or contradiction. This basic ideological conflict is the foundation of every dramatic narrative controversy. We find such binary oppositions between the individual and the community in westerns, like *Stagecoach*, or between order versus anarchy in gangster films, like *Scarface*. Other genres, featuring romantic couples, depict the conflict between the sexes. Each genre narrative poses the problem and then undertakes a particular narrative strategy to resolve the conflict. Thus the audience is provided with a vicarious experience in which a chaotic world is brought back to order by the

actions of the protagonist. In this manner, the genre films of the 1930s and 1940s temporarily relieved the anxieties and fears of the audience aroused by the prominent social and political problems during the Depression. During the war years (1941–1945) these tensions accelerated and some Hollywood directors like Frank Capra and Alfred Hitchcock developed film narratives that explored and tested the strength of these myths.

Thomas Schatz (1981) categorized genre films as addressing two major social conflicts related to two different narrative strategies. One, dealing with rites of order, emphasized violence; the other, dealing with rites of integration, emphasized romantic relationships. In the rites of order category were westerns, gangster or action-adventure thrillers that externalized the conflict in a contested space through physical violence in which the threat to the social order is eliminated in a climactic gunfight. In the rites of integration, musicals, family melodramas, screwball comedies and light romances were placed in a domestic or "civilized" space where emotions were internalized. Interpersonal rivalries between men and women yielded to romantic love. Differences were resolved when the feuding couple were integrated into the community. Either as rites of order or as rites of integration, all genre films gained their fundamental audience appeal because they were designed to resolve basic human tensions and reinforce important cultural values and beliefs of the American viewer.

In relation to historical and cultural conventions, the rites of order in genres such as the western, gangster, detective or horror film involved a male or female protagonist who dealt with conflicts that arose within American history. The reader must remember that although historical incidents provided story material, writers freely reconstructed history according to a formulaic plot. Each genre film turned some known historical event into a fictional melodrama in which certain outlaws were perceived as a threat to the social and political order of the community. These social-historical conflicts are externalized in the film narrative through the visual imagery or iconography that invests the genre film with historical or cultural resonances. The iconography is familiar to the audiences, since genre films use recurrent images. The setting, the time and place of the action, as well as the physical attributes of the characters, their costumes and the tools of their trade (if westerns, then guns and horses) are all readily recognized by the audience.

As generic conventions, the iconography that identifies the individual genre carries more information than simple visual imagery. When these objects are placed within a series of narrative sequences, a certain dress or gesture will connote a specific character. These images also generate a set of expectations when viewed by the audience as well as compress information about the "good guys" and the "bad guys." This visual identification of characters initiates certain plot developments for the audience to follow as the hero succeeds in resolving the conflict through violence, most probably in a showdown with guns. In westerns, once the hero eliminates the threat of the bad guys to the social order, as in *Stagecoach*, he will depart from town. In most cases, he does not settle down to the lifestyle of the community, thus maintaining his mythic status. It is important to remember that genre films are fictions usually based on some historical fact, but have been transformed into an ideological construct by writers to carry a moral message.

Westerns, for example, carry powerful messages about the settlement of the West by the European pioneers in search of land. The fight for land against the native Indians became a thematic conflict as depicted in the expulsion of the evil snake from within the Garden of Eden. The battle for "Civilization" against the primitive Savages in the Wilderness as rendered in early John Ford westerns becomes one of several interpretations easily comprehended by the audiences of the 1930s. Film viewers must also consider the fact that the meanings or interpretations of genre films produced during this period are generated not as a direct reference to actuality or historical accuracy. The revisionist westerns of the 1950s prove this point. Yet genre films are related to other genre films and are recognized because of their visual associations. They also reinforce the ideological constructs of the dominant society using the aesthetic conventions of motion picture making.

With this in mind, the meanings drawn from genre films when viewed, whether they are westerns or gangster films or other similar genres, depend upon the spectators' response to the plausibility of the social reality constructed in the film and how effectively the film addresses the problems of the real world. The solution advocated by the writers may temporarily relieve the fears aroused in the audience or may simply be accepted as an entertaining fantasy. In the early 1930s, with the election of Franklin D. Roosevelt, movie producers like David O. Selznick and Darryl F. Zanuck, in facing the anger of the Legion of Decency, according to Robert Sklar began "producing pictures

Fred Astaire and Ginger Rogers in *The Gay Divorcee* (1934), directed by Mark Sandrich for RKO. This Astaire-Rogers film musical is based on a classic Cole Porter stage show that included songs such as "Night and Day," and "The Continental." The film was in keeping with the romantic genre of integration where lovers express their union through a display of brilliant dancing in the dark.

Victor Fleming's *Gone with the Wind* (1939) stars Clark Gable as Rhett Butler and Vivien Leigh as Scarlett O'Hara in David O. Selznick's epic romantic saga of Southern belles and their suitors caught in the days before the American Civil War and in the war's aftermath.

that appealed to the ideals, ambitions and sentiments of the moviegoers." In their acknowledgment that audiences sought release from the throes of the Depression, they directed Hollywood's "enormous powers of persuasion to preserving the basic moral, social and economic tenets of traditional American culture" (p. 175). While reaping huge profits, these producers returned to genre films that constructed problems and solutions supporting the status quo.

In his essay, "The Gangster as a Tragic Hero," Robert Warshaw argues that the importance and meaning of a gangster film precedes the facts concerning the nature of the crimes or

urban lifestyle. The gangster, as hero, is depicted as a person caught in a paradoxical situation. He strives toward the American dream of wealth and power, but uses unorthodox methods, including violence and murder, to succeed. These films express the dynamics of such a life, creating an aesthetic and emotional impact upon the audience. The genre conventions of the form make this representation distinct from its social reality; thus it is experienced as an art form. In this manner, the gangster film allows for multiple interpretational criticisms by an audience within the cultural context of period.

Before the new production code came into

Frank Capra's *It Happened One Night* (1934) features Claudette Colbert as a spoiled but attractive rich girl to Clark Gable's poor but aggressive reporter who uses his wily ways to get a front page scoop. Here they bed down for the night in a motel, but Colbert's character insists on the "Walls of Jericho" to protect her. A Depression Era fairy-tale in which love conquers more than hunger.

effect, gangster films of the early 1930s such as *Little Caesar* (1930), *Public Enemy* (1931) and *Scarface* demonstrated the results of a work ethic in which a person attempted to rise within a capitalistic society to achieve wealth and political success. The genre resolves the contradictory feelings of fear and desire when the gangster becomes more vulnerable as he becomes more successful. This brings about his downfall after he challenges the basic economic structure of society, and loses his perspective on the moral nature of his own enterprise.

With violence as the trademark of the gangster film, the western genre permits the use of violence as morally acceptable for agents of law and order. Within the confines of a code of be-

havior, executions, revenge killings or killings in defense of one's life and property allow a system of justice to be served, without review. Horror films like *Frankenstein* and *Dracula* depict how people become victims of uncontrollable forces that defy the conventions of the community. Two ways are proposed to solve the crisis and help bring the community back to normal. One solution attempts to discover the cause of the abnormality and control it; the other relies on one's confidence in traditional beliefs to save the faithful. In each film, hidden sexual desires place attractive women in mortal danger, who are rescued by townspeople through the townspeople's faith and knowledge of some sacred rites. *Frankenstein*, more of a

In Howard Hawks' *Bringing Up Baby* (1938), Cary Grant plays into the hands of Katharine Hepburn in a classic screwball comedy that depends upon a reversal of social identities to revel in the mating game. For laughs a "baby" is already present and ready to add to the confusion.

science-fiction tale, finds the scientist destroyed by his own creation; in *Dracula*, the forces of light (knowledge) destroy the forces of darkness. In both cases, aliens or foreigners are looked upon as a menace; the only solution proposed is to destroy them. While some attempts to communicate and understand the intruders are debated, the irrational fears of the people condemn the other to death. In taking this action, such films suggest that "aliens or foreigners" are dangerous, and all attempts must be made to destroy or conquer them. Only in later postwar films, such as Robert Wise's *The Day the Earth Stood Still* (1951), does the fear, menace and paranoia surrounding "humanoid aliens" subside after nuclear destruction is threatened, stressing a pacifist retreat relating to the Cold War.

These predictable formulas of genre cinema are the basis of a variety of historical action-adventure films undertaken by the major studios before the entrance of the United States into World War II. Their best leading actors were featured in a series of historical films, based upon popular novels of the day culminating in the David O. Selznick production of *Gone with the Wind* in 1939.

Before that epic retelling of the American Civil War, MGM produced a powerful sea saga, *Mutiny on the Bounty*, starring Clark Gable and Charles Laughton. The dominant political theme for this film and other sea epics, like Warner Bros.' *The Sea Hawk* (1940), starring Errol Flynn, are the same. From a diverse group of men, a microcosm of society is brought together to challenge and then to overturn by

In Alfred Hitchcock's *Shadow of a Doubt* (1943), Joseph Cotten plays Uncle Charlie, the "Merry Widow" serial killer, leading his adoring niece, young Charlie (Teresa Wright), to question his motives for seeking refuge in this typical middle-class American town. Here the two Charlies share an intense moment.

force the despotic rule of a captain or king. Because this task becomes the major concern of this new society-at-large, the film centers on the democratic leadership of men and on issues of freedom of choice that will determine the success or failure of the mission. These films center upon differentiating relationships between characters who will precipitate the action, such as the coward, the brute, the braggart, the authority figure and the revolutionary. Typical incidents reveal to the audience whether or not these characters will succeed. Being at sea and isolated from civilized society encourages crew members to challenge authority and its despotic rule from the start of the voyage for humanitarian reasons. Both these sea epics demonstrate a somewhat subversive

stance, since the leading characters act as champions for a revolution to free men from the totalitarian rule of their officers. Errol Flynn starred in similar action-adventures such as *The Charge of the Light Brigade* (1936), and *The Adventures of Robin Hood* (1938), in which he displayed his expert swordsmanship.

Among the films categorized in the genre of integration, the most energetic and farcical was the "screwball" comedy created by scriptwriters such as Robert Riskin, Charles Brackett and Billy Wilder during the 1930s. These comedies depended upon a basic plot structure that combined the antics of slapstick farce, sound effects and a fast and witty dialogue that shaped the action into a sequence of surreal escapades on the part of the films' lovers. In these comedies,

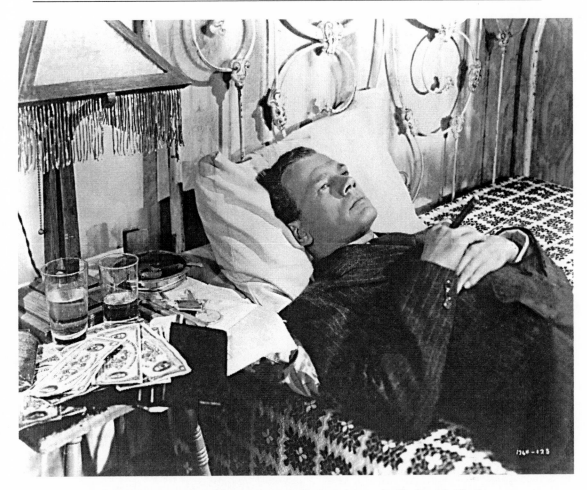

Joseph Cotten as Uncle Charlie reflects on his dark dreams in *Shadow of a Doubt*.

the traditional male and female roles are reversed: The woman plays the aggressive romantic role in opposition to the traditional expectations of male dominance in the battle of the sexes. The first Hollywood success in this genre was *It Happened One Night* (1934), featuring Claudette Colbert and Clark Gable, directed by Frank Capra. Howard Hawks and Preston Sturges advanced the style in the late 1930s and early 1940s in a number of notable films. Cary Grant was involved in a series of them, first co-starring with Katharine Hepburn in Howard Hawks' *Bringing Up Baby* (1938), in which Hepburn seduces Cary Grant with the aid of a baby leopard. In *His Girl Friday* (1940), Grant taunts Rosalind Russell, who plays a no-nonsense career reporter. The sexual permissiveness demonstrated in these "screwball" comedies indicated that directors like Hawks

challenged the limits of screen morality with regard to the Production Code.

Hitchcock in Hollywood — Shadow of a Doubt *(1943)*

Alfred Hitchcock's Hollywood career began in 1940 when David O. Selznick invited the successful British director to America to direct a murder mystery, *Rebecca* (1940). Hitchcock follows the work of the German Expressionist filmmakers of the 1920s, combining the mystery thriller with definite psychological probing that consciously involves the audience in the sexual undercurrents of the drama. Hitchcock draws especially on serial killers as depicted in *The Cabinet of Dr. Caligari* and Fritz Lang's *M* (1931). His early Hollywood films included *Suspicion* (1941), *Shadow of a Doubt* (1943) and *Spellbound* (1945).

In all three films, Hitchcock develops a sense of fear and helplessness for his protagonists when they are subjected to powerful feelings of sexuality and violence. The darkest and most disturbing film of this period is *Shadow of a Doubt*, in which a young woman learns that "ordinary life depends on the rigorous and unnatural suppression of a powerfully seductive underworld of desire." Teresa Wright plays young Charlie, who discovers to her own horror that her same-name uncle is a mass murderer. This film uses many film noir visual motifs and camera techniques to contrast the seemingly normal life in a middle-class California community with the dark incestuous feelings of Uncle Charlie, played by Joseph Cotten, toward his niece. The visual motifs Hitchcock uses in all his films suggest the malevolent aspects of victims being trapped within shadows of their "doubles" creating deceptive environments that imprison them while forewarning the audience of corruption and duplicity in the narrative.

References

Mast, Gerald, and Bruce F. Kawin. 1996. *A Short History of the Movies*. 6th ed. Boston and London: Allyn and Bacon.

MPPDA. 1930. "The Motion Picture Production Code of 1930." In *The Movies in Our Midst: Documents in the Cultural History of Film in America*. Edited by Gerald Mast. Chicago: The University of Chicago Press, 1982.

O'Conner, John E., and Martin A. Jackson (eds.). 1988. *American History/American Film*. New York: Ungar Publishing Co.

Schatz, Thomas. 1981. *Hollywood Genres: Formulas, Filmmaking, and the Studio System*. Philadelphia: Temple University Press.

_____. 1988. *The Genius of the System: Hollywood Filmmaking in the Studio Era*. New York: Pantheon Books.

Sklar, Robert. 1975. *Movie-Made America: A Cutural History of American Movies*. New York: Random House.

Warshow, Robert. 1954. "The Westerner." In *Film: An Anthology*. Edited by Daniel Talbot. Berkeley: University of California Press, 1959.

CHAPTER 11

Italian Neorealist
Cinema: 1945–1954

Introduction

Roberto Rossellini was one of a handful of Italian documentary filmmakers in Rome, with Vittorio De Sica and Luchino Visconti, who decided to use the power of narrative films to influence postwar Italians against the return of the Fascists after the collapse of the German army. The narrative films directed by Rossellini and De Sica focus upon a neorealist style in which each film portrays fictional events as if they were actual happenings without calling attention to the role of the hero or heroine in the story. A common theme running through neorealist films is a documentation of the devastating effects war and poverty had upon the moral growth and development of children who survived despite the severe hardships in postwar Italy. Each film takes a humanitarian position whose emphasis is on questioning all social forces that influence a person's values and actions, actions that may jeopardize one's life as well. The neorealist aesthetic is a political commitment to the humanist and reformist ideologies supported by the writings of Cesare Zavattini. Thus, a neorealist film scenario concentrates more on the economic and environmental conditions that result in poverty and social inequalities

than on an unjust political system which traps everyone in immoral acts of deceit and guile.

As neorealist films, Rossellini's *Roma, città aperta / Rome, Open City* (1945) and De Sica's *Ladri di biciclette / Bicycle Thieves* (1948) obtain their intensity and immediacy from the stress and consequence of documentary filming of "real people" occupied in everyday events. Through this "direct cinema" style the spectator becomes aware how unpredictable events happen to alter the way one commonly accepts

Anna Magnani plays an Italian housewife reacting to the discovery that her lover is part of the Resistance movement against the Nazis that may cause his death in Roberto Rossellini's *Rome, Open City* (1945). (The stills from this movie are rather poor quality, but their historical importance merits a close look at each.)

141

A Catholic priest (Aldo Fabrizi) secretly involved with the Resistance movement in *Rome, Open City*, is questioned by an Italian soldier as to the whereabouts of some parishioners.

human destiny. Because the background of *Rome, Open City* is so stark and realistic, Rossellini's scenario becomes more persuasive in depicting the trials of a Catholic priest trying to help members of the Italian Resistance. The powerful finale refuses to compromise the authenticity of this drama with an heroic ending. In its place, the director focuses upon the children departing the scene, leaving the spectator aware of deeply held human values common to them and to everyone witnessing the film.

Postwar Italian Filmmaking

In the closing days of World War II, after the overthrow of Mussolini, the interim Italian government surrendered to the invading Allied armies in the south of Italy and signed a separate peace agreement. The Germans continued fighting as they slowly retreated into northern Italy while the Allied Forces advanced from the south. When the Allies reached the outskirts of Rome, they began shelling the Eternal City. To avert its destruction, an agreement was reached with the Germans to demilitarize Rome and declare it an open city.

The internal struggle against the German invaders inspired a group of Italian writers and documentary film directors to produce films depicting the work of the Church and the Resistance movement in hopes of shaping a social reality necessary for the reconstruction of a new Italy. The task was to repudiate the lies and rhetoric created by Mussolini's dictatorial Fascist

Anna Magnani fights off German soldiers in *Rome, Open City*, as she attempts to enter her apartment to warn her friends. The documentary treatment of the incidents and Magnani's naturalistic acting style infused this drama with a heroism of common people as they resisted Nazi brutality in their occupation of Rome.

regime and replace it with a cinema that dealt with life-restoring human values. Cinematically, these filmmakers drew inspiration from the documentary style of Soviet cinema found in the work of Dziga Vertov and Sergei Eisenstein and the concept of *agit-prop*, as well as from the early silent films of F. W. Murnau, G. W. Pabst and Erich von Stroheim. Some directors were influenced by the "poetic realism" and rhetoric of Jean Renoir and his epic film *La Grande Illusion*. The thematic concerns involved a number of Italian journalists such as Giuseppe De Santis, Pietro Germi, Federico Fellini and Zavattini. Zavattini provided the humanist rationale for the neorealist movement and later co-authored with director Vittorio De Sica in his depiction of postwar life in

Sciuscià / Shoeshine (1946), *Ladri di biciclette / Bicycle Thieves* (1948) and *Umberto D* (1952).

Rossellini, De Sica, Visconti and other neorealist directors addressed the contemporary moral issues confronting Italians after the fall of Mussolini. Having years of experience working with screenwriters and technicians from the Cinecittà studios near Rome, they used an unpretentious documentary style to establish a postwar reality of economic turmoil which in itself became the dramatic focus of their films. They remained faithful to these images and let the melodrama unfold in its own way. This technique became the major reason for the international success of their work. Their films also rejected the Hollywood genre formulas that raised the same social and political concerns

Aldo Fabrizi, as the Catholic priest, prays for the tortured Resistance man in front of Gestapo agents in *Rome, Open City.*

but only provided stock solutions. Instead, Rossellini and De Sica were interested in film narratives that presented the moral paradoxes and contradictions inherent in a fascist state by focusing upon the conflicts arising between a human being and any given political order. With an emphasis on a reflexive questioning of all social and moral values, the neorealist movement illuminated the philosophical pathway of Sartre and Camus on the nature of human existence and on motivations for social action.

Against this background Roberto Rossellini sets his brilliant film *Roma, città aperta / Rome, Open City.* The narrative documents the activities of a group of underground anti–Fascist Italian partisans, of different political and religious persuasions, uniting in their struggle to free their country from the Germans and the Italian Fascists. Roberto Rossellini (1906–1977) was the first neorealist film director to rise to international acclaim with the release of *Rome, Open City.* Real locations were used for most of the film but Rossellini also constructed sets at Rome's Cinecittà studios for the priest's room, one apartment and the Gestapo headquarters, somehow breaking the authenticity of a real environment. Another theoretical rule was sidestepped when several leading roles were acted by professionals, notably Anna Magnani and Aldo Fabrizi. Yet, for the rest of the cast, Rossellini managed to stay within the principle that roles be played by nonprofessional actors.

After *Rome, Open City*, Rossellini completed two significant neorealist films in the next few years, *Paisà / Paisan* (1946), concerning relationships among members of the American Army with different Italians in the liberation of Italy, and *Germany, Year Zero* (1947), which explores the life of a young boy trying to comprehend his struggle for life in the ruins of Berlin. This trilogy of postwar films dealt with the problems faced by individuals encountering the collective action of a society that attempts to dominate one's life and death. By exploring the never-ending relations between an individual and a given society in a contemporary context, Rossellini asks whether or not a film narrative can mediate an understanding of the societal and political forces influencing a person's choices and actions. Although social criticism may have been one objective of these films, Rossellini defined neorealism in an interview with Eric Rohmer as follows: "For me it is above all a moral position from which to look at the world. It then becomes an aesthetic position, but at the beginning it was moral." Then, as a director, "you have to exert a critical judgment" (Rossellini 1954, p. 209).

In this manner, Rossellini expresses his opposition to the Vertov dictum of a Kino-Eye and the concept of documentary film as a neutral "window on the world." Rossellini knows that filmmaking cannot ignore the presence of a director. Experimentally one may separate the two, as the film work of Andy Warhol and Michael Snow has done, and simply allow the camera to record events mechanically. But again, Rossellini asks the viewer to comprehend that before one looks at "reality" one must have a moral vision; otherwise, the facts and images remain inert and meaningless.

Rossellini's style emphasizes directness, sincerity and a lack of self-conscious artifice. A viewer who sees a Rossellini film will perceive that his neorealist style of documentary filming involves a *mise-en-scène* with endless establishing shots, and long neutral takes that allow each viewer to judge the character within the situation. From his approach to documentary filmmaking, Rossellini evolved new methods of narrative exposition through the use of "unconditioned images." These images appear to capture the historical moment within the political context to give a viewer an insight into the narrative. Rossellini demonstrates this technique in the last episode of *Paisan*, in which contingency plays an arbitrary role in the outcome of guerilla warfare. Again, in *Germany, Year Zero* this detachment of the camera from a controlling view of the action lends a sense of fantasy and a surreality to the happenings. In *Rome, Open City,* the sense of shock aroused by the daylight shooting on real streets with real people is another instance of the viewer becoming aware of how unpredictable events can affect and change human life.

Introduction to Rome, Open City

Rossellini wrote in 1956, "We began our film only two months after the liberation of Rome, despite the shortage of film stock. We shot it in the same settings in which the events we recreated had taken place. In order to pay for my film I sold my bed, then a chest of drawers, and a mirrored wardrobe. *Rome, Open City* was shot silent, not by choice, but by necessity. Film stock cost 60 liras a metre on the black market and it would have involved an additional expense if we had recorded the sound. Also the Allied authorities had only given us a permit to produce a documentary film. After the film was edited, the actors dubbed their own voices."

> The film's intensity and immediacy is derived principally from its depiction of war in terms of human values and relationships. With its subtle blend of documentary and fiction, an anger arises within its narrative that still gives the film an everlasting power. Apart from Anna Magnani and Aldo Fabrizi, the cast was non-professional, but they all give superbly authentic performances against the backdrop of Rome's dismal topography [Bawden 1976, p. 602].

Georges Sadoul writes: "...the latter half of the film is weaker but it regains its power in the finale: the small black-frocked figure of the priest tied to a chair, waiting for death as the local children whistle a resistance song to comfort him. Its realistic treatment of everyday Italian life heralded the postwar renaissance of Italian cinema and the development of neorealism. In addition, as Rossellini jokingly said: '*Rome, Open City* was worth more than the persuasion of our Ministry of Foreign Affairs in helping Italy regain its place in the concern of nations.' As his country's spokesman in this film, Rossellini showed that Italians had fought as hard as anyone against fascism and for freedom" (Sadoul 1972, p. 317).

Zavattini's Essay, "Some Ideas on the Cinema" (1953)

Cesare Zavattini, the scenarist for Vittorio De Sica's major films, was the leading proponent of the theory of neorealism. In his manifesto he requires filmmakers "to excavate reality, to give it a power, a communication, a series of reflexes, which until recently we never thought it had." He urges them "to steer away from plots that try to make 'reality' spectacular or palatable for the viewer. The invention of plots is an aversion and flight away from the richness of real life." Further he claims that the problem with previous filmmakers is their inability to observe reality. "Substantially, then, the question today is, instead of turning imaginary situations into 'reality' and trying to make them look true, to make things as they are, almost by themselves, create their own special significance. Life is not what is invented in 'stories'; life is another matter."

Thus, filmmaking for Zavattini requires a true and real interest in what is happening, a search for the most deeply hidden human values. A script is unnecessary, for he believes, "any hour of the day, any place, any person, is a subject for narrative if the narrator is capable of observing and illuminating all these collective elements by exploring their interior value." Zavattini insisted upon the natural affinity between film expression and "reality," despite the fact that the cinematic apparatus can alter what the camera has recorded in order to convince the spectator of the "reality" of the

image. He was aware that the entire question of cinematic realism was merely a convention, and that the neorealist style was only one of many approaches a filmmaker could take in cinema.

Zavattini's reaction against films made from novels and plays is based upon the concept that they entertain the audience without dealing with the moral issues of contemporary life. His neorealist theory suggests that these values are necessary for the revitalization of people. His approach to cinema may contain Marxist attitudes insofar as films must confront both the audience within a social environment and the ideological systems that underlie and support such an environment. Questions should arise from this confrontation, since it describes how political forces interact negatively and unjustly with essential human needs for food, clothing and shelter as well as self-esteem and dignity. An open-ended narrative based upon a person's experience, such as buying food or searching for a job, could demonstrate certain social problems that create poverty, unemployment or poor housing. When films contain such situations, an audience becomes aware of the social relationships causing the adverse conditions and, upon reflection, would demand a political solution to the problem.

The Films of Vittorio De Sica

Vittorio De Sica (1902–1974) was a well-known screen actor in the 1930s before turning to directing. In 1946, he directed *Sciuscià / Shoeshine*, a film that shaped the neorealist movement. The film concerns the corruption of young children who learn to survive on the black market, only to be sent to a reformatory which turns the boys against each other. In *Bicycle Thieves*, De Sica deals with an unemployed laborer whose bicycle is stolen on the first day of a new job. In his hopeless search for the bicycle he finally resorts to stealing another bike only to be caught while his young son witnesses the act. *Umberto D* is a portrait of a senior citizen trying to retire without a sufficient pension to continue life. When he is evicted from his rented room, he gradually realizes his

In Vittorio De Sica's *Bicycle Thieves* (1948), a working-class father wanders around Rome with his son in search of his stolen bicycle. This elemental story displays Zavattini's new-realist theory in a documentary film style.

predicament and contemplates suicide. *Miracolo a Milano / Miracle in Milan* (1950) is a populist fable that injects a sense of fantasy and pathos when down-and-out tramps escape eviction with the help of angelic intervention.

Throughout these films, De Sica engages the viewer in a drama of survival in which there is no individual villain, but an insensitive and uncaring social and economic system invisibly destroying the lives of young and old alike. Sentimentally, he focuses upon the severe loss of dignity and self-esteem of the central character in each film. As a form of social criticism, however, De Sica's scenario never attempts to examine the root causes behind the poverty, nor does he criticize the "system" that creates the inequalities and injustices. Unfortunately, in each of De

Sica's films it is not the economic conditions that interest us as viewers, but the moral and human relationships operating in a postwar society trying to rebuild, yet unaware of the ideological forces that underlie and structure it.

The strength of *Umberto D* and the other neorealist films is the method of on-location shooting which brings about the illusion that situations seem to arise spontaneously from the people themselves, so that what appears to be a series of fortuitous events is in fact a carefully planned and rehearsed scene. André Bazin, the French critic, spoke highly of this kind of narrative pattern which respected the actual structure of events as well as the films of De Sica and Rossellini for using natural settings and non-professional actors.

The Films of Luchino Visconti

A search for human values and social justice dominated Luchino Visconti's (1906–1976) early decision to devote himself to a career in films. His apprenticeship began with a close relationship with Jean Renoir in prewar Paris during the making of *Une Partie de campagne / A Day in the Country* (1936). Following his political indoctrination in Marxism with the Popular Front and its anti-fascist movement, Visconti returned to Rome to become involved with the film journal *Cinema*, which advocated a new cinematic realism based upon the novels of Giovanni Verga. Visconti directed his first film, *Ossessione / The Postman Always Rings Twice* in 1942. His adaptation of James M. Cain's thriller, shot on location in the Po Valley, depicted a gritty slice-of-life romantic triangle. Visconti followed Renoir's technique in using the moving camera to capture this erotic love affair between a young wife and a transient laborer. As a tale of lust, greed and murder, it contained enough operatic dimensions to fascinate the director while avoiding political commentary. The film was hailed as a precursor to neorealism. After the war, Visconti continued his work in the theatre and opera, then agreed to make a film trilogy on the exploitation of fishermen, miners and farmers in postwar Sicily. Visconti based the first part of the trilogy, *The Sea Episode,* upon his adaptation of a 19th century Giovanni Verga novel, *I Malavoglia / The House by the Medlar Tree,* which he called *La terra trema / The Earth Trembles* (1948). Visconti shot the entire film on location using non-professional actors in the conventions of neorealism. With overtones of Marxism, the narrative focused upon a poor Sicilian fishing family being forced into poverty by a monopolistic combine of marketeers and wholesalers. While the film is neorealistic in theme and environment, the careful staging is more operatic as Visconti chose to highlight scenes of drunkenness and passion with formal patterns of dramatic lighting. When this long epic tale failed at the box office both at home and abroad, Visconti made a second neorealist film, *Bellissima* (1951), starring Anna Magnani as a working class woman trying to get her daughter into the movies. The original script was crafted by Zavattini, but Visconti used it primarily to make a satire about the movie industry at Cinecittà, the Roman film studios.

Visconti then planned his next films using the new color technology and began a series of historical films about the 19th century origins of the Italian state. His first color film, *Senso / The Wanton Contessa* (1954), is a tragic opera about lovers caught in the throes of revolution and betrayal during the fall of the Risorgimento. However, with *Rocco e i suoi fratelli / Rocco and His Brothers* (1960), Visconti produced and directed his last tale of working-class life, this time regarding the displacement of a Sicilian peasant family to a northern industrial center in Italy. He then returned to his historical critique of European aristocracy, stressing its rise and then its moral and financial corruption in a series of powerful operatic narratives such as *Il Gattopardo / The Leopard* (1963), *Vaghe stelle dell'orsa / Sandra* (1965) and *La caduta degli dei / The Damned* (1969). His last films carry themes of marital infidelities and political dissolution: *Morte a Venezia / Death in Venice* (1972), *Gruppo di famiglia in un interno / Conversation Piece* (1974) and *L'innocente / The Innocent* (1976).

Bazin's Essay — "What Is Cinema?"

In his essay on Fellini's *Cabiria* (Bazin 1971, p. 87), André Bazin further explains that "realism" is not defined in terms of ends but of means, that "what De Sica, Rossellini and Fellini have in common is the pride of place that all give to the representation of reality at the expense of dramatic structures." He concludes that it is not the naturalism attributed to novels or to the structure of theatrical plays but to what he calls "phenomenological" realism, which he claims never adjusts reality to meet the needs imposed by the psychology of the drama. "In Neo-realist films, the appearance and meaning [of images] have in a sense been inverted. Appearance is always presented as a unique discovery, an almost documentary revelation that retains its full force of vividness and detail" (p. 87).

Bazin's commentary that neorealist film practice teaches us something new about the basic structure of reality is contested by other film critics. They state that this theory ignores the ambivalence and ambiguity essential to any film or artwork that attempts to convey the impression of naturalness through the cinematic apparatus. That feeling of ambivalence comes about by one's own subjective state of mind, which Rossellini calls a moral position with which one looks at the world. This perspective is shaped by the differences in our beliefs about what society ought to be and what it actually is. By focusing on the social injustices caused by the postwar economic system, these neorealist films promoted a sense of an underlying neo–Marxist ideology. Thus, the movement came to a swift end with the passage of the Andreotti Law in 1949, which gave the government wide-ranging power over the cinema. As Undersecretary of Public Entertainment, Giulio Andreotti influenced "the ministry concerned with the cinema. He controlled government subsidies and restricted them to more optimistic motion pictures about Italy" (Bondanella 1990, p. 87). He vetoed loans to films which were "infected with the spirit of Neo-realism." But the ban placed upon the exportation of domestic films that Andreotti and others thought maligned Italy cut the neorealist movement off from foreign markets and the huge earnings on which its film productions depended (Bondanella 1990, p. 87).

References

Bawden, Liz-Ann (ed.). 1976. *The Oxford Companion to Film*. Berkeley: University of California Press.

Bazin, André. 1971. *What Is Cinema?* Vol. II. Translated by Hugh Gray. Berkeley: University of California Press.

Bondanella, Peter. 1993. *Italian Cinema: From Neorealism to the Present*. New York: Continuum.

Rossellini, Roberto. 1954. Eric Rohmer interview in *Cahiers du Cinéma: The 1950s: Neo-Realism, Hollywood, New Wave*. Vol. I. Edited by Jim Hillier. London: Routledge & Kegan Paul: BFI, pp. 209–212.

Sadoul, Georges. 1972. *Dictionary of Filmmakers*. Berkeley: University of California Press.

Zavattini, Cesare. "Some Ideas on the Cinema." From *Sight and Sound*, October 1953, pp. 64–69. Published in *La Revista del Cinema Italiano*, December 1952. Translated by Pier Luigi Lanza.

"Some Ideas on the Cinema"

by Cesare Zavattini

From *Sight and Sound*, October 1953, pp. 64–69. Edited from a recorded interview published in *La Revista del Cinema Italiano*, December 1952. Translated by Pier Luigi Lanza. Copyright © 1953. Reprinted by permission of *Sight and Sound*.

"The true function of the cinema is not to tell fables."

In this ringing manifesto, Cesare Zavattini, who wrote such neorealist films as *Shoeshine* and *Bicycle Thief* for the Italian director Vittorio De Sica, laid down a challenge to all film makers "to excavate reality, to give it a power, a communication, a series of reflexes, which until recently we had never thought it had." Like Kracauer, he declares that the camera has a "hunger for reality," that the invention of plots to make reality palatable or spectacular is a flight from the richness of real life. The problem, he says, "lies in being able to observe reality, not to extract fictions from it." Zavattini wants to "make things as they are, almost by themselves, create their own special significance," and to analyze fact so deeply that we see "things we have never noticed before." A woman buying a pair of shoes can become a drama if we dig deep enough into her life and the lives of those around her.

Zavattini denies that we need to be bored by facts, or that we may get tired of poverty as a theme, or that there is anything beneath the notice of a film audience. In the manner of the postwar Marxists, he belabors bourgeois attitudes; declares himself against the "exceptional" man or hero; calls for a sense of solidarity, equality, and identification with the common man in the crowd. He wants the viewer to contribute an intensity of vision that will "give human life its historical importance at every minute." He wants the director to take both the dialogue and the actors from real life, from "the street." And in a momentary forecast of the work of Antonioni, he speaks of the film maker's need to "remain" in a scene, with all its "echoes and reverberations."

1

No doubt one's first and most superficial reaction to everyday reality is that it is tedious. Until we are able to overcome some moral and intellectual laziness, in fact, this reality will continue to appear uninteresting. One shouldn't be astonished that the cinema has always felt the natural, unavoidable necessity to insert a "story" in the reality to make it exciting and "spectacular." "All the same, it is clear that such a method evades a direct approach to everyday reality, and suggests that it cannot be portrayed without the intervention of fantasy or artifice.

The most important characteristic, and the most important innovation, of what is called neorealism, it seems to me, is to have realized that the necessity of the "story" was only an unconscious way of disguising a human defeat, and that the kind of imagination it involved was simply a technique of superimposing dead formulas over living social facts. Now it has been perceived that reality is hugely rich, that to be able to look directly at it is enough; and that the artists's task is not to make people moved or indignant at metaphorical situations, but to make them reflect (and, if you like, to be moved and indignant too) on what they and others are doing, on the real things, exactly as they are.

For me this has been a great victory. I would like to have achieved it many years earlier. But I made the discovery only at the end of the war. It was a moral discovery, an appeal to order. I saw at last what lay in front of me, and I understood that to have evaded reality had been to betray it.

Example: Before this, if one was thinking over the idea of a film on, say, a strike, one was immediately forced to invent a plot. And the strike itself became only the background to the film. Today, our attitude would be one of "revelation": we would describe the strike itself, try to work out the largest possible number of human, moral, social, economic, poetic values from the bare documentary fact.

We have passed from an unconsciously rooted mistrust of reality, an illusory and equivocal evasion, to an unlimited trust in things, facts and people. Such a position requires us, in effect, to excavate reality, to give it a power, a communication, a series of reflexes, which until recently we had never thought it had. It requires, too, a true and real interest in what is happening, a search for the most deeply hidden human values; which is why we feel that the cinema must recruit not only intelligent people, but, above all, "living" souls, the morally richest people.

2

The cinema's overwhelming desire to see, to analyze, its hunger for reality, is an act of concrete homage towards other people, towards what is happening and existing in the world. And, incidentally, it is what distinguishes "neorealism" from the American cinema.

In fact, the American position is the antithesis of our own — while we are interested in the reality around us and want to know it directly, reality in American films is unnaturally filtered, "purified," and comes out at one or two removes. In America, lack of subjects for films causes a crisis but with us such a crisis is impossible. One cannot be short of themes while there is still plenty of reality. Any hour of the day, any place, any person, is a subject for narrative if the narrator is capable of observing and illuminating all these collective elements by exploring their interior value.

So there is no question of a crisis of subjects, only of their interpresentation. This substantial difference was nicely emphasized by a well-known American producer when he told me: "This is how *we* would imagine a scene with an aeroplane. The 'plane passes by ... a machine-gun fires ... the 'plane crashes.... And this is how you would imagine it. The 'plane passes by.... The 'plane passes by again ... the 'plane passes by once more...."

He was right. But we have still not gone far enough. It is not enough to make the airplane pass by three times; we must make it pass by twenty times.

What effects on narrative, then, and on the portrayal of human character, has the neorealist style produced?

To begin with, while the cinema used to make one situation produce another situation, and another, and another, again and again, and each scene was thought out and immediately related to the next (the natural result of a mistrust of reality), today, when we have thought out a scene, we feel the need to "remain" in it, because the single scene itself can contain so many echoes and reverberations, can even contain all the situations we may need. Today, in fact, we can quietly say: give us whatever "fact" you like, and we will disembowel it, make it something worth watching.

While the cinema used to portray life in its most visible and external moments—and a film was usually only a series of situations selected and linked together with varying success—today the neorealist affirms that each one of these situations, rather than all the external moments, contains in itself enough material for a film.

Example: In most films, the adventures of two people looking for somewhere to live, for a house, would be shown externally in a few moments of action, but for us it could provide the scenario for a whole film, and we would explore all its echoes, all it implications.

Of course, we are still a long way from a true analysis of human situations, and one can speak of analysis only in comparison with the dull synthesis of most current production. We are, rather, still in an "attitude" of analysis; but in this attitude there is a strong purpose, a desire for understanding, for belonging, for participating—for living together, in fact.

what we might call their "dailiness," their longest and truest duration. The cinema has everything in front of it, and no other medium has the same possibilities for getting it known quickly to the greatest number of people.

As the cinema's responsibility also comes from its enormous power, it should try to make every frame of film count, by which I mean that it should penetrate more and more into the manifestations and the essence of reality.

The cinema only affirms its moral responsibility when it approaches reality in this way.

The moral, like the artistic, problem lies in being able to observe reality, not to extract fictions from it.

3

Substantially, then, the question today is, instead of turning imaginary situations into "reality" and trying to make them look "true," to take things as they are, almost by themselves, create their own special significance. Life is not what is invented in "stories," Life is another matter. To understand it involves a minute, unrelenting, and patient search.

Here I must bring in another point of view. I believe that the world goes on getting worse because we are not truly aware of reality. The most authentic position anyone can take up today is to engage himself in tracing the roots of this problem. The keenest necessity of our time is "social attention."

Attention, though, to what is there, *directly*: not through an apologue, however well conceived. A starving man, a humiliated man, must be shown by name and surname; no fable for a starving man, because that is something else, less effective and less moral. The true function of the cinema is not to tell fables, and to a true function we must recall it.

Of course, reality can be analyzed by ways of fiction. Fictions can be expressive and natural; but neorealism, if it wants to be worthwhile, must sustain the moral impulse that characterized its beginnings, in an analytical documentary way. No other medium of expression has the cinema's original and innate capacity for showing things, that we believe worth showing, as they happen day by day — in

4

Naturally, some filmmakers, although they realize the problem, have still been compelled, for a variety of reasons (some valid, others not) to "invent" stories in the traditional manner, and to incorporate in these stories some fragments of their real intuition. This, effectively, has served as neorealism for some filmmakers in Italy.

For this reason, the first endeavor was often to reduce the story to its most elementary, simple, and, I would rather say, banal form. It was the beginning of a speech that was later interrupted. *Bicycle Thieves* provides a typical example. The child follows his father along the street; at one moment, the child is nearly run over, but the father does not even notice. This episode was "invented," but with the intention of communicating an everyday fact about these people's lives, a little fact — so little that the protagonists don't even care about it — but full of life.

In fact *Paisà*, *Open City*, *Sciuscià*, *Bicycle Thieves*, *La terra trema*, all contain elements of an absolute significance — they reflect the idea that everything can be recounted, but their sense remains metaphorical, because there is still an invented story, not the documentary spirit. In other films, such as *Umberto D.*, reality as an analyzed fact is much more evident, but the presentation is still traditional.

We have not yet reached the center of neorealism. Neorealism today is an army ready to start; and there are the soldiers—behind Rossellini, de Sica, Visconti. The soldiers have to go into the attack and win the battle.

We must recognize that all of us are still only starting, some farther on, others farther behind. But it is still something. The great danger today is to abandon that position, the moral position implicit in the work of many of us during and immediately after the war.

5

A woman is going to buy a pair of shoes. Upon this elementary situation it is possible to build a film. All we have to do is to discover and then show all the elements that go to create this adventure, in all their banal "dailiness," and it will become worthy of attention, it will even become "spectacular." But it will become spectacular not through its exceptional, but through its *normal* qualities; it will astonish us by showing so many things that happen every day under our eyes, things we have never noticed before.

The result would not be easy to achieve. It would require an intensity of human vision both from the creator of the film and from the audience. The question is: how to give human life its historical importance at every minute.

6

In life, in reality today, there are no more empty spaces. Between things, facts, people, exists such an interdependence that a blow struck for the cinema in Rome could have repercussions all over the world. If this is true, it must be worthwhile to take any moment of human life and show how "striking" that moment is: to excavate and identify it, to send its echo vibrating into other parts of the world.

This is as valid for poverty as for peace. For peace, too, the human moment should not be a great one, but an ordinary daily happening. Peace is usually the sum of small happenings, all having the same moral implications at their roots.

It is not only a question, however, of creating a film that makes its audience understand a social or collective situation. People understand themselves better than the social fabric; and to see themselves on the screen, performing their daily actions—remembering that to see oneself gives one the sense of being unlike oneself—like hearing one's own voice on the radio—can help them to fill up a void, a lack of knowledge of reality.

7

If this love for reality, for human nature directly observed, must still adapt itself to the necessities of the cinema as it is now organized, must yield, suffer and wait, it means that the cinema's capitalist structure still has a tremendous influence over its true function. One can see this in the growing opposition in many places to the fundamental motives of neorealism, the main results of which are a return to so-called "original" subjects, as in the past, and the consequent evasion of reality, and a number of bourgeois accusations against neorealist principles.

The main accusation is: *neorealism only describes poverty*. But neorealism can and must face poverty. We have begun with poverty for the simple reason that it is one of the most vital realities of our time, and I challenge anyone to prove the contrary. To believe, or to pretend to believe, that by making half a dozen films on poverty we have finished with the problem, would be a great mistake. As well believe that if you have to plough up a whole country, you can sit down after the first acre.

The theme of poverty, of rich and poor, is something one can dedicate one's whole life to. We have just begun. We must have the courage to explore all the details. If the rich turn up their noses especially at *Miracolo a Milano*, we can only ask them to be a little patient. *Miracolo a Milano* is only a fable. There is still much more to say. I put myself among the rich, not only because I have some money (which is only the most apparent and immediate aspect of wealth), but because I am also in a position to create oppression and injustice. That is the moral (or immoral) position of the so-called rich man.

When anyone (he could be the audience, the director, the critic, the State, or the Church) says, "STOP the poverty," i.e., stop the films about poverty, he is committing a moral sin. He is refusing to understand, to learn. And when he refuses to learn, consciously, or not, he is evading reality. The evasion springs from lack of courage, from fear. (One should make a film on this subject, showing at what point we begin to evade reality in the face of disquieting facts, at what point we begin to sweeten it.)

If I were not afraid of being thought irreverent, I should say that Christ, had He a camera in His hand, would not shoot fables, however wonderful, but would show us the good one and the bad ones of this world — in actuality, giving us close-ups of those who make their neighbors' bread too bitter, and of their victims, if the censor allowed it.

To say that we have had "enough" films about poverty suggests that one can measure reality with a chronometer. In fact, it is not simply a question of choosing the theme of poverty, but of going on to explore and analyze the poverty. What one needs is more and more knowledge, precise and simple, of human needs and the motives governing them. Neorealism should ignore the chronometer and go forward for as long as necessary.

Neorealism, it is also said, *does not offer solutions. The end of a neorealist film is particularly inconclusive.* I cannot accept this at all. With regard to my own work, the characters and situations in films for which I have written the scenario, they remain unresolved from a practical point of view simply because "this is reality." But every moment of the film is, in itself, a continuous answer to some question. It is not the concern of an artist to propound solutions. It IS enough, and quite a lot, I should say, to make an audience feel the need, the urgency, for them.

In any case, what films *do* offer solutions? "Solutions" in this sense, if they are offered, are sentimental ones, resulting from the superficial way in which problems have been faced. At least, in my work I leave the solution to the audience. The fundamental emotion of *Miracolo*

a Milano is not one of escape (the flight at the end), but of indignation, a desire for solidarity with certain people, a refusal of it with others. The film's structure is intended to suggest that there is a great gathering of the humble ones against the others. But the humble ones have no tanks, or they would have been ready to defend their land and their huts.

8

The true neorealistic cinema is, of course, less expensive than the cinema at present. Its subjects can be expressed cheaply, and it can dispense with capitalist resources on the present scale. The cinema has not yet found its morality, its necessity, its quality, precisely because it costs too much; being so conditioned, it is much less an art than it could be.

9

The cinema should never turn back. It should accept, unconditionally, what is contemporary. *Today, today, today.*

It must tell reality as if it were a story; there must be no gap between life and what is on the screen. To give an example:

A woman goes to a shop to buy a pair of shoes. The shoes cost 7,000 lire. The woman tries to bargain. The scene lasts, perhaps, two minutes. I must make a two-hour film. What do I do?

I analyze the fact in all its constituent elements, in its "before," in its "after," in its contemporaneity. The fact creates its own fiction, in its own particular sense.

The woman is buying the shoes. What is her son doing at the same moment? What are people doing in India that could have some relation to this fact of the shoes? The shoes cost 7,000 lire. How did the woman happen to have 7,000 lire? How hard did she work for them, what do they represent?

And the bargaining shopkeeper, who is he? What relationship has developed between these two human beings? What did they mean, what interests are they defending, as they bargain?

The shopkeeper also has two sons, who eat and speak: do you want to know what they are saying? Here they are, in front of you...

The question is, to be able to fathom the real correspondences between facts and their process of birth, to discover what lies beneath them.

Thus to analyze "buying a pair of shoes" in such a way opens to us a vast and complex world, rich in importance and values, in its practical, social, economic, psychological motives. Banality disappears because each moment is really charged with responsibility. Every moment is infinitely rich. Banality never really existed.

Excavate, and every little fact is revealed as a mine. If the golddiggers come at least to dig in the illimitable mine of reality, the cinema will become socially important.

This can also be done, evidently, with invented characters; but if I use living, real characters with which to sound reality, people in whose life I can directly participate, my emotion becomes more effective, morally stronger, more useful. Art must be expressed through a true name and surname, not a false one.

I am bored to death with heroes more or less imaginary. I want to meet the real protagonist of everyday life, I want to see how he is made, if he has a moustache or not, if he is tall or short, I want to see his eyes, and I want to speak to him.

We can look at him on the screen with the same anxiety, the same curiosity as when, in a square, seeing a crowd of people all hurrying up to the same place, we ask, What is happening? What is happening to a real person? Neorealism has perceived that the most irreplaceable experience comes from things happening under our own eyes from natural necessity.

I am against "exceptional" personages. The time has come to tell the audience that they are the true protagonists of life. The result will be a constant appeal to the responsibility and dignity of every human being. Otherwise the frequent habit of identifying oneself with fictional characters will become very dangerous. We must identify ourselves with what we are. The world is composed of millions of people thinking of myths.

10

The term neorealism — in a very Latin sense — implies, too, elimination of technical-professional apparatus, screen-writer included. Handbooks, formulas, grammars, have no more application. There will be no more technical terms. Everybody has his personal shooting-script. Neorealism breaks all the rules, rejects all those canons which, in fact, exist only to codify limitations. Reality breaks all the rules, as can be discovered if you walk out with a camera to meet it.

The figure of a screen-writer today is, besides, very equivocal. He is usually considered part of the technical apparatus. I am a screen-writer trying to say certain things, and saying them in my own way. It is clear that certain moral and social ideas are at the foundation of my expressive activities, and I can't be satisfied to offer a simple technical contribution. In films which do not touch me directly, also, when I am called in to do a certain amount of work on them, I try to insert as much as possible of my own world, of the moral emergencies within myself.

On the other hand, I don't think the screenplay in itself contains any particular problems; only when subject, screenplay and direction become three distinct phases, as they so often do today, which is abnormal. The screen-writer as such should disappear, and we should arrive at the sole author of a film.

Everything becomes flexible when only one person is making a film, everything continually possible, not only during the shooting, but during the editing, the laying of tracks, the post-synchronization, to the particular moment when we say, "Stop." And it is only then that we put an end to the film.

Of course, it is possible to make films in collaboration, as happens with novels and plays, because there are always numerous bonds of identity between people (for example, millions of men go to war, and are killed, for the same reasons), but no work of art exists on which someone has not set the seal of his own interests, of his own poetic world. There is always somebody to make the decisive creative act, there is always one prevailing intelligence, there is always someone who, at a certain moment, "chooses," and says, "This, yes," and "This, no," and then resolves it: reaction shot of the mother crying Help!

Technique and capitalist method however, have imposed collaboration on the cinema. It is one thing to adapt ourselves to the imposed exigencies of the cinema's present structure, another to imagine that they are indispensable and necessary. It is obvious that when films cost sixpence and everybody can have a camera, the cinema would become a creative medium as flexible and as free as any other.

11

It is evident that, with neorealism, the actor — as a person fictitiously lending his own flesh to another — has no more right to exist than the "story." In neorealism, as I intend it, everyone must be his own actor. To want one person to play another implies the calculated plot, the fable, and not "things happening." I attempted such a film with Caterina Rigoglioso; it was called "the lightning film." But unfortunately at the last moment everything broke down. Caterina did not seem to "take" to the cinema. But wasn't she "Caterina"?

Of course, it will be necessary to choose themes excluding actors. I want, for example, to make a report on children in the world. If I am not allowed to make it, I will limit it to Europe, or to Italy alone. But I will make it. Here is an example of the film not needing actors. I hope the actors' union will not protest.

12

Neorealism does not reject psychological exploration. Psychology is one of the many premises or reality. I face it as I face any other. If I want to write a scene of two men quarrelling, I will not do so at my desk. I must leave my den and find them. I take these men and make them talk in front of me for one hour or for twenty, depending on necessity. My creative method is first to call on them, then to listen to them, "choosing" what they say. But I do all

this not with the intention of creating heroes, because I think that a hero is not "certain men" but "every man."

Wanting to give everyone a sense of equality is not leveling him down, but exalting his solidarity. Lack of solidarity is always born from presuming to be different, from a *But:*

"Paul is suffering, it's true. I am suffering, too, but my suffering has something that ... my nature has something that..." and so on. The *But* must disappear, and we must be able to say: "That man is bearing what I myself should bear in the same circumstances."

Others have observed that the best dialogue in films is always in dialect. Dialect is nearer to reality. In our literary and spoken language, the synthetic constructions and the words themselves are always a little false. When writing a dialogue, I always think of it in dialect, in that of Rome or my own village. Using dialect, I feel it to be more essential, truer. Then I translate it into Italian, thus maintaining the dialect's syntax. I don't, therefore, write dialogue in dialect but I am interested in what dialects have in common — immediacy, freshness, verisimilitude.

But I take most of all from nature. I go out into the street, catch words, sentences, discussions. My great aids are memory and the shorthand writer.

Afterwards, I do with the words what I do with the images. I choose, I cut the material I have gathered to give it the right rhythm, to capture the essence, the truth. However great a faith I might have in imagination, in solitude, I have a greater one in reality, in people. I am interested in the drama of things we happen to encounter, not those we plan.

In short, to exercise our own poetic talents on location, we must leave our rooms and go, in body and mind, out to meet other people, to see and understand them. This is a genuine moral necessity for me and, if I lose faith in it, so much the worse for me.

I am quite aware that it is possible to make wonderful films, like Charlie Chaplin's, and they are not neorealistic. I am quite aware that there are Americans, Russians, Frenchmen and others who have made masterpieces that honor humanity, and, of course, they have not wasted film. I wonder, too, how many more great works they will again give us, according to their particular genius, with actors and studios and novels. But Italian filmmakers, I think, if they are to sustain and deepen their cause and their style, after having courageously half-opened their doors to reality, must (in the sense I have mentioned) open them wide.

CHAPTER 12

Hollywood at War and Postwar Paranoia: 1940–1954

Introduction

During the war years, Hollywood directors produced different genre films to support the war effort for the government. The major studios also changed Hollywood into a powerful propaganda agency that made new combat films to wage a psychological war against the known enemies of the United States. In the postwar period, a large number of films were made depicting a new awareness of the social and political conditions within the United States. These socially conscious films critically examined American beliefs surrounding racism, political corruption, and power, yet the postwar years for the American film industry were plagued by the fear and paranoia embedded in the Cold War between the United States and the Soviet Union. The political tensions created by this situation brought about investigations by the House Committee on Un-American Activities (HUAC) of Hollywood studios in 1947. This congressional subcommittee claimed that Hollywood and the film industry were secretly infiltrated by subversive members of the Communist Party who worked as screenwriters and directors. This alleged Communist conspiracy in Hollywood allowed the general fear and paranoia over the "Red Menace" to influence right-wing producers such as Louis B. Mayer and Jack Warner to bring about a witch hunt that found ten prominent writers guilty of contempt of Congress.

Hollywood studios also began a series of postwar melodramas in the genre known as film noir that depicted a dark, seedy world of moral corruption where the central hero is caught by unseen sinister forces that either betray, sell out or double-cross him. Jacques Tourneur's *Out of the Past*, made in 1947, displays the visual characteristics of a film noir with a depiction of a nightmarish "big city" where the central hero makes a fateful connection with a *femme fatale*. Under her influence, he is led to commit a criminal act on her behalf. Once he commits the act, the woman betrays him. Now corrupted, he becomes trapped either by other criminals or by the police.

HUAC and the Crusade Against Subversives

The propaganda war against Nazi Germany and, later, Japan began before the United States entered World War II. It started with a B-movie melodrama, *Confessions of a Nazi Spy* (1939), directed by Anatole Litvak, with Edward G. Robinson leading FBI agents against a Nazi fifth column in America. In this anti-fascist Hollywood film, the German secret agents appear as ruthless and efficient gangsters, men without morals, who worked behind enemy lines to spread their fascist lies and ideology. This and other similar anti–German propaganda films began to influence American attitudes toward Nazi Germany, foreign spies, subversives and tyrants in general. Hollywood's interest in making propaganda films in favor of Great Britain against Nazi Germany persuaded a U.S. Senator, Martin Dies, to form a Senate committee in 1940 to investigate why studios like Warner Bros. refused to remain neutral. This initial probe into the political agenda of Hollywood producers was suspended when the United States entered the war after the Japanese attack on Pearl Harbor on December 7, 1941. After the war a congressional probe was revived, but for other reasons.

With the American declaration of war, the U.S. government quickly brought Hollywood under the Office of War Information with the creation of the Bureau of Motion Picture Affairs (BMPA). Producer-directors such as Frank Capra, John Ford and John Huston were recruited to cooperate voluntarily with the War Office to produce a series of combat films that included documentary footage of the fighting on both the Pacific and European fronts. Capra headed the *Why We Fight* series of films that included *Battle with Russia* and *War Comes to America* in 1942 and *Tunisian Victory* (1943). John Ford contributed several shorts: *The Battle of Midway* (1942), *Torpedo Squadron* (1942), and *We Sail at Midnight* (1943), on naval action in the Pacific. He then completed a feature film, *They Were Expendable* (1945), starring Robert Montgomery and John Wayne. Although Ford's docudrama focused on the heroics of naval officers leading their men into battle, his future cavalry dramas would question themes of sacrifice and teamwork. In many other commercial American war epics, German and Japanese soldiers were stereotyped by directors as sadistic and pitiless soldiers, a class of subhuman animals, who committed all kinds of atrocities. John Wayne became the Hollywood icon for American heroism as a Marine fighter. He starred in *Wake Island* (1942) and *Guadalcanal Diary* (1943). Other prominent war films were *The Moon Is Down* (1943), dealing with the German occupation of Norway, and *The Seventh Cross* (1944), starring Spencer Tracy as an anti–Nazi German escaping from a concentration camp in 1936. Tracy also starred in *Thirty Seconds Over Tokyo* (1944), a reconstruction of the American raid on Tokyo led by General Jimmy Doolittle. Two other major films dealt directly with the war and the common foot soldier. *A Walk in the Sun* (1945) was directed by Lewis Milestone, the maker of *All Quiet on the Western Front* (1930), but without the earlier film's special pleading against war. The other was *The Story of G.I. Joe* (1945), starring Robert Mitchum, about the life of war correspondent Ernie Pyle and his coverage of a platoon of foot soldiers fighting in Italy.

John Huston's Battle of San Pietro *(1945)— From* Why We Fight *Series*

The U.S. War Department and its Pictorial Service commissioned John Huston to write, direct and narrate a documentary film that would explain why the conquest of Italy was so long and costly. At the time the Allies were trying to liberate Italy from German troops before attempting landings in France. During a bitter winter, limited Allied forces found the Germans dug in at the little village of San Pietro, about 100 miles below Rome, thus stalling American troop advancement. Huston, at first, presents the military strategy to engage the enemy, then proceeds with a visual account of the ground fighting and artillery barrages. Documentary photography takes the viewer alongside American infantry soldiers as they mount a series of attacks on hidden German machine gun emplacements. Before the town is secured, Huston's narration takes a skeptical tone that questions the purposes of the fighting. The heavy toll in casualties provokes the viewer to wonder about the price paid for the final American victory in the actual scenes of this war against the Germans.

The Potsdam Agreement

In the summer of 1945, the Allied leaders held a conference in Potsdam to implement the unconditional surrender of the German Army. Here, Harry Truman, Clement Attlee and Josef Stalin agreed on the division of Germany into four allied zones including the city of Berlin, thus assuring the dissolution of all German political and military authority. These decisions resulted as part of a moral crusade against the brutality of the Nazi war machine, the concentration camps, and Germany's devastating

The Battle of San Pietro (1945). Filmed with a handheld 16mm camera, John Huston's war documentary for the *Why We Fight* series captured the deadly battle against entrenched Nazi positions below Rome.

occupation of other European countries. The division of Germany into Eastern and Western zones soon became a permanent boundary. Tensions between the Soviets and the British, French, and U.S. zones grew as the Soviet Union installed Communist regimes in all the Eastern European countries it had liberated from Nazi occupation. In 1949 the three Western zones of Germany were united and a parliamentary democracy came into power as the Federal Republic of Germany. To counter this move, the Soviets placed their Eastern zone under a puppet government known as the German Democratic Republic. Later, to stop the emigration of East Germans to the West, the Soviets erected the infamous Berlin Wall in 1961.

Led by President Truman, the American government countered this political strategy with the Marshall Plan in 1947, providing economic and military aid to many European countries threatened by communist military action. When Czechoslovakia fell to a communist coup in 1948, a betrayal of wartime agreements on self-determination, the Western powers established a military defense system called the North Atlantic Treaty Organization (NATO). However, by 1949, the Soviet Union had placed Eastern Europe securely under its sphere of influence. It then contrived a military and political barrier that became known in the West as the Iron Curtain, to counteract the NATO alliance. This new Stalinist strategy created warnings of a nuclear war in a bipolar world, and both sides began an extensive buildup of military weapons, including nuclear missiles.

The bipolar politics of this era marked the beginning of the Cold War, the political struggle emerging between the democratic Western powers led by the United States, and the Communist-led Eastern bloc. The East-West division of Germany also caused both sides to break the Potsdam agreements, leading to a communications blockage and a diplomatic break-down between the United States and the Soviet Union. New restrictions between the two world powers grew as the ideological warfare rendered the infamous Iron Curtain more impenetrable.

The House Committee on Un-American Activities (HUAC)

The climate of fear and paranoia created by the possibility of Communist Party members infiltrating American unions led Congress to bring Hollywood under investigation again. In September 1947, the House convened a special subcommittee on Un-American Activities, known as HUAC, to investigate communist subversion in the motion picture industry. It was chaired by J. Parnell Thomas. The congressional hearings of HUAC were nationally publicized as Thomas and other House representatives probed into the political practices, beliefs and loyalties of leading screenwriters, directors and actors in Hollywood. Investigators subpoenaed 41 witnesses, including Walt Disney, Ronald Reagan and Gary Cooper, who were asked to identify "leftist sympathizers" working in the industry. The committee knew of earlier war films such as *Mission to Moscow* (1943) that could be interpreted as propaganda for communist goals. Jack Warner, who produced the film with Louis B. Mayer, testified to the committee, arguing that these pro–Russian films were made in a "spirit of patriotism" to inform Americans about the war efforts of America's ally in the fight against Nazi Germany. Yet, the House committee used witness testimony to show that films had been made

that were now perceived as part of an insidious plot to undermine Americans with communist ideology, betray "American democracy" and lead to a possible overthrow of the government.

The opening remarks by Chairman J. Parnell Thomas indicated the concerns of the committee, stating that:

> It is the very magnitude of the scope of the motion-picture industry which makes this investigation so necessary. We all recognize, certainly, the tremendous effect which motion pictures have on the mass audiences.
>
> With such vast influence over the lives of American citizens as the motion-picture industry exerts, it is not unnatural — in fact, it is very logical — that subversive and undemocratic forces should attempt to use this medium for un–American purposes [U.S. House of Representatives, Committee on Un-American Activities 1947, p. 497].

With the general fear of communists promoting the use of force and violence to achieve their goals, a young California Congressman, Richard M. Nixon, questioned Jack Warner on the kinds of anti-communist films Hollywood had produced. Warner replied that to his knowledge, none had been produced to date. However, as one of the "friendly witnesses" called to testify before the subcommittee, Warner heard the inference by the members of the committee that Hollywood would be well advised to generate films of this kind. Another producer-director, Sam Wood, responded to a question regarding the degree of influence he thought communists in Hollywood had in making and producing motion pictures. Wood replied that "they are always trying, so you have to be a watchdog." But like other right-wing producers in Hollywood, Wood stated that Jack Warner or Louis B. Mayer and other studio heads would not willingly permit propaganda, communist propaganda, in their pictures. Ironically, Sam Wood had recently produced a film based upon Ernest Hemingway's novel, *For Whom the Bell Tolls* (1943), co-starring Gary Cooper and Ingrid Bergman. Cooper portrays an American soldier-of-fortune fighting for the socialist cause against fascist forces during the Spanish Civil War of 1936–1939.

Liberal voices from the movie industry were at first united in their opposition to such an inquiry, stating through their Committee for the First Amendment that such a probe was itself un–American and an infringement on their civil liberties and rights to free speech. But Hollywood producers and directors soon found themselves divided by liberal and conservative politics on the identity of certain "leftist" writers and directors. Film directors William Wyler and John Huston entered the hearings as unfriendly witnesses hopeful for public support for those screenwriters and directors already named by Sam Wood, Jack Warner and Louis B. Mayer, especially John Howard Lawson, Dalton Trumbo and Ring Lardner, Jr., of the Screen Writers Guild.

When these witnesses came to testify before the subcommittee, the new president of the Motion Picture Producers Association (MPPA), Eric Johnston, was going to deliver a written speech before the questioning to defuse the damaging impression created by earlier testimony on the dangers of communist infiltration in Hollywood. His speech called for tolerance of political differences and for freedom of speech. Instead, the congressmen decided to call upon the 11 witnesses whose alleged ties and sympathies with the Communist Party had been confirmed by the earlier testimony. Except for Bertolt Brecht, who cleverly sidestepped the issues, but was forced to leave the country, the other witnesses refused to answer questions on their political beliefs and associations. Since the witnesses were so hostile and uncooperative they were cited for contempt of Congress and drew one-year prison terms.

Hollywood studio executives were shaken by the defiance of the Hollywood Ten and their refusals to testify before HUAC. Subsequent publicity in the news media caused them to rethink their responses to the communist threat and public pressure. The Hollywood executives publicly deplored the tactics of the ten writers and directors held in contempt. The MPPA reversed previously held policies with regard to the intentions and procedures of the investigations by HUAC. The MPPA declared: "We will not knowingly employ a Communist or a member of any party or group which advocates the overthrow of the government of the United States by force, or by any illegal or unconstitutional method" (Kahn in Mast 1982, pp. 541–542). This statement by MPPA created the first blacklist used as part of a public relations campaign to restore public opinion in Hollywood motion pictures.

The main reason behind Hollywood's new position regarding HUAC was the fear of a boycott of motion picture theatres. These economic interests overshadowed any possible anxieties over communist propaganda emanating from Hollywood films. Dore Schary of MGM at the Screen Writers Guild argued that the accused should be judged innocent until proven otherwise. Still, he dismissed two of his writers while claiming they had never attempted any subversive attacks in their films. In the face of huge financial losses, the producers felt the need to heed public opinion and follow HUAC's advice. These studio executives also recognized the growing paranoia of the American public toward the unknown Red Menace. The film industry responded to this threat of subversives by producing several anticommunist films "educating" the public on how the communist conspiracy works. Films like *The Iron Curtain* (1948), *The Red Menace* (1949) and *I Was a Communist for the FBI* (1951) propagandized the dangers of communism to the American way of life. Another assortment of war films showed how America was capable of defeating any enemy that threatened the security of the United States. These included *Battleground* (1949), *The Sands of Iwo Jima* (1950) and *The Steel Helmet* (1951). Later in the 1950s, science-fiction films would reflect the Cold War rhetoric using aliens or mythological beasts as enemies similar to subversive communists that were taking over "earthlings." These films found strong support from right-wing pressure groups who endorsed HUAC's aims and its moral attack on subversives of any kind in America. Yet the fracture of the democratic process by this witch-hunt is reflected in a number of films that introduced a "cinema of moral anxiety" produced by the hearings. They were part of an anti–HUAC reaction found in revisionist westerns such as Fred Zinnemann's *High Noon* (1952) and John Sturges'

In Fred Zinnemann's *High Noon* (1952), Gary Cooper and Grace Kelly discuss the dangers of staying in town to fight a killer and his gang who are intent on eliminating Cooper as the town's sheriff.

Humphrey Bogart stars as Sam Spade in an archetypal film noir detective thriller with Peter Lorre as Joel Cairo in John Huston's *The Maltese Falcon* (1941). Mary Astor is the *femme fatale* and Sidney Greenstreet is the Fat Man. Huston demonstrates how obsessive greed turns every character into a bizarre human being fetishizing a black Maltese Falcon.

Bad Day at Black Rock (1954). In answering his critics, Elia Kazan directed a Budd Schulberg script, *On the Waterfront* (1954), about a dock worker (Marlon Brando) who testifies against corrupt labor bosses in a government inquiry and pays a heavy price. But the blacklist became an index of the paranoia and treachery that divided and destroyed the creative spark of the old Hollywood.

The Film Noir Tradition, Visual Style and Thematic Content

A group of postwar films were produced in Hollywood that echoed this sense of moral cor-ruption and betrayal in the motion picture in-dustry. In general, these films were dark melo-dramas whose typical protagonist is an average working-class guy "caught in contradictory dreams ... that create problems rather than re-solve them" (Telotte 1989, p. 1).

As if in an existentialist nightmare, these people are trapped in a complex labyrinth cre-ated by their own greed or lust, or other im-pulses that psychologically dislocate them in the hollow dark world they inhabit. It is a world of violence where all human values are seri-ously called into question, and suggests a per-vasive sense of fear and helplessness in the face of threats from unseen malevolent forces. The films envision a world where political corrup-

Jane Greer emerges from the darkness as the *femme fatale* to complete the entrapment of her prey, ex-detective Robert Mitchum, in a classic example of a film noir thriller, Jacques Tourneur's *Out of the Past* (1947).

tion and paranoia indicate a continuing disintegration and destruction of all social relationships.

Film noir evolved from a number of crime films produced by Warner Bros. in the late 1930s, first by Fritz Lang in *You Only Live Once* (1937), followed by Raoul Walsh with *The Roaring Twenties* (1939). These films look back upon a fatalism captured by the dark tonality of a film noir visual style brought to Hollywood by German Expressionist film directors like Fritz Lang and Josef von Sternberg. The French poetic realist style found in the films of Marcel Carné also contributed to a film noir sense of pessimism. One of the influences on the content of film noir was a group of hardboiled detective thrillers typical of the style,

beginning with John Huston's *The Maltese Falcon* (1941), Stuart Heisler's *The Glass Key* (1942), Frank Tuttle's *This Gun for Hire* (1942), Otto Preminger's *Laura* (1944) and Billy Wilder's *Double Indemnity* (1944), based upon a James M. Cain story. Each film depicts shadowy characters driven by lust, greed or psychotic reasons to lie, betray, kill or be killed in order to obtain whatever they secretly desire.

As a visual style film noir displays the hallucinatory, nightmarish criminal world of the big city where the detective protagonist tries to comprehend the deceptive appearances of persons with whom he comes into contact. Visually the style uses high-contrast, low-key lighting techniques and non-traditional compositions and camera angles to create feelings of alienation,

Glenn Ford as a police detective, Sergeant Bannion, after he discovers police corruption in Fritz Lang's *The Big Heat* (1953). In a battle against crime bosses in collusion with police commissioners, he takes on Lee Marvin, assassin for the mob, and forces a confession.

claustrophobia and entrapment. This dark and sleazy urban environment also suggests hidden and malevolent forces lurking in the shadows, stalking their prey. This metaphor of the city as an asphalt jungle or human jungle reveals the sense of danger and doom for characters caught in the oppressive confines of this urban world. The occasional use of flashing neon lights to intermittently break up the shadows also aims to distort any physical reality and to suggest a subjective state of mind.

Postwar realism accentuated the authenticity of film noir productions in which producers like Louis de Rochemont of "March of Time" newsreel fame used actual locations to indicate a harsher, more alienating environment peopled by social misfits. Together with director Henry Hathaway he produced *House*

on 92nd Street (1945), *Kiss of Death* (1947) and *Call Northside 777* (1948). Mark Hellinger teamed with directors Robert Siodmak in *The Killers* (1946) and Jules Dassin in *Brute Force* (1947). Both films starred Burt Lancaster and used flashbacks extensively. From 1949 to 1952, the portrait of a psychotic killer is forcefully rendered by actors such as Richard Widmark (*Kiss of Death*), James Cagney in *White Heat* (Raoul Walsh, 1949) and *Kiss Tomorrow Goodbye* (Gordon Douglas, 1950), Kirk Douglas in *Ace in the Hole* (Billy Wilder, 1951) and *Detective Story* (William Wyler, 1951), Lee Marvin in *The Big Heat* (Fritz Lang, 1953), Gloria Swanson in *Sunset Boulevard* (Billy Wilder, 1950), Jack Palance in *Panic in the Streets* (Elia Kazan, 1950), and Robert Mitchum in *Pursued* (Raoul Walsh, 1947) and *Out of the Past*

(Jacques Tourneur, 1947). In all these films, the moral disintegration of the protagonist is visually depicted as a sociological reflection of the corruption of the American dream during the postwar paranoia of the Cold War. Orson Welles directed and starred in two important film noir melodramas that defined this style using a voice-over, flashback structure. In *The Lady from Shanghai* (1948), co-starring Rita Hayworth, and *Touch of Evil* (1958) with Charlton Heston and Janet Leigh, Welles portrays characters that are corrupted by the chaos of moral ambiguities of human law and order. The most brutal critique of Cold War paranoia and despair using film noir style is *Kiss Me Deadly* (Robert Aldrich, 1955), starring Ralph Meeker as Mickey Spillane's unprincipled detective, Mike Hammer. He is attempting to find the Great Whatsit, a Pandora's box of destruction that everyone pays dearly to possess. As a psychological thriller, it is comparable to the science-fiction drama of *Repo Man* (Alex Cox, 1984), starring Harry Dean Stanton and Emilio Estevez, who get involved with a 1964 Chevy carrying a lethal cargo (Telotte 1989, pp. 209–213).

Commentary on Jacques Tourneur's Out of the Past

This story is based upon Geoffrey Homes' 1946 novel, *Build My Gallows High*. In adapting the detective thriller to the screen, Tourneur follows the subjective world of the protagonist using a voice-over and flashback technique that recollects how past events propel the story. As a classical film noir, the film follows a three-part movement beginning with a present-day set-up to introduce the enigmatic codes or threats being posed, then a series of flashbacks to produce a search of past events where characters enter the narrative to solve the enigma. When the past catches up to the present, a third stage is reached as the protagonist attempts to overcome the threat and resolve the issue. Tension and suspense are maintained throughout, since relationships among the characters are incoherent and ambiguous, creating a further mystery and disorganizing the narration. Performances by Robert Mitchum as the fated detective, Kirk Douglas as a businessman mobster and Jane Greer as the *femme fatale* form an obsessive deadly triangle, leading the viewer to believe that desire and lust can motivate any person into criminal action and away from a normal life in this dark, shadowy and hallucinatory underworld.

References

Kahn, Gordon. 1948. "Hollywood on Trial." In *The Movies in Our Midst: Documents in the Cultural History of Film in America*. 1982. Edited by Gerald Mast. Chicago: The University of Chicago Press, pp. 541–542.

Koszarski, Richard. 1977. *Hollywood Directors: 1941–76*. New York: Oxford University Press.

Navasky, Victor S. 1991. *Naming Names*. New York: Penguin.

Telotte, J. P. 1989. *Voices in the Dark: The Narrative Patterns of* Film Noir. Urbana and Chicago: University of Illinois Press.

U.S. House of Representatives. Committee on Un-American Activities. 1947. "Hearings Regarding the Communist Infiltration of the Motion-Picture Industry in the United States." In *The Movies in Our Midst*. Edited by Gerald Mast. 1982. Chicago: The University of Chicago Press, pp. 496–512.

Warshow, Robert. 1952. *The Immediate Experience*. New York: Doubleday.

CHAPTER 13

Postwar Japanese Cinema: 1950–1990

Introduction

This chapter surveys the postwar renaissance of Japanese films of the 1950s, when the cinematic traditions of the Japanese film industry gained recognition in the Western world after Akira Kurosawa's *Rashomon* (1950) won the Grand Prize at the Venice Film Festival in 1951. The other important master directors were Yasujiro Ozu and Kenji Mizoguchi, both leaders of Japanese prewar sound films. For the international market, the Japanese studios promoted films that followed two major genres: historical films called *jidai-geki* featuring stories about samurai warriors, and films on modern life, or *gendai-geki*. Western audiences found the action-packed samurai or warrior films made by Kurosawa, such as *Rashomon* and *The Seven Samurai* (1954), comparable to American westerns.

Postwar American occupation and censorship dictated against cinematic depiction of militarism, feudalism or imperialism in Japanese films. Most influential was the influx of American films of Frank Capra, John Ford and Orson Welles that Japanese filmmakers absorbed into their own cinematic styles. Their later films also were infused with humanistic ideals for individuality and democracy. Akira Kurosawa's postwar films, especially *Nora Inu / Stray Dog* (1949) and *Ikiru / Living* (1952), are contemporary existentialist dramas that established his international status as one of the leading postwar directors in Japan, with Ozu and Mizoguchi.

Kurosawa continued his filmmaking prowess well into the 1980s and 1990s with a series of films that portrayed the ethical dilemmas facing postmodern society. *Ran / Chaos* (1985), adapted from *King Lear*, and *Rhapsody in August* (1991) both situate characters in a vacuum facing moral ambiguities that appear to lead to the destruction of all human values.

The Influence of Japanese Noh and Kabuki Theatre on Japanese Cinema

Noh Theatre emerged during the Edo period of the 17th century with its highly stylized dance-dramas that evolved from ceremonies and rituals concerning all aspects of life and death. As drama they contain the literature of the mythic and historic past of the Japanese people. They employ symbolic settings, masks and expressive gestures for the presentation of major characters. The staging and actions of these characters are choreographed into a series of mimes and dance movements that establish relationships between themselves and their cultural situation.

During the 1920s, Japanese filmmakers developed a cinematic style based upon the rich theatrical traditions of the Noh and Kabuki. These traditions brought with them a powerful visual style for mood and atmosphere that reinforced universal themes on love and violence. Two important features from this theatre are incorporated in most postwar Japanese

In *Ran / Chaos* (1985), Kurosawa's adaptation of Shakespeare's *King Lear*, he explores the tragic conse-quences when an old warlord decides to divide his kingdom among his three sons, resulting in a chaotic battle for power that destroys all of them.

films: the *benshi*, or narrator, and the *oyama*, or female impersonator. The major characters are costumed in oversized kimonos and head-dresses to gain a theatrical presence. A male chorus chants the actor's lines. A *benshi* nar-rates the tale as the actors perform the dance-ritual. Noh plays are short stories concerned with the actions of five different types of char-acters: Gods, warriors, women, spirits using mad persons as a medium and supernatural demons. An all-day theatrical performance of Noh drama would consist of a five-act struc-ture of short plays depicting a ritualized enact-ment of a dramatic situation from the mythic past.

The formalized staging with masked actors is a symbolic representation of human beings or gods. As an art form, each dance has been transformed into a ritual. This breaks down any sense of accepting the reality of the action. The ritual is complemented by the visual pres-ence of a chorus and a narrator who comments

upon it. The theatricalization of the dance-drama is important because it keeps the audi-ence aware that it is watching a story unfold-ing on stage as a sacred place. Both Mizoguchi and Kurosawa include many classical Noh ele-ments in their respective samurai films, notably a chorus or a replica of the stage as in *Rashomon*, *Ran / Chaos* and *Kumonosu-Jo / Throne of Blood* (1957). Western directors such as Bertolt Brecht and Sergei Eisenstein also acknowledged the ritual aspects of Noh drama by adopting many anti-realistic features of Noh drama in the 1930s. Both men incorporated these features into their own historical dramas and films.

Kabuki theatre also contributed stories and plays to the traditional drama of Japan. As a popular song and dance theatre, kabuki is com-parable to Broadway musical theatre, which draws most of its stories from contemporary romantic melodramas. The dance movements and acting are stylized into narrative gestures, movements and postures. Actors wear mask-like

Set in 12th century Kyoto, Akira Kurosawa's *Rashomon* (1950) brings a modern moral dilemma to a traditional folk-tale. With Toshiro Mifune as the bandit, Kurosawa interweaves four different versions of an attack on a samurai warrior and his bride, each version relating a different point-of-view.

makeup that conveys specific character types, and men perform all the roles because women were banned from the stage in 1629. Again, as in the Noh theatre, Kabuki uses an on-stage chorus and narrator providing songs, musical accompaniment and commentary. Although the settings are usually stylized, they also indicate place scenically through flat illusionistic paintings and use elaborate stage effects to change scenes, whereas the Noh stage is formal and non-scenic.

The Films of Akira Kurosawa

When the Western film world honored Akira Kurosawa (1910–1998) and his film *Rashomon*, and indirectly Japanese filmmaking, at the Venice Film Festival in 1951, Western filmmakers were astonished to find a sophisticated cinematic culture behind the new Japanese film

industry. But Kurosawa was not the only Japanese director hailed as a distinguished filmmaker. His older friend, Kenji Mizoguchi (1898–1956), made two films, *The Life of Oharu* (1952) and *Ugetsu* (1953), that won awards at the Venice Film Festival in the following years. With Yasujiro Ozu (1903–1963), who made *Tokyo Story* in 1953, Japan revealed three master film directors who developed different cinematic styles for film narratives based upon the rich theatrical traditions set by the Noh and Kabuki theatres.

During the postwar years, Kurosawa saw the national recovery of Japan as a moment in history when his own cinematic voice could respond to the new political and social climate. He attempted a didactic cinema that would express his own thematic concerns about human moral responsibility to others and the emotional desire for power. Kurosawa's heroes combat the ethical and psychological dilemmas that influence their beliefs and actions. Kurosawa drew upon the Zen Buddhist teachings and conventions of Noh theatre to use this art form for ethical or moral instruction. His films, like *Rashomon,* deal directly with the difficulty of separating one's dreams from reality. All of Kurosawa's heroes become preoccupied with differentiating illusion from reality when faced with moral choices for action, to illustrate the basic theme of self-deception. Further, each story carries a lesson involving a relationship between a master and his disciple learning to overcome human misfortune and suffering in an absurd and uncertain world.

Kurosawa is one of many Japanese filmmakers who borrowed heavily from the moral teachings of Noh theatre. Like Ozu and Mizoguchi before him, he also developed cinematic sequences influenced by American cinema to capture the general mood and atmosphere of this tradition. His cinematography is choreographed to capture long passages of action that integrate visual metaphors through a play of light and shadow accompanied by musical support of drums and flutes. Compositions carry a painterly visual elegance and beauty emphasizing the emotional atmosphere of the scene. Long tracking and traveling shots capture a depth of field to support a carefully designed *mise-en-scène.* This cinematic style continued the developments of early Japanese cinema, in which long takes of entire sequences allowed the action within the frame to command the narrative.

Although the early Japanese filmmakers knew of Western modes to represent time and space in a realistic manner, they followed a direct style of presentational cinema. Here their cameras simply recorded the stylized actions of a Kabuki theatre piece using a fixed frontal view and a long take. The traditional *benshi* or voice-over narrator became an important feature in silent Japanese motion pictures as he continued the conventions of Kabuki theatre throughout the silent era of films.

Moreover, this presentational style of filmed staging, employing the iconography of the settings and actors, gave Japanese movie audiences something close to the "magic" films of Méliès with their one-scene, one-take productions.

Only with the influx of Western silent films from Germany and France did Japanese directors begin to use other camera techniques that could manipulate time and space. Yet the Japanese film industry was slow to adopt modern Western ideas on filmmaking. Only Teinosuke Kinugasa (1896–1982) adopted expressionist and surrealist cinematic techniques in directing two avant-garde silent films, *Page of Madness* (1926) and *Crossways* (1928). In the 1950s Kinugasa used wide-screen processes and color to direct *Gate of Hell* (1953), which won best film of 1954 at the Cannes Film Festival and an Oscar for the best foreign film of the year. Foreign silent films became accepted as part of mass entertainment and Japanese filmmakers held on to their own stylistic devices past the introduction of sound technology.

The Japanese government took control of film production during World War II. Most filmmakers, including Mizoguchi and Ozu, made propaganda films to support the war effort. After the war, the American Occupational Forces censored all Japanese films that promoted any return to the military or imperial goals of the emperor. New filmscripts had to promote beliefs in individualism and the productivity of capitalism to secure the redevelopment and growth of the country's economy.

Japanese Films and Western Audiences

Akira Kurosawa is acknowledged as the most respected and renowned Japanese film director today. He first achieved international recognition when his samurai film *Rashomon* won the Venice Film Festival award. This film introduced Western audiences to a new visual style that changed the form and content of film narratives. Thematically, the film also raised philosophical questions regarding the moral responsibilities of human beings when life is challenged by chaos and change.

The film offers four different versions of the same incident involving the death of a samurai warrior. Each protagonist has a different version of what happened according to the character's subjective viewpoint. If truth becomes subjective in a court of law, Kurosawa asks, how can a person continue living in a moral way after committing criminal acts? Further, how does one maintain faith in the trustworthiness of human beings when each is caught in one's own self-deception?

Kurosawa also introduces three distinct visual styles to affect the atmosphere and mood of the major scenes that add to the symmetry of the narrative. Such diversity of styles in a historical film was quite unusual. It is Kurosawa's artistry that

In Akira Kurosawa's *The Seven Samurai* (1954), farmers, trained as foot soldiers by samurai warriors, encircle a raiding bandit on horseback.

reveals the subjective interests of the protagonists as they recall their own stories. Yet the "courtroom" scene allows the audience to become members of the jury, in effect, and pass judgment on the guilt or innocence of the bandit. Indirectly, Kurosawa can prove that the discrepancy in what a person is and what that person does is dependent upon the illusions or myths attributed to a stereotype. A samurai warrior may attempt to live up to the *bushido* code of conduct, but when it comes down to war and chaos, there are no heroic battles, and there are no heroes.

This existentialist outlook on life reveals the pessimism Kurosawa displays in greater detail in his later samurai films, first in *The Seven Samurai* and *The Throne of Blood*, and later, in *Kagemusha* (1981) and *Ran*. In each film, Kurosawa's multiple camera coverage captures the terrible suffering of samurai warriors in battle, sacrificing their lives in a bid for power and dominance.

As in *Ran*, Kurosawa charts a symmetrical course of action that runs full circle as the heroes set themselves the task of combating the forces of evil they have unwittingly unleashed. Their dreams of power and glory turn into nightmares of murder and betrayal when each

protagonist faces his or her own evil ways. Lord Hidetora is struck with the death of his youngest son, Saburo, at the moment when reconciliation occurs. Kurosawa's dark pessimism runs through this entire film. It is demonstrated time and again in the death and destruction of one army after another. Behind the slaughter is the treachery of Lady Kaede, a wife to the eldest brother. A strong desire to avenge the murder of her family by Lord Hidetora motivates her as she seeks to set brother against brother. In contrast to Lady Kaede is the portrait of Lady Sue. She became a believer in the Amida Buddha when her family was murdered by the same Lord Hidetora. Now she attempts to cease her suffering and pain by following the path to enlightenment through Zen Buddhism. Her attempt is to accept a spiritual path in life, away from the corrupting influences of family feuds. Ironically, she meets the same fate as Lady Kaede and is beheaded by an assassin while her blind brother wanders untended toward a dangerous precipice (Prince 1991, pp. 284–291).

Kurosawa's perspective and commentary on the social and moral dilemmas facing humanity continue in his later films. His films always show his concern for humanistic values that

Set in the 16th century civil wars in Japan, Kurosawa's *Hidden Fortress* (1958) places a proud samurai warrior (Mifune) with two clownish peasants as he attempts to rescue a princess. The plot is partly Shakespearean, reaching for a moral solution in times of chaos.

reflect psychological truths about people. Sometimes he parodies the samurai warrior, as in *Yojimbo* (1961) and *Sanjuro* (1963), in which this solitary warrior avoids taking sides. In each film the samurai eliminates the evil forces controlling the town, especially those with capitalist motives as in American westerns like *Shane*.

Western viewers became more familiar with an adaptation of Kurosawa's *Hidden Fortress* (1958) and samurai warriors when they appeared in George Lucas' *Star Wars* (1977). The original story retells the efforts of a samurai warrior, Han Solo, escorting a princess and two peasants to safety during the civil wars of the 16th century. Lucas carries the analogy further into Zen Buddhist beliefs and values when he brings the mythical powers of Jedi knights and the Force into action. The spiritual battle between Darth Vader and Ben (Obi-Wan) Kenobi and the training of Luke as a Jedi warrior com-

plete the master-discipline legends like those found in most Kurosawa films. As the screenwriter and director, Lucas places the action in a past galaxy whose denizens use light swords and other electronic weapons in an unending battle between the forces of good and evil, thus playing on the moral sensibilities of a mass audience. However, unlike Kurosawa, Lucas avoids dealing with the moral dilemmas of a world torn by war and strife.

The Films of Kenji Mizoguchi

Kenji Mizoguchi's later films contain a similar moral philosophy akin to that of Kurosawa. Yet a common social theme arises in his postwar films that examine the sacrificial role Japanese women play to redeem their morally weak men. His last trilogy, *Life of Oharu* (1952), *Ugetsu Monogatari* (1953) and *Sancho Dayu /*

Ohama threatens a customer who attempts to skip out without paying for the service in Kenji Mizoguchi's *Ugetsu Monogatari* (1953). In the background is Tobei, in armor, who shows astonishment in realizing Ohama, a prostitute, is his wife.

Sansho the Bailiff (1954), draws upon medieval morality plays to examine the strength and weaknesses of family bonds that reflect larger social issues of exploitation and oppression of women. These films are set in the past when civil wars shattered communal relationships. They describe the absurdities of human ambition, greed, selfishness and lust that overcome the men and affect the unprotected women left behind. These postwar films reiterate his concerns for the social welfare of women attempting to survive in a male-dominated society. Mizoguchi's stark and realistic depictions of these women as they are degraded, prostituted and discarded are more specifically Japanese in thematic content and outlook than in other films by Kurosawa or Ozu.

Mizoguchi's visual style is poetic and painterly, following his training as a painter.

He succeeds in visualizing the past on both a realistic and mystical level. His style is comparable to the illustrations of legends or folk tales displayed in Japanese picture scrolls (*emakimino*). *Ugetsu Monogatari* is typical of this style as it demonstrates Mizoguchi's use of the long take (one scene, one shot) to compose in depth, framing the dramatic action within the *mise-en-scène*. He uses frequent pans to pick out the action rather than employing tracking shots. He establishes low-key lighting effects to create different moods and atmosphere in his films. These lighting effects are supported by acoustical sounds that help Mizoguchi move deliberately from a natural environment to a supernatural one, as he does in the boat scene in *Ugetsu*. Here the sound track suggests the symbolic nature of the action. The ghostly apparitions of Lady Wakasa follow the

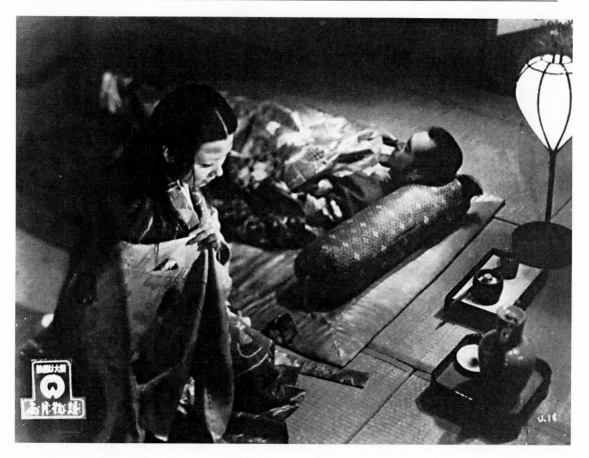

Lady Wakasa sets the stage to possess Genjuro, the potter, as she performs a magical ceremony while he sleeps in *Ugetsu Monogatari.*

Noh tradition of stories about spirits and mad people. Even the eerie groans of Lady Wasaka's father add to the depiction of the otherworldliness of Noh theatre. Throughout his films, Mizoguchi uses cinematic devices that invite a sense of involvement with the characters or create a sense of detachment from the scene to allow time for a viewer's contemplation of the action.

ATMOSPHERE AND CONFLICT IN MIZOGUCHI'S UGETSU

Keiki I. McDonald describes how Mizoguchi's use of the long take, low-key photography, with a static camera using long and medium shots and acoustic effects, evokes a mood and atmosphere to help support the thematic conflicts of this film. She contends that this integration of form with content allows Mizoguchi to dramatize two major themes in

his film: dislocation and dissolution. Mizoguchi divides his film narrative into two parts. The first shows the involvement of the men leaving their farms to acquire wealth and status during the civil war. The second depicts the violence war has upon the unprotected women who attempt to survive. Throughout the film, Mizoguchi indulges in images that contrast illusion and reality, and interweaves the spirit world with the natural world. These two features merge harmoniously during the homecoming sequence in which the husband, Genjuro, recognizes the spiritual presence of his wife, Miyagi (McDonald 1983, pp. 104–119).

The Films of Yasujiro Ozu

Yasujiro Ozu, as the other master Japanese director, adopted a cinematic style that is

Yasujiro Ozu's cinematic style displays the gaps between the generations in this family portrait of visiting parents dealing with the emotional strains of separation in *Tokyo Story* (1953).

unique in the history of cinema. Ozu's style is more austere and contained. His camera is fixed parallel to the room as in early silent cinema and in later Andy Warhol films of the 1960s. However, Ozu departs from the classical Hollywood style that dictates that the camera stay parallel to the picture plane, the 180-degree space of the action. This gave the viewer a sense of proper screen direction and a continuous space. Ozu's camera jumps over the 180 degree line to produce a number of unusual framing situations that relocate the actor within the space. Ozu, by using the entire 360-degree space of the room, can allow the spectator to view the action as if seated within the space. Actions are minimal but the emotional content resides in the restrained performances of the parents or children who contain their desires according to custom as in a tea ceremony. Rituals are the means to pleasure, either

through eating, drinking or mating, but respect and companionship is most sought after.

Ozu is an astute observer of family life. His films deal with the loss of patriarchal authority after the defeat of Japan in the Second World War. These family melodramas concern the dissolution of family life as the young refuse marriage partners or seek alternatives to the traditional ways. Although at times he is critical of the social code, he advocates family solidarity. This major thematic interest produces the primary conflicts in his films, a tension between traditional Japanese ways of life and the freer modern society of Japan. These tensions are set in motion at the family level when grandparents and older children meet. Most typical is *Tokyo Story* (1953). A coming together of the family at the beginning of the film finds the grandparents acutely aware of the differences between their children and themselves. This universal story ends with the children mourning the death of the mother.

References

Burch, Noel. 1979. *To the Distant Observer: Form and Meaning in Japanese Cinema* (rev. ed.). Edited by Annette Michelson. Berkeley and Los Angeles: University of California Press.

McDonald, Keiko I. 1983. *Cinema East: A Critical Study of Major Japanese Films.* Rutherford, N.J.: Farleigh Dickinson University Press.

Prince, Stephen. 1991. *The Warrior's Camera: The Cinema of Akira Kurosawa.* Princeton: Princeton University Press.

CHAPTER 14

Hollywood in Transition and Decline: 1955–1962

Introduction

Three major postwar factors changed the power structure and practices of Hollywood filmmaking. First, the ruling by the 1947 U.S. Supreme Court in *United States v. Paramount* found that vertical control was monopolistic and in restraint of trade. The major studios were forced to discontinue "block bookings" and had to divest themselves of their theatre holdings. A second factor involved halting the steady decline in movie attendance by introducing new technical innovations, such as wide-screen projection with Cinemascope, stereophonic sound, 3-D movies and color, to meet the challenge and growth of television. The third factor related to the competition of European "art" films for the postwar market. After the 1952 Supreme Court decision on *The Miracle* in *Burstyn v. Wilson* affirmed for motion pictures the right of free speech, many independent producers began making films on controversial subject matter. Independent producers and directors like Billy Wilder, John Huston, Fred Zinnemann and Elia Kazan adapted popular stage plays and novels into narrative films. Social dramas such as *On the Waterfront* led to a series of "youth films" that rebelled against the norms of a decaying middle-class America. Serious antiwesterns such as *High Noon* and *The Searchers* reflected concerns about the origins of community beneath the myth of white America. Other films made covert political statements about the HUAC blacklisting and the tyranny of the McCarthy hearings, such as *Bad Day at Black Rock* and

Invasion of the Body Snatchers. In New York, a new group of talented directors and screenwriters from television, such as Arthur Penn and Paddy Chayefsky, began making intimate psychological portraits of typical urban dwellers using techniques borrowed from the Italian neorealists. On the other hand, independent producers like Sam Spiegel made deals with American studios for worldwide distribution of their blockbuster films, namely David Lean's *The Bridge on the River Kwai* and *Lawrence of Arabia*.

Hollywood in Transition and Decline (1952–1962)

Some film historians claim that 1952 was a turning point for the American film industry as it struggled to halt the decline of movie audiences in the postwar years. The major studios quickly realized the financial losses that accompanied their divestment of their theatre chains and the outlawing of block-booking. The *United States v. Paramount* antitrust court ruling of 1947 thus ended the vertical integration of production, distribution and exhibition in the studio system. Without a guaranteed income from their theatrical chains, the companies had to market their films separately to independent exhibitors. For this reason, the major studios stopped producing pictures, let go their contract players, and engaged independent producers and directors who, in turn, had to raise their own capital and agree to rent Hollywood studios in exchange for distribution

David Lean's *Lawrence of Arabia* (1962) stars Peter O'Toole as T. E. Lawrence in a film adaptation of Lawrence's book, *The Seven Pillars of Wisdom.* The controversial film depicts Lawrence as a misguided Arab symphathizer and a knowing British agent uniting Arab tribes riding with Omar Sharif, a chieftain.

rights to their films. Yet, when independent producers undertook the risks of film production, exhibitors knew that Hollywood had to make further technological changes to reverse the loss of box-office revenues and bring audiences back to the theatres.

New marketing strategies were devised allowing banks to provide funds for independent production. Studios like MGM, Paramount, United Artists and 20th Century–Fox agreed to handle worldwide distribution of each film. MGM conducted a survey to discover what films most audiences wanted to see. They discovered that musicals starring Gene Kelly or Fred Astaire headed the list. This choice was followed by war pictures, crime stories and costume romances, an apparent return

to the familiar genre forms of the past. The survey also uncovered the fact that movie audiences were educated and affluent, and that as many men as women went to the movies. What was already known about the Hollywood product was confirmed by the survey as the movies attracted young people more than older people (Sklar 1975, p. 269).

3-D Experiments and Wide-Screen Projection

In taking note of this survey, Hollywood producers decided to make films that included a more adult attitude toward the depiction of social and sexual relationships to match the sophistication and thematic content of European and Asian films that were attracting more mature audiences. Further, they realized that not only better films, but bigger films, were required that could give their audiences sights and sounds unavailable on television, especially including motion picture spectacles that were longer, in full color (i.e. not black and white or tinted), and on a screen with a greater illusion of three-dimensional depth. Hollywood packaged all of this thinking into a Madison Avenue slogan, hoping that audiences would believe "that bigger films are better films."

With the novelty of illusionistic depth in mind, producers called upon Arch Oboler, a radio mystery writer, to produce a feature film in 3-D, one which the advertisements claimed "would land a lion in your lap." Oboler's *Bwana Devil* was released in the fall of 1952. The 3-D effect was initially successful with audiences who came to view this novelty. Within the year, other 3-D films were marketed successfully, including *House of Wax* (1953), a mystery thriller starring Vincent Price, directed by Andre de Toth, and *Creature from the Black Lagoon* (1954), directed by Jack Arnold. Both films paid careful attention to settings and props to authenticate the reality of the environment and establish atmospheric effects common to horror stories. But production values did not save these films. There were three major problems associated with them. First, they were based upon routine genres or banal stories without properly developed characters. Second, viewers had to wear polarized glasses to see the stereoscopic 3-D effect. Third, they overused various cinematic tricks and gimmicks that assaulted the audience, sensationalizing the film narrative.

In September 1952, Warner Bros. introduced its multiple-screen film process, Cinerama, in the attempt to recreate a three-dimensional depth of vision. Fred Waller, Cinerama's inventor, designed a curved, wraparound screen using a three-strip projection process that exploited peripheral vision. The new screen, with a 2.85 to 1 aspect ratio of width to height was curved and vast, presenting audiences with panoramas of mountains,

oceans and deserts. The film *This Is Cinerama* (1952) became a hit with audiences mostly as a novelty. As a forerunner of today's IMAX, it suffered as 3-D films did from the lack of dramatic features and narrative drive. While films made for *Cinerama* continued ongoing chase sequences as in 1962's *How the West Was Won*, directed by Henry Hathaway, John Ford and George Marshall, the spectacle placed far too much importance on the spectacular landscapes than on the dramatic appeal of the narrative. *Cinerama* did draw significant crowds to witness this visual and aural spectacle, yet only a few theatres in major cities were equipped to show such films. *Cinerama* was financially rewarding over a span of time but this wide-screen technique lacked dramatic narratives and its novelty soon wore itself out with the public.

A technological breakthrough at 20th Century–Fox produced the wide-screen medium of CinemaScope. This process was designed by Henri Chrétien in the 1920s. He used anamorphic lenses on both projectors and cameras. This system had one major advantage over other wide-screen processes: Films shot with these lenses could compress a wide-screen image into a 35mm frame that could be exhibited with projectors already in place at most movie theatres. In 1953, Fox introduced CinemaScope to audiences with Henry Koster's film adaptation of Lloyd Douglas' best-selling novel, *The Robe*, starring Richard Burton and Jean Simmons. As an historical-religious epic, the story involves a Roman tribune choosing between Christian martyrdom or obeying Caligula's directives. The film is a blend of earlier DeMille-like fascination with religious spectacle, and a display of Roman power, aided by a stereo soundtrack.

The Biblical epic received wide audience approval, convincing studio heads like Spyrous Skouras at Fox that this wide-screen system would prove a financial bonanza for his studio. Other historical epics were made using CinemaScope's new screen aspect ratio of 2.55 to 1. Leading the parade of hits were wide-screen films that combined Westerns with romantic love stories set in exotic locales. Anthony Mann's *El Cid* (1961) and David Lean's *Lawrence of Arabia* (1962) fared well, as did musicals like

Joshua Logan's *South Pacific* (1958) and Robert Wise's *The Sound of Music* (1965), starring Julie Andrews.

Hollywood producers also set up European companies in Spain, England, Italy and Yugoslavia to exploit cheap labor and foreign motion picture facilities in making a number of epic historical spectacles like *Alexander the Great* (1956), *The Vikings* (1958), *Ben-Hur* (1959) and *Spartacus* (1960). All these films were heavily costumed action-dramas featuring all-star casts. Some films had weak narratives and reverted to the Film d'Art productions of Sarah Bernhardt's day, substituting spectacle for drama. This happened to the opulent Elizabeth Taylor–Richard Burton version of *Cleopatra* (1963), a box-office disaster directed by Joseph L. Mankiewicz.

The Miracle Case and Freedom of Speech

In 1950, the Italian film *The Ways of Love* opened in New York City at an "art house" cinema. The film contained three unrelated one-act stories: Jean Renoir's *A Day in the Country,* Pagnol's *Joffroi,* and Rossellini's *The Miracle,* starring Anna Magnani, with a screenplay by Federico Fellini. As a modern allegory on the birth of the Christ child, the last story is a frank tale about a simple-minded peasant woman, Mary, who believes she has been visited by St. Joseph.

Rossellini's *The Miracle* focuses more upon a compassion for human nature than on the morality of these people as individuals in conflict with the codes of society. For his central protagonist, Mary, the director presents a psychological problem that becomes a political problem for the individual. His emphasis on the emotional state of this person caught in a crisis raises questions about a person's security within her own society. Moreover, the film addresses all social and moral norms as it searches for the most basic but deeply-sought human values. As a neorealist film, *The Miracle* raises questions about the confining nature of today's social and political culture, and its supporting ideological value system which directly governs a person's moral existence.

After bomb threats provoked by the film, and pressure from the Legion of Decency and other Catholic agencies, the New York State Board of Regents revoked the license of the theatre and banned the film, calling it "sacrilegious." Its American distributor, Joseph Burstyn, took Lewis A. Wilson, the Commissioner of Education, to court. After losing his case in New York, Burstyn appealed to the U.S. Supreme Court, which overturned a 1915 decision, *Mutual v. Ohio,* and in 1952 delivered its landmark ruling on motion pictures. The case asked whether the motion picture is within the protection of the First Amendment as a form of "speech" or "the Press." The Court overturned its 1915 decision declaring motion pictures "a business, pure and simple." The judges concluded in 1952 that "expression by means of motion pictures is included with the free speech and free press guarantee of the First and Fourteenth Amendments" (Mast 1982, p. 618). The decision further held a state may not ban a film on the basis of a censor's conclusion that it is 'sacrilegious'" (Mast, p. 619).

The Supreme Court decision opened the public debate on film content, challenging Hollywood's Production Code. A leading Hollywood producer-director, Otto Preminger, sought to exploit popular novels and stage plays by converting them into controversial social and political films. After directing *Forever Amber* (1947) to poor reviews, his screen adaptations of *The Moon Is Blue* (1953), *The Man with the Golden Arm* (1955), *Anatomy of a Murder* (1959), *Exodus* (1960) and *Advise and Consent* (1962) tested the Production Code in light of the *Miracle* decision. After Preminger released *The Moon Is Blue* without the MPPDA's Production Code seal of approval, he succeeded in establishing a precedent for a franker interpretation of code restrictions that other producers of maturer European films from England, France and Italy had followed.

The Rise of Independent Producers

The rise of independent producers followed in the wake of the major studios divesting themselves of their theatre holdings. By 1951, as movie audiences declined and television expanded into a powerful competitor, 40 percent of the movie houses in major cities began to close down. Two factors contributed to this phenomenon: the postwar growth of suburban housing developments where cinemas did not exist, and the accessibility of TV programming for children and adults in these new affluent communities.

The changing social fabric of cities in the early 1950s made the major Hollywood studios soon realize they could not maintain their production practices in the face of the overwhelming decline in revenues. Moreover, the *Paramount* decision of 1947 forced them to give up their cinemas and the cash flow they produced, making these Hollywood studios less "bankable." Coupled with the 1952 House of Representatives investigation into the alleged subversive activities of Hollywood workers, and the flight of many top screenwriters and directors from the United States, the major studios were forced to release their employees from long term contracts and to rent out their studio properties to former producers and directors.

The new alliance between independent producer-directors with the major studios guaranteed worldwide distribution of their respective independent films. However, the major studios took a healthy percentage of the profits. This kind of deal making had become the norm between the major studios and independent producers. The films of the 1950s and 1960s were thus controlled by a worldwide market rather than by Hollywood vice-presidents in charge of production. However, deal making pressured independent directors such as Billy Wilder and John Huston into organizing commercially sure scripts and stars for their films of the 1950s. Since they produced only one picture at a time on borrowed money, each film had to be a well-known literary property that could be made into a successful motion picture. Billy Wilder stopped making films noirs after *Sunset Boulevard* (1950) and *Ace in the Hole* (1951), and turned to romantic comedies that hinted at illicit romances in films like *Sabrina* (1954) and *The Seven Year Itch* (1955),

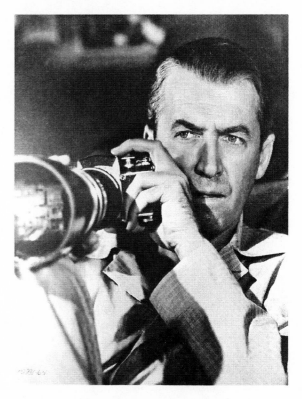

Alfred Hitchcock's *Rear Window* (1964) shows James Stewart watching various stages of married life in different apartments from his rear window overlooking a courtyard. He believes he has witnessed a murder.

based upon hit Broadway comedies. *Some Like it Hot* (1959), starring Marilyn Monroe, Tony Curtis and Jack Lemmon, and *Love in the Afternoon* (1957) took a satiric point-of-view on the conventions of popular romantic mores. Wilder continually played with themes relating American capitalism to promiscuity, adultery, and sexual seduction in each of these romantic comedies. On the surface, the films appeared like earlier screwball comedies through a setup of confusing sexual mismatches, yet underlining each story were obvious suggestions of covert moral corruption in sexual games that are played out with a touch of film noir coldness.

Only Alfred Hitchcock (1899–1980) attained a directorial brilliance in shocking an audience by projecting sexual guilt, suspense and voyeurism using expressionistic film noir techniques. In a series of psychological thrillers, beginning with *Strangers on a Train* (1951), starring Robert Walker and Farley Granger, the director exposes the audience to the dark, sexual aberrations hidden beneath the facade of apparently comfortable middle-class men and their cool, fashionable women. His trilogy on sexual deviancy begins with *Rear Window* (1954), starring James Stewart and Grace Kelly, then after *The Wrong Man* (1956) with Henry Fonda, ends with *Vertigo* (1958), again starring Stewart. His next trilogy begins with his exploration of schizophrenia in *Psycho* (1960), notable for the montage of the shower murder sequence, then features Tippi Hedren in *The Birds* (1962) and *Marnie* (1963).

John Huston (1906–1987) traveled with his film crew to Africa to make *The African Queen* (1952) with Humphrey Bogart and Katharine Hepburn. He worked with a British producer, Sam Spiegel, to bring into focus the movement toward the internationalization of movie making. His interest in placing actions within authentic locations followed the new trend for producers to leave Hollywood studios and make films in exotic locales to add glamour and spectacle to basic romantic comedies. But Huston's films usually concern a central character who sacrifices his or her life to a powerful obsession or quest. His most successful films are placed in quasi-wartime conditions. These films include *The Treasure of the Sierra Madre* (1948), *The Asphalt Jungle* (1950), *The Red Badge of Courage* (1951), set in the American Civil War, and *The African Queen* at the start of World War I. Huston's antiheroes deconstruct the myths of bravery and heroism. These values are betrayed through the characters' cowardice or greed when placed in the line of fire. This theme is demonstrated in both his adaptation of Rudyard Kipling's *The Man Who Would Be King* (1975) and *Prizzi's Honor* (1985). Huston's last film, a remarkable adaptation of James Joyce's novella, *The Dead* (1987), starred his daughter, Anjelica Huston, as a married woman who reveals to her husband a long-lost lover evoked by a song at a dinner party.

The noted British director David Lean (1908–1991), also teamed with producer Sam Spiegel and adapted two popular novels about war, *The Bridge on the River Kwai* (1957), starring Alec Guinness and William Holden, and *Lawrence of Arabia* (1962), starring Peter O'-Toole and Omar Sharif, using the wide-screen process CinemaScope and four-track stereo sound. Although commercially successful, these two films blended romantic heroism with realistic tensions that questioned the myths about heroes and heroic sacrifice. To secure worldwide distribution, Spiegel assembled a cast of international stars from the United States, Italy, Spain and England. This tactic helped the producer secure financing and gave exhibitors star attractions for the box office. Another reason for filming away from Hollywood was to spread the financial risk through co-production with British companies. Later, American producer-directors, like Stanley Kubrick in 1961, set up production offices in London as British companies to meet minimum requirements for financial assistance from the government. This strategy allowed films made under this system to be considered home product, thus eluding the foreign quota system imposed by European countries and protecting their own reestablished film industry. Behind the government strategy was a policy to prevent huge revenues from leaving the country as they did before the war through American-owned film companies.

At the end of the decade, Samuel Bronston became the major independent producer, working through MGM to finance a program of epic historical spectacles by preselling distribution rights throughout the world. His epic films included *El Cid* (1961), *55 Days at Peking* (1963) and *The Fall of the Roman Empire* (1964). Each film exploited wide-screen images in color with synchronous sound to excite movie audiences. Finally the epic dramatizations reached their zenith with Stanley Kubrick's *Spartacus* (1960), and Nicholas Ray's *King of Kings* (1961). Both films depicted an open rebellion against the oppressive forces of pagan Rome. Thematically these two films supported messages of personal freedom in showing the parallels between Roman fascism and present-day America. The two directors were precursors of the antiestablishment directors who produced films in the 1960s in the United States.

The antiestablishment attitude flourished in

Gary Cooper, as a town marshal who puts his life on the line, faces a freed killer and his goons. He seeks a posse but his friend and former sheriff (Lon Chaney, Jr.) refuses to help in Fred Zinnemann's *High Noon* (1952).

the mid–1950s as part of the evolving youth culture. It focused upon juvenile delinquency, teenaged gangs, rock 'n' roll music, motorcycle gangs and a set of values clearly in rebellion against the conventional wisdom of adult conformity and the status quo. The two leading Hollywood stars who typified teenage idols of rebellion were Marlon Brando and James Dean. In the musical world of rock and roll, it was Elvis Presley. Brando's first movie was *The Men* (1950), directed by Fred Zinnemann (1907–1997). The film deals with a study of paraplegic war veterans frustrated by confinement and impotence in an army hospital. Zinnemann uses documentary techniques to suggest government incompetence that creates conflict by testing a man's moral conviction in his fight against an oppressive system. Later Zinnemann

directed *High Noon* (1952) as an allegorical western (with references to the McCarthy witch hunt). It starred Gary Cooper as a sheriff caught in a moral dilemma with his community when he is called upon to face a band of vengeful outlaws. He cast Burt Lancaster, Montgomery Clift and Frank Sinatra as career soldiers in the Academy Award-winning *From Here to Eternity* (1953), in which Lancaster feels morally charged to defend his men facing the wrath of incompetent officers. Zinnemann, who won his first Academy Award for the 1938 short, *That Others Might Live*, won a third with his film adaptation of Robert Bolt's play, *A Man for All Seasons* (1966), starring Paul Scofield as Sir Thomas More, a man of conscience in the realm of Henry VIII.

Marlon Brando's screen image as a rebel

In John Ford's *The Searchers* (1956), John Wayne, as Ethan Edwards, surveys a Comanche village from afar in hopes of finding his rival, Scar.

grew with his performance as a revolutionary Mexican outlaw in Elia Kazan's *Viva Zapata!* (1952), and the biker in Lazlo Benedek's *The Wild One* (1953). He played the lead in Kazan's *On the Waterfront* (1954), in which as the central character Terry Malloy he takes an unpopular stance and testifies to a crime commission against a mob-ridden labor union, exposing the gangsters in control of the waterfront. Some critics have noted that this film reflected Kazan's personal attitudes toward the HUAC investigations. In April 1952, when HUAC began another inquiry demanding witnesses "name names" of Communist Party members, Elia Kazan testified in a climate ruled by Senator Joseph McCarthy and his raging paranoia about the Soviet Red Menace. Kazan named eight colleagues who, in the 1930s, belonged to a Moscow-led U.S. Communist Party cell with

him. Kazan's decision to inform, when so many of his friends had, at great cost, refused, transcended the actual content of his testimony. At the end of this third inquiry, hundreds of Hollywood professionals were added to the blacklist, destroying their chances of making a living in American films. Acrimonious controversy about Kazan continued into 1999, when he accepted an Academy Award from no less than Martin Scorsese for lifetime achievement in motion pictures. Yet *On the Waterfront* earned six Academy Awards, including best picture, best actor and best direction. In *East of Eden* (1955), Kazan directed James Dean as a rebellious son fighting against an authoritarian father. Dean became a teenage icon with his strong angst-ridden performance in *Rebel Without a Cause* (1955), directed by Nicholas Ray, a protégé of Kazan.

John Wayne, on horseback, preparing for a five-year odyssey to find his missing niece kidnapped by Indians in *The Searchers*. John Ford shot the film in Vista-Vision to exploit the natural beauty of Monument Valley.

The Searchers *(1956)* *by John Ford*

John Ford's mid–1950s film, *The Searchers* (1956), is a landmark western that poses more questions on the loss of American values in the settling of the West than any other film. The plot concerns two men and their long five-year odyssey in an obsessive quest to find a young niece kidnapped by Indians. John Ford sets the story in a mythic past where a returning Civil War veteran, Ethan Edwards (John Wayne), is depicted as a loner caught in a battle both with his own Confederate ideals and a renegade Cheyenne named Scar. As an allegory on the racist tensions and attitudes plaguing the United States in the mid–1950s, the film reex-plores the American myth of opening the West and the cost to a society of bringing civilization into a savage world. In doing so, Ford's narrative deals with a number of complex themes concerning the white settlement of this territory, such as illicit sexual desire, racism, capitalism and miscegenation, with each theme threatening the survival of the white family. The film also strives to make us critically aware that historical events can be narrated from many different perspectives, according to the storyteller. The importance of *The Searchers* in film history is apparent as it influenced several young screenwriters and directors of the 1980s, including Paul Schrader, John Milius, Martin Scorsese, Steven Spielberg, George Lucas and Michael Cimino. All have adopted

Spencer Tracy plays a one-armed war veteran on a mission to pay respects to a Japanese-American farmer when he meets some white racists in a small-town hotel in John Sturges' *Bad Day at Black Rock* (1954).

the basic narrative structure of *The Searchers* for their own films, such as *Taxi Driver, Close Encounters of the Third Kind* and *The Deer Hunter*.

Bad Day at Black Rock *(1954)* *by John Sturges*

This film follows the other morally charged westerns of the 1950s like Henry King's *The Gunfighter* (1950), Nicholas Ray's *Johnny Guitar* (1954) and Delmer Daves' *The Hanging Tree* (1959) in using the western genre to expose contemporary problems besetting postwar America. It is not concerned with how the West was won, but more about the price one pays

for the exploitation of the land. While the film delivers a powerful message on civic responsibility and moral integrity, it also carries a second message in its theme of protest against reactionaries who use patriotism as an excuse for ritual murder and revenge. There is a direct analogy to the use of the blacklist in Hollywood. This analogy allows the film to explore the pathological traumas that arise when other members of the community, aware of the injustices, remain silent, held hostage by fear of reprisal. *Bad Day at Black Rock* is a contemporary western set in California. It depicts a returning World War II veteran attempting to bestow an honor on a soldier who died in action. This unexpected visit brings the town back from its self-imposed isolation. The veteran, portrayed by Spencer Tracy, then discovers those very reactionary forces that are hostile to his life and others.

Sturges continued his interest in reconstructing action adventures with western locations with a retelling of *Gunfight at the O.K. Corral* (1957), then adapting Kurosawa's *The Seven Samurai* (1954) into *The Magnificent Seven* (1960). Later in the 1960s he turned his attention to Cold War strategies in his provocative adaptation of Alistair MacLean's thriller, *Ice Station Zebra* (1968).

References

Mast, Gerald. 1982. "Burstyn v. Wilson." In *The Movies in Our Midst: Documents in the Cultural History of Film in America*. Edited by Gerald Mast. Chicago: The University of Chicago Press, pp. 614–620.

Sklar, Robert. 1975. *Movie-Made America: A Cultural History of American Movies*. New York: Random House.

Warshow, Robert. 1966. "The Westerner." In *Film: An Anthology*. Edited By Daniel Talbot. Berkeley: University of California Press, pp. 148–162

CHAPTER 15

Symbolist Traditions in the Cinema: 1950s–1970s

Introduction

Ingmar Bergman became the most prodigious stage and film director in Sweden during the 1950s, gaining international status with his metaphysical film narratives on the nature of being in a Godless world. Instead of continuing the Romantic, imaginary, or subjective interpretations of the world as earlier Swedish and German Expressionist films had done, Bergman preferred to have his central characters face existence phenomenologically. In *The Seventh Seal* and *Wild Strawberries*, Bergman questions the values of life in a postwar world unconcerned with human suffering. His films advance the psychic realities found in the symbolist dramas of Ibsen and Strindberg, utilizing, at times, surreal dream imagery to project the strangeness of a meaningless world. This existential reexamination frees the individual from dehumanizing constructs that alienate one's feelings and creativity. Bergman's later films of the 1960s consider the difficulty of interpersonal communication and the role of the artist in projecting images of reality. As Andrew Sarris notes, "If modern man must live without the faith that makes death meaningful, he can at least endure life with the aid of certain necessary illusions."

Buñuel takes an atheistic approach to a world indifferent to human sufferings. His Catholic upbringing and a lifelong association with the Surrealist movement find expression through the use of dream sequences and surreal images in all his films. His Surrealist vision disrupts modern reason with manifestations of unconscious desires that appear in hopes of regenerating the spirit of human beings trapped by outworn ideologies and rituals. As a Spanish director, Buñuel's desire is to circumvent rational or positivist thinking by placing his major characters within a series of chance situations that compel them to violate all bourgeois morality.

The Existentialist Cinema of Ingmar Bergman

The cinematic work of Ingmar Bergman (b. 1918) concentrates upon the effects on his characters of a metaphysical disorder caused by a psychological fall from grace and salvation. His films explore this human condition through existentialist themes of doubt, guilt and alienation in a postwar world indifferent to human suffering. This problem becomes the focus of the dramatic conflict in his films. Bergman's screenplays gain their dramatic intensity from the attempts of their central characters to restore a spiritual foundation to life when confronted by an existence without meaning. Bergman's films of the 1950's, *Det Sjunde Inseglet / The Seventh Seal* (1957), *Smultronstället / Wild Strawberries* (1957) and *Ansiktet / The Magician*, also titled *The Face* (1958), reveal three consistent themes in his work: the symbolic use of visual imagery as corresponding metaphors to illuminate the psychic condition of mankind; the depiction of emotional crises in which one's inquiry into the meaning of existence becomes dependent upon personal acts of love; and a critical attack on rational thought and hypocrisy in institutions which negate a person's freedom. Bergman's later films, such as *Persona,* reveal a different cinematic style to reflect the irony of motion pictures and the necessity of role-playing to help one establish an understanding of one's being or identity.

Bergman draws upon the existentialist thought of the French novelist and philosopher Jean-Paul Sartre. Sartre claims that human reason alone is inadequate to explain the enigma of the universe. The significant fact is that people and things, in general, exist but they have no meaning for us except when we create meaning through acts of engagement. Various strategies of being are devised in adopting roles, even multiple ones, to help define our relationships to ourselves and to others. But there is an irony in this activity, for it neither defines one's purposefulness nor helps one arrive at an understanding of one's being or self. In his first novel, *La Nausée* (1938), Sartre's protagonist, an historian, realizes that the external world is a mass of solid "brutal facts" in which experience tells us "what-is" is what we appear to perceive. Further, he realizes that individual existence cannot be comprehended if systems of thought and institutions become a set of rational functions and obligations that force out the consciousness of one's own being. Sartre argues that these conceptual systems about the universe blind the individual to what the world really is like. One easily loses sight of oneself by accepting a social duty to some stereotyped role or concept that one happens to adopt or employ.

Sartre's Existentialism also recognizes the contingency of human existence as part of the unpredictability of the universe. He states that human existence is dependent on chance happenings or uncertain conditions for being. For him, to exist is simply *to be there*, but following logic, existence is not a necessity. There is a moment of existence when one reflecting on one's situation does not allow oneself to be absorbed into functions and duties set up or constructed by society, thus avoiding being cast into a particular role. When a person is engaged or trapped in an unforeseen event or happening, accidental and contingent upon other events of chance, a dilemma of engagement is curtailed by duties to societal goals. When one disengages oneself from past history and disconnects oneself from previous social duties and functions, then one can be free to choose what is of value for one's future. For Sartre, human beings who exist for themselves have a consciousness and freedom to chose whether or not to be caught in a cultural structure or system that will determine their actions. Therefore, the existentialist thoughts of Sartre bring forth a subjective, self-creating person who initially is not endowed with a character or goals, but must choose them by acts of pure chance or irrationality, since each individual must decide what is of personal value (Passmore 1970, pp. 491–492).

INGMAR BERGMAN'S
EARLY CHILDHOOD

In a recent interview Bergman recalled a number of influences that he identifies with his family and the world of childhood. He stated that his parents were "sealed in iron casks of duty," his mother running a meticulous household in the Swedish university city of Uppsala for his father, a Lutheran pastor who was chaplain to the Royal Swedish court. The severe conditions of his upbringing in the vicarage gave Bergman an early acquaintance with the conflicts between faith and doubt that appear to be analogous to those of the 19th century existentialist Danish theologian Søren Kierkegaard (1813–1855), who wrote *Fear and Trembling*, a series of books on what it meant to be a Christian. Bergman vividly recalls these childhood memories in his discussion of filmmaking:

> A child who is born and brought up in a vicarage acquires an early familiarity with life and death behind the scenes. Father performed funerals, marriages, baptisms, gave advice and prepared sermons. The devil was an early acquaintance, and in the childmind there was a need to personify him. This is where my magic lantern came in. It consisted of a small metal box with a carbide lamp — I can still remember the smell of the hot metal — and colored glass slides: Red Riding Hood and the Wolf, and

all the others. And the Wolf was the Devil, without horns but with a tail and gaping red mouth, strangely real yet incomprehensible, a picture of wickedness and temptation on the flowered wall of the nursery [Bergman 1970, pp. 6–7, 12].

At the age of ten, Bergman received a toy film projector, and he describes how the film images continued to mystify and fascinate him:

> This little rickety machine was my first conjuring set. And even today I remind myself with childish excitement that I am really a conjurer, since cinematography is based on deception of the human eye. When I show a film I am guilty of deceit. I use an apparatus which is constructed to take advantage of a certain human weakness, with which I can sway my audience in a highly emotional manner — make them laugh, scream with fright, believe in fairy stories, feel shock, be charmed, deeply moved or yawn with boredom [Bergman 1970, p. 12].

INGMAR BERGMAN'S THEATRICAL BACKGROUND

Bergman's film career followed directly from his theatre studies at the University of Stockholm, where he directed productions of Shakespeare and Strindberg at several local theatres. He also wrote novels, plays and filmscripts usually fashioned as Strindbergian chamber dramas. His script *Hets / Torment* (1944) was made into a successful film by his mentor, Alf Sjöberg, and began a renaissance in Swedish filmmaking, bringing Swedish films into international prominence. Bergman scripted and directed his first film, *Kris / Crisis*, in 1945. He continued his theatrical career at that time directing for municipal theatres such plays as Camus' *Caligula*, Tennessee Williams' *Streetcar Named Desire* and in 1948, Sartre's *No Exit*. Bergman's next filmscript, *Fängelse / Prison* (1948), reflected his exposure to the existentialist themes of Camus and Sartre. These films and plays take as their central theme the plight of an individual becoming or seen to be a rebel or loner, unable to conform to oppressive codes of school or an

adult society. Bergman adopted an expressionist film noir style to visualize a dark and traumatic environment that threatened the psychological security of his characters caught in a conflict between an absurd world and their own emotional needs. These early films focused on troubled adolescents and their awareness of their being-in-the-world, their sexuality and the "vicissitudes of passion" in relationships with others.

Bergman's childhood film experiences of illusionism are resurrected in a number of his films, sometimes becoming surrealistic in their dream-like powers to confront the central character, like demonic visitations of Death. In *The Magician*, a nightmarish exploration into the act of conjuring and deception in the 19th century, Bergman portrays the magician-mesmerist casting images upon a wall thrown by a magic lantern for a dying actor. The major confrontation is between this conjurer and a scientist. In *Persona* (1966), Bergman repeatedly demonstrates the way projected images create believable illusions in place of what is actual. This ambiguity becomes the major struggle of the actress in her attempts to find an authentic self instead of playacting.

Bergman uses cinema as a creative art form in his quest to reveal the nature of being and reality. Creative filmmaking for Bergman acknowledges the deep psychological drives of each character in a symbolic I-Thou relationship that defines the character in terms of the other. In *Persona*, the nurse, Alma, attempts to relate herself to the actress, but fails. The film orchestrates mental states of being in which games of chance occurrences express the tensions and complications of life itself. From these chance experiences of life evolve questions of being and the nature of existence in an authoritarian and patriarchal Christian society.

Bergman's films of the 1950s continually deal with the existentialist quest to find meaning in life when confronted with Nothingness in all its guises, whether as an apprehension of emptiness, a sense of meaninglessness or sorrow or tragedy. This occurs when the aged professor, Isak Borg, awakens from a premonition of death that spurs him on to reflect upon the meaning of his life in *Wild Strawberries*. Bergman's films also explore the predicament of humanity searching for some hope, meaning and purpose in a modern world that has lost faith and security in its own ethical foundations. His characters substitute role-playing for authentic being to avoid terrifying experiences of inner life. Bergman focuses his dark and disturbing narratives on some psychic breakdown of his central character with commonly held beliefs and understandings with a parallel breakdown in personal communication between lovers, or within a family group. These powerful breakdowns catch the characters unaware, and reflect the personal torment and anguish suffered in losing one's sense of identity or being faced with the absurdities of life.

BERGMAN'S FIRST TRILOGY

Bergman's early trilogy of films beginning with *Sommarlek / Summer Interlude* (1951), *Sommaren med Monika / Monika* (1952) and *Gycklarnas Afton / The Naked Night* (or *Sawdust and Tinsel*, 1953) features ill-matched lovers whose marriage is depicted as a futile attempt for them to realize their sexual dreams and desires. They only find that such an alliance leads to mutual destruction. In these films Bergman contrasts a character's subjective state of mind with the outer world, cinematically through dream episodes or flashbacks, as interruptions into a couple's dreary everyday reality. This state of mind becomes a sexual and emotional projection of the other person by the character to counteract the individual's publicly assigned role. *The Naked Night* was influenced by E. A. Dupont's *Variety*, a German Expressionist film of the 1920s. Bergman uses the same metaphor of the circus as a series of acts that men and women perform to carry out their own sexual fantasies and desires. (A similar fantasy reappears in Wim Wenders' *Der Himmel über Berlin / Wings of Desire* (1987) when an angel reappears in human form to help a lonely trapeze artist).

In *The Naked Night* Bergman's sense of theatre comes to the fore with a dramatic visual style that corresponds to a symbolist mode of expression, linking the *spiritual* world with *natural* world. Bergman uses a film noir lighting approach, by contrasting rich black shadows with high-key pastoral scenes. Actors may play scenes totally in shadow or in silhouette against an illuminated background. Interior sets in the film are always dark and low-key with foreboding shadows lacing the walls. This constant visual opposition of light and dark areas allows the small areas of light to appear surrounded by a darkness always threatening to overwhelm the actors. As part of his chamber cinema to exploit a rich suggestiveness of images, Bergman uses deep focus photography for a *mise-en-scène* that creates an analogous world that is never stable or secure. It appears off-balance, ready to change drastically and in some ways, unexpectedly. Bergman constantly uses framing devices such as doors, windows, stairways, bedframes or cast shadows to separate characters from each other or from one world and another. Camera movements are sparingly used while editing is done for an effective ellipsis from a close-up to a long shot quickly bridging space and time.

THE SECOND TRILOGY

In the late 1950s, Bergman directed a trio of films that concern the role of religion in his thinking and filmmaking. As a clergyman's son, Bergman finds that "religious problems are continuously alive. I never cease to concern myself with them; yet this does not take place on the emotional level, but on an intellectual one. Religious emotion, religious sentimentality, is something I got rid of long ago" (Bergman 1970, p. 12).

The Seventh Seal is a modern allegory set in medieval times in which Bergman tries to exorcise his religious doubts through the character of Antonius Block, an archetypal Knight returning home from the Crusades. As an intellectual, the Knight has lost his innocence and unquestioning faith in the tenets of Christianity. His homecoming is marred by his encounter with Death and a deadly plague overrunning his country. The Knight wrestles with

Max von Sydow, as a returning knight from the Crusades, is challenged to a game of chess by Death as a plague spreads over the land and Judgment Day nears in Ingmar Bergman's *The Seventh Seal* (1957).

symbolic shadows as he seeks some proof of God's existence that will furnish a reason for human suffering and death. His squire Jöns provides an answer. He simply states that God does not exist and the universe is absurd. His commitment is to his Knight, a code of chivalry, and the pleasures of the flesh. He is not a doubting Thomas, nor a questioner of the nature of life; he accepts life as it is and becomes a man of action, satisfying his own needs. Only when Death becomes a certain victor in the game of life does the doomed Knight's quest for meaning turn upon a search for life-sustaining values. His commitment to life and his compassion for others will, one hopes, allow him to perform one significant act of faith that restores a sense of purpose to his life. As his final act, he alerts Josef and his fam-

ily to the coming danger awaiting them in the forest and forestalls their deaths.

As Mast and Kawin (1996, p. 398) note, the game of chess becomes the visual metaphor running through the narrative, a life and death struggle between the Knight and Death. Throughout this match, Bergman raises questions about faith, God, death and salvation, showing the Knight defeated, and knowing that these questions cannot be answered.

In *Wild Strawberries*, Bergman's film narrative deals with a retired doctor and professor confronting his fear of death. In a series of flashbacks, reveries and surrealistic dream sequences, Bergman takes the viewer on a psychic journey with the professor as he relives past experiences that have contributed to his present state of being. The absorption in his

In Ingmar Bergman's *Wild Strawberries* (1957), a family doctor (Victor Sjöström) listens to a young hitch-hiker and recalls his own early loves en route to a college town to receive an academic award.

own psychic past reveals those chance moments of self-discovery that caused his estrangement from his wife and family and the austerity of his relationships. Time and memory reveal a man trapped in a sterile past of duty and obligation. An existential quest, initiated by his daughter-in-law, forces the professor to recognize the death-in-life existence he has led. The film's car journey parallels his confrontation with a dream-like double to reveal the causes of the professor's estrangement from life itself. Again, like the Knight, the professor chooses to make a new commitment to life to affirm the lives of his immediate family. But this compassionate act, while concluding the drama, still does not resolve the metaphysical anguish and despair arising from the paradox of existence.

Bergman's film *The Magician* (1958) again takes us on a journey into a dark and brooding land full of Gothic visions of the uncanny and the macabre. Bergman presents a psycho-spiritual world haunted by illusions and doubts.

The magician, Vogler, is a man without faith. He appears to have a dual identity, first as a practicing doctor using Mesmer's hypnotic practices and then as a magician who creates deceptive images and illusions. He is confronted by a scientist, Vergerus, who tries to prove Vogler a charlatan without any healing powers. Again this confrontation provides Bergman with an opportunity to compare the mysteries of life within the limited meanings of language. The possible allegorical relation to Christ, regarding His ability to heal the sick, and His powers to provoke visions are suggested by Bergman. In this drama, illusion and deceit on the one hand compete with a cold, emotionless science on the other. The power of silence does not negate questions on the history of being nor can it avoid the hostility and violence of those in power.

In the 1960s, Bergman's third great trilogy of films included *Persona* (1966), *Vargtimmen / Hour of the Wolf* (1968) and *Skammen / Shame*

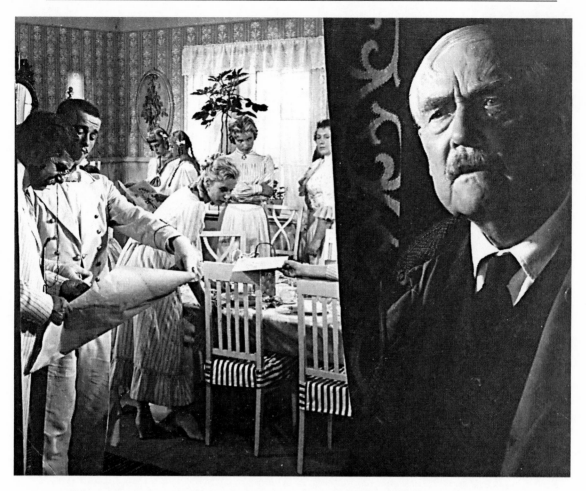

In *Wild Strawberries*, the doctor is seen revisiting a luncheon party at the family's summer cottage, where he hears about the amorous actions of his sweetheart toward his own brother.

(1968). Each film explores themes directly associated with The Theatre of the Absurd on the difficulty of human communication, a person's loss of identity and the isolation of the individual. *Persona* follows Bergman's *Tystnaden / Silence* (1963) on the tortured sexuality of two women trapped in an unknown city. In *Persona,* an actress withdraws into a world of silence, perhaps in search of her own identity. *Hour of the Wolf* is a parable, with nightmarish creatures haunting the imagination of an artist. In *Shame* Bergman gives the viewer an apocalyptic vision of war that destroys the beliefs and values of a husband and wife living a sheltered existence on a remote island. These films share some of the existentialist views of the human condition, making all actions in life senseless and useless: in a word, absurd.

Mythmaking and Narratives

In the light of Jean-Paul Sartre's postwar Existentialism, Luis Buñuel brings forward a pessimism in each of his films toward any chance encounter that would alleviate the human condition. As a Surrealist filmmaker, he asks how it is possible for a person to avoid the unconscious desires and obligations already demanded by the culture in which he or she lives. How can one avoid being cast into a particular role? While Buñuel depicts the isolation of his characters trapped in unforeseen events, accidental and contingent upon other events of chance, his films raise the moral dilemma of social intercourse being diminished by repressive religious or political conventions based upon given societal myths. Buñuel's films thus attempt to display the impossibility of disengaging oneself from history except through suicide. On the other hand, Sartre believes it is possible to disconnect oneself from previous social duties and functions, so that one can be free to choose what is of value for one's future. Yet for Buñuel, it is the very nature of the bourgeois imagination that "wants to keep reality without keeping the appearances: it is therefore the very negativity of bourgeois appearance, infinite like every negativity which solicits myth infinitely" (Barthes 1972, p. 149). If Sartre seeks emancipation or liberty, and hopes of transforming society as a choice open to the oppressed, the myth of the oppressor is theatrical, where the style is "rich, subtle, with all the possible degrees of dignity at its disposal" (p. 149). It is within the given codes and conventions of this myth that Buñuel depicts his surrealist world view in attempts to reconcile a binary opposition of the ideal and universal with the personal and immediate circumstance. Here Buñuel chooses to depict the various forms of sexual deviance, perversion and violence that come into play, exposing bourgeois hypocrisy and decadence.

Buñuel knows that every film narrative is a work of fiction that constructs ways of seeing and thinking. Narratives also demand a structure that organizes events into sequences of time, defining the site where one acts out one's place in society, a position that one accepts as natural. It is within his narratives that Buñuel chooses to move into cinematic techniques that expose physical reality in a harsh, documentary, neorealist style while representing his characters engaging in intense experiences of social and political intercourse. These are his ways of representing reality in an imaginary

In Ingmar Bergman's **Persona** (1966), Liv Ullmann (right) plays an actress who suffers a breakdown and refuses to communicate with others. Bibi Andersson, as the nurse, tends to her silence with her own tales of woe.

form. The French Marxist philosopher Louis Althusser argues that in the dominant ideology people are represented not by their real conditions of existence, but in an imaginary relationship. Buñuel exploits this distinction by reconstructing past events in his films, where he can challenge the dominance of this ideology against an imaginary account of that reality as a truth.

Roland Barthes (1974) contends that everything in a narrative is functional, "everything in it signifies; 'art is without noise' detaching art from life, the latter knowing only 'fuzzy' and 'blurred' communications. Art is a system which is pure, no unit ever goes wasted" (pp. 89–90). Barthes also believes that "if everything in the narrative signifies, it does so at the level of myth." He argues that bourgeois society exists today through the various associations assigned to each and every rhetorical figure it uses as it displaces History by Ideology. The power of ideology constantly performs as an interpellative force that attempts to eternalize norms itself by becoming mythic, i.e. being accepted as a common-sense, ordinary way of seeing. Myth, for Barthes, "turns history into nature" (1972, p. 129).

Luis Buñuel's *Los Olvidados* (1950) is a caustic account of poverty, juvenile delinquency and sexual obsessions drawn from the modern slums of Mexico City. Here an older blind man is stoned by a gang of youths set on robbing him, displaying the mercenary and venal side of human nature.

Buñuel's Films of the 1960s and 1970s

After surviving the vicissitudes of the Spanish Civil War and the fascist dictatorship of Franco, Buñuel started his second phase of filmmaking in Mexico, where he sought refuge with many other Spanish intellectuals in 1946. His daring exposé of shanty towns in Mexico City, *Los Olvidados / The Lost Ones / The Young and the Damned* (1950), followed a neorealist style interspersed with powerful dream sequences. The film won Buñuel a best director award in Cannes and international acclaim and acceptance in Paris. The film reflects the influence of Vittorio De Sica's *Shoeshine* with its focus on young children living in poverty in the slums of Mexico City. The scenario involves a caustic account of a socio-political situation emphasizing the cruelty and violence of juvenile gangs with a precise depiction of their own inner dreams and sexual desires. From this film, certain psychological truths about the human condition are depicted which Buñuel explores in his continuing commitment to a surreal narrative.

In 1960, Buñuel's aggressive, surreal views on the mores of the Catholic church found resonance upon his invitation to return to Spain to direct *Viridiana* (1961). Having won the full cooperation of Franco's fascist authorities, Buñuel sets out to retell the story of St. Viridiana, a young nun, who brings her own idealistic pride and Christian charity with her when

Luis Buñuel's *Belle de jour* (1967) stars Catherine Deneuve as a married woman who decides to spend her afternoons in a high-class brothel. Another Buñuelian surreal comedy on the relationship of one's desire to reality.

she visits her widowed uncle and tries to turn his estate into a sanctuary for the poor. However, her uncle is struck by the likeness of Viridiana to his former wife, and asks her to don a wedding dress, which she does. He then drugs her to evoke the lustful memories of his bridal night. When his seduction fails, he turns to suicide. His death brings about the arrival of his illegitimate son, who moves in and begins to improve the property. Viridiana then finds her efforts at charity cannot control the beggars who respond by becoming greedy, selfish and cruel. With the famous parody of Leonardo da Vinci's *Last Supper*, Buñuel depicts the drunken beggars committing lewd acts, including Viridiana's rape and another beggar's murder, as they attempt to pillage the estate. When order is restored, Viridiana's idealistic illusions are

shattered and she renounces the convent. She is then invited to join her cousin and his wife in a three-handed card game as a new ritual of married life, a *ménage à trois*.

In *Le Journal d'une femme de chambre / Diary of a Chambermaid* (1963), Buñuel cast Jeanne Moreau as Célestine, a beautiful but ambitious young woman who takes a position in an aristocratic manor house full of eccentric and decadent aristocrats. Again, eroticism is the wellspring of the various games Célestine plays to manipulate the desires of three older men who reside in or next to the estate. Her relationship to the bestial gamekeeper, Joseph, becomes the focus of her attention after he rapes and kills a little girl in contempt, not lust. To avenge this death, Célestine seduces Joseph and betrays him to the police. Throughout this

In Luis Buñuel's *That Obscure Object of Desire* (1977), an older man lusts after an attractive young woman, but is frustrated in his attempts to achieve sexual fulfillment. Connecting sexual drives with random guerrilla violence gives Buñuel the opportunity to expose the religious, social, and political dogmas that distort and destroy human relationships.

power struggle, the contrary impulses to control and dominate in a fascistic manner are played out, with sexual aggression but a physical side of political aggression and fetishism.

In *Belle de jour* (1967), Buñuel continues his study of female desire in his adaptation of a Joseph Kessel novel, a comic fantasy on the immorality and degeneracy of bourgeois marriage. The film depicts the erotic fantasies of Séverine, a beautiful but strange wife, played by Catherine Deneuve, who decides to engage in humiliating sexual encounters with a variety of characters to atone for her inner fantasy life. During the afternoons she visits an upscale brothel and engages in sexual fantasies with a depraved Duke, a gangster with whom she falls in love, and an Asian client with a mysterious erotic box; all becoming unquenchable objects of desire. The film continues on a double level where it is difficult to separate the real world

from the imaginary one until the end, when Buñuel fuses them together. Even then, the ending is ambiguous when the husband rises from his wheelchair. As a study in female sexuality, *Belle de jour* depicts the erotic fantasies of a woman seeking expiation from her inner feelings of moral crisis.

With the success of *Belle de jour*, Buñuel directed three films that are thematically linked to the empty rituals of bourgeois ideology, and that relate sexual repression with terrorism and violence. Beginning with *Le Charme discret de la bourgeoisie / The Discreet Charm of the Bourgeoisie* (1972), Buñuel uses film techniques to enter various bourgeois dreams that appear as a continuation of daily life, and introduces the play of chance to change their outcomes. Each film plays upon *l'amour fou*, provoking an object of desire for each male character.

The Discreet Charm of the Bourgeoisie depicts

what happens when the guests at a dinner party are given a chance to speak their minds whatever the consequences. Thus language disrupts the social reality of the ruling class as the partygoers find themselves confused and frustrated by their own social codes of conduct. Switching roles is part of the narrative in this comic satire in which everyone realizes that one's unconscious thoughts are incomprehensible, with a myriad of sexual associations suggested. In this poetic rendering of socialites trapped in their own fantasies, Buñuel plays illusion against reality as sexual violence erupts to erase the boredom of bourgeois existence.

Le Fantôme de la liberté / The Phantom of Liberty (1974) continues the abortive attempts of bourgeois society members to reconcile or even humanize their own lives as they battle with the rules of logical thinking. Buñuel depicts scene after scene where his characters attempt to communicate with each other only to find they are lost in their own rituals. An inn serves as a place for chance encounters with such people as friars, a sadomasochistic couple, and a young man with his older aunt. Buñuel easily interconnects the various narratives to show that such persons cannot perceive the world they live in without the mental filters of Christian morality. Although there is irony in the film, there also is a pessimism holding any hope for "freedom" as just another illusion.

Buñuel's last film is a combination of surreal fantasy within a romantic satire that becomes a study in frustration amid the outbreak of terrorist bombings perpetuated by the Revolutionary Army of the Infant Jesus, (R.A.I.J).

Cet Obscur Objet du désir / That Obscure Object of Desire (1977) is an intimate study of an older man enamored with a young woman, Conchita, who deliberately takes advantage of his desire to possess her. As a running gag, Conchita frustrates his sexual strategies by switching roles, first amorous, then cool and rebellious, as she enjoys her sadistic games with her lover. Christian terrorism also surfaces as a corresponding object of desire, as a secret revolutionary sect undertakes various forms of social and political acts that couple sex and violence, however mysteriously encoded by the R.A.I.J. (Colina and Turrent 1992, pp. 170–232).

References

Barthes, Roland. 1972. *Mythologies.* Translated by Annette Lavers. New York: Granada.

_____. 1974. *S/Z.* Translated by Richard Miller. New York: Hill and Wang.

Bergman, Ingmar. 1970. *Wild Strawberries: A Film.* Translated by Lars Malmstrom and David Kushner. New York: Simon & Schuster.

_____. 1988. *The Magic Lantern: An Autobiography.* Translated by Joan Tate. London: Hamish Hamilton.

Colina, Jose De La, and Tomás Pérez Turrent. 1992. *Objects of Desire: Conversations with Luis Buñuel.* Edited and translated by Paul Lenti. New York: Marsilio Publishers.

Mast, Gerald, and Bruce F. Kawin. 1996. *A Short History of the Movies.* 6th. ed. Boston and London: Allyn and Bacon.

Passmore, Golen. 1970. *A Hundred Years of Philosophy.* Baltimore: Penguin Books, Inc.

CHAPTER 16

The French New Wave, Part One: 1957–1968

Introduction

The next two chapters focus on the historic importance of the New Wave (*nouvelle vague*), a radical film movement that changed the way we think about and understand film narratives as an art form and cultural construct. The movement was initiated by a young, talented group of French film critics, namely, François Truffaut, Jean-Luc Godard, Claude Chabrol, Eric Rohmer and Jacques Rivette, whose first feature films in 1959 revolutionized film production in Western Europe. Their improvisational approach to acting, directing and scriptwriting followed the documentary techniques of filmmakers like Jean Rouch, Alain Resnais and Chris Marker, using handheld cameras, on-location shooting, and small crews. As writers and directors they followed André Bazin's concept of the long take and *mise-en-scène*. The unifying principle behind these films was French Existentialism, in which they expressed a personal vision of the world. They merged this philosophy with the dramatic theories of Bertolt Brecht. The New Wave displaced the postwar French commercial cinema, the Tradition of Quality, in which studio writers adapted novels into filmscripts to produce a cinema of "psychological realism."

The Influence of French Existentialism on the New Wave

During the postwar years French Existentialism, through the writings of Jean-Paul Sartre and Albert Camus, became part of a significant philosophical reflection on the nature of being and the absurdity of the human condition. Sartre and Camus proposed a concept of human freedom based upon the possibility of a deliberate and conscious choice in which the actions of human beings are not limited or determined by powerful cultural forces. On the contrary, it is the experiential choices they make that fully bring whatever endowments they have into being. "Man is a self-creating being who is not initially endowed with a character and goals," notes Sartre, "but must choose them by acts of pure decision ... [and make] existential leaps into being" (Sartre 1943). Contrary to Plato, Sartre places one's existence before the idea of essence. By acknowledging that people are temporal beings conscious of their own mortality, a person must strive to live *authentically* with the understanding of this fact as leading to a person's own ultimate destiny.

These concepts were born out of the philosophers' own experiences during the French struggle against German occupation during World War II. For some documentary French filmmakers such as Alain Resnais, Georges Franju and Alexandre Astruc, it was necessary to depict on film these atrocities, symbolically or otherwise, if only to document them. This political commitment to documentary filmmaking began with the early short documentaries of Georges Franju (1912–1987), the co-founder of the Cinémathèque Française with Henri Langlois. His *Les Sang des bêtes / The Blood of the Beasts* (1949) is a surreal documentary on a

Alain Resnais in *Last Year at Marienbad* (1961) uses shots of gardens and statues of a hotel where remembrances of times past confuse time present.

Paris slaughterhouse that becomes an allegory of the Nazis and their butchery of French Resistance fighters. His other short films, one on Georges Méliès, the other on Madame Curie, deconstruct myths about heroism and heroes. His first feature film, *La Tête contre les murs / The Keepers* (1958), a partly surreal documentary on the French insane asylums, is cited as a forerunner of New Wave attacks on traditional institutions and structures that Michel Foucault revisits in his account of mental institutions in *Madness and Civilization* (1965/1981).

Alain Resnais (b. 1922) is another important documentary filmmaker to influence the New Wave filmmakers and critics. His early work included short documentary films about Van Gogh and Gauguin. In *Nuit et brouillard / Night and Fog* (1955), he interweaves past with present in a political documentary on Nazi concen-

tration camps. Resnais uses brief, almost subliminal, flash cuts as a method to pursue the effects of time and memory and how they play upon our present sense of reality. A somber voice-over narration throughout the film leads to his warning for viewers to remember the horrors of the death camps. His meditations on the effects of time upon memories and how we perceive them became the theme of his first feature film, *Hiroshima, mon amour* (1959), followed by *L'Année dernière à Marienbad / Last Year at Marienbad* (1962) whose intersection of past and present affects our sense of the future. These themes are taken up by another documentary filmmaker, Chris Marker (b. 1921). In his science-fiction short, *La Jetée / The* Pier (1962), we become involved in a time-travel adventure of a man revisiting his past only to discover his own death. In *Le Joli Mai* (1963) Marker focuses upon

Impersonal relations between lovers, indicated by long tracking shots of empty corridors and outdoor vistas, disorient the viewer trying to sort out the flashbacks and present-day actions in *Last Year at Marienbad*.

the political strife in Parisian life as he mixes present time with fading memories. Resnais and Marker and other documentary filmmakers were part of the Left Bank group associated with the New Wave, but were committed to a more existential approach to documentary films.

Alexandre Astruc (b. 1923) championed the *direct cinéma* style of Franju and Resnais. He expressed his critical thoughts on filmmaking in his 1948 essay, "The Birth of a New Avant-Garde: La Camera-Stylo" (camera-pen). According to Astruc, this new cinema would "gradually break free from the tyranny of what is visual, from the image for its own sake, from the immediate and concrete demands of the narrative, to become a means of writing just as flexible and subtle as written language" (Astruc, quoted in Graham 1968, p. 18).

By breaking away from a traditional narrative technique, and more into a surreal stream-of-consciousness approach, the director would use the camera as a pen to express his own thoughts and ideas independent of a given scenario, as opposed to adopting a style from literature or the theatre. This "writing with the camera" would see filmmaking as a spontaneous happening, in which the director would face the problems of expressing ideas and thoughts through the very activity of filmmaking. Using this cinematic technique, Astruc believed young French filmmakers would be able to find a personal style and form of expression comparable to a written language. Thus, they could discover a new audiovisual language that abandoned the classical style of montage editing and linear narration. This new cinema would give the filmmaker the status of author, or *auteur*, since the mode of filmmaking investigated natural phenomena according to the director's personal attitude and beliefs. As a film style, it would emphasize the use of the "long-take" and *mise-en-scène*.

The French New Wave Directors, 1956–1968

The critical comments of Alexandre Astruc on a personal, first-person filmmaking technique were advanced by André Bazin (1918–1958) in the influential film journal *Cahiers du Cinéma* which he founded as *La Revue du Cinéma* with Jacques Doniol-Valcroze in 1951. The term to describe this filmmaking practice became known as the *politique des auteurs,* and was defined by Bazin in his own essay as follows:

> The *politique des auteurs* consists, in short, of choosing the personal factor in artistic creation as a standard of reference, and then of assuming that it continues and even progresses from one film to the next. It is recognized that there do exist certain important films of quality that escape this test, but these will systematically be considered inferior to those in which the personal stamp of the *auteur,* however run-of-the-mill the scenario, can be perceived even minutely [Bazin, quoted in Graham 1968, p. 151].

Under the guidance of Bazin, a group of young writers and critics who wanted to become filmmakers began studying film at the Cinémathèque Française. This film theatre was founded by Georges Franju and Henri Langlois in 1937 as a film archive designed to promote film study and film culture. After the war, André Malraux, the Minister of Culture, provided funds to maintain the collection and provide public screenings of the experimental silent French films of the 1920s and the sound films of the 1930s, especially films directed by Jean Vigo, Abel Gance and Jean Renoir. Besides these classical French films, American films of the 1930s and 1940s, particularly those of Alfred Hitchcock, Nicholas Ray and Howard Hawks, also were screened.

Another important influence on the development of these film critics was Roberto Rossellini (see Chapter 11), who became their film mentor. They followed his advice and made their own independent short films, using his semidocumentary techniques including on-location shooting, nonprofessional actors and lightweight 16mm cameras, and remembered his dictum to show people as they are. Godard made *Tous les garçons s'appellent Patrick / All the Boys Are Named Patrick* (1957), Truffaut directed *Les Mistons / The Mischief Makers* (1958) and Chabrol produced and directed *Le Beau Serge / Bitter Reunion* (1958).

The New Wave and Jean-Luc Godard

The French New Wave was a provocative exploration into commercial cinema at a time when film that relied on traditional stage techniques was seen as a sterile creative movement. The personal styles of these young critics of *Cahiers du Cinéma* challenged this "cinema de papa." They became filmmakers to examine the relationship of one's own identity with the role assigned by society. They followed two basic tenets emerging from *Cahiers du Cinéma* and André Bazin. One was the use of the long take, and a *mise-en-scène* that respected the unity of time and place, as opposed to montage. The second tenet related to the use of the camera as an instrument for personal expression as advocated by Alexandre Astruc. Thus universal themes on life, love and identity would receive a personal interpretation as a dialectical play between the representation of self in the cinema and in real life, a play between illusion and reality.

Jean-Luc Godard and François Truffaut practiced a *cinéma des auteurs*, calling attention to itself as cinema through the process of its own making. Thus, New Wave cinema becomes self-reflexive of filmmaking itself, unmasking the process of its own apparatus. These two directors advocated a freewheeling, improvised style that called attention to the cinematic tricks of filmmaking. They reveled in appropriating cinematic techniques from the silent films of the 1920s and the sound films of the 1930s. As Godard's cinematic anti-heroes rebel against the norms and conventions set up by a popular culture and consumerism, Truffaut's misfits try to understand the forces that repress individuality. The goal of their film experiments was to deal with the question of authenticity, and the coming together of an inner subjective consciousness within a social-political reality.

In this conscious intellectual striving, Godard and Truffaut not only borrowed from American B-movies but also drew upon the modernist tendencies of James Joyce, Bertolt Brecht and William Faulkner. Godard and Truffaut extended the experimental forms of the novel in their exploration of cinema as an art form as well as its role in education and communication. With these two young directors, Claude Chabrol, Eric Rohmer and Jacques Rivette also used a self-reflexive style to establish their roles as *auteurs*. As directors and screenwriters, they established various narrative strategies to explore the moral and social values in a changing existential world of contingency. In this world the personal experiences of life are often alienated by the depersonalizing forces of modern society. The problem is to unmask these forces and liberate oneself from their tyrannies.

The Influence of Bertolt Brecht

Bertolt Brecht (1898–1956) was a German dramatist and poet who developed an epic or narrative theatre during the late 1920s in Berlin. His theatre employed anti-illusionistic devices to break down the Aristotelian theatre of illusion, one based upon the theory of catharsis, an empathic identification by the spectator with the stage actor. This response purged the audience of its emotions of fear and pity created by the drama. Such dramas easily brought the audience under their spell, and it became anti-critical of the stage actions. "These powerful empathic responses depended upon stage illusion and served as mental foodstuffs, quickly enjoyed and consumed by the viewer, then forgotten" (Willett 1968, p. 172).

Brecht claimed that the function of theatre should be to challenge the cultural perceptions of the audience. It should communicate, not only provide entertainment. A theatre is a symbolic place where the audience should be made to think, to question and to become politically conscious of the contradictions behind the events taking place on stage. To insure that his dramas achieved the necessary critical detachment, Brecht advanced his theory of *Verfremdung,* translated as "distanciation" or "estrangement" and referred to as the V-effect. It does not mean alienating spectators in the sense of making them hostile to the play. According to Wright:

> *Verfremdung* is a mode of critical seeing that goes on within a process by which man identifies his objects. Further, it sets up a series of social, political and ideological interruptions that remind us that representations are not given but produced. Contrary to popular belief, *Verfremdung* does not do away with identification, but examines it critically, using the technique of montage which shows that no representation is fixed and final [Wright 1989, p. 19].

In 1948, after years in exile from Nazi Germany, Brecht returned to East Berlin, where he became director of the state-supported Berliner Ensemble. Here he directed his own plays, notably those written while he was living in the United States. During this period, Brecht decided to replace the term epic with the term dialectical to further his political awareness "that the spectator is never only at the receiving end of a representation, but is included in it" (Wright 1989, p. 19). He produced and directed three major plays that became world famous: *Mother Courage* (1941), *The Good Woman of Setzuan* (1943) and *The Caucasian Chalk Circle* (1955). In each drama, Brecht shows how his "dialectical" theatre, using the V-effect, discourages and agitates against audience identification with stage characters, thus helping the spectator to realize the parts they play in the fictional narrative itself.

For each of these plays, Brecht "developed a variety of effects to present his themes and motifs: songs, inserted texts, self-reference, and the self-presentation of characters." These effects were all designed to promote a new way of seeing, a new attitude to be shared between the stage and the audiences. Brecht's dramas aimed at "transforming 'fear' and 'pity' into a 'desire for knowledge' and a 'readiness to help'" (Wright

Anna Karina plays a prostitute in a series of Brechtian episodes detailing her lifestyle in Godard's *Vivre sa vie / My Life to Live* (1962).

Jean-Paul Belmondo and Jean Seberg as lovers strolling down the Champs-Élysées in *Breathless* (1959), directed by Jean-Luc Godard.

1989, p. 33). Brecht's techniques kept the audiences constantly aware that they were being presented with a report of past events. As historical reconstructions his plays openly declared the stage as just a stage, and not a place to be mistaken for the actual world itself. The main function of the enactment was to produce living illustrations that could foster a critical attitude in the audience in hopes of changing the powerful social, economic and historical forces operating upon people's lives.

For Brecht, the art of the drama was to place familiar things, attitudes and situations "into a new fresh and unfamiliar perspective so that the spectator is brought to look critically at what has been taken for granted" (Willett 1968, p. 177). Brecht points out that when the "natural" is made to look surprising or creates won-

derment, then audiences become discoverers of the relationships that exist between people and realize that nothing will seem inevitable. Brecht sought to demonstrate how his characters can develop and grow out of a social function. As that social function changes, so does the action and identity of the person. The idea he explores in his dramas is that nothing is fixed, that there is no absolute role or identity created that is unchangeable. His characters, through their actions and experiences, are in the act of becoming in association with their social and political functions.

In this context, Jean-Luc Godard, in his assimilation of Brechtian theatre, became the foremost experimenter of narrative form in the cinema. He constantly reminds us, as spectators, that we are watching a filmed reality, one that shares resemblances to actual life but is a constructed reality. Through the use of jump-cuts, elliptical editing, and the elimination of transitional scenes, Godard violates the invisible editing developed by film directors in the classical Hollywood style.

In its place he deliberately creates a self-reflexive cinema. This cinema, which appears to have temporal and spatial continuity through editing is, in reality, a very discontinuous process. In a radical departure from the narrative films of the past, Godard's films become a series of cinematic essays deconstructing the myths that control the social relations of people within modern industrial society.

In the early films of Godard and Truffaut, the central character is always trying to shed an assigned social role, especially in Truffaut's *400 Blows* and in Godard's *Vivre sa vie / My Life to Live* (1962). Further, as in Brechtian theatre, the New Wave films always pose this question: How will a given person act in a specified set of circumstances and conditions? Godard, like Brecht, reverses a psychological drama which focuses upon a character caught in a suspenseful Aristotelian plot with a narrative drama which concentrates on a character caught in a particular political situation. By showing a series of episodes, each detailing a different set of circumstances, the writer-director can place familiar characters into new or unfamiliar positions, thus contrasting episodes.

Further, Godard allows the non-literary elements, including the decor, the sound effects, the music and the *mise-en-scène*, to retain their autonomy. In this manner they enter into a dialectical relationship with characters in each episode. Godard uses these non-literary elements to their full extent as he demonstrates in *Breathless, My Life to Live*, and *Weekend* (1968). As cinematic techniques, the jump-cuts, slow fades and wipes, the use of titles, newspaper headlines, interviews and voice-overs interrupt the flow of the action and thus break the illusion of reality. In many cases, Godard used different sound effects either from a music score or actual sounds coming into the scene from the environment, to comment upon or contradict the mood of the scene.

À BOUT DE SOUFFLE / BREATHLESS

Breathless is the first feature film directed by Jean-Luc Godard. It is based upon an idea for a love story written by François Truffaut, but Godard scripted and edited the film. Godard dedicated *Breathless* to Monogram Pictures, a minor Hollywood studio that made B gangster movies. As a New Wave critic and filmmaker, Godard exploited this gangster-thriller model and its familiar plot to set up a self-reflexive cinema, making films about the process of making films.

When *Breathless* was first reviewed in the *New York Times* by Bosley Crowther in 1961, he criticized the sordidness of the love affair, and the fact that the key character, Michel, as portrayed by Jean-Paul Belmondo, was "an impudent, arrogant, sharp-witted and alarmingly amoral hood." He cited Jean Seberg's character, Patricia, as a "cold, self-defensive animal in a glittering, glib, irrational, heartless world." For Crowther, these two lovers were fearsome characters since their animalistic drives "were completely devoid of moral tone, and they were mainly concerned with eroticism, and the restless drives of a cruel young punk." But Crowther seems not to be aware that Michel was one of the first film antiheroes, the outsider from the fictions of Sartre and Camus, living immorally in an antisocial world.

The first close-ups of Michel show him reading a newspaper containing erotic photos of bathing beauties. By an association of his image with the newspaper images, we are led to believe that Michel is motivated or driven by lust. This sexual desire, called *l'amour fou* by the Surrealists, removes the person from any rational behavior. Michel is an anarchist who acts impulsively and irrationally. He models himself on movie-made gangsters like Bogart and Cagney to show his contempt for law and order. Michel has no qualms about committing petty crimes to obtain money, including a car theft, which accidentally leads to the death of a police officer.

It is the irrational nature of this character in an absurd world that interests Godard. As in a film noir, Godard creates tensions in *Breathless* as part of a gangster-thriller narrative whose male character is fated to "live dangerously to the end." In this fashion then, Godard can ask the audience a series of moral questions regarding the nature of contemporary society and its middle-class preoccupations with sex and wealth. As lovers, Michel and Patricia are trapped by different jobs in order to gain what they most desire. In fact, Michel steals cars to pay for their amorous activities. Patricia works for the *Herald Tribune* as a novice reporter, but she uses her sexuality to gain advantage over Michel and other men. Both in their own ways prostitute themselves, hoping to gain an economic edge in their obsessive love affair.

In his films made before May 1968, Godard turned to parables in a Brechtian manner to demonstrate the myriad problems of modern industrialized society. In *Une Étrange Aventure de Lemmy Caution / Alphaville* (1965), he devised a science-fiction thriller using film noir techniques to retell the legend of Orpheus and Eurydice. His major character, Lemmy Caution, becomes involved with Alpha 60, a master computer that controls a city where a show of human emotions is punishable by a firing squad. Again, the concern is with alienation in a technological world where human beings are robotized and dehumanized. *Weekend* is a more apocalyptic parable about a modern Garden of Eden turned into a monumental nightmare where the landscape becomes a highway of burning cars and corpses overrun by Maoist revolutionaries. Here the consumer society is reduced to savages engaged in rape, murder and cannibalism in order to survive.

After the May-June student riots in Paris in 1968, Godard immersed himself in a four-year collaboration with the Dziga-Vertov Group, making 11 agit-prop films. This work went mainstream in 1972, when he cast Jane Fonda and Yves Montand in *Tout va bien*, co-directed by Jean-Pierre Gorin. The characters are journalists committed to a revolutionary struggle. Using Brechtian techniques Godard examines the nature and uses of propaganda and the cultural packaging of capitalism throughout all media, especially television. In a second film, *A Letter to Jane* (1972), Godard explores the power of images through the use of Fonda's photograph found in the magazine *L'Express* and its impact on the Vietnam War. Godard turned to a television format to continue his rebel spirit to unmask the Victo-

rian melodrama and morality which he believes informs the social constructs of modern society and the world of cinematic "illusions."

Dudley Andrew:
"Breathless: Old as New"

Dudley Andrew's essay explores the decade of the 1950s, in which the cultural forces in postwar Europe underwent dramatic changes as found in New Wave filmmaking. Andrew describes the innovations in editing techniques Godard employs in *Breathless* to jolt the viewer as his camera moves from long-takes and pans to staccato jumps and quick cuts. These techniques give Godard the opportunity to explore the romantic possibilities of a world of contingency where chance, accident and random elements collide and play havoc with bourgeois traditions. Andrew analyzes the ways Godard incorporates many surrealist elements to fantasize sex and violence as examples of *l'amour fou*. The complementary emotions of fear and love become the irrational forces that bring the lovers together. Patricia even compares her involvement with Michel to the affair of Romeo and Juliet, lovers who are fascinated by their strange attraction to each other. The parodic elements are also presented in *Breathless* through an interview with a writer who discusses the politics of French and American women and their different concepts of love.

References

Andrew, Dudley (ed.). 1987. "Breathless: Old Is New." In *Breathless: Jean-Luc Godard, Director.* London: Rutgers University Press, pp. 3–20.

Godard, Jean-Luc. 1972. *Godard on Godard.* Translated and edited by Tom Milne. New York: Da Capo Press, Inc.

Graham, Peter (ed.). 1968. *The New Wave.* Garden City, N.Y.: Doubleday.

Sartre, Jean-Paul. 1943. *L'Être et le Néaut* (Gallimard). Translated by Hazel Barnes. *Being and Nothingness.* New York: Simon & Schuster, 1956.

Willett, John. 1968. *The Theatre of Brecht.* London: Methuen.

Wright, Elizabeth. 1989. *Postmodern Brecht.* London and New York: Routledge.

CHAPTER 17

The French New Wave, Part Two: 1959–1980

Introduction

The early films of François Truffaut (1932–1984) display his sense of rebellion against cinematic conventions, his joy of play, and his love of sexual relationships. His work as a critic for *Cahiers du Cinéma,* with Godard and Bazin, led him to reevaluate the history and aesthetic of cinema. His *Politique des Auteurs* argued for a cinema that displayed the creative force of the screenwriter and director. His films are metaphysical journeys into a formidable existentialist world where he playfully explores the relationships of characters attempting to find communion with others and avoid the pain of existence. In this absurd world, unsuspected chance and accidents cause havoc with all human relationships, However, Truffaut's love of cinema is joyfully expressed in all his films, especially *La Nuit américaine / Day for Night* (1973) and *Le Dernier Métro / The Last Metro* (1980). Cinema helped him explore how irrational desires and impulses of human beings may one day triumph over the absurd conditions of modern society.

A Certain Tendency in the French Cinema

In 1954, a young film critic of the *Cahiers du Cinéma* wrote a scathing article on the state of the commercial French postwar cinema. In this essay, "A Certain Tendency in the French Cinema," François Truffaut asserted that French motion pictures were in the control of literary screenwriters who manufactured well-wrought scenarios based upon popular French novels. These adaptations, notably for such films as Jean Delannoy's *Symphonie pastorale* (1946) and Claude Autant-Lara's *Devil in the Flesh* (1947), were stylish enough to win prizes at film festivals but were lacking in confronting the social and political problems arising in postwar France. More important to Truffaut was the lack of optimism and extreme cultural conservatism of the role art played in cinema. In his own way, Truffaut saw cinema as a means to return to the romantic freedom of the arts, outside the influences of any particular ideology or dogma.

Truffaut claimed that French commercial cinema had reached a stage of stagnation in attempting international co-productions with big-name stars to guarantee box office results for producers attached to Hollywood studios. The French followed the American example in making adaptions of popular literary and stage material using trite clichés and conventions of filmmaking. In Truffaut's essay, he protests against the deterministic view of life which had its origin in Émile Zola's naturalism. Furthermore, most of these films demonstrated the anticlericalism and left-wing ethos of the successful co-writing team of Jean Aurenche and Pierre Bost. In its place, Truffaut offers a different history of film that emphasizes the emergence of the highly original and individual expressive style of directors and scriptwriters, like the work of Jean Renoir in *Le Carrosse d'or / The Golden Coach* (1952), Robert Bresson in *Le Journal d'un curé de campagne /*

Diary of a Country Priest (1951) or Jacques Tati with *Les Vacances de Monsieur Hulot / Mr. Hulot's Holiday* (1953).

Truffaut argues that French cinematography has become an imitation of American cinema, moving from the school of *poetic realism* that dealt with love, destiny, and the confrontation of good and evil, to the postwar French cinema of *psychological realism*, in which the central character is affected and misled by the social context, displaying how society itself is the cause of human evil and suffering. In both scenarios, there was a tendency to use conventional approaches to filmmaking based upon the classic Hollywood style. These French films depended on dialogue and elaborate settings in which a static camera framed traditional stage acting. Truffaut described this popular cinema as representing *The Tradition of Quality*. In its place, Truffaut supported a *cinéma des auteurs* that not only took advantage of the dynamic possibilities of film techniques used by the great silent filmmakers of the 1920s, but also provided a return to the filmmaker's own personal views in thinking and reflecting about the modern world. Here, Truffaut informal manifesto establishes his own interest in filmmaking, one that can introduce audiences into the mystification and absurdity life itself embraces.

Albert Camus and the Theatre of the Absurd

The Theatre of the Absurd, as a theatrical part of the existentialist philosophical movement, emerged after the horrors of the Second World War as a rebellion against the beliefs and values of idealism and rationalism, and the goals of traditional bourgeois culture. Eugène Ionesco, a leading French writer of absurd drama, defined the absurd as "that which is devoid of purpose. When man is cut off from his religious, metaphysical and transcendental roots, he is lost; all his actions become senseless, useless, absurd" (Esslin 1961, p. xix). Ionesco's comic-tragedy, *The Chairs* (1952), dramatizes how human perseverance and courage function only to confirm human impotence in the face of death.

According to Martin Esslin, this sense of metaphysical anguish, and the absurdity or senselessness of the human condition is, broadly speaking, the theme of the French plays of Samuel Beckett, Jean Genet and other writers of this mode. The theatre of Beckett, Ionesco and Genet does not argue about the absurd condition. Their plays present a familiar situation of humankind living in a world where communication is impossible and appearances or illusions are accepted and preferred to reality. Often what occurs on stage contradicts the words spoken by the characters. Beckett's *Waiting for Godot* (1953) is a prime example. For all the action and words spoken in the play, nothing happens. In *Endgame* (1958), Beckett shows his central character, Hamm, a blind knight, desperately seeking his place or center on the last days of his life but to no avail. These playwrights reject any causality that motivates the well-made play and the logical development of character and rational speech. The theatrical form relies on the description of objects, unconscious sexual hostilities, and brutal, nonsensical language that disconnects characters from past happenings and creates a denial of empathy from the audience.

The Theatre of the Absurd derives its major catalyst from the work of Albert Camus and his 1942 novel, *The Myth of Sisyphus*. Camus defined the absurd as the tension created when humanity continually seeks to discover purpose and order in a universe which refuses to provide evidence for encouragement or success in this search. Camus' diagnosis creates the sense of ambiguity and paradox that leaves human actions and aspirations merely ironical.

A world that can be explained by reasoning, however faulty, is a familiar world. But, in a universe that is suddenly deprived of illusions and of light, man feels a stranger. His is an irredeemable exile, because he is deprived of memories of a lost homeland as much as he lacks the hope of a promised land to come. This divorce between man and his life, the actor and his setting, truly constitutes the feeling of Absurdity [Camus 1955, p. 18].

In writing for the theatre during the Occupation, Camus recognized the dominant characteristics of the human condition. He represented human existence as one of isolation, moving from the Nothingness it came from toward the Nothingness where it must end, perhaps in anguish and absurdity. He conceived the universe as being alien to human beings, possessing no inherent value or meaning. Human beings thus are cast into a life of uncertainty and insecurity and forced to seek a balance between the forces of life and death, love and hate, justice and mercy. His novels suggest the frightening premise that each human being can only liberate himself or herself from the tyranny of existence through the acceptance of the idea that life is without meaning of any kind. Although it may be full of sound and fury, it signifies nothing.

Camus also adds that when one recognizes that the world is absurd, one can achieve personal freedom through compassion or love. Camus, as a new humanist, understands that one cannot be free at the expense of others, for no person can save himself or herself all alone without becoming an outsider. For Camus one cannot be a Christian in a modern world and be indifferent to the sufferings of humanity without questioning the meaning of grace and salvation.

Existentialism in Truffaut's Early Films

Existentialism plays an important role in Truffaut's early films as they explore the ideological climate in postwar France. He claims that these early films function as an art form that "deranges our way of perceiving experience (including the experience of art itself) and changes the space within which experience may be represented or perceived" (Thiher 1979, p. 143–163). Here a "new means of filmic representation" probes the modern absurdist sensibility that conditioned the Existentialist movement of the late 1950s. This "absurd condition" led to three basic structures in cinematic representation. First, any sense of being or presence could exist without a transcendental view

toward a final cause or meaning. Second, each film represented the notion of a rupture between the metaphysical nature of the universe and any attempts by human beings to gain a rational basis for existence. Thus, causality is undermined by the accidents and unpredictability of life. Third, the old modes of representation become dysfunctional, failing to designate or confirm one's role in life. Filmic modes of representation within this absurd condition thus tend toward irony and incongruity as human identities shift aimlessly among various forms of self-awareness.

Within these three configurations, Truffaut's early films rejected traditional narratives and cinematography by going on a spree with a mobile camera and improvisational sequences as demonstrated in the Italian neorealist films. His first film, *The 400 Blows*, uses various gratuitous camera shots that parallel the irony of the young hero of the film, Antoine Doinel. These episodic meanderings support a series of discontinuous events reflecting the sense of freedom enjoyed by this central character. Similar cinematographic techniques and loose structuring of filmic events occur in *Tirez sur le pianiste / Shoot the Piano Player* (1960) and *Jules et Jim / Jules and Jim* (1961) in which each situation indicates a precarious existential world. Each location or place confronts the characters with an absurdist sense of being as chance events and accidents undermine their rational and responsible actions.

This early trilogy demonstrated two major themes in Truffaut's work: first, the role freedom and romance play in a celebration of life, and second, a fatalistic awareness of the paradoxes of life in an existential world. As the work of an auteur critic and filmmaker for the New Wave, Truffaut's major films are semiautobiographical, examining the emotional life of a troubled young man who withdraws into a solitary existence, as in *L'Amour à vingt ans / Love at Twenty* (1961), *Baisers volés / Stolen Kisses* (1968) and *Domicile conjugal / Bed and Board* (1970). This self-conscious act attempts to remove the unpredictability of life and somehow diminish the pain of familial and social obligations. Some of Truffaut's characters try in turn to escape from their past identities,

In François Truffaut's *The 400 Blows / Les Quatre Cents Coups* (1959), two rebellious boys decide to skip school and invent their own games to play.

especially in *Jules and Jim*, when poets and artists lived in a bohemian age in which they could invent new values for conducting their own lives. In their search for love and freedom, however, they are depicted facing the unpredictability and absurdity of life itself, from which there is no defense.

The New Wave Films of François Truffaut

As a modern fable about a young boy, Antoine Doinel, *The 400 Blows* is semiautobiographical. The narrative displays Antoine's continual attempts to free himself from the "prison-like schools" and "school-like prisons" which his parents have consciously forced him to attend, first at home, then at school, which

in turn leads to a penal system that disregards Antoine's personhood. He is caught in an unending series of confrontations with various forms of tyranny that dehumanize him. Like a character in an absurdist drama, Antoine is "cut off from his religious, and transcendental roots, and thus his actions appear to be senseless, absurd and useless" (Ionesco, cited in Esslin 1961, p. xix). In Antoine's being cut off from human love and compassion, Truffaut illustrates the absurd dilemma facing a young man trying to come of age only to find himself dehumanized and oppressed in an alienating society unwilling to communicate with him.

Truffaut's second feature film, *Shoot the Piano Player,* is based upon the American gangster thriller *Down There*, by David Goodis. The story again deals with the intentions of the central character to escape from the pain of human

In Truffaut's ***Tirez sur le pianiste / Shoot the Piano Player*** (1960), Charles Aznavour plays a lonely pianist hiding from his own past and gangsters who threaten his life in the most unpredictable ways.

intimacy. As played by Charles Aznavour, Charlie Kohler is a timid and shy honky-tonk piano player in a sleazy Parisian bar. Accidents of birth and involvement with two gunmen who are after some stolen money lead to a shoot-out between the gangsters and Charlie's brothers at a snow-laden farmhouse. The misfortune and pain that Charlie was hoping would not strike again does happen. Truffaut says he conceived the film from one single image in Goodis' novel, one in which a car was running down a sloping road in the snow with no noise from the engine. That surreal image of a helpless car sliding through the snow, unable to control its fate, was what Truffaut wanted to visualize in his film.

With that single image, Truffaut began playing with the American gangster thrillers, those B-movies that both he and Godard loved to imitate. But Truffaut intentionally inverted the gangsters' character and their actions. He inserted the customary chase scene involving the two gangsters, but their reactions are similar to those of characters found in a Chaplinesque farce. Instead of creating the requisite suspense and dread of killers, the scene shows the gangsters acting like children craving some new thrills. Further, by interlocking the past events in Charlie's life with his present love affair, and the bungling interference of the gangsters, Truffaut is able to keep the viewer disengaged from any empathic identification with these characters. The commercial success of these two films marked the international ascendence of Truffaut and the New Wave.

Henry Serre, Oskar Werner and Jeanne Moreau as young, romantic bohemians engaged in a playful *ménage à trois* before World War I in Truffaut's *Jules and Jim* (1961).

JULES AND JIM

In this film Truffaut focuses upon the enigmatic quality of the central character, Catherine, as portrayed by Jeanne Moreau. In the eyes of her two suitors, Jules and Jim, Catherine is the embodiment of a Greek goddess of love. Her face carries the mysterious smile of Eros, and her amorous nature dominates the whimsical lovemaking rituals she plays with both men. She is a free spirit who possesses an eternal feminine nature that changes constantly when forced to conform to conventional human behavior. She is forever willing to challenge social conventions, deliberately breaking societal norms by inventing new rules to the games she plays. At first she defines how each man must engage in the game of love with her. Soon she discovers other forces that prohibit the men, notably Jim, from meeting her expectations. Jim is self-conscious of his role in so-

ciety, and thus cannot decide whether to accept the given rules or continue his liaisons with Catherine under her rules. When Jim returns from World War I, Catherine tries various schemes to lure Jim back into her game of love. This time the results are different.

Truffaut's representation of *l'amour fou* is similar to Godard's, but for one important difference. Truffaut represents the contradictions and complexities of human existence as shifting from a celebration of life with all its potential for gaiety and happiness toward an awareness of pain and sadness together with the reality of death.

As in historical drama, Truffaut's characters also suffer from the absurdity of human experience. They are cast into a world full of uncertainty and are forced to seek choices between the forces of life and death, In this way cinema expresses Truffaut's interest in achieving "a vibration or trembling" within his narratives in

A dinner party after the war to celebrate their reunion and hopes of more amorous adventures in *Jules and Jim*.

these spaces. The frightening premise that emerges from *Jules and Jim* is that the lovers can only liberate themselves from the tyranny of existence through playing out adult games and rituals that lessen the unpredictability of their lives.

Chabrol, Rohmer and Rivette

Claude Chabrol (b. 1930) with Eric Rohmer (b. 1920) and Jacques Rivette (b. 1928) also were critics for *Cahiers du Cinéma* with Godard and Truffaut. They used Hitchcock as a model for their own dark studies of the sexual obsessions of the petite bourgeoisie. Chabrol and Rohmer wrote a monograph on the films of Alfred Hitchcock, *Hitchcock* (1957), that became the turning point in early New Wave films. It was

Chabrol, as director-scriptwriter of his film, *Le Beau Serge / Bitter Reunion* (1958), who established the concept of an *auteur* as the creator of a cinematic text. His next film, *Les Cousins / The Cousins* (1959), proved to be a daring tale of decadent Parisian students that displayed different narrative strategies to explore changing moral values in an existential world of contingency. The influence of Hitchcock on Chabrol's obsessions with the ambiguous nature of characters who commit murder subverted the traditional genre conventions of the "villain." By the late 1960s, Chabrol directed three powerful tragic thrillers concerning moral corruption and violence: *La Femme infidèle / Unfaithful Wife* (1968), *Que la bête meure / This Man Must Die!* (1969) and *Le Boucher / The Butcher* (1969). Chabrol made his most critically acclaimed film, *Une Affaire de femmes / Story of Women* (1988), as a psychological exploration of a woman doctor trapped in a moral dilemma of performing illegal abortions in order to survive under the Vichy government during World War II.

While Chabrol was making films, his colleague Eric Rohmer served as editor of *Cahiers du Cinéma* from 1956 to 1963. Chabrol's film successes helped him produce Rohmer's first feature film, *Le Signe du lion / The Sign of the Lion* (1960). More interested in the studies of characters who wish to uphold their own ethical and moral beliefs while preoccupied by romantic liaisons, Rohmer directed a series of moral tales including *Ma Nuit chez Maud / My Night at Maud's* (1969), *Le Genou de Claire / Claire's Knee* (1970) and *L'Amour l'après-midi / Chloe in the Afternoon* (1972). In each film Rohmer sets his comedies in an ever-changing existential world where the experiences of his characters seemingly are alienated by the depersonalizing forces of modern society.

> *My Night at Maud's* is the perfect antidote to faux-intellectualism. The three main characters are supremely self-conscious adults, all professionals in their thirties. The protagonist is making an effort to stop drifting and settle into a permanent philosophy, a difficult task when the main social talent of each of his peers seems to be the clever dissection of each other's ideas. They pretend they have nothing to hide, but they are all social deceivers.... Just as in real life, people have personal motivations that must be carefully hidden [Erickson 2003].

Jacques Rivette is known for creating a cinematic style that is both innovative and mysterious. His stories play with the simple fact that cinematic images are both illusive yet realistic. This illusion/reality characteristic of cinema gives his stories a dualistic nature that encourages the use of doubles or pairs through which the spirit and the flesh are set within the narrative metonymically to make various and unexpected connections. In *Céline and Julie Go Boating / Céline et Jule vont en bateau* (1974), he casts two pairs of women as actresses. The first pair, a magician and a librarian, share an apartment and an identity. Their imaginations evoke another pair of women who simply exist as spirits or phantoms in a haunted house with a man and child. With a surfeit of narrative possibilities, Rivette appropriates film footage from past genre films to further speculate on how past illusions still haunt our imaginations. As the New Wave directors perceive cinema, the critical problem for them is to unmask the power projected by these forces in a self-reflexive manner to help liberate people from their tyrannies.

References

Camus, Albert. 1955. *The Myth of Sisyphus.* New York: Knopf.

Erickson, Glenn. 2003. "*My Night at Maud's.*" www.dvdtalk.com

Esslin, Martin. 1961. *The Theatre of the Absurd.* New York: Doubleday.

Thiher, Allen. 1979. *The Cinematic Muse.* Columbia and London: University of Missouri Press, pp. 143–163.

"*L'Année dernière à Marienbad*: The Narration of Narration"

by Allen Thiher

From *The Cinematic Muse: Critical Studies in the History of French Cinema* by Allen Thiher, by permission of the University of Missouri Press. Copyright © 1979 by the Curators of the University of Missouri.

Resnais and Robbe-Grillet's *L'Année dernière à Marienbad* is perhaps the most interesting filmic example of how the creative displacement of artistic limits can go suddenly beyond critical theory and bring about an enigmatic opening in our experience of art. We can speak of an opening, since such a work compels the viewer to enter into an open experience that no critical awareness can immediately close off. Our categories for the perception of experience seem to be suspended, and yet, since we cannot deny the fascination of this work it is imperative that we find new theoretical bases that account for the way this film entices our vision. This film is a seduction, then, not only of the unknown woman whom the narrator pursues throughout the film, but also of our vision. Like every seduction, the film draws us into an unknown realm where unfamiliarity is a source of both fear and pleasure, of both exhilaration and insecurity. The immediate effect is to bring about a desire for total possession, a need to grasp fully the film's paradoxical surfaces, to transform its strangeness into familiarity.

Perhaps the best starting point for a theoretical possession of *L'Année dernière à Marienbad* is to situate it immediately within the context of the postmodern artist's quest to redefine the relationships between art and perception, between the work and the work's understanding of itself, between mimesis and the limits of representation. By postmodern we mean those artists whose works, both novels and films, have since the late fifties broken with the modernist canons of representation. Writers as diverse as Beckett, Borges, Pynchon, filmmakers as diverse as Godard, Robbe-Grillet, and Berman, all seem united in a common refusal of the modernist belief in art as a form of revelation. They refuse to accept the possibility of mimesis as an unquestioned and unquestionable given; indeed, they seek to redefine the way in which the work can enter into relations with any form of referential reality or with itself.

Yet most critical commentary on *L'Année dernière à Marienbad* has attempted to understand the film within the canons of modernist theory. And it is more than a little interesting to note that Resnais and Robbe-Grillet, especially in their earliest comments on the work, were particularly guilty in this respect. Their comments, in fact, established the categories that most subsequent critics have repeated with little variation. By declaring *L'Année dernière à Marienbad* to be an extreme experiment in "subjective" cinema, they made of their work an essentially modernist attempt to find the means for directly representing some form of psychic reality. In effect, they suggested that the film was another variation on such modernist techniques as stream of consciousness or manipulation of narrative points of view. Seen in this light, *L'Année dernière* is a modernist attempt to find filmic epiphany, or the revelation of privileged psychic moments. By placing the emphasis on the film's revelation of immanent experience, rather than on the film's formal structures, the filmmakers as well as a good many later critics were able to take seriously the rather bizarre idea that the film takes place in someone's head.

This point is worth pursuing, for the desire to delimit the locus of mimesis by some privileged space is most characteristic of modernism — and of much of the early criticism to which Robbe-Grillet's work gave rise. In fact, it now appears that it was only because of such critical pressure that Robbe-Grillet theorized about his film in terms of "mental realism" or other modernist categories of "realism." But it is obvious that these categories belong to the theory of literary modernism, and, I believe, they can do little to account for the way we actually experience *L'Année dernière à Marienbad*.

Our first experience of the film is, in fact, a questioning born of our desire to find the locus of mimesis and to delimit the representational space. The film opens a region of experience and, in one sense, forces us to ask what images are about. Our first answer must be that the status of these images is ambiguous, for they blatantly refuse to obey the laws of verisimilitude and casual relation that we often take to be inherent in the nature of narration itself. This does not mean that they are irrational or that they can only be explained in terms of the kind of subjectivity represented in literature by an interior monologue.

In fact, it seems dubious that images can represent any kind of subjectivity by direct mimesis, for images never take place inside anyone's head. The images we see either occur in the world or, in the case of so-called mental images, occur nonspatially. Thus mental images cannot be *in* anything. In fact, one might

be tempted to turn the relationship about and say that it is the perception of images that allows us to localize our heads. In any case, critics who resort to the metaphysics of inner and outer, of subjective and objective, to describe what images purport to represent have allowed outmoded philosophical categories to obscure the way in which images create the world they represent. *L'Année dernière à Marienbad* forces us to ask why we wish to speak in metaphysical terms about images or, equally important, why we wish to think of them in terms of literary categories such as *point of view*. It is by demonstrating the failure of such categories that the film opens up new possibilities for the experiencing of films.

Categories such as *subjectivity* and *point of view* have such surface plausibility that it is difficult not to wish to apply them. Thus Bruce Morrissette, one of the best-known critics of Robbe-Grillet's work, can unhesitatingly explain his films in the same terms that he uses to describe Robbe-Grillet's novels:

> It is well known that the theory and practice of *point of view*, in novels as in cinema, are closely tied to the metaphysics of each novelist or scriptwriter. Thus Robbe-Grillet chose at the beginning of his literary career to place himself on the side of Sartre and existentialist metaphysics and declared that every novelistic image must exist or come forth by being grounded in a narrating consciousness.[1]

Morrissette's point-of-view analogy annexes film to literary technique without questioning how this can be so. How can a film be grounded in a narrating consciousness when there is nothing in the structure of a projected image that allows it to be assigned to a consciousness? Language, to be sure, in the very process of enunciation, always presupposes a voice that offers the utterance and thus springs from what one can call a narrating (or narrative) consciousness, even if it is mediated by a third-person pronoun. But it is very difficult to see how the process of enunciation can be applied to the projection of images that, by their projection, create their autonomous world.

It is true, of course, that from its beginnings film has tried to grant itself the status of literary work by using various conventions that designate the film as a transcription of a verbal narration. To take popular examples, one need think of the shot of the book and the narrating voice-over that open *Red River* or, more recently, the presence of the tape recorder at the beginning of *Little Big Man*. These naive conventions usually add little to the film and, in any case, in no way endow the film with a narrative point of view. More interesting of course are more complex films, such as *Citizen Kane* and *Rashomon*. In these works, too, it seems apparent that there is no existential bond between a narrator and the various narratives each film sets forth. Rather, the presence of a narrator serves only to designate each narrative as different from or complementary to the other narratives in the film. The narrator in the film thus serves an epistemological function, for his presence indicates that each individual narrative is a part of the quest for knowledge or truth that the total film undertakes. In *Citizen Kane* it is especially evident that the filmic world overflows, perhaps inevitably, what a narrator could really narrate from a limited point of view. Each narrative goes well beyond a single memory, not only in terms of remembered detail, but in terms of the very being of the image, its ontological fullness, its presence. Moreover, it is obvious that in this film the various narratives that make up the quest fit neatly together to form a linear chronology that purports, in the modernist sense of recapturing the past, to reveal the essence of a life.

Narration as a form of epistemological quest is central to our understanding of *L'Année dernière à Marienbad*, for it seems clear that the only narrative point of view present in the film is the one offered by the narrating voice, a first-person narrative that must be considered in juxtaposition to the world of images. However, we must first take into account one other approach to the film that has found a great deal of acceptance, the approach that takes *L'Année dernière* to be a dream. It does seem true that film can imitate dream images or, more precisely, that filmmakers have developed a series of conventions that allow us to accept certain kinds of images as a representation of dream. We are not disturbed when the autonomous

world of the film is replaced by an oneiric world that, for purposes of narrative coherence, we then usually attribute to one of the characters within the film. *Wild Strawberries* and *8½* come readily to mind in this respect, though both Bergman and Fellini have demonstrated in other works that they need not have recourse to dream conventions in order to use irrational images — irrational in terms of the canons of verisimilitude — for narrative purposes. Dream conventions often seem, in fact, a way by which a filmmaker integrates irrational ruptures into his narrative, for few directors are interested in the mimesis of dream for its own sake.

L'Année dernière à Marienbad is characterized by precisely the kind of ruptures that seem to designate the filmic world as a representation of dream. Yet dream convention usually demands that there be a filmic world against which the irrational images stand out as "dream," and this film world is not present in *L'Année dernière à Marienbad*. There are in effect no indices to designate one image as a "real" image and another, in contrast, as an oneiric image that must be attributed to one of the characters. The conventions objective and subjective, inner and outer, substantial and oneiric, are simply not present, and the film forces us to situate its images in some other space than that demanded by the modernist aesthetics of representation. *L'Année dernière à Marienbad* is, in fact, one of the seminal works for a definition of postmodern art, and only by turning away from such categories as *mental realism* and *degrees of reality* can we begin to understand the film.

If one of the postmodern tasks is to find a means by which to designate the work's functioning as a fiction, to force the reader or viewer to evaluate critically the mimetic constructs that seek to represent "reality," then it would appear that a work that lays bare its own genesis as a fiction best fulfills that critical task. The postmodern artist thus often strives to go beyond the ironic self-consciousness of the modernist to create a work of metanarration that can account for its own unfolding. Self-reference becomes a means by which the work designates its awareness of itself as a fiction. It is in this sense that we can call *L'Année dernière à Marienbad* a metanarrative that proposes a series of narrative hypotheses that finally coalesce into a past, a history, a plausible story. It is an exploration of the labyrinth, to use a favored postmodern metaphor, that designates both the quest for fiction and the fiction itself. And the representational space is the space of the labyrinth of the film itself, the space of the narration.

As the metaphor of the labyrinth points out, subject matter and motifs are metaphorical doubles for the metanarration itself. The quest for narration is thus an attempt to narrate a seduction at the same time it is a seduction — both of the woman who hears the tale and of the viewer who seeks to construct the fictional past out of the elements the film offers. The metaphorical equation of seduction-narration is another aspect of self-reference by which the narrative project designates its own functioning and telos. "X," the stranger who is the narrator-seducer, is then, in one sense, a surrogate artist who must seduce both viewer and woman through the creation of a story, through the elaboration of a preterit narrative that represents the creation of a "past of marble" that can authenticate the seduction.

In *L'Année dernière à Marienbad* Resnais and Robbe-Grillet have, in effect, "deconstructed" the myth of passion. One might well compare the film to the myth of Tristan and Isolde to see how the film uses the archetypical elements of myth to construct the metanarration. In his later works Robbe-Grillet prefers to call upon the popular myths of sex, drugs, secret agents, and the like for his narrative deconstruction. In his first film, however, he seems to have chosen the most perdurable of European myths as a basis for the film's motifs. *L'Année dernière*'s metanarration might be likened to the situation in which Tristan must convince Isolde of the reality of their passion by telling her its story, its legend, so as to create a past that can validate his present desire. In the film as in the myth, the passion depends upon a third party for its forbidden existence. The woman's companion, "M" — possibly a *mari*, possibly a *Marc* — thus fills the role of the interdictor against whom the narrative is directed. The goal of narration is thus given as a subversion

of the order we find in the narration itself and, by analogy, in the hotel's rigid order as well. Our Tristan's task as metanarrator is to lead the object of his passion through the labyrinthine meanderings of his quest, through the halls and gardens, to an acceptance of the new order that he proposes in his narrative. His passion informs his narrative, for ultimately we see that the genesis of fiction is in the service of desire, just as desire or possession is another metaphor for the fiction itself.

The film's final seduction is to draw the viewer into the labyrinth so that he, too, participates in a narration that by laying bare its own genesis, its own functioning, reveals the dangers attendant upon the metaphorical seduction. In this respect Robbe-Grillet's own critical commentary can be useful, for he has always been aware of how the formal possibilities of constructing a representation have conditioned his novelistic or filmic vision. In the creation of *L'Année dernière à Marienbad*, the idea of negotiating a labyrinth seems to have been in his mind from the very inception of the film:

> I began with this idea: a form of itinerary that could be just as well a form of writing [*écriture*], a labyrinth, which is to say, a path that always appears to be guided by strict walls, but which nonetheless leads at each moment to impasses that then force one to go back several times over the same places, over greater or lesser distances, to explore a new direction, and to come again upon new impossibilities.[2]

One might well ask why the labyrinth has become a privileged metaphor for designating the postmodernist creation. It would appear that this metaphor can show the equivalence between the creator's quest and his creation as well as between the act of appropriating the creation and the act of understanding it. The work as a labyrinth is a circle that depends only on its own structures for its coherence; the reader or viewer is detached from all outside frames of reference and must explore the labyrinth in terms of its own presuppositions. And if the labyrinth's paths ultimately go nowhere, perhaps the labyrinth is a metaphor that denounces a naive acceptance of mimesis and warns that one enters only at one's own risk.

The film thus portrays the struggle that the narrating voice undertakes as it contends with the manifold hypotheses and possibilities its narration evokes. This struggle is mirrored in the relationship between the voice — the work — and the images. The images sometimes duplicate the narrative that the voice proposes as though they were offering a confirmation in an experiential world of the narrative hypothesis. At other times they serve as a framework that offers the narrating voice a concrete locus from which to speak. But they can also contradict the narrating voice and reject the narrative order that the voice would impose. The autonomous world of filmic space provides the arena in which the narrative voice must confront its desires as it seeks to negotiate the labyrinth.

The film's opening tracking-shot, accompanied by the sonorous voice repeating that once again the narrator is advancing through these halls, brings the viewer into the metaphorical labyrinth at the same time it sets forth the struggle in which the narrative voice will attempt to master the image. The plastic tensions and irrational patterns of the baroque decor are another analogy for an experiential world that the narrator must order. This order would seem to find an analogical presence in the various images presenting the formal, French gardens whose Cartesian rationality stands in opposition to the baroque profusion. The quest for narration might then be seen as the effort to suppress this labyrinthine exuberance and to create the seemingly ordered space of rational representation. Yet as the film's end, set in the geometric gardens, seems to show, such a rational order is also a maze. Indeed, the end is given in the beginning when we see the play-within-a-play, or the theatrical performance, that sets forth the film's denouement. The play-within-a-play here takes place in a Cartesian decor that points to the circularity of the representational order. The end is given in the beginning, so that every beginning is already a form of conclusion. Cartesian order turns in upon itself as another labyrinth that offers only an illusory openness onto some other referential realm.

The opening sequence is especially important, too, for establishing how every element in the film stands in analogical relation to every other element in this self-contained quest. In structuralist terms, the work self-consciously proclaims that all relations derive their meaning only from each other, for every element mirrors every other, as we see in the mirrors that line the walls and in which we often see the film's characters reflected. In this respect one is struck by the way the hotel's inhabitants are first presented in rigid poses, recalling the statues in the film that in turn double the characters themselves. One might also consider again the pictures that present the French gardens; they seem to point to an order beyond this baroque palace but in effect are but another image of the maze that designates the filmic world.

In the first part of the film, the various posed groups and couples also offer various bits of anecdotes that are doubles for the metanarration itself. One couple speaks of freedom; another group speaks of last year's weather; others speak of a certain "Frank" who the year before had apparently entered a woman's room and attempted to seduce her. All of these doubling fragments stand in analogical relation to the narrative quest, though the references to a certain "Frank" seem to allude to narration in an even larger sense. Through the paronomasia *Frank-Franz*, Robbe-Grillet appears here to be invoking, as he does more explicitly in his later film *L'Homme qui ment*, the patron saint of all postmodernists, Franz Kafka. (The inventor of the Castle, it should be noted, once vacationed in Marienbad with his fiancée.) Here we may again seem another mirror image that refers to the narrative quest. In *The Castle*, Kafka's "K." loses himself in a proliferating textuality that never allows him to reach the Castle or the narrative to reach an end. Robbe-Grillet's Frank, a double for his own narrator, may have reached the castle, but narrative proliferation continues, and there appears to be no narrative finality that can vouchsafe the past that can guarantee there was an entrance into the woman's room, that there *was* a last year at Marienbad.

Robbe-Grillet's narrator must therefore

negotiate the various hypotheses that the narration generates much as K. must deal with the texts, suppositions, and hypotheses that emanate from the Castle's bureaucratic order, an order that is as problematic in its existence as is Marienbad's past. Let us consider in this respect how certain sequences function. Take, for example, the shooting gallery in which the men fire their pistols with such accuracy. These images are unaccompanied either by spoken text or by dialogue and thus seem to emerge as an unconnected possibility that bears little relation to the various hypotheses about "last year." On reflection, however, it is apparent that these images of men shooting methodically at targets show the controlled violence that underlies the order of this rigid world. Moreover, these images clearly foreshadow one of the major narrative hypotheses: that the passion the narrator feels for the woman could result in her death or his. The eros that informs the narrative quest could bring about destruction. These images are thus related thematically to a hypothesis that could, if realized, destroy the entire search for a past and the authentication of desire.

These images of violence are related in turn to the various hypotheses concerning the woman's chamber — the locus of desire — and the kind of reception the narrator might have received there. The narrator first introduces the image of the woman's chamber by telling her that he came there one night. We then see the chamber in a series of flash frames that many spectators might take to be a flashback (as Resnais probably did) or perhaps as a flash forward, since this is the way these kinds of ruptures are usually coded. But, as later images of the room show, there is no single fixed image of the chamber, nor is there a fixed "past" chamber about which one of the characters might be thinking. Rather, there are the multiple rooms, with their varying decors, that offer themselves as hypothetical possibilities in the narrative construction of the past. The various chambers illustrate how difficult it is for the narrator to control the multiple experiential possibilities that besiege him, for each one forces him to modify his approach, to weigh other possibilities, and to struggle to maintain

the inner coherence that will create the verisimilitude necessary for persuasion.

The first room, for example, is rather plain. In it we see a pile of shoes and a glass. These objects find their doubles in other parts of the narrative space and ambiguously relate the room to other aspects of the experiential world that the images propose. A second chamber contains no shoes, though it does contain a glass, while a third presents a more baroque decor in which a mirror reveals the woman's image as a kind of double to the other mirror images. Another chamber presents a painting, another image of the iconic double that recurs throughout the film, while the woman in these shots holds herself against the baroque mirrors that line the wall. This room in particular shows how the proliferation of possibilities risks destroying the narrative project. The narrator here insists that the room's door was closed and that the woman returned to the bed. The image shows quite clearly that the woman stays by the mirror and that the door is open. The room baffles the narrator, and his story seems unable to account for these plausible developments. And so the narrator breaks down, saying that he cannot remember any more. The room is thus the locus upon which the narrative quest is centered. For it is here that the full range of hypotheses are developed, ranging from rejection to death to joyous acceptance.

The various contradictory hypotheses represent what we might call the comedy of narration or, from another point of view, narration as a ludic function. The woman's multiple poses when she is dead, for example, seem to be a farcical aggression against the need for a single, coherent order. One readily thinks of Beckett in this respect, for these various hypotheses call to mind the epistemological games that Beckett's narrators play in *Watt* and *Molloy*. For Beckett's narrators the rules of the narrative game are given by the now-impossible metaphysics that once guaranteed knowledge, and narration now becomes a series of epistemological impasses in which one wonders if one can even know that one knows nothing can be told. Though Robbe-Grillet uses this same kind of speculation in this novel *Le Labyrinthe*, it would seem that *L'Année dernière à Marienbad* may well be the first film to have integrated into its structure this postmodern refusal of the certainty that traditional narration has been founded on. The systematic undermining of the various hypotheses that could make up a narration reflects the postmodern suspiciousness of fictions. Yet this destruction of narrative certainty goes beyond mere skepticism. It would seem that in the case of Robbe-Grillet it aims perhaps at the creation of an uncertainty principle that might become a new way of defining and representing experience.

In any case, the central figure in this constellation of uncertainties is the stone couple, the statue that stands in an analogical relation with the film's couple. The analogy is immediately established when the narrator invokes the statue for the woman as a form of evidence that might verify their common past:

> Remember: quite near us there was a group of stone figures on a rather high base, a man and a woman in classical dress, whose frozen gestures seemed to represent some specific scene. You asked me who these characters were, I answered that I didn't know. You made several suppositions, and I said that it could just as well be you and I.[3]

As is the case with the very presence of the couple in the vacation palace, the camera offers images of the statue as a present *hic et nunc* that can support innumerable suppositions that might explain its existence. Every hypothesis is the beginning of a new narration about the past that can culminate in the present moment, for present identity — be it that of Pyrrhus and Andromache, Helen and Agamemnon, or of two strangers that a dog happens to meet — demands the creation of the narration whose causal chain will guarantee the existence of a substantial self through time. The need for an identity is, then, a generator of fictions, or at least of narratives, and in this respect the stone couple stands in a metaphorical relationship not only with the living couple, but with the entire narrative quest.

The relationship is perhaps made clearest in visual terms through one of the important changes that Resnais made in the script. By adding the suggestion that the couple had

stopped before the sea, he was then able to add a tracking shot up and over the statue. The shot isolates a portion of a pond in such a way that the statue does seem to be standing before a vast expanse of water that could fill the entire visual field. The camera thus converts the narrative hypothesis into a visual reality that we know in a conventional sense to be false, for it is merely the change in perspective that has created the "sea." Yet in terms of pure perception the image has validated the hypothesis, and thus the narrative possibility is upheld as one that could apply to the statue. The autonomy of the image is of course responsible for the seeming truth of the shot, but by revealing how the image can change narration merely by the change in perspective, the camera undermines its own credibility in the game of narrative hypotheses. It can seemingly substantiate any supposition the narrator offers.

The alternative to this trickery seems to be given when the woman's companion appears and offers an explanation of the statue, an image of which the couple is contemplating in an engraving:

> Excuse me, sir. I think I can supply you with some more precise information: this statue represents Charles III and his wife, but it does not date from that period, of course. The scene is that of the oath before the Diet, at the moment of the trial for treason. The classical costumes are purely conventional.[4]

The introduction of "historical" past, one based on dates and a publicly accepted chronology, is comic in its precision and yet as baffling in its dispersion in time as any other form of explanation. Temporal layers overlap in a proliferation of dates and periods, and the statue's identity seems to dissolve into a series of pasts that can scarcely provide the unique series of events that will offer a necessary narrative order.

This is a film about last year, however, and in some sense one should be able to speak of the past. Robbe-Grillet has claimed, among other things, that the film takes place in the present and that it lasts exactly the time that it takes to see it.[5] In other words, there is no symbolic representation of time. We might say, then, that the film's time is the duration of the metanarration. The drama of narration lasts only as long as the narrator is undertaking the narrative quest. It takes place in a virtual present that is generated every time the film is projected.

In a sense, however, every narrative is a present act that aims, in phenomenological terms, at a past it seeks to reconstruct. One might even say that the past exists only as a present project that attempts to seize it. With this understanding in mind, one can turn then to the conclusion of *L'Année dernière à Marienbad*, where we find that the narration ends in the past tense, which seems to endow the entire film with a preterit dimension. It would seem that when the metanarration reaches its goal, one has effectively created or seized a past that exists in function of the present narrative project. In a sense, the metanarration is then sublimated into a "pastness" that is the aim of its quest. Once the woman-viewer has been seduced and led into the labyrinth of narration, then we can say that the story *was* as it *is* told. As Robbe-Grillet suggested, one is at Marienbad throughout the film, at the only Marienbad that can exist, which, however, is the one sought in the present by the narrative consciousness as it undertakes the quest to order a past.

From the moment the narrative voice shifts to the past tense, we know, as does the woman's companion, M, that she has accepted the seduction and that the stranger has created the past into which she will enter. All the elements of the myth of passion fall into place to create the mythic past that validates passion. The myth of passion and narration are one and the same in their metaphorical identity, for it is the narration that has created the legendary past, just as it is passion that has informed the narrative quest. And just as the other side of passion, according to the myth, is death, so the acceptance of a fixed past is entrance into the maze that can lead only to death. To fix a past, to order it as a finality, is to offer a death, since it is only as death that a past can be finally given. As Lucien Goldmann has pointed out, the film's final images are those of a cemetery.[6]

When we turn from a consideration of the film's motifs and their metaphorical relations, we may feel inclined to ask why Robbe-Grillet and Resnais should have taken so much effort to construct a convoluted work that ultimately designates only itself and its self-representing function. One might even claim that such a work should be branded a form of intellectual narcissism. Such a view would not be entirely beside the point, for any work that points out how it works to seduce the spectator, or the spectator's metaphorical surrogate, is a work that reveals itself as an erotic project. In the case of such a circular work, of a film that aims at itself in its narrative project, narcissism would be another term for the erotic project. In the case of such a circular work, of a film that aims at itself in its narrative project, narcissism would be another term for the erotic circularity that animates the work. Yet this self-conscious narcissism is also another sign that the critical intelligence at work in a film like *L'Année dernière à Marienbad* is attempting to lay bare the mechanisms that realistic works seek to hide so that they do not destroy the illusion of representation. By revealing its narcissism *L'Année dernière* denounces in effect the seductions of mimetic conventions that hide their persuasion behind a metaphysics of substantial reality. By proclaiming its tentative hypotheses to be only forms of seduction, by revealing its codes, the construction of its myth, and its narcissistic gratuity, *L'Année dernière à Marienbad* forces us to evaluate all our responses to the guiles of mimesis.

In more positive theoretical terms, *L'Année dernière* points to Robbe-Grillet's more recent thought concerning the function of art. We have already said that the film springs from a series of epistemological games, and it is in fact this ludic aspect of art that has come increasingly to dominate Robbe-Grillet's theoretical views on his work, as it has dominated postmodern works in general. In retrospect, it seems clear that *L'Année dernière à Marienbad* is quite close to such works by Robbe-Grillet as *Projet pour une revolution à New York* or *Éden et après*. All spring from a view of art as a closed game space in which certain combinative rules allow the genesis of fictions. The ludic functioning of art, as Robbe-Grillet now sees it, is another aspect of the postmodern rejection of various bourgeois forms of mimesis. He has, in fact, become quite explicit about how the "ideology of play" aims at the creation of new modes of representation that will liberate us from the repressive modes that characterize realistic art and what he sees as its concomitant bourgeois ideology:

> Often I have thought that the disappearance of the old myths of depth [*profondeur*] has created a determining vacuum [*vide*]. What people call seriousness, that is, that which is underwritten by such values as work, honor, discipline, and so forth, belongs in reality to a vast code, one well situated and dated, outside of which the idea of profundity has no meaning. Seriousness supposes that there is something behind our gestures: a soul, a god, values, bourgeois order ... whereas behind play there is nothing.[7]

Declaring that it is play that defines the field of our liberty in such a work, Robbe-Grillet goes on to say, "In short, play [*le jeu*] is for us the only possible way of intervening in a world that is henceforth deprived of all profundity."[8]

Already in *L'Année dernière à Marienbad* we find in the film's central ludic image a metaphor that is a double of the metanarration. The enigmatic game of pim, at which the stranger loses several times to M, sets forth an analogy with the narrative game of hypotheses. The stranger must defeat M in order to win the woman, and each failure at the game seems to be a metaphor for the narration's failure to carry out the persuasion. Moreover, the game stands as an analogy for the narrative quest in that the viewer can no more decipher the rules of the game than he can fix a past for the couple. The game's enigma designates the narrative's uncertainty, as narrative and game coincide in their drawing the viewer into a ludic space where the rules of the game must be worked out in the course of play itself.

The game's enigma also seems to designate the enigmatic opening in our experience of art that *L'Année dernière à Marienbad* has brought about. Robbe-Grillet's ideology of play may well be the basis for new modes of artistic experience. Certainly his and Resnais's work in film is among the most important postmodern work in this respect. By designating the conventions of realistic mimesis as myth —conventions such as causal necessity, depth or substantiality of character, psychological continuity, and so forth — and by using these conventions as he sees fit in his various combinative games, Robbe-Grillet in particular has displaced the perimeters of the space of mimesis. Perhaps most interestingly, he has also forced us to see that it is not only the subject and conventions of narration that are mythic, but also the narration itself. The myth of narration, which in France has become the dominant postmodern myth today, stands as one limit to the expansion of mimetic space, for the myth stands there as the self-conscious limit of every narrative project.

Notes

1. Bruce Morrissette, *Les Romans de Robbe-Grillet*, p. 226. (All translations are mine, unless otherwise indicated.)
2. Quoted in Gaston Bounoure, *Alain Resnais* (Paris: Seghers, 1962), pp. 79–80.
3. Alain Robbe-Grillet, *Last Year at Marienbad*, trans. Richard Howard, pp. 51–52.
4. *Ibid.*, p. 69.
5. *Ibid.*, p. 13.
6. Lucien Goldmann, *Pour une Sociologie du Roman*, p. 323.
7. Quoted in *Nouveau Roman: Hier, Aujourd'hui*, 1:127–28.
8. *Ibid.*

References

Duras, Marguerite. 1961. *Hiroshima, Mon Amour.* Translated by Richard Seaver. New York: Grove Press.

Goldmann, Lucien. 1975. *Pour une Sociologie du Roman.* [*Towards a Sociology of the Novel.*] Translated from the French by Alan Sheridan. London: Tavistock Publications.

Robbe-Grillet, Alain. 1962. *Last Year at Marienbad.* Translated by Richard Howard. New York: Grove Press.

_____. 1965. *For a New Novel: Essays on Fiction.* Translated by Richard Howard. New York: Grove Press.

CHAPTER 18

Postwar British New Cinema: 1956–1972

Introduction

British cinema after the end of World War II represented traditional adaptations of literary classics to film form. Laurence Olivier emerged as a successful director and actor with his excellent film adaptations of Shakespeare's *Hamlet* (1948) and later *Richard III* (1955). The most highly successful adaptations were made from the novels of Charles Dickens, *Great Expectations* (1946) and *Oliver Twist* (1947), both skillfully directed by David Lean. All of these films preserved the upper-middle class social and political values and norms reflecting prewar attitudes and sense of empire.

During the late 1950s and early 1960s the British New Cinema developed from the documentary tradition of John Grierson and his social programs. Here, the films of Lindsay Anderson, Tony Richardson and Karel Reisz carefully detailed how the changing social and historical times reflected the consumer society of the 1950s. Their attention to the new working-class environment revitalized the filmmaking practices in Britain and brought attention to the growing tensions emerging from the youth cultures and the commodification of leisure activities. With the box-office success of transitional films, including Jack Clayton's *Room at the Top* (1959) and his own *Look Back in Anger* (1959), Tony Richardson founded Woodfall Films, and the Free Cinema movement gained commercial sponsorship. He produced a series of New Wave films, including *Saturday Night and Sunday Morning* (1960), and *This Sporting Life* (1963). The Free Cinema movement continued the neo–Marxist critique of the working-classes in a docudrama style that gave a realistic rendering of their lives. These films focused on the loss of traditional moral and cultural values for the affluent working-class heroes, who attempt to overcome their fears of a growing conformist culture symbolized by the television set and liberate themselves from the traditional class structures in postwar England.

The Documentary Tradition in England

The documentary tradition in filmmaking continued to use the film medium as a powerful source of information for social control and mass education. The founder of the documentary tradition in England and later in Canada was John Grierson (1898–1972). Grierson claims he conceived the film medium as capable of many forms and functions, but he looked "on cinema as a pulpit, and used it as a propagandist" (Hardy 1966, p. 16). He clearly saw the advertising potential of the medium since it "is capable of direct description, simple analysis and commanding conclusion, and may by its tempo'd and imagistic powers, be made easily persuasive" (p. 16). In the heyday of the 1920s, Grierson undertook a three-year intensive study of the film industry in the United States. Here he came into contact with Robert Flaherty (1884–1951) of *Nanook of the North* (1922) fame, and the work of Eisenstein and the Soviet cinema. He returned home to Britain in 1927 and persuaded Sir Stephen Tallents of the Empire Marketing Board to create a documentary film unit to promote the sale of British products throughout the Commonwealth.

The only film Grierson directed was the silent documentary *Drifters* (1929), which traced the heroic saga of a single trawler and its crew catching fish in the North Sea. While his cameraman captured the physical hardships of this voyage, Grierson abstained from any social or economic context in the inter-titles. Since written texts were an important element in documentaries, Grierson brought together a group of politically conscious writers and poets, among them W. H. Auden and Stephen Spender, all Cambridge-educated, with his young filmmakers. Further, he brought Robert Flaherty to England to shoot footage for *Industrial Britain* (1933) and for Flaherty to act as adviser and mentor on their own film projects. Flaherty also stayed in England to make *Man of Aran* (1933) for Michael Balcon.

When Grierson adopted Flaherty's documentary methods of filming, he began manipulating and shaping the realities of life not as a neutral observer or ethnographer but for social purposes agreed upon with his sponsors. Paul Rotha, one of his young film directors, criticized these films as propaganda for big business, and accused them of advancing a conservative ideology. Grierson, however, maintained that the camera records reality faithfully and that a documentary film "opens up the real world by photographing the living scene and the living story" (Hardy 1966, p. 146). Moreover, by exploiting the raw materials in the real world, "cinema has the power to interpret more complex and astonishing happenings than the studio mind can conjure up" (p. 146). Like André Bazin, Grierson placed his faith in capturing unmediated reality within the scope of the story and the skill of the director's *mise-en-scène.* This style of realism, as a "window on the world," became a means for Grierson to apply socialist theories in an interpretation of the visible world, thereby controlling the end results to some degree.

In 1933, Grierson took his young film unit to work for the government's General Post

Office, which became their principal sponsors. In 1934, Alberto Cavalcanti, a Brazilian director who made experimental films in France during the 1920s, joined the film unit and fostered a move to dramatize documentary films in the style of Flaherty. He also introduced a more poetic and lyrical style bordering on the surreal. His *Coal Face* (1935) studies the effects of coal mining on the lives of the miners, with lyrical elements added by poet W. H. Auden and composer Benjamin Britten. *Night Mail* (1935), directed by Basil Wright and Harry Watt, achieved a more dramatic fusion of image and realistic observation with Auden's voice-over commentary that Cavalcanti edited into a powerful rhythmic climax. Grierson departed from the General Post Office (G.P.O.) in 1937, when he was invited to Canada to set up and run the National Film Board and to promote the Mackenzie King government.

With the start of the Second World War in 1939, the G.P.O film unit became the Crown Film Unit as part of the Ministry of Information. In their attempts to aid the British war effort, the documentary film directors developed a stronger poetic style to detail the struggle and victories of the common soldier at war. These films were carefully scripted by Cavalcanti and Harry Watt to inform and indoctrinate viewers. They used lightweight 16mm cameras to obtain documentary footage and mixed actual fighting scenes with historical reenactments to represent real-life incidents that led toward an Allied victory.

Of all the well-trained documentary filmmakers, Humphrey Jennings (1907–1950) most lifted the spirits of the British people at war with his work. His personal and creative interpretation of the Battle of Britain was much admired. His sense of personal expression was later to influence Lindsay Anderson and the Free Cinema movement of the 1950s. Jennings' first war film was *The First Days* (1939) in collaboration with Harry Watt. Here he carefully depicted civilians responding to the threat of the coming war with Germany. This film was followed by *Listen to Britain* (1942), *Fires Were Started* (1943) and *Diary for Timothy* (1945). Each documentary emphasized the common humanity of the people undergoing tremendous

In Jack Clayton's *Room at the Top* (1959), Laurence Harvey uses his mistress, Simone Signoret, to fight his way to success in a northern English town.

stress in surviving air-raids, fire bombings and the general madness of modern warfare. Watt took a different approach by showing the British soldier in combat. His *Target for Tonight* (1941) cleverly reconstructed a bombing mission over an oil refinery and storage center in Germany. Watt used real servicemen, bombers and fighter planes but the raid was a simulation. However, the message of the film was clear: Britain had the manpower and machines that could win the war. In 1943, Roy Boulting and his film crew went to North Africa to cover the Battle of El Alamein and the defeat of Rommel's Afrika Korps for their powerful documentary film, *Desert Victory*. The reception on the home front was impressive leading to further *Victory* documentaries, which

served the same purpose as Frank Capra's *Why We Fight* series made for the United States government.

The mixture of fact with fiction during the war was a common practice in documentary filmmaking. A more precise term for these films would be docudramas, for most of them were biased toward the point-of-view of the filmmaker. These docudramas were infused with propaganda to create support for the Allied war effort against the German forces then attacking England. Most British filmmakers followed the Aristotelian dramatic formula showing the basic life and death struggle and final victory. After the war, Michael Balcon (1896–1977), as head of Ealing Studios, used this semidocumentary technique for a number

Richard Burton as Jimmy Porter argues with his wife (Mary Ure) about the coming of the consumer society and his chances for a traditional life in Tony Richardson's *Look Back in Anger* (1959).

of feature-film comedies about middle-class life in Britain. The success of these films was worldwide, supported by the crafty and clever performances of Alec Guinness and Alistair Sim. These comedies depended upon a surreal construction of plots in which human conduct goes out of control, unchecked by law or order or conscious planning.

Alexander Mackendrick (1912–1993) directed *Tight Little Island* (1949) and *The Man in the White Suit* (1951). Local citizens were hired to play extras for the second film, and on-location shooting heightened its realism. Charles Crichton directed Guinness in *The Lavender Hill Mob* (1951), a crime caper that uses slapstick comedy routines akin to those of Mack Sennett but with an English tilt toward the unforeseen, playing on the trustwor-

thiness and honesty of the people. Crichton returned to filmmaking in 1988 when he directed John Cleese, of Monty Python fame, and Kevin Kline in another surreal comedy-farce, *A Fish Called Wanda* (1988). As in his earlier films, Crichton delights here in showing how the unexpected can debilitate criminal intentions.

Despite the success of the comedies made during the 1950s, Ealing Studios faced a box-office crisis and found it could not compete with the rise of television in Britain. When the "telly" took over as the primary form of entertainment in many middle and working-class households, the Ealing brothers decided to sell their studios to the BBC in 1955. Only two major producers, distributors and exhibitors remained in England, the Rank Organization and the Associated British Picture Corporation

Defiant Albert Finney plays a factory worker seeking to break away from the traditional working-class system with the aid of his fiancée, Shirley Anne Field, in Karel Reisz's *Saturday Night and Sunday Morning* (1960).

(ABC). They began backing independent producers to acquire the necessary commercial films for their own cinema circuits.

The "Angry Young Man" Movement

The characteristic reaction to the shift from the traditional values of the middle-class culture to the new postwar consumer culture is dramatically represented by playwright John Osborne in *Look Back in Anger*, directed by Tony Richardson at London's Royal Court Theatre in 1956. In this play, Jimmy Porter (Albert Finney) is a representative of the angry young men who suffer from psychological frustrations and doubt when confronted by the moral and

social upheavals generated by the new postwar consumer world. As an articulate university graduate, he gives voice to his feelings about the erosion of certain cultural values and beliefs brought about by mass advertising and the establishment, which, he claims, sold out his birthright. Porter attempts to free himself from these invisible marketing forces that use the media to daily invade and debase his contemporary world. He urgently wants to return to an earlier Edwardian time where his "usefulness" as a vital member of society will be evident. Within this cultural situation, however, Porter senses he has no chance of making any worthwhile contribution as a member of this new society, and he demonstrates his anger in a continual show of violence, attacking and destroying any meaningful social relationship he

Tom Courtney displays his hatred of the British class system by refusing to win a cross-country race for the benefit of his upper-class sponsor in *The Loneliness of the Long Distance Runner* (1962), directed by Tony Richardson.

has with other people, notably his wife. This destructiveness is based upon his own sense of impotence in justifying the expectations of his middle-class heritage. He simply refuses to undertake any constructive action toward the future.

The growing antagonism toward the new reality of popular culture and its consumer values was further accentuated by the demoralizing defeat of British imperialism in 1956, as the British invasion of Egypt failed to take control of the Suez Canal. With this defeat, Britain's role as a world power collapsed. In the same year, the Soviet Union exercised its control over Eastern Europe when Soviet tanks invaded Hungary and put down a Hungarian revolution.

British New Wave and Free Cinema

The arguments put forth by the "angry young man" movement in Britain became part of larger protests and demonstrations taken up by the younger working classes against the establishment. It was led by a group of politically radical young men at Oxford University. They were inspired by a neo–Marxist political ideology, and published their ideas in a journal, the *New Left Review*, in a reaction to the global changes in the power structures of the world during 1956. As social Marxists, they called for a fundamental restructuring of the economic system that exploited and oppressed people's lives through means of wealth, privilege and class. They protested against unfair labor practices and justified acts of violence against the power structures and institutions that maintained the status quo. Moreover, they attacked the values of the middle class and its materialistic interests in promoting a hedonistic and immoral popular culture. Further, they advocated a dissolution of the rigid class structures and a recognition of the virtues and solidarity of the working class.

A group of young film critics and independent filmmakers, Lindsay Anderson (b. 1923), Karel Reisz (b. 1926) and Tony Richardson (b. 1928) were sympathetic to the aims of the New Left. Anderson co-founded *Sequence,* at Oxford with Karel Reisz, which he edited from 1947 to 1952 . He then began making industrial documentaries for an engineering firm in the early 1950s. Later, a personal note came through two short films, *Wakefield Express* (1952) and *Thursday's Children* (1953), about the problems children face in a world of silence at a school for the deaf. It won an Oscar in 1954 and illustrated the central themes of Free Cinema productions: One, the director should impose his own personal observations and ideas in recording the lives of working-class people; two, a "poetic realism" should emerge from the raw material; and three, the director as artist should be selective in the choice of documentary material to support his or her views on the true nature of social reality. With *Every Day Except Christmas* (1957) and *O Dreamland* (1953), Anderson was able to emphasize his interest in working-class values and sense of community. He co-directed and produced *Momma Don't Allow* (1955) with Tony Richardson, about a London jazz club. Later he directed *We Are the Lambeth Boys* (1958) and his first feature, *This Sporting Life* (1963). Both films examined with greater interest the newly emerging youth culture, showing fresh observations on leisure activities of the new working class. Underlying these docudramas was a continuity with the film theories of John Grierson, who advocated the use of documentary techniques as a means to inform and educate the public to a new social awareness.

All three directors contributed critical essays for *Sight and Sound*, a magazine published by the British Film Institute (BFI), an educational organization formed to disseminate information and critical reviews on film theory and filmmaking and to encourage experimental non-commercial filmmaking. The public awareness of Free Cinema grew out of BFI sponsorship of six Free Cinema programs shown at the National Film Theatre in London between 1956 and 1959. In addition to these British documentaries, a selection of foreign films and documentaries by European filmmakers, including Claude Chabrol, François Truffaut, Roman Polanski and Georges Franju, were featured in these Free Cinema programs. During this time Anderson wrote several articles for *Sight and Sound* that proposed films should be socially committed to illuminate the problems of contemporary life. Before long, he joined Karel Reisz and Tony Richardson in bringing documentary realism to feature film production.

In 1959, after Tony Richardson's stage success with John Osborne's play, *Look Back in Anger*, Richardson formed Woodfall films with Harry Saltzman to produce films based on Osborne's plays. As one of the independent production companies, Woodfall found commercial distribution through British Lion and in America through Walter Reade. With financial backing in place, *Look Back in Anger* was followed by *The Entertainer* in 1960, starring Sir Laurence Olivier as an out-of-date music hall comic. With the production of Alan Sillitoe's novel *Saturday Night and Sunday Morning* (1960), Karel Reisz was able to bring the "poetic realism" of Free Cinema to the commercial screen. Location shooting of working-class homes inside the ominous industrial cities of Britain brought documentary qualities to this film. The star system was abandoned and the leading roles were given to rising stage actors like Albert Finney, who played Arthur Seaton. The success of this film is due to the audience's identification with the attitudes expressed by this character. At the beginning of the film, he says, "What I'm out for is a good time. All the rest is propaganda." For its language and frank representation of sex and violence, the film received an X certificate from the censor. It focused on a working-class rebel who is hostile to

Richard Harris (center) plays an arrogant but insecure English rugby star in a clash of identities. He displays his disillusionment with the postwar British society at a Christmas party given in his team owner's posh new home in *This Sporting Life* (1963).

the inequalities of the class system but lacks the imagination and education to free himself of it. Reisz's mobile camera documents the working environment of the factory and the oppressive lifestyles within the industrialized city. The film is organized around the leisure activities of Seaton as he tries to satisfy his sexual appetite while rebelling against the codes and communal values of traditional working-class life. Various episodes reveal his discontent with the crowded conditions at home, where his parents are trapped by the "telly," and the ways he spends his weekends at the local pub, where he engages in various sexual liaisons.

Saturday Night and Sunday Morning

There are a number of pop songs that infiltrate the pub where Arthur and his friends meet after work. The small pub band plays "I'm gonna grab it — I'll have it. Why not? Why not?" Such pop songs provide the contrast between the youth culture and the traditional working-class culture of the older men who frequent the downstairs bar and sing group songs. Later the pop band sings "What do you want if you don't want money?" alluding to the women who attend to the needs of the young men. In this new consumer culture of the working-class male, one's identity is revealed by one's wardrobe, spending money, and relationships with young women. Here the rules are defined in terms of the aggressive heterosexual male and satisfaction of his desires. Women are split as characters. Either they are other men's wives or potential wives seeking marriage and a home, or they become mistresses and lovers intent on continuing sexual intercourse with men. The film is explicit and direct about these sexual relationships but the narrative takes a conservative moral stand against these extra-marital affairs.

The discovery of Seaton's illicit love affair with his boss' wife becomes the turning point in this narrative. He is found out and severely beaten by the husband's army buddies. These scenes, coupled with Seaton's futile attempt to secure an abortion for this woman, destroy any positive images of a possible family or married life. Instead, the film celebrates an individual's resistance to arbitrary acts of repression used to maintain the status quo. In this way, *Saturday Night and Sunday Morning* becomes a drama organized around a playboy-type hero, whose fantasies are devoted to a good time through a variety of sexual escapades. As a rebellion against the status quo—"Don't let the bastards grind you down"— Finney's portrayal of a defiant factory worker, who appears to resist settling down in a new suburbia being built at the edge of town, confirms the emerging tastes and values of a youth culture ready to change an outdated society (Hill 1986, pp. 145–176).

The irony of the angry young man movement occurs when we find that the traditional hero of *Look Back in Anger* seeks to hold back the coming of the consumer society to ensure his traditional middle-class birthright. On the other hand, the new affluent working-class hero, although discouraged by the advent of pop culture, sought to defy the traditional mores of his class.

Changes occurred in the British film industry in the early 1960s as the New Wave films, such as *A Taste of Honey* (1961) and *The Loneliness of the Long Distance Runner* (1962), were released by Woodfall Film productions. Under Tony Richardson's direction, both films are explorations of adolescent rebellion in which working-class people attempt to find a new life in a changing social and political climate. In 1963, Richardson then directed John Osborne's screenplay of Joseph Fielding's novel *Tom Jones*. The film is a bawdy 18th century rendering of a country rustic's adventures when he comes into a fortune. With a lusty performance by Albert Finney in the lead role, Richard-

son adopted some of the intrigues of the French New Wave in his irreverent but playful rendition of the youthful rebel. This film garnered Richardson Oscars for best picture and best direction, and brought American money and producers into "swinging London."

Lindsay Anderson continued his documentary interests in his first feature film, *This Sporting Life*, starring Richard Harris as a rugby star whose overnight wealth brings him into conflict with his working-class values. Adapted from David Storey's novel, the film gave Anderson an opportunity to paint a brutal picture of the rat race hidden behind sober middle-class society. In his next three feature films, he attacks the degeneracy and decadence of the British class system in no uncertain terms. With Malcolm McDowell playing the central character, Mick Travis, Anderson directed *If...* (1968) about a youthful rebellion in an English private school using Vigo's *Zéro de conduite / Zero for Conduct* (1933) as his model of student insurrection. He followed this film with *O Lucky Man!* (1972), using a disconcerting Brechtian style to pursue his accusations of the absurdity and arrogance of greedy politicians in collusion with the medical profession. The final film of this trilogy, *Britannia Hospital* (1982), becomes a nightmarish version of British pomp and ceremony brought to life via BBC television crews. The media visitation causes havoc and allows Anderson to depict the decay and deterioration of the medical establishment.

References

Hardy, Forsyth (ed.). 1966. *Grierson on Documentary*. New York: Praeger.

Hill, John. 1986. *Sex, Class and Realism: British Cinema 1956–1963*. London: BFI Publishing.

CHAPTER 19

The Italian Cinema of Fellini and Antonioni

Introduction

This chapter surveys the work of Roberto Rossellini, Federico Fellini, and Michelangelo Antonioni as they moved away from the post-war problems of working-class people struggling against poverty and unemployment. The artistic and commercial success of Italian films after the neorealist period was primarily the result of two major factors developed by the Italian film industry. One was the popular appeal of genre films, mostly romantic comedies and westerns that competed with American films on the international market. The second was the emergence of highly profitable "art" films from Italian filmmakers such as Visconti and Fellini, whose highly personal cinematic styles rose above their neorealist concerns to earn prestigious film awards at major international film festivals. Rossellini was the leader of this new perspective; his films examine the psychological traumas of contemporary marriage and the resulting emotional alienation and despair. Following Rossellini's lead, Antonioni and Fellini began to create a cinema of Reconstruction with their own personal films on the effects of solitude and alienation upon human beings. Both these directors introduced new narrative techniques blending a surreal fantasy with reality. Fellini's major works of this period are *La strada* (1954), *La dolce vita* (1960), *Otto e mezzo / 8½* (1963) and *Giulietta degli spiriti / Juliet of the Spirits* (1965).

Antonioni produced a highly acclaimed trilogy—*L'avventura* (1960), *La notte / The Night* (1961) and *L'eclisse / The Eclipse* (1962)—that broke away from more conventional narrative techniques to explore the emotionally sterile lives of characters alienated by modern society. In *Blow-Up* (1966) Antonioni plays with camera images whose visual aspects displace the narrative, shifting it toward abstraction and an ambiguous relationship to one's identity.

Rossellini's Break with Neorealism

Roberto Rossellini (1906–1977) began the shift away from neorealism with his production of *The Miracle,* written by Fellini, in 1947. This story is about a simple-minded peasant girl, depicted by Anna Magnani, who believes she is made pregnant by a man she takes to be St. Joseph. Rossellini relies on the virtuoso performance of Magnani to bring this religious allegory into focus. More important is Rossellini's belief that modern society has lost touch with an understanding of a religious experience. In his next film Rossellini explores the theme of a "saintly fool" in *Francesco, Guillare of God* (1950). This theme is later transposed by Fellini in his two early films *La strada* and *Le notti di Cabiria / The Nights of Cabiria* (1956). Rossellini also began developing a new cinematic technique, *plan-sequence*, in which the director organizes the action into a long single take to concentrate on an actress to reveal her psychological state of mind. His reliance upon professional actresses continued as he cast his wife, Ingrid Bergman, in a series of films that explored the pain and suffering of a woman alienated and estranged by a modern marriage.

In Michelangelo Antonioni's *Blow-Up* (1966), David Hemmings as a mod fashion photographer checks film strips *(opposite)*, and mounts model Veruschka for an orgiastic photo session in the "swinging London" of the 1960s.

Rossellini directed two robust films in the early 1950s, *Europa 51* (1952) and *Viaggio in Italia / Voyage to Italy* (1953) that completed the break with the neorealist aesthetic. In these films, Rossellini's *mise-en-scène* techniques use the natural locations and sites as impersonal realities that mirror the estrangement of the cen-

tral characters from an emotional life. With these films Rossellini "shifted the focus of Italian neo-realism perceptively toward psychological analysis and emotional behavior and away from themes directly associated with the war" (Bondanella 1993, p. 108). Such a decisive shift of Italian neorealist cinema evolved to-

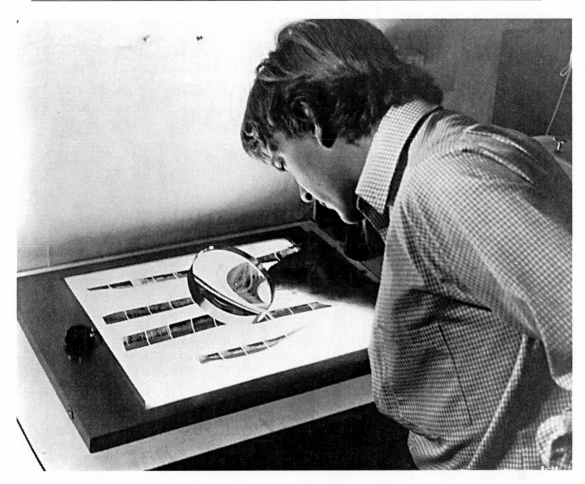

ward a postwar Italian cinema characterized by an existentialist examination of solitude and alienation in the work of Fellini and Antonioni and their own anti-linear film narratives. Fellini works within parables while Antonioni takes on ideological, existential constructs.

Rossellini recovered critical approval in the later 1950s, first with his documentary *India* (1958), then with *Il generale Della Rovere / General Della Rovere* (1959), starring Vittorio De Sica as an Italian Resistance fighter, signaling a return to the neorealist style. Rossellini's interest in historical docudramas brought him into French and Italian television where he directed *L'età del ferro / The Age of Iron* (1964), *Atti degli apostoli / The Acts of the Apostles* (1968) and *La Prise de pouvoir par Louis XIV / The Rise of Louis XIV* (1966), which received critical praise in its theatrical release. His detached style, using a *mise-en-scène* with extensive long takes emphasizing slow zooms and panning, presented his elliptical narratives with remarkable historical detachment and authenticity as in *The Age of the Medici* (1972) and *Blaise Pascal* (1974). By then Rossellini had achieved canonization by New Wave filmmakers, like Godard in France and Bernardo Bertolucci in Italy, as a man devoted to the persuasive uses of the cinema.

The Films of Federico Fellini

Though Federico Fellini (1920–1993) adopted the cinematic techniques of *mise-en-scène* and the long take, he followed the aesthetic of the neorealists. His first film *Luci del varietà / Variety Lights* (1950), co-directed with Alberto Lattuada, displays his great interest in music halls and vaudeville acts. He combined this interest with early mating games of young men in *Lo sceicco bianco / The White Sheik*

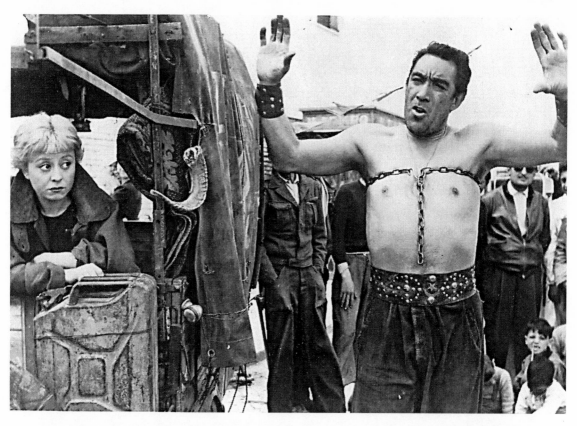

Giulietta Masina plays Gelsomina, a clown performer and concubine to Zampano (Anthony Quinn), a roguish strongman who betrays her in a callous manner without compassion in Federico Fellini's *La strada* (1954).

(1952) and *I vitelloni* (1953). In two of his most popular films of the 1950s, *La strada* and *Nights of Cabiria*, both starring his wife, Giulietta Masina, in the leading role, Fellini adopted Rossellini's theme of the "saintly fool." Yet while Fellini uses neorealist themes, these two films add a sense of surreality to the mystery and spectacle in the life of a street performer. *La strada,* a parable about a young woman sold into bondage to a circus strongman, was the turning point in Fellini's film career when the film won an Oscar for Best Foreign Film and brought him international acclaim.

These films are motivated by Fellini's recurrent theme of finding some meaningful spiritual values that will convert or redeem one's existence in a world of spiritual poverty and alienation. His films indirectly touch upon the economic and social forces that act upon human relationships, but they focus on the human values of self-worth and faith neces-

sary to sustain existence amid a harsh, insensitive world corrupted by personal greed and selfishness, one devoid of human compassion and understanding. In both *La strada* and *Nights of Cabiria*, Fellini uses allegory to demonstrate how the gifts of life and love are destroyed by the forces of ignorance, greed and selfishness. This baseness and cynicism of the adult world is personified by the two male characters, Zampano, the strongman in *La strada,* and Oscar, a would-be marriage partner in *Nights of Cabiria.* In both situations, the childlike innocence of the woman is shattered by the betrayal and duplicity of the man. In *La strada,* Gelsomina is abandoned, her gift of love destroyed by Zampano. Rejected, she now drifts in a world made meaningless, without comfort or compassion, to die alone. Yet Fellini shows us that in the end, even the brutish Zampano, in his own loneliness, will finally be touched by the selfless love of Gelsomina. The ending of

Marcello Mastroianni rides a playgirl in an act of sensuality as part of a wild night on the town in Fellini's *La dolce vita* (1960).

Nights of Cabiria differs greatly from *La strada.* Cabiria is not defeated nor set back by Oscar's betrayal, but instead she is redeemed by an awareness of a life-affirming vision. Thus, Cabiria recovers her self-esteem as she meets a procession of youthful players starting down a symbolic road of life we all travel.

In his films of the 1960s and 1970s, Fellini's stature as a filmmaker grew with each successive film. *La dolce vita* (1960) or "the sweet life" achieved huge profits at the box office in Italy and abroad for its controversial depiction of the decadent lives of Italian intellectuals and the bourgeoisie, and its anticlerical stance toward the Church. The Vatican newspaper quickly classified the film "unsuitable for all" for its debasement of family values and its depiction of casual sex and suicide. Moreover, the Italian government decried the way Fellini sat-irized the Church and the TV media for manipulating human spectacles for their own interests. Throughout the controversy raised by this film, Fellini maintained that he used the cinema as a means toward a personal expression, a vision that affirmed and accepted a person's humanity in the celebration of life. Thus, Fellini attacked those institutions and social conventions that inhibited the freedom of a person toward self-fulfillment. Fellini (1976) contends that:

> What I care about most is the freedom of man, liberation of the individual man from the network of moral and social conventions in which he believes, or rather in which he thinks he believes and which encloses him and limits him and makes him narrower, smaller, sometimes even worse than he really is [pp. 157–158].

Marcello Mastroianni, as director, makes up his mistress as a prostitute so that he can engage in his own sexual fantasies in 8½.

In his later films, Fellini combines the energizing forces of life to emancipate his central characters from the decadent and life-inhibiting mythologies and institutions of modern society. In all his works, the city of Rome becomes the center for an unending conflict between decadence and rebirth. Thematically, the contradictions of modern life encouraged Fellini's directorial imagination to develop his love of the circus, a place of mystery and magic, into a metaphor of modern life, where one kind of activity or illusion overlaps with another in a continuing cycle without any apparent beginning or end. In many of his films, the corruption and prostitution of life for material rewards is countered with the childlike innocence of his characters, who provide us with an insight on and faith in the wonders of existence.

La dolce vita is organized around the quest by a reporter, an alter ego of Fellini played by Marcello Mastroianni, seeking life-supporting values in the hedonistic world of modern Rome. There are many encounters with different representatives of this society but each experience demonstrates how gravely modern humanity is disconnected from the generative source of psychic energy that focuses meaning in life. In its place Fellini depicts several artificial social structures that impede meaningful communication. Christian mythology appears hollow and reflects the emptiness of human values in modern life. The absurdity of existence is personified in the suicide of the intellectual Steiner, who has detached himself from human needs. The tawdry love affairs are sexual games performed without passion by Mastroianni as public relation stunts.

The later films of Fellini, especially *8½* and

In Federico Fellini's *8½* (1963), Marcello Mastroianni plays Guido, a film director searching for material for his next film, partly based on his own personal relationships with his wife, his mistress and other associates.

Amarcord (1974), are a combination of autobiographical details and childhood fantasies that contrast a sense of wonder and joy in the mysteries of life with a sense of malignant, nameless images that emerge from the darkness threatening or even destroying life. These shadowy figures appear and reappear constantly in the action of *8½*. They are surreal phantoms that psychologically condition human response. *Amarcord* serves Fellini as a nostalgic return to his boyhood days in Rimini when fascism was on the rise in Italy. Part of the film is his examination of the social and political causes of fascism. He concludes that fascism arrests development of a person during adolescence, where children remain children for eternity, leaving responsibility to others, and feeling a sense of security in having someone

else do one's thinking, first one's mother, then, in another time and place, Il Duce.

While both *Amacord* and *8½* draw heavily upon autobiographical experiences, *8½* spotlights a director's struggle to find the creative inspiration required to bring about his own spiritual redemption. At times it is a surreal fantasy in which Guido, as portrayed by Mastroianni, is a film director attempting to escape from the reality of the film's production. In this manner, the film is self-reflexive on the fears that the director must face as he develops the script for the film. With no apparent solution at hand, Guido attempts suicide to escape from his inability to resolve the terrifying conflict between his commitment to his art and to the commercial demands of his new film. Some critics have considered this motion picture a

The director Guido, wondering where he is as he recovers from a nightmare in a fashionable health spa in *8½.*

"film within a film," but that explanation overlooks the exploration by the director of his past nightmares, fantasies and fears that have produced the material that is the basis of this mid-life crisis.

Fellini says that *8½* is a "film in which parts of the past and imaginary events are superim-posed on the present." The episodic narrative is structured like a three-ring circus with the director's alter ego, Guido, as the ringmaster, moving characters from present events to memories, then to fantasies. Again, Fellini uses the circus as a metaphor for a human comedy that objectifies his own subjective state of mind. The film centers on his quest for identity, self-definition and liberation from the restrictive codes and conventional forces of society, from his parents to his schoolteachers to his wife and associates. Entrapment occurs in the first surreal sequence that opens the film. In this scene Guido is trapped in his car, then magically he escapes into the clouds only to be pulled back to earth by his producers.

Throughout the film, Fellini dramatizes episodes in which he fantasizes how these various forces, from church to family, tyrannize him. In Guido's first appearance at the hotel, we realize that "dream spaces" exist side by side with "real" spaces depicted in the film. Episodic scenes flow into one another repeating the theme of the self-reflexive spirit seeking to unlock the mystery of creativity. In the end, Guido understands that his film must include all of the past obsessions and experiences of his authentic self.

Guido, as director and Fellini's alter ego, awakens to the fact that his quest for spiritual renewal resides in the circus, a spectacle where magic and mystery energize his imagination. In this arena, the conflicting forces of illusion and reality, innocence and experience meet and restore order to his life. The circus also brings together the opposing forces of containment and liberation representing the psychic wholeness of union. Thus, the director symbolically returns to life as he disregards his critics and strikes up the band. Then he unites all hands, family and cast alike, into a magical circle to reaffirm the joyous forces of life itself (Affron 1990, pp. 109–124).

Fellini's later films of the 1970s and 1980s were equally self-reflexive as he turned to Italian literature to seek comparative social satires that brought into play memories of containment and flights into liberation. He began with *Juliet of the Spirits* (1965), which contained a strong feminist tract on the role of a housewife fantasizing her escape into new worlds. This was followed quickly by his adaptation of the *Satyricon* by the Roman author, Petronius. *Fellini Satyricon* (1969) is a sensuous odyssey of two young men first joining, then escaping from the myriad bacchanals within the Roman empire. More phantasmagoric in surreal,

dream-like spectacles than Fellini's previous films, *Satyricon* shifts between the imaginary and symbolic restrictions on the libido that jeopardize the lives of these men as they travel through ancient Rome.

The Films of Michelangelo Antonioni

The films of Michelangelo Antonioni (b. 1912) also evolved from his awareness of the existentialist crises in modern life. Where Fellini informs his films through his own visions of Christian humanist philosophy, Antonioni avoids the romantic, fantasy world constructed within the powerful imagination of a director. In its place his films project the existentialist dilemma facing displaced characters searching for identity in a completely alienated, urbanized society. Antonioni's films thus contemplate what happens to men and women when moral systems are absent from human relationships. In the same year that Fellini's *La dolce vita* appeared, Antonioni released his film *L'avventura*, starring Monica Vitti. The film deals with bored middle-class people whose loss of contact with each other leads to promiscuity and philosophical speculation. The plot of this film is a simple one: a woman mysteriously disappears and her two friends go on a search for her. After a time, the two friends forget about the missing person and instead begin their own love affair. Thus, the "search" for someone becomes a thematic excuse for Antonioni to transform traditional narrative cinema into an exploration of feelings between a man and a woman caught in their own psychological landscapes. Suffering from a sense of meaninglessness, absurdity and boredom, they respond by attempting to find relief through sexual liaisons. But these sexual encounters fail to overcome their own need for some meaningful human relationship and the unexplained absence of the other.

In this manner, Antonioni creates similar situations that illustrate a variation on the problems inherent in today's society. Antonioni does not advocate any predetermined solution. As a documentary filmmaker, he uses the long take and long focal length lenses that flatten the space and confine his characters in an environment while distancing his camera from the action. In his presentation of the enigma of modern life, his characters appear to be displaced within the theatricality of an outdoor setting. They are like "found objects" lacking identity, purpose or meaning. They are stranded in a new kind of existence in which significant action within moral standards and human values have atrophied. These characters have been cast adrift in the time-space medium of cinema, into the absurdity of modern technological life where images and appearances control social activities.

In his own minimalist style, Antonioni has explored the existentialist dilemmas of Sartre and Camus: one, that life is merely a sum of the actions one lives; two, that our modern society depersonalizes and alienates us from ourselves and each other insofar as the ability to communicate meaningfully with one another has failed; three, that our faith and belief in the purpose of life has been lost, and with it our ability to distinguish between love and lust.

L'avventura, *La notte* and *L'eclisse* form a trilogy advancing the same theme of aliena-tion. They entertain the ambiguities of modern life in the midst of uncertainty and change and the pervasiveness of chance and disorder. The film narratives are tautological and thus the action is circular. The characters end up where they have started without being able to come to grips with or advance any answers to the socio-political problems they encounter in their journey through an urbanized Western world.

A spectator's response to their explorations makes us more aware how a person's life in a post-industrial society becomes sterile. Destructive acts of sex are seen in this cold and empty world as diversions through which anxieties are discharged. In *Professione: Reporter / The Passenger* (1975), chance happenings and puzzling accidents are the means for a TV reporter to make contact with revolutionaries, but in the end all significant actions become self-centered or self-inflicted, as seen in his interview with the rebel leader who reverses the questions asked. In this film we become passengers, and like the TV reporter, willingly exchange identities in hopes of entering a new world of political adventure and daring.

Although his early trilogy gave Antonioni international prominence as a filmmaker, popular acceptance of his films occurred with the release of *Blow-Up* (1966), made in England for MGM. Again, Antonioni takes us on an extended search, this time with a photographer who tries to find some meaning and connection through a series of still photographs. Behind this narrative, the director clearly indicates how our lives are shaped by our fragmentary ways of seeing, and the manner in which we attempt to construct meaning from supposedly documentary facts. However, the true drama of Antonioni's films depends upon our emotional reactions to the undecipherable chance occurrences one encounters in life itself.

Blow-Up is an English adaptation from Julio Cortázar's short story, "Las Babas del Diablo," or "Devil's Drool." As Spanish slang, the title refers to a person having a close call with evil. The moral of the story involves saving the soul of a human being from Satan.

In the film version, Antonioni follows a story line with a photographer, Thomas, as a voyeur who gazes upon a lovemaking tryst and takes a series of photographs of the primal scene. But a spectator's attention to Thomas' acts of voyeurism, which lead to a possible enactment of an Oedipal plot, is only an entry into understanding some of the actions in the narrative. In his many attempts to interpret these photos, Thomas realizes that he was a witness to more than just an embrace of lovers alone in an Arcadian setting. Thomas proceeds to blow up several shots, then sections from these shots, without revealing to the audience any connections. Then, when the camera pans to view these series of blow-ups in a particular sequence, a story unfolds. To enjoy *Blow-Up*, one must realize that these images are susceptible to various interpretive acts by the viewer. They do not depend so much on the replication of external reality, but more upon the social contexts in which they are perceived. Thomas, after witnessing a primal scene, attempts to understand his unconscious reactions to this scene. Here the interplay between past memories and consciousness comes into play, between the voyeur and the image, since Antonioni demonstrates how such images of real events symbolically alter how we respond to their reality. Thus, the true subject of this film concerns understanding how one's consciousness of self is shaped by an imaginary fantasy of desire which misrepresents one's fragmentary ways of perceiving the outside world, whether from a journalistic, objective stance or by accepting a given interpretation of this world through the images of another (Eberwein 1990, pp. 262–281).

References

Affron, Charles. 1990. "Order and the Space for Spectacle in Fellini's *8½*." In *Close Viewings: An Anthology of New Film Criticism*. Edited by Peter Lehman. Tallahassee: Florida State University Press, pp. 109–120.

Bondanella, Peter. 1993. *Italian Cinema: From Neorealism to the Present*. New York: Continuum.

Eberwein, Robert. 1990. "The Master Text of *Blow-Up*." In *Close Viewings: An Anthology of New Film Criticism*. Edited by Peter Lehman. Tallahassee: Florida State University Press, pp. 262–281.

Fellini, Federico. 1976. *Fellini on Fellini*. New York: Delacorte Press.

CHAPTER 20

Hollywood Revival and the Anti-Myth Era: 1964–1976

Introduction

New cinematic trends from Europe helped Hollywood reemerge as a production center for commercial filmmaking. One trend recognized the impact of the New Wave films by Godard, Truffaut and Antonioni on younger American audiences. To offset television dramas and sitcoms, these new films broke away from the traditional genre films of Hollywood and began to explore the sexual and psychological conflicts of offbeat heroes using Brechtian episodic structures and improvisational techniques similar to those of Godard. Producers also targeted their films to the particular interests of the youth culture and younger audiences within urban centers. The second trend capitalized on the success of the New Independent Cinema and the experimental films of Andy Warhol and Stan Brakhage in New York. Their films introduced new cinematic forms of elliptical construction and controversial depictions of sex, drugs and violence. More important was the introduction of the antihero protagonist, who as a misfit, loner or outlaw, challenged the norms and values of modern industrial society. From these trends, a new Hollywood cinema arose that responded to the social and political changes in society created by the Civil Rights Movement, the assassinations of Robert Kennedy and Martin Luther King, Jr., and the student protests against the Vietnam War. By May 1968, large student protests in America and Europe demanded the powerful industrial-military complex end the war. Commercial films such as Arthur Penn's *Bonnie and Clyde*

(1967), Mike Nichols' *The Graduate* (1967), and Stanley Kubrick's *A Clockwork Orange* (1971) appealed to a new generation of moviegoers by reflecting the spirit of the counter-culture. Each film presents different social accounts of the antihero protagonist during this period of film history.

Pop Art and the Play of Images in the 1960s

In the 1960s, Pop Art and later manifestations of this work known as postmodern art incorporated machine-processed images and objects that are produced by an urban, industrial society and transformed them into collages and assemblages. In the United States, Robert Rauschenberg and Jasper Johns were precursors of Pop Art. They were the first American artists to dramatize the ambiguities between an image as a "signifier" and a verbal representation. This dramatic shift in modern painting follows the semiotic concept that pictures or images of reality are to be read as part of the "text" of language games. A Pop artist was thus seen as a player who makes a game of metonymic connections out of a selection of pre-existing symbols, signs and icons. These visual signifiers change their meaning according to the contexts in which they are placed. The effect of collage is to displace these images from their ordinary contexts and allow them to take on new signification or identity. By taking them out of their ordinary contexts, one can reflect upon the power of the image and the

Dustin Hoffman as Ben breaks sexual taboos as he meets Mrs. Robinson for an extramarital affair in *The Graduate* (1967), directed by Mike Nichols.

influence it holds upon one's sense of truth. By displaying them as documentary facts, these artists deconstruct such images and expose the controlling visual elements that mediate our daily perceptual experiences. Pop artists, then, use the icons of Hollywood and re-combine them into new disguises to reveal the true artifice behind the image.

Part of the artists' response, especially in Antonioni's *Blow-Up*, was inspired by Marcel Duchamp's philosophy of a *readymade* and an *objet trouvé*. Antonioni plays out the Freudian game of repressed memory by the unexpected juxtaposition of photographic images that recall past lived experiences. These images create a visual language game that unconsciously contributes to the roles played by the central character in this film. In some ways, Antonioni, like other Pop artists of the 1960s, plays with the ambiguities of the self and the other. This con-

cept shapes his films, and is reminiscent of the Dadaist collages of Kurt Schwitters, a German artist from the 1920s. Schwitters' work consisted of collected bits and pieces of industrial refuse and waste that triggered past memories and unconscious relationships.

A leading British artist, Richard Hamilton, adopted both Duchamp's philosophy of art and the collage technique of Schwitters to create a small collage, *Just What Is It That Makes Homes So Different, So Appealing?* (1956). The collage shows a nude muscle-man in a Charles Atlas pose holding a large lollipop, with the word "pop" covering his private parts. Seated on a couch nearby is a nude female with a television set behind her showing a woman on the phone. Products of the consumer culture adorn the walls and floors of the apartment, including a Ford emblem, a tape recorder, an enlarged poster of Romance comics, a Warner's Theatre movie marquee featuring Al Jolson in *The Jazz Singer*, and a large tinned ham on the coffee table.

The term *Pop Art* was coined by the English critic Lawrence Alloway in 1952 at a conference in London where artists like Richard Hamilton and others discussed the effects folk art or popular culture had upon the fine arts. Pop Art is also called Neo-Dada because it tries to attack the power of popular art or kitsch. Kitsch is a term that is applied to mass mechanical reproductions of original works of art. Kitsch also appears to be folk art that appeals to the romantic desires of the populace. The most powerful forms of kitsch are found in detective thrillers and gangster novels. However, kitsch is a substitute for the "real thing." It is empty and sterile, since it devalues and replaces actual experiences (Richardson and Stangos 1974, pp. 224–237).

In the history of cinema, the pioneering film of the 1960s was Godard's *Breathless*. He appropriated the popular American "B" movies made by Monogram Pictures and incorporated all the images associated with advertisements and their kitsch qualities to parody romantic illusions based upon gangster heroes. By undercutting the illusionism of a gangster and juxtaposing the real life of Paris with a fictitious hero, Godard accomplishes the same goal as Pop Art. With humor and irony, he displaces his hero from the expected role model, in the fashion of Marcel Duchamp. He allows his characters to show evidence of a self-awareness by becoming bored with the "taken for granted" ways of living as a criminal. Godard thus forces the viewer to question who is really controlling the film fantasy. Moreover, Godard's films encourage a debate on the banality of consumer culture. Hence, the viewer needs to look at the problems caused by modern culture within such genre films and understand the ways these film narratives conditioned the viewers' perceptions of themselves as well as of others, and further, how cinema itself appears to communicate what is "the truth" about the modern world.

Andy Warhol (1927–1987), as a visual artist and filmmaker, also used minimalist strategies in his art and film work. He produced over 50 films in his Factory in New York. As one of the leading figures of an underground film movement for a New American Cinema, he experimented with new theories on film time that broke away from the traditional narrative forms established by Hollywood. By returning to the one-shot, one-reel cinema of Lumière, Warhol forces the viewer to take a new attitude toward the repetition of sequences through long, fixed camera shots of an immobile subject. *Sleep* (1963) is a six-hour long film document on a man asleep. *The Empire State Building* (1964) becomes a dusk to dawn film document about the slow visual change from artificial to natural light which alters the building's character.

Chelsea Girls (1967) became a satirical Warhol study of erotic decadence of the 1960s that found popular appeal and commercial distribution. His camera becomes a true voyeur and spy, seeking a narcissistic identification with the objects photographed, and capturing a mirror image of the sexual intrigues happening in various rooms at the Chelsea Hotel at any given time. Warhol used a split-screen projection system to allow viewers to see different actors play out the same scene simultaneously as they would in real life. As a subversive strategy, Warhol's documentary camera effectively deromanticized the sexual act, making it as sterile as a tomato soup can. Warhol produced films directed by Paul Morrissey, such as *Flesh* (1968) and *Trash* (1970), in which actors play out their sexual fantasies with others when they are self-conscious of their roles and improvise their situation, disregarding plot structure. In these films, Warhol parodies the relationships between the sexes to show clearly that sex, violence and drug-taking are over-dramatized and glamorized by many Hollywood image-makers (Brougher 1996, pp. 138–187).

American Directors in England

Three American directors, Joseph Losey (1909–1984), Richard Lester (b. 1932) and Stanley Kubrick (1928–1999) brought film techniques from the French New Wave and Pop Art to their films of the 1960s. Of the three, Lester settled in England as a director of television commercials. His association with Peter Sellers and *The Goon Show* led to the direction of an experimental short film, *The Running, Jumping, and Standing Still Film* (1959). From this encounter with Sellers and his surrealist antics, he made two feature films about life on the road with the Beatles. *A Hard Day's Night* (1964) and *Help!* (1965) are a mixture of improvised cinematic sketches to display the music-making of this popular rock band caught in a surreal world of their own. In *A Hard Day's Night* Lester captures the paradoxical rise of the Beatles to media fame as a surreal fantasy. Fully exploiting cinematic devices such as jump-cuts, telephoto zooms, flashbacks and transformations, Lester achieves a fresh, exhilarating style of screen comedy by showing how each member of the band attempts to escape not only from his rabid fans but from the effects of daily media exposure. These episodic juxtapositions are carried out with the performances by John, Paul, George and Ringo of their popular songs such as "All My Lovin'," "I Wanna Be Your Man" and others.

As part of the New Wave counter-culture, the Beatles parodied the roles of proper Englishmen from a working-class perspective. Lester's freewheeling film style emulated the rock and roll beat and avoided the conventions of Hollywood musicals. Chance encounters liberate the actions of this talented singing group just as the Beatles urged their fans to escape from the restrictions of their established culture. In *The Knack* (1965) Lester achieved further recognition in adapting Ann Jellicoe's stage play to the screen using similar cinematic tricks to underline the eccentric actions of the lovers. Lester applied this free-flowing film style in a number of stage musicals he adapted to the screen, including *A Funny Thing Happened on the Way to the Forum* (1966) starring Buster Keaton, and *How I Won the War* (1967), starring Beatle John Lennon. Lester's films are now seen as precursors to the surreal comedies of the Monty Python troupe. Lester's unique cinematic techniques remain a seminal influence on the making of contemporary music videos on MTV today.

Joseph Losey was blacklisted in 1951 when he refused to testify before the House Un-American Activities Committee in Washington. He moved to England and worked under a variety of names, such as Victor Hanbury and Joseph Walton. His film collaborations with Harold Pinter brought out his skills in dealing with the ideological forces inherent in the rigid English class system. *The Servant* (1963), *Accident* (1967) and *The Go-Between* (1971) reflect the influence of Samuel Beckett and the Theatre of the Absurd on his interpretation of unconscious, irrational forces at play. These dark and probing psychological studies are given a more symbolic and intellectual treatment for film audiences. *Accident* moves from the civilized behavior of a group of men and women living at Oxford to the unmasking of the emotional pain and darkness beneath each person's facade. It is exciting to watch Losey use Brechtian stage techniques to distance the viewer from empathic responses and to reveal the destructive side of the English class system in a narrative discourse controlling the sexual behavior of each person.

Stanley Kubrick (1928–1999) was brought to Europe by actor Kirk Douglas to help complete a wide-screen film epic in Italy, *Spartacus* (1960). Douglas had previously starred in Kubrick's anti-war film *Paths of Glory* (1957), a film that criticizes the misguided political strategies of French generals in World War I. Kubrick's cinematic style won over Douglas as he attempted to save another biblical epic from disaster. By joining Dalton Trumbo, one of the blacklisted filmmakers now working in Europe, Douglas hoped the theme of the film would also erase the stigma that Hollywood producers attached to alleged communist screenwriters. Trumbo eventually returned to work in Hollywood, but Kubrick's interest took a different turn. He decided to emigrate and settle in London in 1961. There he began the translation of a series of novels into film narratives dealing with repressed psychosexual forces that, when unleashed, lead to the destruction of moral and spiritual values. His screen adaptation of Vladimir Nabokov's novel *Lolita* (1962) succeeds both as a serious social commentary and dark, cynical comic farce. Kubrick follows

Keir Dullea, an astronaut, disengages the HAL 9000 computer after it malfunctions in *2001: A Space Odyssey* (1968), directed by Stanley Kubrick.

this tendency toward ironic farce in three important films that he produced and directed: *Dr. Strangelove or: How I Learned to Stop Worrying and Love the Bomb* (1964), starring Peter Sellers, *2001: A Space Odyssey* (1968) and *A Clockwork Orange* (1971).

Kubrick teamed with Arthur Clarke to create *2001,* based upon Clarke's science-fiction short story "The Sentinel." The film is set in the near future when the moon is already colonized and exploration of the galaxy is underway in search for possible life in the solar system. A master computer, HAL 9000, becomes a major protagonist in the narrative as it guides the spaceship toward Jupiter on a secret mission to make contact with extraterrestrial intelligence. With a brilliant display of future technology and cinematic innovations, Kubrick's journey into space retains his pessimistic outlook on humankind ever resolving its basic conflict between the self and the other.

The future world constructed by Kubrick in *A Clockwork Orange* seems to reflect his concerns about the counter-culture that developed during the late 1950s and early 1960s in France, England and Italy. In his adaptation of the Anthony Burgess novel, Kubrick emphasizes the chaos, lawlessness and anarchy of a Western society gone mad. Gang sex and violence reach a point at which it is seen as a horror show with

a mixture of black comedy and social protest. Kubrick shows his disdain for a totalitarian society controlled by cynical men who desire power at all costs. What he is wary of is the destructive nature of those who create weapons and tools for domination of others under the pretext of patriotism, national defense or justice. This near-future science-dominated society is based upon the premise that there is a way to control humankind's instinctive sexual habits and acts of violence. Our narrator Alex, a leader of a gang of Droogs, enjoys nights of ultra-violence mixed with acts of rape and murder. Medical treatment is given to Alex in hopes of reversing his psychological desires and needs.

The Ludovico treatment uses sexual violence as reenacted in motion pictures to produce a repulsive reaction of fear and terror in Alex, so much so that he attempts suicide. However, the film does not end at this point. The roles of politicians and behavioral scientists come under review as they attempt to psychologically restructure a human being. How does society decide when it is necessary to use such measures on others? And why does Kubrick use this film as an anti-authoritarian attack on the traditional values of law and order? Where does this romanticization of sex and violence originate? Why rebel against the

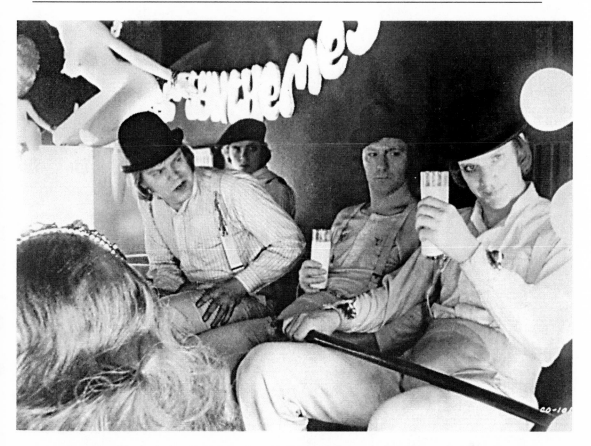

In Stanley Kubrick's *A Clockwork Orange* (1971) Malcolm McDowell (right) sits with his Droogs in the Milk Bar, checking the action.

social and political systems that regulate and control our Western culture? Is our antihero just another victim?

Looking Back at the 1960s

As these questions are posed, we have to place them in the context of the 1960s in the United States, where the Cold War reached a fever pitch and the fear of nuclear war was prevalent. The possibility of a nuclear Armageddon was brilliantly satirized by Kubrick in *Dr. Strangelove*, in which a military maniac decides to launch an air strike against the Soviets. While Kubrick was making this film, President Kennedy was assassinated in 1963 and an increase in military spending followed the launching of the Apollo space program. Kubrick decided to attack this space initiative in his own version of a venture into space with

2001: A Space Odyssey. Again, the political nature of the trip unfolds as the computer becomes the agent of totalitarian control against the astronauts.

The start of the 1960s saw John Kennedy replace Dwight D. Eisenhower as president of the United States. With this change in leadership, new hope arose for ending the Cold War. The Civil Rights Movement gained momentum in America. But in 1964, anti-black forces in the South reacted against the peace marchers and the decade's first race riots in many urban ghettos were ignited. John Kennedy's assassination brought Lyndon Johnson to the presidency. Johnson worked with a strong Democratic legislature which passed his Great Society program of social reform. Johnson also escalated the Vietnam War. The escalation of the unpopular Vietnam conflict started a powerful wave of student activism in universities throughout the country which eventually turned into an

In Arthur Penn's *Bonnie and Clyde* (1967), Clyde Barrow, depicted by Warren Beatty, impresses his new girlfriend, Bonnie Parker, played by Faye Dunaway, with a careful display of his revolver to prove he robs banks.

anti-war movement with peace rallies drawing hundreds of thousands of protesters. Many young people sought alternative lifestyles outside the norms of the established society, forming a youth counter-culture of "flower children" and "hippies."

Two important films of the late 1960s, *Easy Rider* (1969) and *Woodstock* (1970), documented this antiestablishment counter-culture. *Easy Rider* is an odyssey detailing the violence, paranoia and drug dealing occurring in a segregated America at that time. The film was directed by Dennis Hopper (b. 1936), a young actor-director who found distribution with a major Hollywood studio. Peter Fonda and Dennis Hopper portray two motorcyclists wandering across the country from California to New Orleans seeking the ideal America, some utopia where they can live unrestricted by rules

and regulations. As they search for this paradise, they are often confronted by different groups of people, many of whom are intolerant of long-haired tramps, drug addicts and scroungers. The real world rejects their alleged ideals of freedom on the road and their end is tragic.

Easy Rider caught the attention of European filmgoers and was cited by critics at Cannes before it successfully captured the attention of the American youth market, becoming a box-office surprise. The carefree anti-rule attitude displayed by its actors combined a musical score of popular folk-rock songs with the reality of the story. In its own way the film reflected the concerns of the counter-culture trying to exist in America. *Woodstock* was more of a documentary film of a pop-culture music festival held in a farmer's field in Bethel, New York.

The Barrow gang is caught in an ambush where Bonnie is wounded as Clyde avoids bounty hunters in *Bonnie and Clyde.*

The hundreds of thousands of people who gathered there gave a truer picture of the counter-culture generation and its views of peace, freedom and love. Some Woodstock visitors did drugs, destroyed private property and behaved accordingly, in their own fashion toward others. *Woodstock* was one of the first large music festivals that featured Joan Baez, Jimi Hendrix, Arlo Guthrie, Joe Cocker and The Who, among many others.

Arthur Penn's
Bonnie and Clyde *(1967)*

Arthur Penn (b. 1922) is one of many stage and television directors from New York who moved to Hollywood, where he directed *The Left-Handed Gun* in 1958, starring Paul New-man. His psychological interpretation of Billy the Kid compared the traditional myth to the reality of this Western outlaw and killer. By 1967, after directing *The Miracle Worker* (1962) and *Mickey One* (1964), a film noir caper of a stand-up comic on the run from the mob, Penn pursued his interest in social misfits as he compared the myth of Bonnie and Clyde with the real-life story of the Barrow gang. Penn's version of the myth introduced American film audiences to many innovations in a film narrative drawn directly from Godard's *Breathless*, a combination of Brechtian principles of "distanciation" within an episodic structure. But unlike *Breathless*, Penn quietly evoked the past with a soundtrack of popular tunes from the 1930s.

Visually the film presents itself as nostalgia. The introductory titles are interspersed with sepia photographs of the real Bonnie Parker and Clyde Barrow. After the names of these characters are projected on screen, the lettering of the names turns into a symbolic red. This prologue not only evokes the past but sets the way Penn will retell this history, partly as a surreal fairy tale and partly as a series of brutal and violent confrontations with law and order. Penn mixes historical fact and fantasy in a series of episodes that recreates the legend of Bonnie and Clyde for the audience to reflect upon the sociopolitical discourses operating behind the modern myth of these bank robbers.

Bonnie and Clyde is set in the Depression days in Southwest Texas and Arkansas, part of a weird landscape of the American desert of dusty and derelict towns somehow suspended in time and space. In this environment, our two protagonists emerge, destined to become legends through Bonnie's poetry about how they rob banks. Their flagrant lawlessness brought great media attention and a manhunt. By presenting Bonnie and Clyde as social misfits and outlaws in the form of a legend or myth, Penn skillfully unmasks the economic and political systems in America and how they affected the lives of many impoverished people during the 1930s.

Penn follows the French New Wave films, which reversed the standard genre formulas produced in Hollywood with the law and the police depicted as respectable defenders of the system. This film depicts the state police as corrupt and devious bounty hunters who use the law for their own self-interest. Penn also restructures the legend of the Barrow gang, looking at the action from the outlaw's perspective. From this viewpoint, the argument is made that capitalism and the banking system deny the average citizen the fruits of his or her labor. During the Great Depression, such a dynamic appeared to defeat the hope of any economic solution.

In rebellion, Bonnie and Clyde decide to go against the grain and not accept or play the passive roles assigned to them. They become folk heroes to the dispossessed and homeless by learning to rob banks and defy the system. Unfortunately, they also become murderers. Yet,

Bonnie is able to raise the consciousness of the public by writing descriptions of their exploits. Penn carefully integrates the use of newspapers and other media into the film, so that Bonnie and Clyde become legendary figures in their struggle for identity and freedom. Penn also questions the moral values in play at that time, and the forces of oppression that devalued many people's land and their opportunities for a livelihood. Thus, he asks, what do the forces of law and order uphold and protect? Whose interests do they serve? These questions were raised by prewar Marxist writers like Brecht and other radical writers in the 1930s and 1950s, especially by Lindsay Anderson and the Free Cinema in England and Jean-Luc Godard in France.

Penn's *Bonnie and Clyde* was not hailed by the critics at the time as a seminal film of the 1960s. One critic said "This is a bunch of decayed cabbage with leaves smeared with catsup." The *New York Times* claimed the film was corrupt, accusing the director of making graphic violence palatable. Penn defended himself by characterizing violence as an element in human nature. What he attempted to do was to juxtapose comedy with mayhem in each episode to show how violence erupts arbitrarily. At first, film critics were dismayed by the presentation of these outlaws in relationship to the conventions of society at that time. Only *Time* magazine reappraised the film in a second review, stating that "it is a ballad, a blending of the real with the fictitious, a gangster flick that turns dark, a romance that suddenly is ended in a horrific death."

Penn follows Brecht's dictum to distance the audience from empathetic involvement with the central characters. He attempts to create a visual environment arranged as a vision of the past, more like a dream than a precise reconstruction of the 1930s. For Penn, the film is more like a myth that works upon our imagination and memory, rather than history or fact. It is a haunted vision of a curiously empty world in which characters appear only to play out their roles in the mythical drama and then disappear. So, while the viewer is pulled in by the temporal events and the reality of the action, the visual environment, the surreal landscapes and empty streets and houses as well as the slapstick car chases, create for the viewer a sense of distance and myth. By returning us to the legend, we appear to react to witnessing the tragic actions of characters having a larger, more portentous significance. Bonnie is the true tragic figure in the film. It is her quest to achieve dignity and fulfillment that drives the legend. It is her responses to Clyde's fantasies for wealth and power that create the Barrow Gang. Yet, it is the vitality of Bonnie's poetry that shows us her increased awareness of her situation and her impending death with Clyde that creates the legend (Cawelti 1972).

References

Agel, Jerome (ed.). 1970. *The Making of Kubrick's 2001.* New York: New American Library, Inc.

Brougher, Kerry, ed. 1996. *Art and Film Since 1945: Hall of Mirrors.* Los Angeles: The Museum of Contemporary Art and The Monacelli Press.

Cawelti, John G. (ed.). 1972. *Focus on* Bonnie and Clyde. Englewood Cliffs, New Jersey: Prentice Hall.

Richardson, Tony, and Nikos Stangos (eds.). 1974. *Concepts of Modern Art.* New York: Harper & Row.

"*Blow-Up*, Swinging London, and the Film Generation"

by Peter Lev

From *The Euro-American Cinema* by Peter Lev. Copyright © 1993. By permission of the University of Texas Press.

Blow-Up, like *Contempt*, can be approached from the dual perspectives of art and commerce. It is certainly a key work in the distinguished artistic career of Michelangelo Antonioni, one of the world's great film directors. *Blow-Up* has excellent credentials as an art film: script and direction by Antonioni, based on a story by the Argentine modernist Julio Cortázar, and with an emphasis on theme and visual imagery rather than on genres or stars. Yet *Blow-Up* must also be considered an entry into the world of big-budget commercial filmmaking: produced by Carlo Ponti for MGM, made in London at a time when that city was exporting popular culture around the world.

The artistic aspects of *Blow-Up* have monopolized critical discussion. Article after article has delved into the film's ambiguities. The film seems to be particularly attractive to American critics, perhaps because it is one of the few widely admired art films to have achieved extensive distribution in the United States. Without denying the interest of *Blow-Up* criticism, I will concentrate in this essay on the film's social and cultural backdrop. I believe that social and cultural factors can illuminate the film's distinctive look and feel, and can solve some, though not all, of its mysteries. *Blow-Up*, like other Euro-American art films, can be understood as a response to a particular period and to particular film-industry conditions.

The film *Blow-Up* was based not only on Cortázar's short story "Las Babas del Diablo" (the English translation was titled "Blow-Up" after the success of the film), but also on the article "The Modelmakers," written by Francis Wyndham for the *London Sunday Times Magazine*.[1] Wyndham's article is a long interview with three successful young photographers—Brian Duffy, Terence Donovan, and David Bailey—which describes the milieu of British fashion photography circa 1964. A handful of fashion photographers, with David Bailey perhaps the best-known, were among the new celebrities of London in the 1960s. Young, wealthy, creative, impatient with tradition (most came from working-class backgrounds), they cut dashing figures in the era of the Beatles. Their professional and personal innovations included a more directly sexual approach to fashion, a breakdown of the gap between fashion photography and art photography, and a similar coming together of documentation of an event and creation of an event. The photographers observed the London scene but also helped to create it.

As Alexander Walker notes, the idea of a feature film about the life of a fashion photographer set in London, and based in part on Wyndham's article, did not originate with Antonioni. The highly commercial Italian producer Carlo Ponti, working on a multi-picture production deal with MGM, began discussions on such a film in 1964. At one time David Bailey himself was scheduled to direct the film. However, Bailey turned to other projects, and the "photographer film" was stalled until Antonioni and Ponti came to an agreement on it.[2]

Although Antonioni was not involved in the earliest stages of the "photographer film," he did have ample opportunity to shape it to his own artistic needs. Antonioni conducted extensive research on the lives of London's young fashion photographers, using Francis Wyndham as a consultant. Antonioni and Tonino Guerra, his longtime script collaborator, wrote a screen play which made the "photographer film" a loose adaptation of the Cortázar story (which concerns a photographer, a mystery, and a crucial scene of making enlargements; it is otherwise quite unlike Blow-Up).[3] Antonioni also cast the picture, directed it, and supervised the editing.

The plot of Blow-Up presents twenty-four hours in the life of a successful young photographer (David Hemmings). We first see him leaving a flophouse where he has spent the night taking pictures for a book. He jumps into a Rolls-Royce convertible and goes to his studio/living space for photo sessions with the glamorous Veruschka (a celebrity model of the time, who plays herself) and with a group of bizarrely dressed fashion models. Then he leaves to scout an antique store for possible purchases. He visits a park across from the antique store and films a tryst between a young woman (Vanessa Redgrave) and an older man. The woman is disturbed about being filmed, but the Hemmings character says photography is his job. After lunch with his agent Ron, the photographer returns to his studio to develop the pictures from the park. The young woman from the park appears and asks for the film. She eventually leaves with a roll of film (not the right one). The photographer starts developing and enlarging the park photographs and finds in a stand of trees what appears to be a gun pointed at the lovers. In another enlargement he discovers what appears to be a body. He is interrupted by a visit of two miniskirted young girls asking to have their picture taken. He ends up undressing both girls in a sprawl of photo backdrop paper (and presumably having sex with them).

Waking up from this "orgy," the photographer visits the park at night and sees the body. He returns home and finds his studio has been burglarized. The negatives and most of the prints from the park are gone. When he goes next door to talk to his neighbors, a painter and his girlfriend (wife?), they are making love. The photographer then drives to meet his agent at a party. On the way, he thinks he sees the Vanessa Redgrave character; looking for her, he finds himself in a rock club, but she has disappeared. He arrives at the party, but Ron, the agent, is not interested in his story. Ron passes the photographer some marijuana joints, and both men evidently spend the evening getting high. In the morning, the photographer revisits the park; the body is gone. Leaving the park, he encounters some mimes playing a tennis game. At their gestured request, he returns an imaginary tennis ball (invisible, though not inaudible) to the players. The photographer then disappears in mid-frame.

Why was Antonioni interested in such a "trendy" subject? Without undue psychologizing, a few answers are possible. First, Antonioni had observed the London art and fashion scene in 1964, when he accompanied Monica Vitti to England for the filming of Modesty Blaise. At that time he saw something in mod London that intrigued him. In doing interviews about Blow-Up, Antonioni several times expressed interest and even a qualified support for the freedom and iconoclasm of mod London. Second, despite his critical reputation, Antonioni had not at this time established himself as a commercial filmmaker. A proud man, he insisted on being treated as a major artist. In a notorious interview with Rex Reed in the New York Times (which Antonioni later complained about in a letter to the Times), Antonioni expressed resentment about being underpaid and under-recognized in comparison to star actors and to other directors.[4] He may have turned to the fashionable subject of Blow-Up in a conscious attempt to make his mark in commercial filmmaking. The success of *Blow-Up* did, in fact, have this result. Antonioni reached a broader public with *Blow-Up* than ever before or since in his career, and the film's success led to a contract for three more English-language films with MGM (only two were ever made: *Zabriskie Point* and *The Passenger*).

Many critics have noted that *Blow-Up* is strikingly different in visual style from Antonioni's earlier films. *Blow-Up* is more colorful, more rapid, more active then the gray-toned, languidly paced Italian films Antonioni made in the early 1960s. The change of style and mood can be attributed to both commercial and artistic attributes of *Blow-Up*. Commercially, *Blow-Up* is a film of "swinging London," of a free and creative youth culture which reached a worldwide audience in the mid-sixties. Academic critics may easily overlook the extent to which the subculture presented in *Blow-Up*—fashion, rock music, pot parties— was in itself attractive to audiences of the time. The film is a detailed look at the successful artists of the British "youth culture," and may have positive connotations independent of Antonioni's personal interpretation of the London scene. MGM's press releases on *Blow-Up* heavily emphasize the youth appeal of modern London, "where teenage pop singing groups have their records sold in shops owned by people their own age, and photographers who have barely started showing drive Rolls-Royces with radio-telephones."[5] Even incidental details of the film may have a powerful attraction; for example, a former student tells me that *Blow-Up* is an important record of sixties rock and roll because it is "the only film with Jimmy Page and Jeff Beck playing together" (in the brief scene of the Yardbirds at the rock club).

Blow-Up can be enjoyed for its beautiful surfaces: the photographer's airy, modern studio; the modeling session with the statuesque Veruschka; the quiet neighborhood park, the rock club, and so on. But the attractive visuals of swinging London are only one part of a complex artistic construction. For Antonioni, swinging London represents at least a possible way out of the social world in crisis he had analyzed in his Italian films. In the tetralogy of *L'avventura* to *Red Desert*, Antonioni had shown a fragmented, confused, anomic society where intimate relationships in particular had lost their meaning. Antonioni told interviewers in the early 1960s that his films portrayed a situation where concepts of love and morality were profoundly out of touch with the actual conditions of life.[6] *Blow-Up* brings a new freedom to these problems. The photographer, with his aesthetic sensibility and his willingness to act on impulse, seems to be less conflicted and less blocked than the protagonists of *L'avventura* or *La notte*. Casual, sexually available, open to experience, he suggests a breakout from conformism, a new morality. He is also an artist in a society that values the artistic (note the Rolls-Royce). The visually exciting environment of *Blow-Up* expresses the new possibilities of the character and his milieu.

Blow-Up also, however, contains a critique of this character and of the 1960s youth culture he represents. In this course of the film the photographer's new morality turns out to be severely limited. The photographer lives in an environment where things are often not what they seem, and where no one standard of values prevails. Indeed, as Andrew Tudor has pointed out, reality itself is mutable: a love scene becomes a murder because of a changed "vantage point."[7] In this situation, how does one follow through on a personally and socially meaningful action? The photographer fails to do this, allowing himself to be distracted from reporting the murder. He is ultimately a weak character, limited to the aestheticism and hedonism of his profession and his subculture. The bright colors and rapid movements of *Blow-Up* might thus be seen as distractions and illusions rather than as unambiguous representations of an attractive, mod London.

Another cultural context influencing the production and reception of *Blow-Up* was the evolution of motion picture censorship in the 1960s. The restrictive Motion Picture Production Code governing Hollywood films was rapidly eroding in this period. Many foreign-made films were being successfully released in the United States without a Code seal of approval. In response to this competition, the Code was reorganized and simplified in 1966, with many specific prohibitions eliminated. As part of the reorganization, the category "Suggested for Mature Audiences" (SMA) was added to accommodate films on the margin of the new Code's limits.

A key argument in the censorship debates of the mid–1960s was that rigid censorship codes unduly restricted the possibilities of film art. *Blow-Up* was very much in the middle of this debate, since it was made by an internationally prestigious director; it contained sexually explicit scenes that had not, to this point, been acceptable in a film released by a major Hollywood company; and it was produced by MGM, which had traditionally been one of the Code's staunchest supporters. *Blow-Up* was submitted to the Production Code Administration in 1966, and a deal was worked out with MGM as to what cuts would be needed to qualify for a Code seal with the AMA proviso. The cuts involved two scenes: the photographer's erotic tussling with the teenaged girls, and the lovemaking between the painter and his girlfriend as witnessed by the photographer. However, Antonioni refused to make any changes, saying that he had a contractual right to final cut. MGM backed Antonioni, with a company official commenting that *Blow-Up* was "an artistic masterpiece, which could only be flawed by cutting even such brief deletions as requested by the Code office."[8] *Blow-Up* was ultimately released without a Code seal by "Premier Films" (a subsidiary company of MGM) and under the heading "Carlo Ponti Presents." This was done to avoid putting MGM in explicit conflict with the Production Code, which all the major studios ostensibly supported. MGM thus resorted to a subterfuge in order to release a film which in its explicit sexuality was more akin to the art film than to traditional studio product.

A curious sidelight to this censorship controversy is that MGM actually did cut the film, and a Code-approved SMA label was still being negotiated one month after the film's release in December 1966. MGM cut a few seconds of the lovemaking between the painter and his girlfriend to tone down the implication that the girlfriend (Sarah Miles) gets excited by having the photographer watch. But MGM made the cut quietly, without a public statement; a *Variety* article suggested that this was done to avoid unfavorable publicity for censoring a filmmaker's work.[9] With the one cut plus *Blow-Up*'s strong commercial opening, MGM asked for a reconsideration of the Code seal decision. The Production Code Administration agreed to reconsider, but MGM quickly withdrew its request.[10] Since *Blow-Up* was doing so well without a Code seal, there was no reason for MGM to continue negotiations with the PCA. The Production Code was fast becoming irrelevant. It was replaced by a ratings system in 1968.

The censorship controversy surrounding *Blow-Up* created a great deal of free publicity and thereby contributed to the film's commercial success. *Blow-Up* grossed about $7,000,000 in its 1966–1967 American release, an excellent figure for an art film.[11] It was equally controversial and successful in Italy, where a nationwide ban on the film was quickly overturned. As in the United States, the Italian censorship battle highlighted weaknesses in the existing censorship mechanism and generated enormous interest in the film.[12]

Although there is much merit in the argument that censorship of sexually explicit material restricts film's artistic possibilities, it is important to note that film art and sex in cinema are linked for commercial reasons as well. Historically, the popularity of the foreign film in the United States after World War II — and continuing to the present — can be explained at least in part by the frank attitudes toward sexuality presented by the European imports. This does not mean that foreign films are necessary calculating and exploitative in their use of sexuality. In *Blow-Up*, the sexually provocative material is integral to the milieu being studied, and to Antonioni's thematic concerns. But viewer interpretation can separate and emphasize the sexual display, making *Blow-Up* an arty backdrop for several sexually daring scenes. This possible "reading" undoubtedly was a factor in the film's box office success.

A third social and cultural context of *Blow-Up* was the motion picture audience of the 1960s. Antonioni's broadening of interests beyond the ennui of the Italian upper-middle class came at a moment when film audiences were unusually open to artistic and philosophical dimensions of motion pictures. The mid–1960s was the era of the "Film Generation." Stanley Kauffmann used this phrase in a 1966 essay to describe "the first generation that has matured in a culture in which the film has been of accepted serious relevance, however that seriousness may be defined." According to Kauffmann, "Even its [the Film General's] appreciations of sheer entertainment films reflect this overall serious view." Kauffmann and others have described the 1960s as the period in which film replaced the novel as the preeminent cultural form in the United States and Europe.[13]

In this situation, audiences were willing to accept *Blow-Up* as both popular entertainment and philosophical exploration. Audiences and critics enjoyed playing the game of what the film might mean. In some cases, *Blow-Up*'s meaning and value were heatedly debated in the popular press. In Baltimore, Anne Childress of the *News American* described *Blow-Up* as "the best movie I have ever seen," but Andrea Herman of the same paper responded by labeling the film "a weary senseless sequence of events that never add up to anything artistically or otherwise."[14] Pauline Kael's negative review of the film in the *New Republic* was met by a salvo of complaints from angry readers.[15] In *Playboy*, Antonioni was accorded not only a review, but a lengthy and serious "Playboy Interview" as well.[16] And *Blow-Up* criticism appeared in any number of literary and philosophical journals. It is difficult to imagine any film of the early 1990s being so hotly debated in both popular and specialized publications.

Charles Eidsvik suggests that *Blow-Up*'s audience appeal depends on Antonioni's respect for the "hypothesizing and perceptual processes" of narrative cinema. Antonioni engages the viewer with two fascinating puzzles: first, the identity of a protagonist who shifts roles frequently; and second, the nature and consequences of the murder revealed by the protagonist's enlargements. With the viewer "seduced" (Eidsvik's term) by these two rather traditional puzzles, which would not be out of place in a Hitchcock film, Antonioni's film pro-

ceeds to more unsettling developments. It shows that perception, understanding, and action depend on numerous subjective and social elements; there is no one clear path for the photographer to take in responding to the murder. The film concludes with the thoroughly enigmatic scene of the imaginary tennis ball. At this point the viewer is still trying to "solve" the narrative puzzle; since the puzzle is unsolvable, the spectator has been transported from a traditional to a modernist film-viewing experience.[17]

I would add two historical-cultural factors to Eidsvik's formalist account of *Blow-Up*'s appeal. First, the film's "difficult" themes of ambiguous perception and multiple levels of reality were familiar to audiences of the time. *Blow-Up* was made in the period when pop culture figures such as Timothy Leary, Carlos Castaneda, and innumerable rock stars were playing with levels of perception and reality in relation to the use of psychedelic drugs. In *Blow-Up*, the pot party is a negative moment which blocks the photographer from taking action about the murder. However, the viewer can choose to avoid Antonioni's moralism (which, itself, is presented in an ambiguous context) and to concentrate on the film's mutable surfaces. This reading of the film brings it close to the perceptual play of the drug-influenced pop culture of the 1960s.

A second factor to emphasize is that only the serious audience described by Kauffmann, an audience willing to look beneath the surface of a film narrative, would have followed *Blow-Up*'s trajectory from conventional to philosophical mysteries. As Kauffmann's article states, film and audience are interdependent.[18] The imaginative and challenging narrative strategy described by Eidsvik requires a serious and receptive audience. Conversely, the Film Generation audience needs films like *Blow-Up*. Without this symbiotic relationship between art film and film audience in the 1960s, *Blow-Up* would have been an inaccessible, elitist film.

The point to be made is not that a film can be reduced to a few historical and social conditions. But I do object to criticism that looks at *Blow-Up* as the timeless masterpiece of the great filmmaker Antonioni adapting the great writer Cortázar. Instead, *Blow-Up* is the point of convergence of a number of important trends. It is Antonioni, Ponti, and MGM's foray into the youth culture of swinging London. It is carefully balanced between the prestige of the art film and the commercial appeals of fashion, sex, and rock and roll. It is a conservative Hollywood studio's experiment with an English-language art film and with sexually explicit scenes. In its mix of youth culture and philosophy it is specifically aimed at the audience Kauffmann dubbed the "Film Generation." The extraordinary achievement of *Blow-Up* lies in its rich synthesis of Europe and Hollywood, sex and philosophy, art and entertainment.

Notes

1. Francis Wyndham, "The Modelmakers," *London Sunday Times Magazine*, May 10, 1964.

2. Alexander Walker, *Hollywood U.K.: The British Film Industry in the Sixties*, pp. 316–317, 320–322.

3. British playwright Edward Bond was added to the scriptwriting team to help with English-language dialogue.

4. Antonioni specifically refers to Elizabeth Taylor and Franco Zeffirelli. Rex Reed, "After the 'Blow-Up,' a Close-Up," *New York Times*, January 1, 1967.

5. Publicity release, *Blow-Up*, prepared for Director's Guild of America screening, Los Angeles, December 14, 1966.

6. See, for example, Joseph Morgenstern, "How De-Dramatizer Works," *New York Herald-Tribune*, April 2, 1961; Ian Dallas, "Antonioni on Seeking Love," *Observer* (London), February 4, 1962.

7. Andrew Tudor, "Death Valley," *Cinema* (London) 6–7 (1970): 27–28.

8. "Approval Denied to Antonioni Film," *New York Times*, December 17, 1966.

9. "MGM Prunes Print on QT," *Variety*, January 26, 1967.

10. Memo, Geoffrey Shurlock to Michael Linden, November 23, 1966; Letter, Michael Linden to Dan Terrell, November 25, 1966; Letter, Terrell to Linden, November 28, 1966; Letter, Robert Vogel to Shurlock, January 27, 1967; File Memo, Ralph Hetzel, January 31, 1967. G. Shurlock was head of the Production Code Administration. M. Linden was head of the Code for Advertising. D. Terrell and R. Vogel were MGM executives. R. Hetzel was a PCA employee.

All letters and memos listed in this note are from the MPAA Collection, Margaret Herrick Library, Academy of Motion Picture Arts and Sciences.

11. "Gross of $7 Million," *Hollywood Reporter*, May 23, 1967.

12. "'Blow-Up' Calms Down; No 'Criminal Angle,'" *Variety*, November 11, 1967; Andrew Rhodes, "Censorship Blowup over 'Blow-Up,'" *Los Angeles Times*, November 5, 1967.

13. Kauffmann, "The Film Generation," pp. 415–417.

14. "'Blow-Up' Able to Rile Baltimore," *Variety*, March 8, 1967.

15. Pauline Kael, "Tourist in the City of Love," *New Republic*, February 11, 1967, pp. 30, 32–35; "Correspondence," *New Republic*, February 25, 1967, pp. 39–41.

16. "Playboy Interview: Michelangelo Antonioni," *Playboy*, November 1967, pp. 77–88.

17. Charles Eidsvik, *Cineliteracy*, pp. 229–230.

18. Kauffmann, "The Film Generation," pp. 426–427.

References

Eidsvik, Charles. 1978. *Cineliteracy: Film Among the Arts*. New York: Horizon Press.

Kauffmann, Stanley. 1966. "The Film Generation: Celebration and Concern." In *A World on Film*. New York: Harper & Row, pp. 415–428.

Walker, Alexander. 1974. *Hollywood UK: The British Film Industry in the Sixties*. New York: Stein and Day.

CHAPTER 21

New Italian Cinema of Pasolini and Bertolucci

Introduction

Pier Paolo Pasolini and Bernardo Bertolucci are the leading representatives of Italian directors following Fellini and Antonioni. Both directors are neo–Marxists who made allegorical films comparing sexual relationships with political structures. While Pasolini deals with an aggressive political strategy to uncover the sociopolitical systems that dominate human lives, Bertolucci uses a more familiar narrative structure to explore family traumas based upon the sexual and political conflicts between father and son. Strongly influenced by the films of the French New Wave, these two directors combine classical myths with modern ideology to examine the complex structure of Italian postwar society. The psychoanalytical theories of Freud are mixed with Marxian theories of alienation in dealing with taboos, Christian myths, capitalism and sexual politics.

Pasolini, a poet and film theorist, reinterprets classic literary works, including Sophocles, Euripides and the Bible, from a neo–Marxist political perspective. Visually, he compares a Renaissance one-point perspective associated with one's perception of space which situates the viewer in a fixed relationship to space-setting, with those perceptions related to a flat two-dimensional surface, where one's perception is open to numerous relationships and ambiguities. Bertolucci, as a disciple of Pasolini, examines the psychosexual crises of his characters within the context of social and political change in which the ideological functioning of the state, church, police, family and media operate on a person's identity within totalitarian strategies. Each director seeks to ameliorate personal dehumanization with film narratives that critique fascist ideology through a comparison with sexual politics.

The Use of Myths in Film Narratives

In the history of film, most film narratives have their roots in folklore, legends or myths that interpret natural events to shape a particular cultural perception of human life. Usually they are shaped within specific cultural groups that share common beliefs in the meanings of existence. Myths, in a traditional sense, are ahistorical, unlike legends or fables. Essentially they are religious formulations that explain universal or supernatural truths through the adventures and actions of particular heroes. Older myths are revised and exploited today by screenwriters as dramatic film narratives, such as *Star Wars*, that give cultural meanings to the writers' own personal visions and perceptions of something deep and primitive in all people.

This modern version of the battle between Good and Evil does not assist historians as they inquire into whose interests are served by such myths. Some historians bring into focus the economic and political forces that brought them into existence. As works of fiction, most myths mediate between reality and social consciousness. As narratives, myths are charged to make viewers believe certain social conventions are natural, to be taken for granted when, in fact, they reflect specific social and political values and ideological goals. When they are fashioned by film narratives, myths attempt to dispel the contradictions between illusion and reality. Their role as dramatic narratives is to assign significance and meaning arbitrarily to persons and objects according to some contemporary discourse or cultural convention.

Although myths appear to be independent of these cultural discourses, they actually support ideologies hidden within the work of art to advance a "reality" for the viewer. Narrative films are used as works of art to project particular meanings and values for the construction and manipulation of feelings and emotions. This emotional formation of attitudes and values through film narratives at times reproduces conformity and stereotypes. As contemporary art forms they can lead to distortions and contradictions between an arbitrary "real" world and the mythic construction of a cultural world. Mythic form controls the dynamics of a story in which the viewer "lives the myth as a story at once true and unreal" (Barthes 1973, p. 128). Unlike history, a myth does not provide a reflection of any specific social attitudes or values.

Roland Barthes, a French semiotician and critic, has reflected upon cinematic images and their relationship to myth. He considers the cinema an imaging machine that processes images in which the subject is continually engaged, represented and inscribed within an ideology. Images on film are immediately readable in and of themselves, regardless of the context. Narratives make them more readable in the context of their production and reception. When film images are placed within a myth, they will be read from an all-encompassing context of an ideology, whose mythic values and effects are social and subjective.

In this manner, images as art forms share with writing the attribute of placing the viewer or reader at the furthest point from authentic knowledge. For just as writing is a "sign of a sign," a substitute for speech which in turn stands in or represents the conscious self-presence of thought, so art provides a kind of shadow play on reality, an illusion lacking the

wisdom or virtue to pursue philosophical truths. Plato's "Myth of the Cave" is quoted by Marcello in *The Conformist* while in conversation with his former mentor, Professor Quadri:

> Picture men dwelling in a sort of subterranean cavern with a long entrance open to the light on its entire width ... Picture further the light from a fire burning higher up and at a distance behind them, and between the fire and the prisoners and above them a road along which a low wall has been built, as the exhibitors of a puppet show have partitions before the men themselves, above which they show the puppets [Plato 1963, Book VII, p. 253].

Plato's dramatic metaphor illustrates how we attempt to integrate a single view of the world when there is a belief in the world of change and motion, but perhaps there is some eternal truth or principle underlying all of these images. Nonetheless, people who substitute these illusions or fantasies for truth, give up the quest for authentic wisdom and self-knowledge. In *The Conformist,* Marcello seeks to distort the metaphor and its statement on the human condition. His actions betray his mentor as he closes down the blinds in the room to silhouette the professor as a two-dimensional character, just an illusion of a reality.

These aesthetic considerations have produced controversy on how film narratives can be understood as an art form. Herbert Marcuse (1978) writes on the way he identifies a work of art:

> The truth of art lies in its power to break the monopoly of the established reality (i.e. to those who have established it) and to define what is real. In this rupture, which is the achievement of aesthetic form, the fictitious world of art appears as a true reality.
>
> Art is committed to that perception of the world which alienates individuals from their functional existence and performance in society — it is committed to an emancipation of sensibility, imagination, and reason in all spheres of subjectivity and objectivity [p. 9].

Bruno Bettelheim (1964), a leading Freudian psychologist and critic, relates his experiences

In Bernardo Bertolucci's *The Conformist* (1969), a young woman finds herself involved in a fascist assassination plot in which she is sacrificed as well.

on the importance of fairy tales. He argues that fairy tales state an existential dilemma as opposed to myths, that like religion, impose patterns of behavior. As imaginative images and art forms, he states:

> I also want to indicate what I believe art's unique place to be: that of guiding the individual to a personal vision of the world, and of his or her place in it.
>
> Contrary to theories held by some enemies of art, such as Plato and his followers, art is not an imitation of reality, neither of external reality or inner reality of the unconscious. It is always a vision, an attempt to express visibly what a particular age, a particular society, a particular person has viewed as the true nature and essence of reality, both the essence of mankind and of a person's relations to significant aspects of the world [p. 49].

The Films of Bernardo Bertolucci

The films of Bernardo Bertolucci (b. 1940) follow similar narrative patterns used in myths but have the magic of a fairy tale, with many flashbacks recalling a mixture of fantasy and fact. They are archetypal narratives whose images evoke something familiar but strange. Usually they depict the sexual adventures of young men who believe they are knowingly different from others. The men become split personalities as they desperately engage in "radical impulses" but finally yield and become conformist, trying to follow the norms of their society and be like the others. Each film explores the sexual pathology of the central male character from a strongly Freudian perspective. The quest for one's identity is complemented

Bernardo Bertolucci's *The Conformist* shows decadent dancing between two women who tease their respective mates with sexual innuendoes.

by a search for one's father, an authoritarian figure who is usually anti-conformist and anti-fascist. In relating the personal traumas of an individual to dominant bourgeois values in conflict with neo–Marxist beliefs, Bertolucci's films examine themes of psychosexual deviancy within authoritarian systems.

Bertolucci established his reputation as an international filmmaker with his critically acclaimed film *Before the Revolution* (1964). This film concerns the inability of a young man to break away from bourgeois values after he discovers Marxist ideals. The paradoxical nature of this would-be revolutionary became more prominent in the later films of Bertolucci as his central character struggles to find liberation through sexual or political alliances. In *The Conformist* (1969), Bertolucci adapts Alberto Moravia's novel that exposes the murderous intentions of Italian Fascism during the 1930s into a visually striking film. The film rearranges the chronological narrative into a

In Bernardo Bertolucci's *Last Tango in Paris* (1972), Marlon Brando plays an American loner seeking sexual gratification with an anonymous woman in a barren Parisian apartment. Sexual exploitation is a means by which the film makes a serious political statement on the search for one's identity.

series of flashback memories from the point-of-view of Marcello Clerici, a young Fascist official, as he rides to assassinate an Italian anti–Fascist leader living in exile in France. Bertolucci freely adopts his understanding of Freudian psychoanalysis on a mythic level in dramatizing the Oedipal legend. In relation to this myth, Bertolucci uses a voice-over, film noir presentation to compare and contrast the blind with the sightful. Bertolucci also uses Plato's "Myth of the Cave" as a metaphor and constant reminder throughout the film that illusions are of necessity easily accepted as reality. Yet, Bertolucci's emphasis on a Freudian interpretation allows little or no room for a Marxist analysis of the causes of Italian Fascism and stands more as another illusion displacing the first than an indictment of it.

Rather, Bertolucci succeeds in unmasking the sterility of Marcello as a conformist through the presentation of the character's unconscious drives and desires through carefully placed flashbacks of his early childhood.

Bertolucci's *Last Tango in Paris* (1972) is the first commercial film to revolutionize the cinematic depiction of physical lust. The director takes us into another Oedipal narrative in which explicit sexual relationships are corrupted by the psychological backgrounds of the two main characters. However, the powerful depictions of the sexual encounters created box-office appeal and worldwide commercial success new to the history of cinema. Marlon Brando as a middle-aged man, Paul, seeks a sexual association without emotional entrapments. The young girl, Jeanne, projects her own

Pier Paolo Pasolini's *Teorema / Theorem* (1968) is a religious allegory in which a peasant woman sacrifices herself to a mystical Christ figure.

incestuous Oedipal fantasy upon this older man, who resembles her dead father. The setting is a vacant apartment where the romantic liaisons take place. As the frankness and primitive force of their intense lovemaking break most of society's sexual taboos, including sodomy, we realize we are witnessing "the most powerfully erotic movie ever made," according to film critic Pauline Kael, "and it may turn out to be the most liberating movie ever made" (Reeling 1976, p. 27). The psychosexual turmoil inside Paul, brought on by the suicide of his wife, cannot reawaken his American dream of conquest. His attempts to regain his sexual virility in fantasies with this young girl finally culminate in disaster.

Securing American actress Jill Clayburgh to star as an opera singer in *La luna* (1979), Bertolucci again struggles with the mythic subtext of a son's search for a missing father. The film created further controversy by shocking

audiences with its explicit enactment of mother-son incest. However, despite poor critical response to this film, Bertolucci secured further American financing for a number of epic films, most notably *1900* (1976), with Robert De Niro, Burt Lancaster and Gérard Départieu as leaders of feuding dynasties that herald the coming of communism in Italy. After receiving further poor reviews for this two-part epic, Bertolucci and company traveled to China to produce and direct *The Last Emperor* (1987), starring John Lone, Joan Chen and Peter O'Toole. The epic scope of this film encompasses half a century in the transition of traditional China into a People's Republic. Using flashbacks from the Forbidden City to contemporary Beijing, this complex narrative follows the life of China's last Emperor, P'u-yi, from his exile, to his status as a Japanese puppet governor, then capture, indoctrination and "political rehabilitation" by the Chinese Communists. As an overwhelming spectacle, with the fluid color cinematography of Vittorio Storaro, the film details the psychosexual deviancies of this man's life as he searches for an identity after losing control of his social and political destiny. Bertolucci earned Oscars for Best Director and Best Picture in 1987 for *The Last Emperor*, among other Academy Awards.

The Films of Pier Paolo Pasolini

Pier Paolo Pasolini's (1922–1975) early films followed the neorealist tradition of on-location filming with nonprofessional actors using contemporary sociopolitical themes. But unlike the films of De Sica and Rossellini, Pasolini's dealt directly with the outcasts, beggars and sub-proletariat of Roman low-life without resorting to sentimentality or melodrama. Pasolini's interest in this culturally disinherited group of people stems from the revisionist work of Antonio Gramsci (1891–1937), a Marxist theorist. Gramsci introduced the concept of hegemony, whereby social classes influence other classes through cultural institutions such as schools, churches, films and books using reason and common consent rather than force. Thus, the ruling class becomes the dominant group by influencing the power structure of the culture by its own cultural constructs or dominant discourses.

Gramsci's interest in the language and customs of pre-industrial agrarian farmers in Southern Italy, known as sub-proletariat, provided Pasolini with the mythical and religious consciousness necessary for his poetic narratives. His films follow a basic ritual: a depiction of an outsider's violent encounter with the leaders of a political state. In *Accattone* (1961), *Mamma Roma* (1962) and *Il vangelo secondo Matteo / The Gospel According to St. Matthew* (1964), Pasolini evokes the mythic dimensions of a Christ figure, a person who reveals the turbulence of his or her sexuality. In *Accattone*, this figure parallels the Christ legend. But in the *Gospel*, Pasolini reconstructs a religious sense of awe and mystery around the Christ figure. As a revolutionary figure who attacks authoritarian dogma, he becomes a determined political orator setting out to overturn the social and economic injustices inflicted by the state on the poorest of people. Pasolini's cinematic techniques are simple and direct, and his on-location settings are photographed in a neorealist documentary style to capture the dramatic atmosphere of the barren and rocky landscape. Pasolini's editing emphasizes rapid cutting to juxtapose powerful images of biblical events, shown as natural happenings emerging from the popular culture of that day. The sound track, which uses classical music of Bach and Mozart mixed with Negro spirituals, helps give these events a strong sense of contemporary relevance.

Pasolini's use of myth refers to traditional legends dealing with ancestor worship or supernatural heroes that brought into human consciousness a social awareness and understanding of the phenomenal world. His films examine each myth as part of the ideological constructs of our modern culture. Each myth reveals a recurring theme and character-hero who represents the social consciousness of a people. By embodying its cultural ideals and by giving expression to a deep, commonly held range of emotions, the hero carries with him supernatural powers to perform miraculous events.

In a trio of films produced in Italy in the late 1960s, Pasolini explored various aspects of mythical consciousness as typified in the traditional narratives of Greek tragedy. Pasolini contended that each mythic construction unveiled cultural ideologies that transformed certain Greek legends into classical dramas. The dramas depicted a confrontation between two cultures, each carrying an opposing view on the nature of human reality. Pasolini adapted these Greek tragedies into films for modern audiences. First, he produced *Edipo re / Oedipus Rex* (1967), then *Teorema* (1968), followed by *Medea* (1970). In each of these dramatic films, Pasolini contrasted mythical, pre-rational cultures exemplified by Medea and the Sphinx with rational, ideologically based cultures that featured the problem-solving skills of an Oedipus and a Jason. From Pasolini's viewpoint, rational consciousness creates a dialectical relationship with the psychic or spiritual consciousness of modern humankind.

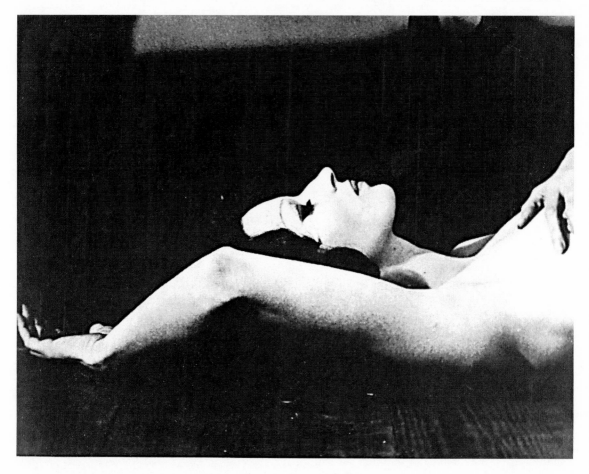

Silvana Mangano plays the wealthy Italian wife after an erotic encounter with the mystical stranger in *Teorema.*

Teorema is a modern parable similar to the legends of Greek tragedy. It is structured like a mystery, introducing the central character as a guest without a fixed identity or name, but who carries with him the power of Eros. His appearance alters the human relationships within a typical modern family. But unlike the raw passion displayed in *Oedipus Rex*, Pasolini contains the anguish and passion within a precise structure that cuts through the surface appearances of life in his search of some fundamental reality underlying human existence that can subvert the artifices of bourgeois life.

In the 1970s, Pasolini incorporated medieval literature and its legends into his own vision of mythic fictions. *The Decameron* (1971) translated Boccaccio's work into a series of earthy and erotic encounters that satirized the rites of the Church and new middle class. With the success of this film, he directed Chaucer's *I racconti di Canterbury / Canterbury Tales* (1972) and *Il fiore delle mille e una notte / The Arabian Nights* (1974) with similar erotic episodes. However, he enraged Italian officials with his rendering of *Salò, or the 120 Days of Sodom* (1975). His allegorical updating of this biblical legend into present-day Italy detailed the sado-masochistic sexual violence committed by the Fascist bureaucrats of the day. The following year, Pasolini was murdered by a youth in a setting similar to those of his films.

Introduction to "Teorema: *Line and Surface*"

Stephen Snyder's essay "Teorema: Line and Surface" focusses on Pasolini's interest in holis-

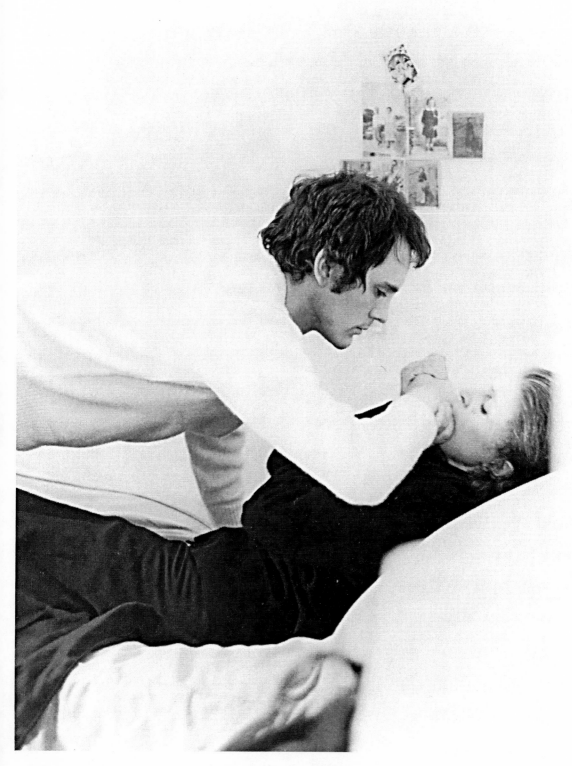

Terence Stamp, as the mystical stranger in *Teorema* who seduces each member of the family, starts with the young daughter.

tic consciousness, a vision of life in which the individual makes a connection with the phenomenal world. According to Pasolini, humankind needs to divest itself of its logocentric views of reality, a surface-depth duality in which rational thought helps establish a linear or perspectival relationship with the external world. For the successful bourgeois family, this cultural perspective represents a fixed, controlling relationship to its world. Pasolini claims that this rational viewpoint negates the possibility of a new surface consciousness with spiritual or psychic values.

According to Snyder, Pasolini styles this narrative visually by contrasting the two visions, the perspectival with the surface vision. The mysterious appearance of the mythical force of Eros into the lives of these characters introduces the new surface consciousness. As we experience his relationships with each member of the family, we see the power of Eros as his appearance plays against the controlling perspective of the rational world. Soon, rationality becomes irrelevant to members of the family. They organize their lives in response to the visitor's aura. However, after making sexual contact with him, they cannot assimilate his life force into their own restricted social imagination. Incapable of escaping from their rational selves, each family member withdraws into painful acts of self-awareness.

In all cases for Pasolini, film is the perfect medium to increase the social consciousness of the spectator, since it is actuated by a surface reflection of the external world and achieves visibility through the projection of light.

Pasolini's "The Poetics of Cinema"

Pasolini's essay departs from the semiotics of language as a sign-system based upon verbal and written texts. In its place he proposes a cinematic language supported by the use of "significant images" that can express different forms of reality. Thus he claims that a "cinema of poetry" can express reality with images of reality itself, but the danger lies in the imposition of formalist techniques that characterize the framing of shots and inhibit a "free indirect subjective" perspective. There are further differences that are encountered by any filmmaker who cannot break away from viewing the world through his or her own perspective and also represent the perspective of another character whose world view is different. More important to Pasolini is the fact that cinematic images relate more to memories and dream images that govern important communications within oneself. These subjective images are compared to archetypal ones that are more objective. He concludes that a poetry of cinema is found in a particular form of discourse he calls "free indirect discourse" in which the director uses a character to project a personal perspective of the world, as Antonioni has done in *Red Desert* (1964).

References

Barthes, Roland. 1973. *Mythologies.* London: Paladin.

Bettelheim, Bruno. 1964. *Art: A Personal Vision.* New York: Museum of Modern Art.

Kael, Pauline. 1976. *Reeling.* Boston and Toronto: Little Brown.

Marcuse, Herbert. 1978. *The Aesthetic Dimension.* Boston: Beacon Press.

Pasolini, Pier Paolo. 1965. *The Cinema of Poetry.* In *Movies and Methods.* Edited by Bill Nichols. Berkeley: University of California Press, 1976.

Plato. *The Republic.* Book VII (370–380 BC). Edited by James Adams. 2 vols. New York: Cambridge University Press, 1963.

Snyder, Stephen. 1980. "*Teorema*: Line and Surface." In his *Pier Paolo Pasolini.* Boston: Twayne Publishers, pp. 105–119.

CHAPTER 22

New German Cinema

Introduction

The history of the New German Cinema, *Das Neue Kino*, emerged from its formulation as the Oberhausen Manifesto in 1962. Inspired by Godard and the French New Wave, the films were low-budget projects sponsored by the West German government and television in attempts to overcome the ideological power of American films flooding the German market. Films of the New German Cinema were deemed cultural or educational products as a means to counteract the dominant American cinema and the older commercial German cinema. The movement produced some outstanding films by reflecting on the political and social situations arising from the postwar American Occupation. The films of three young postwar German filmmakers, Rainer Werner Fassbinder, Werner Herzog and Wim Wenders, gained international prominence with film critics in New York, London and Paris, but their early films were deemed too austere and intellectual to find a German audience. Thematically, each new film was preoccupied with questions of sexual identity, paranoia and disillusionment within a radical left-wing political framework.

Rainer Werner Fassbinder was the most prolific of the new directors, specializing in working-class melodramas satirizing bourgeois society through a sadomasochistic depiction of sexual power relationships. His films are styled on Hollywood's popular romances of the 1950s. *Angst Essen Seele auf / Ali, Fear Eats the Soul* (1974), *Faustrecht der Freiheit / Fox and His Friends* (1975) and *Die Ehe der Maria Braun / The Marriage of Maria Braun* (1978) are notable examples of his work. Werner Herzog's

epic films are haunted by romantic characters obsessed with the power to control one's own destiny. Among his most popular films are *Aguirre, der Zorn Gottes / Aguirre: The Wrath of God* (1972), *The Mystery of Kasper Hauser* (1974) and *Stroszek* (1977). Volker Schlöndorff and his wife, Margarethe von Trotta, specialized in contemporary political issues that defined the social roles played by both men and women. They co-directed *Die Verlorene Ehre der Katharina Blum / The Lost Honor of Katharina Blum* (1975). In her film, *Marianne and Juliane* (1981), von Trotta addresses the political issues of terrorism. Wim Wenders' films echo American westerns and road movies, but his characters are human wanderers, searching to make some meaningful contact with others. *Im Lauf der Zeit / Kings of the Road* (1976), *Der Amerikanische Freund / The American Friend* (1977) and *Paris, Texas* (1984) examine the sterility of American materialism and its cultural values. Fassbinder's *The Marriage of Marie Braun* (1978) and Schlöndorff's *Die Blechtrommel / The Tin Drum* (1979) both critique the history of Nazi Germany and the immediate postwar period. These two films became the most commercially successful motion pictures produced by the New German Cinema.

The New German Cinema

The New German Cinema is a collective term used to describe a group of young filmmakers who, under the leadership of Alexander Kluge, signed the Oberhausen Manifesto in 1962. In the manifesto they declared that the conventional German film industry was dead,

In Volker Schlöndorff's *The Tin Drum* (1979), based upon Günter Grass' epic novel, a young boy watches the rise of the Nazis and their brutal tactics.

and that a new German film was about to be born. The decline of the old film industry was in part brought about by the rapid rise of television during the 1960s in West Germany and the loss of film distribution in Germany to American companies during the 1950s. With the loss of audiences to television and American films, the hope of the young filmmakers was to set out to emulate the French New Wave directors and find new methods of financing, producing and exhibiting their films.

To implement the Oberhausen proposals, the West German government established a Board of Curators or Kuratorium for these filmmakers in 1965 to provide interest-free loans for the production of first and second feature films and to establish a film school. Within three years, well over 20 feature films were made, including Alexander Kluge's first film,

Abschied von Gestern / Yesterday's Girl (1966), concerning a young refugee, Anita G., from East Germany, who resorts to petty crimes and prostitution to survive in a repressive patriarchal society. Kluge's film parodies the historical and political aspects of West Germany and its dependence on American military power and a corporate mentality. He employs many Godardian techniques to break the narrative into quasi-documentary episodes filled with allusions and printed quotations from news headlines, forcing viewers to examine critically the right-wing discourses on materialism that appear to be taken for granted. This film won a Silver Lion award at the Venice Film Festival, giving notice to the international film community that a revival of German cinema had happened.

In 1968, under pressure from the commercial

Volker Schlöndorff and Margarethe von Trotta directed *The Lost Honor of Katharina Blum* (1975), an adaption of Heinrich Böll's novel on the impact of the media upon a young woman unknowingly involved with a terrorist.

film industry, the subsidy system was altered by a new law. Now the Kuratorium became the Film Subsidies Board, and funds could only to go to producers, which, in turn, encouraged directors to establish production companies to produce, distribute and exhibit their own films. In 1971, Wenders, Herzog and Fassbinder with the help of Kluge formed the Filmverlag der Autoren, an authors' film publishing company to assist with the sale and distribution of their films abroad and in Germany. Like the *cinéma des auteurs,* the German directors also considered themselves serious artists who "authored" their own films. Thus, they called the New German Cinema an example of *Autorenkino,* the personal visions of these directors. By 1974, the non-commercial West German television began financing films made for television. Co-production deals were signed with directors, like Fassbinder, who brought *Eight Hours Are*

Not a Day (1972), a new TV series, into international attention.

These directors developed their screenplays out of a conscious awareness and recognition of American film styles and the influence American consumer society had on the lives of postwar Germans. To counter this powerful consumer environment and its ideology, the New German Cinema adopted the distancing effects of Brechtian theatre so that its films would intellectually prompt the viewer. By incorporating collage effects in the film narrative, the directors separated these images from their ordinary contexts, allowing the viewer to reflect upon the social and political messages behind them.

With an appropriation of the conventions and clichés of American genre films, these directors studied the expressionistic film practices of such German silent filmmakers as Murnau

Alexandra Kluge plays Anita G., a refugee girl from East Germany caught up in West Germany's past in Alexander Kluge's *Yesterday's Girl* (1966).

and Lang. Each of the three leading directors chose one of the three basic film genres of the 1920s. Werner Herzog continues the historical-mythological dramas of Fritz Lang, with his central characters possessed by powerful romantic desires that plunge them into death-defying adventures. The films of Wim Wenders follow the Caligari-like themes of sleepwalkers, of men wandering under the hypnotic influence of another mind, unaware of their own identity, or of the purpose of human existence. Fassbinder selects the chamber film or *kammerspiel* style of Murnau, similar to Strindbergian theatre, in which attention is focused upon actors caught in sadomasochistic power conflicts with other protagonists.

For their film narratives, these directors examine the social life of outsiders, foreigners and other marginal people exploited and dehumanized by a powerful conformist society. By distancing the audience from an emotional attachment to the characters, the directors encourage a critical study of the way conventional images and objects take control of people and their sense of reality. As the director depersonalizes these images in the film narrative, the viewer is prompted to gain an understanding of the ideological power struggle being waged during the Cold War to capture the minds of humankind.

The Films of Rainer Werner Fassbinder

Fassbinder (1946–1982) followed Godard's lead into the use of B-movie melodrama mixed with an anti-naturalistic stylization that projected a deliberate form of distancing in the Brechtian tradition. Fassbinder is the only film director and screenwriter coming from a background of "action-theatre" modeled after Julian Beck's Living Theatre that toured Europe. This improvisational acting group worked as radical political activists in Munich when authorities closed down Fassbinder's theatre troupe in May 1968 because they feared the spread of student and worker uprisings.

Fassbinder completed close to 30 feature films. His early works were variations on American gangster genres; the later films were melodramas about manipulative women trapped by their own sexual conflicts. His films cynically undercut the conventional Hollywood code of sexual morality and depicted how subversive sexual relationships are politically exploited as in his *Ali: Fear Eats the Soul*, a Cannes Festival Critics prize winner. In the place of the conventional code, these melodramas exhibit a sense of paranoia because their characters continue to be defeated by living in a fantasy world not of their own making. From *Die Bitteren Traneu der Petra von Kant / The Bitter Tears of Petra von Kant* (1972) to *Die Sehnsucht der Veronika Voss / Veronika Voss* (1982), Fassbinder depicts how women sacrifice their lives to emotional dreams that are removed from reality. With *The Marriage of Maria Braun*, Fassbinder moves beyond these *kammerspiel* dramas to explore the postwar economic "miracle" of West Germany through the life history of its main character, who is defeated by her forfeiture of basic human values. In this film, Fassbinder illustrates the impossibility of such an individual achieving happiness in a social construct of existence that ultimately destroys her.

Fassbinder's impressive television series, *Berlin Alexanderplatz* (1980), examines the life of a working-class man who is trapped by a social system that does not recognize him as a human being. As part of the petty bourgeoisie, he is unaware of the social forces that shape and control his life. Franz Biberkopf is a man lacking the knowledge to help himself analyze his own problems and communicate his needs to others. He is possessed by the romance of the popular culture, and like an outsider, he feels

inadequate to deal with the complexities of modern life. When all hope fails, his frustrations turn into sudden outbursts of violence. He longs for love and companionship, yet he can only develop odd relationships with other people. Lost in his own loneliness, he cannot escape from his desires and their frustrations. He becomes an outsider, without a culture or a tradition to guide him. Unable to articulate his feelings, he returns again and again to confront the same paradoxical human relationships in which his own fear of betrayal and jealousy brings about the death of a loved one.

Fassbinder repeatedly shows us that we are trapped by the illusions we have formed about ourselves. He advises us to distance ourselves from these illusions. To effect social change, human beings must remove themselves from a commitment to dreams of sexual politics. In that way they can defuse the power of illusions and put a hold on unrestrained love. Then, once aware of the effects such objects have over us, we can remain aloof. To illustrate this theme, Fassbinder directed two historical spectacles, *Lili Marleen* (1980) and *Lola* (1980) as postwar narratives depicting how the corrupting forces of prostitution during the miraculous reconstruction of West Germany served as a metaphor for the moral bankruptcy of city officials and profiteers.

The Films of Wim Wenders

While Fassbinder attacks the political power that sexual fantasies hold over his petty bourgeois men and women, Wim Wenders (b. 1945) introduces his characters in a surreal but sterile landscape to demonstrate metaphorically what happens to any person living in a subconscious dream state. His films explore how these characters begin to deny reality and continue to search for an identity that is out of their reach. This quest for a conscious sense of personhood, for an answer to who I am, or who anyone else is, creates a restlessness with life and an endless anxiety that ultimately provokes a person's self-destruction.

Wenders' existential hero is the unadaptable man, both as a dreamer and wanderer caught living in the 20th century, where life is constantly endangered by violence and warfare. To break away from confrontation and violence, the hero seeks the solace of the open road in his attempt to solve the uncertainties of social disillusionment. This hero adapts a schizoid temperament, a split personality, that allows him to become a perpetrator of illogical behavior and actions. His way of life is introspective, for in his quest to accept himself and who he is, or make friends or find some meaning in life, he must analyze all the contradictory social forces that have contributed to the shaping of his identity.

In *Kings of the Road* and *The American Friend*, Wenders demonstrates the way postwar American pop culture, through films, television and rock and roll music, has infiltrated German minds and developed a cultural schizophrenia in that country. The effect of this cultural colonization is depicted by his characters' fascination with all things American. They begin to daydream about America, and emulate American heroes, whether gangsters or cowboys. This "new way of life" begins to alienate the hero from his own German identity, one that has been hidden and repressed by his own government. Because of the contradictory nature of these different cultural forces, Wenders places his characters in a narrative at the moment when their desires and dreams conflict with the difficult realities of life. In their attempts to resolve the disparity between these two cultural forces, Wenders' characters occupy a stark and cold landscape where chance encounters between strangers seem to offer some hope of warmth and intimacy. Some of these encounters are unconventional, and the relationships between strangers succeed. Other traditional relationships, those between parents or between parent and child, fail. It is through these brief periods of contact that Wenders explores the emotional investment we place on human relationships and why human beings need some vision or framework to overcome the sense of fragmentation and isolation they experience in modern society.

These thematic threads are found in his American film, *Paris, Texas*, a rambling narrative written by Sam Shepard. Starring Harry Dean Stanton and Nastassia Kinski, it concerns the struggle of an older man driven by an obsession to find his roots and be reunited with his family. But time has eroded his past, and his new confrontations with his wife and son remind him that to pursue such a life is futile. The film won the Palme d'Or at Cannes in 1984. On his return to Germany, Wenders collaborated again with playwright Peter Handke to direct his script for *Der Himmel über Berlin / Wings of Desire* (1987). Set in contemporary Berlin, it describes a fanciful universe where two invisible angels entertain a return to human existence. One angel, played by Bruno Ganz, is so moved by a sad and lonely trapeze artist that he joins human ranks to rekindle in her a sense of love and wonder. With Peter Falk as an aging writer and "former angel," the spectator visits a movie set where memories of Nazi atrocities are revealed. Wenders carefully follows the action with a highly mobile camera that captures the dividedness of a great city. Within the ruins, Berlin is depicted as a city attempting to reconstitute its own life-spirit from the trauma of social and political upheaval and devastation. In *In Weiter Ferne So Nah / Faraway, So Close!* (1993), Wenders returns to the city after the fall of the Berlin Wall and the unification with East Berlin, this time entrusting a different angel, only to recognize the grim realities of social and economic disparities. The alienation and isolation attest to a call for a reinvention of politics from *either/or* to *both/and* thinking.

The Films of Werner Herzog

In the imaginative film world of Werner Herzog (b. 1942), dreams are more important than a person's everyday existence, where mediocrity and banality deaden one's consciousness. As a director and screenwriter, he removes his heroes from the present-day world into an historical world that tests the limits of human desires. In this world what is believed to be accepted as familiar or normal is suddenly treated as being different, stressing the reality of a dream. While Herzog may consider that dreams are based upon a reality, he is more intrigued at playing out the cosmic dreams of humans. In this arena, heroic romanticism is displayed through a constant struggle against the stultifying norms of civilized society. His films, such as *Aguirre: The Wrath of God, Nosferatu: Phantom der Nacht / Nosferatu the Vampyre* (1978) and *Woyzeck* (1979), help us understand how the grotesque and the abnormal enter human behavior. They are graphic depictions of men suffering under the agony of social or sexual deprivation. Through his own intensely personal vision of film, Herzog removes the viewer from any psychological or social reflection on the ordeals encountered by his central characters. His main purpose is to combine stunning images and haunting music to promote an emotional reaction of wonder and awe as his heroic madmen struggle to change the paralyzing conditions of everyday life and achieve their dreams. Films like *Aguirre* and *Stroszek* (1977) display the creative capacity of humankind to envision a more mystical and spiritual world. Herzog's heroes appear to be obsessed by their own dreams to overcome a hostile and unforgiving world. Through Herzog's vision, we, as viewers, realize how these romantic figures allow us to witness the power of imagination that shapes and controls human destiny. When these forces are repressed by the demands of civilization, society alienates human beings from understanding their own nature. For that reason Herzog believes society forces people into madness, and that we must continue to try to understand the romantic quest for liberation and freedom.

In *Fitzcarraldo* (1982), with Klaus Kinski as the visionary Irish adventurer, we are witness to his obsessive dream of importing opera to the wilds of a Brazilian trading post. The grandiose scheme includes transporting an actual steamship down rivers and across the mountains. This action is chronicled in Les Blank's remarkable documentary, *Burden of Dreams* (1982), capturing the director, actors and film crew making daily contact with local native tribes along the Amazon. It clearly demonstrates why Herzog feels our present society traps us within rational thought, forgetting the powerful creative forces of life itself.

References

Kaes, Anton. 1989. *From Hitler to Heimat: The Return of History as Film.* Cambridge, Mass.: Harvard University Press.

Rentschler, Eric. 1984. *West German Film in the Course of Time: Reflections on the Twenty Years Since Oberhausen.* Bedford Hills, N.Y.: Redgrave.

_____ (ed.). 1986. *German Film and Literature: Adaptations and Transformations.* New York: Methuen, Inc.

CHAPTER 23

American Auteurs:
Allen, Altman and Coppola

Introduction

A number of new American *auteurs* success-fully entered Hollywood studios in the 1970s by producing, scripting and editing films that questioned American myths of fame and success. These directors were predominately film school graduates from California and New York. Andrew Sarris applied the concept of *auteurism* to the filmmaking practices of these young American directors, such as Robert Altman, Francis Ford Coppola, Martin Scorsese, John Cassavetes and Woody Allen. Each film director uses irony to show the contradictions between the past myths and the present social and political situations of the Vietnam-Watergate era of the 1970s. The romantic illusions found in the earlier classical Hollywood genre are transformed into anti-genre film narratives using episodic structures that emphasize character relationships. Frank depiction of sex and violence became the norm for off-beat and innovative Hollywood films, such as *The Godfather* (1972) and *Taxi Driver* (1976). Using improvisational New Wave techniques, each director followed themes comparing illusion to reality, with major characters struggling to overcome defeat and despair. The leading producer-writer-director was Francis Ford Coppola. With George Lucas and Martin Scorsese, they translated the style of the French New Wave and remade older Hollywood genre films into newer Hollywood films by restructuring their film narratives. They were joined by other New York television directors such as Robert Altman, Woody Allen and John Cassavetes to revolutionize earlier Hollywood productions. In 1972, Coppola made box-office history with his phenomenal production of *The Godfather*, starring Marlon Brando as a Mafia chieftain, and followed this film with two successful sequels. Coppola also acted as producer for George Lucas' *American Graffiti* (1973), a film with a rock and roll soundtrack that became one of the most popular films of the decade. Robert Altman, the maverick director who avoided Hollywood producers, found commercial success with his satirical comedy *M*A*S*H* (1969) and the brooding anti-genre western *McCabe & Mrs. Miller* (1971). With *Nashville* (1975), Altman parodies American politics with a loosely structured tale of promoters and performers in the American country music capital in Tennessee.

The Theory of the Auteur

In 1954, when François Truffaut wrote his polemical essay concerning the "Tradition of Quality" within the French cinema, he attacked a French cinema dominated by scriptwriters who adapted literary works for the screen. His *Politique des Auteurs* referred to his policy to regard the director of the film as the creative force in filmmaking. His singling out Hollywood directors of the past as *auteurs* provoked a controversy on how he determined what directors deserved to be praised for their contributions to the history of film. Truffaut's theory stated that the formal qualities of the film, the *mise-en-scène*, carried the distinctive style of the creative personality of the director.

In Robert Altman's anti-western, *McCabe & Mrs. Miller* (1971), Warren Beatty and Julie Christie reach Presbyterian Church, a frontier mining town with girls for the miners and some get-rich schemes before the syndicate moves in.

Andrew Sarris, a newspaper film critic for New York's *The Village Voice*, introduced Truffaut's auteur theory to American film critics in 1962. In 1968, Sarris extended his argument for auteurism in his book, *The American Cinema: Directors and Directions 1929–1968*. He analyzed the films of a number of prominent American and European directors who worked in Hollywood and argued that the person who controlled the entire project and who projected a personal style and vision into a film was a film auteur. Further Sarris stated that the directorial signature could be identified in a series of films through the structure, style and the visual design of these films. Thus, auteur criticism would take into consideration the ways and means the director treated the themes or content in the film in terms of the *mise-en-scène*. In other words, whatever the genre, the director imposes his own visual interpretation on the film, thus earning the director the designation of *auteur*.

As Sarris states, the auteur theory introduces another way to study the history of films. By looking at a cinema of directors within cinematic genres, one achieves a more total history of film. For Sarris "the auteur theory is merely a system of tentative priorities, a pattern theory in constant flux" (Sarris 1976, p. 244). Yet Sarris' emphasis is an appeal to let the film speak for itself. The director's work would be systematically explored to trace the characteristic themes, structures and formal qualities that set a critical standard for all films. But if a person follows this auteur concept, how does that person examine Hollywood films as a sociological construct or study them from a genre-entertainment viewpoint? Auteur criticism deliberately

dismisses the Hollywood studio system production line replication of genre films and
raises films into artworks. Sarris contends that
"the auteur theory is not so much a theory as
an attitude, a table of values that converts film
history into directorial autobiography" (p.
246).

Some critics, notably Pauline Kael, accuse
Sarris of elevating Hollywood kitsch or low-
brow art into a classic highbrow realm. But
that is not the case. Auteur criticism is different
and quite distinct from genre criticism. Genre
criticism utilizes the notion of an idealized
form or structure and how well it is realized by
directors, whether the film is a western or a detective thriller. On the other hand, auteur criticism treats genre films as a method to pursue
personal expression of constant themes. Directors manipulate a genre-formula using variations of one "realist" style or another to make
their own statements about the human condition. Sarris lists a pantheon of great directors
who "transcended" their production problems
to promote their own directorial vision in the
history of film. These include D. W. Griffith,
Robert Flaherty, Buster Keaton, Charlie Chaplin, Fritz Lang, F. W. Murnau, Ernst Lubitsch,
Josef von Sternberg, Max Ophüls, Jean Renoir,
John Ford, Orson Welles, Howard Hawks and
Alfred Hitchcock. Most of these directors came
from the silent film period and withstood the
challenges of a studio-dominated system and
the front-office interference of its powerful
producers. John Ford and Alfred Hitchcock
validate the auteur theory because their own
personalities overcame Hollywood's drive toward a conventional formula-driven commercial cinema.

The American Auteurs

The new American filmmakers of the 1970s
were mainly young directors who graduated
from film schools in the United States. Like
their French New Wave colleagues, they were
trained to write, produce and direct their own
films. As American auteurs, they were able to
merge the commercial aspects of filmmaking
with their own personal styles. Francis Ford

Coppola and Paul Schrader were writer-direc-
tors who graduated from the University of California at Los Angeles. George Lucas and John
Milius graduated from the University of Southern California. Martin Scorsese and Brian De
Palma were trained at New York University,
and Steven Spielberg and Peter Bogdanovich
were college graduates who entered Hollywood
studios as apprentices to directors. Joining this
group of young college graduates was an older
group of television writers and directors from
New York including Robert Altman, Arthur
Penn and Woody Allen. Some historians suggest that the old Hollywood with its genre films
evolved into the new Hollywood through the
development of anti-genre films. These new
"genre genre" films were influenced by the
French New Wave of Godard and Truffaut and
the American underground cinema of Andy
Warhol and Paul Morrissey. Paul Morrissey was
the director of *Flesh* (1968), *Trash* (1970) and
Heat (1971) for the Factory. Each of these films
parodied established Hollywood film romances, turning them into comic charades
about Hollywood, reputing myths of sexual in-
trigue and violence. With *Heat,* Morrissey remade Billy Wilder's *Sunset Boulevard* (1950)
into a soft-porn nightmare of sexual impo-
tency and drug addiction. With other underground American filmmakers, the "glamour"
associated with Hollywood genre films was unmasked and questions were raised about social
and political structures that supported the
American dream of fame and fortune.

The pre-existing ideologies planted in Hollywood genre films of the 1940s and 1950s that
supported stereotypical solutions to given
problems were under attack in the 1970s. The
anti-genre films of the decade redefined the
fixed meanings associated with these older
films and revealed a new context. "These postmodern films parodied the plot structures, stylistic conventions and movie stars of Hollywood Past, usually by compiling a catalogue of
Studio Era clichés" (Mast and Kawin 1996, p.
467). The critical relationship between the cultural myths of the past and the new anti-genre
films of the 1970s is demonstrated in Roman
Polanski's *Chinatown* (1974), whose central
character is asked to find a missing person. But

instead of solving the mystery, the film becomes an exploration of lust, power and greed during the 1930s. Not only is political corruption unmasked, but the investigation demonstrates how political corruption is closely connected to sexual and moral corruption. The film was a reflection of the contemporary Watergate break-in in July 1972, with the cover-up and the eventual indictment and conviction of high-ranking government officials. *Chinatown* also accomplished an ironic commentary on the power of the American dream by referring us back to a traditional era of Hollywood filmmaking. The script by Robert Towne reworks the formal genre elements into a new context to bring the viewer into a self-awareness about the cultural myths that influence how we understand ourselves. The theme of obsessive power corrupting and overtaking traditional authority is explored more fully in the *Godfather* trilogy made by Coppola and in *Apocalypse Now* (1979). In these films, Coppola examines how Mafia warfare becomes part of family business necessary to defend and protect both the stability of the business as well as the family itself.

The Films of Francis Ford Coppola

Of all of these talented filmmakers, Coppola became the most important screenwriter-director-producer in Hollywood during the 1970s. His film career was launched after he won the Samuel Goldwyn award for screenwriting in 1964 while attending UCLA's graduate program in film production. Warners' Seven Arts studios then hired him as a house writer for two projects, *Is Paris Burning?* (1966), directed by René Clément, and *This Property Is Condemned* (1966), based on Tennessee Williams' play. His early draft of *Patton* for 20th Century–Fox was the basis for the success of *Patton* (1970). Then, in 1967, Coppola directed *Finian's Rainbow* for Warner Bros. After good reviews, Coppola gathered a crew to do his own road movie, *The Rain People,* in the style of the French New Wave. This film was based on Coppola's own short story, "Echoes,"

that he developed at UCLA. With George Lucas as his assistant director, Coppola shot the film in sequence from New York to Colorado in three and a half months. From the on-location improvisations using hand-held cameras, Coppola's long takes reveal a self-reflexive mode of cinema and a *mise-en-scène* that he employs in all of his films.

The Rain People (1969) starred Shirley Knight, James Caan and Robert Duvall. It focuses upon a pregnant married woman and her attempts to escape from her husband and the forthcoming responsibilities of family life. In this drama, Coppola explores the contradictions and paradoxes of being a member of a family when suddenly one must choose between being loyal to one's self and learning to serve the needs of one's family. For this young woman, the ironies of having family ties and fulfilling the expectations of others become a nightmare. Her own life appears to be guided by "a tradition of the past," one that haunts her present situation and directs her future activities. In Coppola's major films, *The Godfather, The Godfather: Part II* (1974) and *Apocalypse Now,* the family becomes, paradoxically, the enemy of personal and social development and growth. Fundamentally, the family is shown as a political power machine in which each adult member is expected to play assigned social and political roles.

In *The Rain People,* when Natalie (Shirley Knight) leaves her husband and the entrapment of marriage and motherhood, her revolt becomes a journey of exploration into her own psyche; she attempts to discover who she is, and what her responsibilities are to others. Her voyage of discovery starts with her arriving at her mother's house to explain her actions and why she "wants to be free for five minutes, a half-hour a day." This breakdown of traditional ways leads to a sense of anxiety and moral instability. Her dream of freedom is condemned as Coppola poses other moral questions for her to consider when chance encounters bring her into contact with other people who need her care and support. He asks how deeply are we committed to others' needs, and whether we are responsible for the crimes of others.

Coppola asks these same questions of a

Francis Coppola's *Apocalypse Now* (1979) is set in Vietnam during the war. Starring Martin Sheen and Robert Duvall, the film focuses on the long boat ride upstream and a confrontation between Sheen as the military assassin and a renegade colonel, Marlon Brando, who is waging his own war. Classic scenes of airstrikes combine with a surreal sense of dread as modern man meets, in horror, his dark and violent other.

wiretapper in his later film *The Conversation* (1974), whose central figure, Harry Caul, is hired to spy on the wife of a powerful business executive. After delivering the information, he attempts to remain isolated and anonymous from the tragic consequences of the conversation he recorded. Life, however, is shown to be paradoxical and ironic. Caul's corporate sponsor has silenced him within his own apartment by secretly placing him under surveillance with a wiretap he cannot find, so that he remains a prisoner of the business. Caul and Natalie both realize they must choose a course of action decided upon by the power structure of the family: one cannot be in and out of the family at the same time. Once they choose or reject the traditional ways of the family, they can never become independent of the influence of the

family without suffering alienation and guilt. Past conditioning has embedded a style of life that makes it necessary for one to remain in the family and accept one's place or, if rejected, move into madness.

Coppola explores the possibility of madness caused by an obsession for power that overrides traditional authority in *Apocalypse Now*, a film loosely based on Joseph Conrad's *Heart of Darkness*. We are confronted with the knowledge that a member of the military family, a renegade colonel, has "gone over the edge" and set up his own military base in the jungle. Colonel Kurtz was an exemplary family man who had a brilliant war record. But his decision to operate his own tribal army has become a serious threat to the war now engaging American forces. Again, Coppola takes us on a metaphor-

Francis Ford Coppola's *The Rain People* (1969) is an early film odyssey of a young wife breaking away from the "family" and sexual domination. Starring Shirley Knight as the runaway wife and James Caan as a mentally retarded man, the film uses New Wave film techniques to capture the immediacy and uncertainty of life itself.

ical journey of discovery, this time into a dark continent where a primitive uncivilized society still exists in the jungle. We are confronted with the mystery of Colonel Willard Kurtz and why he broke away from the military. He is considered mad. His state of sanity or insanity becomes the battleground between the dark primitive forces of savages and the calculating forces of modern humanity and its technology. The military man sent to destroy Colonel Kurtz is very much a younger version of Kurtz. What is at stake is the authority of the military family to remain in control of the war. But the obsession with power creates the paradoxes in the film since war, with its unlimited potential for violence and destruction, becomes a form of madness itself. In the creation of an environ-ment of savagery and brutality, Coppola surrounds the film with surreal images of destruction that reflect the disorienting dilemmas faced by characters trying to understand the unpopular war in Vietnam. The abuse of power by men in authority is analogous to the ideological practices of democratic governments producing spies, murderers and assassins out of the darkness. *Apocalypse Now* shared the critics' award at the Cannes Film Festival with Schlöndorff's *The Tin Drum* in 1979.

The Films of Martin Scorsese

In many ways, Martin Scorsese (b. 1942) parallels Coppola's Italian-Catholic upbringing

Martin Scorsese's *Raging Bull* (1980) stars Robert De Niro as Jake LaMotta, an Italian middleweight boxing champion confronting his own lack of sexual identity and his fear of being cuckolded by his wife.

in New York City as a graduate of a film school program. After graduating from New York University, he worked on rock documentaries, editing *Woodstock* (1970), before he traveled to Hollywood to work with Roger Corman. Like Coppola, he made an exploitation film, *Boxcar Bertha* (1972), based on the memoirs of the real Bertha Thompson, a runaway Arkansas farm girl who was caught stealing from railway bosses. On returning to New York, he directed *Mean Streets* (1972), a film about a group of young adolescents, each attempting to "be somebody." They strive to break away from the stifling confines of their Catholic neighborhood and partake in the joys of crime with the Mafia. The film introduced Harvey Keitel as an ambitious nightclub owner and Robert De Niro as the irresponsible Johnny Boy who owes everybody money. Scorsese successfully integrates rock music into the structure of the film to in-

tensify his recurring themes of urban violence and the macho rituals of manhood.

Thematically, Scorsese differs from Coppola in that he looks at the struggles of working-class young men who resort to violence whenever their self-esteem is shattered by a rigid code of masculinity. Themes of madness are integral to the bloody violence unleashed by his protagonists. Robert De Niro starred in the next three Scorsese films, *Taxi Driver, New York, New York* (1977) and *Raging Bull* (1980). In *Taxi Driver*, De Niro depicts a Vietnam veteran who goes on a mad rampage to protect a young prostitute. The ending is a powerful demonstration of a psychotic on the loose, erupting in an orgy of violent bloodshed. With *Raging Bull*, Scorsese uses the biography of middleweight champion Jake LaMotta as a starting point to demonstrate how a sexually insecure man is taunted into becoming a

In Woody Allen's *Annie Hall* (1977), Woody Allen as Al Singer and Diane Keaton as Annie Hall exchange tennis quips related to Singer's hang-ups on his sexual potency, movies, psychoanalysis and his ever-present existentialist angst.

ruthless champion. Still clinging to an old-fashioned notion of masculinity, LaMotta powers his way toward world recognition as he fights a battle within himself that finally brings about the self-destruction of his own family.

The Films of Woody Allen

As an *auteur* filmmaker, Woody Allen (b. 1935) follows Scorsese in probing the myths surrounding romantic heroes with his series of comic adventures as a man lacking sex appeal. His screen persona, whether as illustrated by

Manhattan (1979) is Woody Allen's semi-autobiographical reverie as a TV comedy writer reflecting upon the women in his life. Diane Keaton plays a neurotic intellectual infatuated by Allen's persona.

Alvy Singer in *Annie Hall* (1977) or Isaac Davis in *Manhattan* (1979), finds him alienated as an adult who cannot engage in a serious romantic liaison. His comic awareness of this personal dilemma triggers his struggle to maintain his rational balance when romantic setbacks play havoc with his emotional needs. His comedies are self-conscious psychodramas that allow Allen to become the introspective intellectual seeking various methods and relationships to secure a sexually fulfilling lifestyle.

Allen, as a parodic writer of his times, contrasts the romantic attitudes and lovemaking myths and rituals of the Hollywood Dream Machine with his own ironic versions to show how characters, like himself, pursue these romantic dreams and fantasies. Film critic Roger Ebert, in his review of *Manhattan*, states:

> Woody Allen populates his film with people who are at odds with their own visions of themselves. They've been sold, indeed, on the necessity of seeming true and grave and ethical that even their affairs, their deceptions, have to be discussed in terms of " and "meanings"—the dialogue in this film was learned in psychoanalysis [Ebert 1989, p. 392].

Woody Allen films often take place in New York City, and frequently focus on the sexual mores and hang-ups of white middle-class males. He usually casts himself as the romantic leading man, whose strengths are his bright and witty one-liners that overshadow his lack of physical manliness. Like many male fantasy figures, the Allen persona projects his dream of becoming a man by winning the love and respect of a beautiful woman. But every relationship with a different woman results in the Allen character bemoaning his lack of romantic fulfillment. Allen humorously compares the

Jeff Daniels plays the hero who steps off the screen to woo Mia Farrow in a bizarre relationship that cleverly mixes screen characters with other illusions of reality in Woody Allen's *The Purple Rose of Cairo* (1985).

differences between what people say and do; in *Manhattan* he also supports this contrast with a musical sound track from the 1930s full of melodious songs by George Gershwin. Songs like "S'Wonderful," "Embraceable You," "I've Got a Crush on You" and "Someone to Watch Over Me" romantically resonate the feelings and desires of the hero. But Allen's character is an anti-hero, who has to psychoanalyze everything people do and say in a relationship. Thus, in each film, Allen satirizes these movie fantasies by introducing a sense of reality in which romantic illusions are insufficient to sustain a mature relationship between lovers. In *The Purple Rose of Cairo* (1985), Allen reverses the lead role and shows what happens to a woman who becomes star-struck with a romantic leading man. In this film, an Irving Berlin score provides the musical counterpoint to the action of the film. One scene in particular cap-

tures the nostalgia of the 1930s, when we return to the film version of Rogers and Astaire dancing to the words and music of "Cheek to Cheek."

The Films of John Cassavetes

If Woody Allen plays with the romantic contradictions of contemporary life, John Cassavetes (1929–1989), a fellow New Yorker and professional actor, was an experimental filmmaker and iconoclast who brought into his films the Pirandellian dilemma between illusion and reality. Like Pirandello's plays of the 1930s in which the playwright states "Right You Are, If You Think You Are," we see in Cassavetes' work the battle between the individual self and the persona or mask it adopts as a social entity. Cassavetes' major films also explore the battle between the actors and the roles they perform to illuminate the schizoid or split personality. His films use satire and humor to dramatize the paradoxes that emerge when his characters begin to differentiate between who they think they are and how they are perceived by others. Once these characters realize they are trapped by the roles other people have given them, they reach a point of rebellion to avoid going insane. A similar situation is also found in some of Coppola's dramas.

Cassavetes' series of films in the 1970s displayed his improvisational directing and *cinéma vérité* documentary styles to bring out the personal narratives of his characters. Although *Women Under the Influence* (1975) established his place as an *auteur* filmmaker, *Gloria* (1980) indicated more clearly the existential dilemma confronting the anti-heroine. *Gloria* features Gena Rowlands as a tough talking ex-chorus girl who works for a Mafia gangster. A tragic incident causes her to see a more important role in life to play. Apparently overcome with maternal instinct, she decides to protect the life of a wise-mouthed seven-year-old boy after his family is gunned down by Mafia henchmen. The rest of the film shows how she switches roles back and forth from her former self as a mobster's girl to her newly created one as surrogate mother. A number of times Rowlands puts on the mask to get back at her former employer. Underlying the basic narrative is her newfound commitment to life in which she suddenly finds herself experiencing strong maternal emotions. As these feelings and sentiments are established, Cassavetes' film makes the viewer aware of the importance of self-esteem in maintaining one's own life.

The Films of Robert Altman

Along with Cassavetes, Robert Altman (b. 1925) is another prominent Hollywood maverick. Altman comes to film production through his work in television drama. At age 45, he directed his first revisionist genre film, *M*A*S*H* (1969), in which he satirically questions the carnage created by the Korean War. Altman's directorial style depends upon a multiple series of short happenings to help reveal complex character relationships. The film's cast members usually improvise dialogue as they play eccentric characters caught in absurdly dangerous situations; they cannot explain to themselves why they are doing what they are doing as doctors in a U.S. Army field hospital during the Korean War.

After *M*A*S*H* garnered critical and box-office acclaim, Altman continued developing scenarios based upon deconstructing the myth-making omnipotence of Hollywood genre films. His anti-genre narratives create tensions in human interactions when his characters reveal their weaknesses and are quickly exploited by others. His narratives then explode into violence toward the end of each film, when his characters cannot overcome the overwhelming sense of defeat in spite of the myth of law and order. In his own cynical fashion, Altman uncovers the serious pattern of innocence myths serve in a series of anti-genre films beginning with the western, *McCabe & Mrs. Miller* (1971), then the crime thriller, *The Long Goodbye* (1973), and a musical drama, *Nashville* (1975), which parodies the sentimental romanticism and politics of country music.

In *Nashville*, Altman uses the city metaphorically — the film is really about politics. By cutting between public functions and private scenes, shooting in theaters and studios from offstage and on, he shows what goes into creating a self-image. Much like the political world, the culture in *Nashville* believes that its self-image is what is most important. "We watch the city recording itself, playing itself back to itself and marketing the image to itself. We eavesdrop on the culture's conversation with itself. We're watching people decide how they want to see themselves and how they want to sell themselves" (Sawhill 2000).

Over the course of his career, Altman developed many techniques to allow for inclusiveness. With his sound engineers Jim Webb and Chris McLaughlin, he allowed much more ambient and background noise to pervade his films. His cinematographers — during this period, usually Vilmos Zsigmond and, for this film, Paul Lohmann — used multiple cameras and lighted entire environments rather than single scenes so his actors had unprecedented freedom of movement and, since they didn't know which angle would finally be used, could not play to the cameras (Sawhill 2000).

His later films, *Players* (1992) and *Short Cuts* (1993) continue his cynical exploration of Hollywood producers and media manipulators who try to come up with illusive fairy tale solutions when no one has any right answers.

McCabe & Mrs. Miller is a fine example of Altman's anti-genre crusade against genre films produced during the 1970s. Within a harsh western setting, Altman reconstructs the past as more brutal fact than as Hollywood illusion. Once in this hostile environment, Altman humorously exposes the myth about free enterprise through the affair between a small-time gambler and opportunist, depicted by Warren Beatty, and his opium smoking lady-friend, Julie Christie, the madam of the town's favorite bordello. Their ill-fated business partnership, combining a gambling casino with a bordello, is secondary to the purposes of the film. Altman is not concerned with the success of the new partnership nor in the abilities of his lead characters to overcome adversity in settling the West, as a genre film would normally do. His major objective is to demonstrate the western hero as a lone financier who spreads capitalism and corruption in the new territory with charm and good cheer. Yet he is powerless to protect his own free enterprise operations against the hired guns of big business and comes to an ignominious defeat. Altman removes the heroic dimensions from the traditional western genre story to reveal the workings of human naiveté and folly and to expose a corrupt economic system that destroys the small free-enterpriser. The dramatic tension in the film derives from McCabe's mistaken attempt to ignore the power of the system and to refuse to accept the reality of the nameless company men as they move in to take over this new mining town in the American Pacific Northwest. The attention Altman pays to the harsh conditions of life together with absence of law and order helps him isolate McCabe as an insignificant factor. His chances for survival against the hired guns appears to be only a matter of luck. Altman succeeds in using the film as an allegory about the way myths function in our society. By showing how forces of capitalism devalue law and order for their own personal interests, Altman successfully parodies these accepted notions of western heroes who supposedly are there to fight against injustice and the political forces of evil.

References

Ebert, Roger. 1989. *Home Movie Companion.* New York: Andrews and McMeel.

Mast, Gerald, and Bruce F. Kawin. 1996. *A Short History of the Movies.* 6th ed. Boston and London: Allyn and Bacon.

Sarris, Andrew. 1976. "A Theory of Film History." In Bill Nichols, ed. *Movie and Methods: An Anthology.* Berkeley: University of California Press, pp. 237–251.

_____. 1992. "Notes on the Auteur Theory in 1962." In Gerald Mast, Marshall Cohen and Leo Braudy, eds. *Film Theory and Criticism: Introductory Readings.* 4th ed. New York and Oxford: Oxford University Press, pp. 585–588.

Sawhill, Ray. 2000. "A Movie Called *Nashville.*" www.salon.com

Truffaut, François. 1962. "Notes on The Auteur Theory." In *Film Culture* 27, Winter 1962–63.

CHAPTER 24

Revisiting Genre Films in the 1980s and 1990s

Introduction

In the late 1970s the major Hollywood studios, Columbia, Paramount, Universal, MGM and United Artists, were taken over by larger corporations that began to produce a handful of big-budgeted, mass-appeal feature films. The success of these "blockbuster" films, like *Jaws* (1975), *Star Wars* (1977) and *Superman* (1978), generated new economic growth in the film industry. The films moved from the pessimistic anti–genre films of the early 1970s to the popular myths and cultural values later endorsed by the Reagan administration. These films contained strong discourses promoting "family values," a democracy able to ward off any "evil" empire, and a reestablishment of moral order.

New marketing strategies packaged successful tie-ins of films with other merchandising products to offset the higher production costs. The advent of VCRs and films on video revitalized the commercial base of the film industry. Independent producer-directors like Francis Coppola and George Lucas set a new trend in the history of film by directing powerful sequels to their original film hits. *The Empire Strikes Back* (1980) and *The Return of the Jedi* (1983) completed the *Star Wars* trilogy. Lucas also produced the immensely profitable *Indiana Jones* series for Steven Spielberg. Maverick directors such as David Lynch (*Blue Velvet,* 1986), Spike Lee (*Do the Right Thing,* 1989), and Ridley Scott (*Blade Runner,* 1982), among others, continued producing serious adult films strongly accented by sex, violence and power politics. Some films were a mixture of film noir and science fiction and fantasy.

New Technology and Blockbuster Films

George Lucas and Steven Spielberg were the leading filmmakers who repackaged cultural myths into new action-adventure epics enhanced with computer-generated special effects, and stereo-sound scores resulting in contemporary "feel good" experiences with exciting escapist overtones. *Star Wars* was the first science-fiction blockbuster that successfully integrated a high standard of film technology. George Lucas developed these spectacular special effects from initial technological breakthroughs designed by Douglas Trumbull for Stanley Kubrick's *2001: A Space Odyssey.* New electronic means of producing stereophonic Dolby sound effects complemented these computerized visuals. The invention of the Steadicam enhanced live-action cinematography. With the miniaturization of strange mechanized monsters, Lucas combined all together into a new aural-visual kind of special effects that had never been seen in motion pictures. Lucas proved that almost anything can magically appear to exist or happen in motion pictures in a manner similar to the effects achieved by Georges Méliès, the early French film director-magician.

In the history of film, *Star Wars,* more than *Jaws,* anticipated the new cultural attitudes arising after the Vietnam War. The new film industry had never enjoyed a bigger box office smash, as audiences returned to the movies houses to cheer its fighting heroes again. The rebels in this film were not misfits or losers, alienated characters who dominated American films in the 1970s from *Bonnie and Clyde* to *Taxi Driver.* In place of these serious melodramas was a film that returned the audience to the hero sagas and genre formulas of the past. At its core, *Star Wars* is a basic earlier hero story translated from classical literature; the hero, Luke Skywalker, is without parents, claiming his birthright as a noble knight on a quest. A mythic union with the "Force," an energizing power, enables him to challenge the emperor and his evil empire. Lucas provides us with a new villain, Darth Vader, a fallen Jedi knight who leads "the dark side" in an interplanetary space spectacle that threatens Luke and his allies as he fights for democracy.

Thus, as a cultural myth about American high technology, *Star Wars* became one of the pivotal points marking a change in the American film industry. By tapping into revitalizing powers of action-adventure genre films, Lucas ably combined a strong mass entertainment adventure with a dynamic political message that carried into the 1990s. *Star Wars* and its subsequent sequels (and new prequels) made unprecedented profits from merchandising products with the *Star Wars* label. With the release of Spielberg's *E.T. the Extra-Terrestrial* (1982), Hollywood filmmakers continued to revive past myths and fairy tales as film scenarios. From *Rocky* (1976) to *Rambo: First Blood* (1985), both starring Sylvester Stallone, audiences followed the adventures of heroes who could win, in which monsters could be slain, and good overcame evil. The films recreate a mythical world where the most remarkable actions and deeds can be accomplished. They are distinguished by high tech special effects and "cliff-hanger" action sequences, avoiding when necessary any serious political commentary. More than ever before, American films became market-driven consumer products appealing to younger audiences. *Star Wars* itself heralded all of the major marketing trends that were to become commonplace ten years later and that

today still dominate almost every major Hollywood release, including James Cameron's *Titanic* (1997).

Titanic, arguably, could have been made in 1912, the year the ship sank. That year, D.W. Griffith made *Man's Genesis, The Musketeers of Pig Alley,* and *The New York Hat.* The movie is much closer to Griffith's era than it is to other disaster films made in 1990s and takes itself more seriously than other movies of the time, which seem cynical and self-mocking. "The characterizations of heroes and villains, which appear to be drawn with the utmost sincerity, all seem cut from the same Victorian cloth as those in Griffith's melodramas—among others, there's the dreamy and selfless Irish-American artist-adventurer, the tempestuous and freethinking Philadelphia debutante, the snarling and brutal zillionaire fiancé (with an improbable touch of Brando's Stanley Kowalski), and the fiancé's sadistic and preying valet (David Warner)" (Rosenbaum 1997).

Both Lucas and Spielberg share a taste for coming-of-age adolescent mythology. Spielberg's two science-fiction fantasies made box-office history. In *Close Encounters of the Third Kind* (1977), and *E.T. the Extra-Terrestrial,* the director also moves into a form of popular mythology in which the alien menace becomes the hero. Both films suffer from trivializing the meetings between these unknowable aliens with a maudlin appeal to emotional excess. The extraterrestrials not only have to combat fearful earthly authorities, who insist on capturing them, but must overcome adult authority figures who are shown as paranoid individuals, apparently unaware that they have lost their childlike imaginations. Spielberg depends largely upon highly manipulative emotional encounters with UFOs and aliens to show their benign intentions. He heightens audience response by using special visual effects and a powerful soundtrack to demonstrate the magical forces these aliens possess that can enhance human life. Like Lucas before him, Spielberg is a director who likes to explore the imaginative possibilities of life from a childlike perspective. However, he sacrifices his appeal to serious moral themes by an acceptance of well-worn melodramatic clichés from earlier action-adventure serials. With Lucas as his producer, Spielberg initiated a series of Indiana Jones adventure thrillers starring Harrison Ford in *Raiders of the Lost Ark* (1981), *Indiana Jones and the Temple of Doom* (1984) and *Indiana Jones and the Last Crusade* (1989), all fashioned as quests for a Holy Grail or a magical talisman that once in one's possession would destroy one's enemies. In *Schindler's List* (1993) Spielberg was more faithful to the novel by Thomas Keneally, yet tended to repeat the same melodramatic patterns in dramatizing the Holocaust (Conner 1989, pp. 173–183).

Anti–Vietnam War Films

While the appeal of blockbuster films continued to capture the imagination of audiences, with mega-hits like *Terminator* (1984), *Ghostbusters* (1984), *Back to the Future* (1985) and *Batman* (1989), several veteran filmmakers persevered in directing a number of films dealing with real-life experiences of American soldiers in Vietnam. These films brought home the different ways the Vietnam War affected and altered the lives of the young soldiers and their friends. This cycle of films began with the release of *Go Tell the Spartans* (Ted Post, 1978), followed by *Coming Home* (Hal Ashby, 1978) and *Deer Hunter* (Michael Cimino, 1978). Francis Coppola's *Apocalypse Now* (1979) was followed by Oliver Stone's *Platoon* (1986), and Stanley Kubrick's *Full Metal Jacket* (1987). The awesome reality of war reconstructed in these films seemed to touch an adult audience unaware of the price paid by Americans in Vietnam. *Deer Hunter* appeared to shock the audiences the most as it depicted the physical and psychological torture and violence endured by three buddies from a Pennsylvania steel town. Vivid scenes of Russian roulette spelled out the chaotic nature of this war. Coppola's *Apocalypse Now* went further and truly captured the madness and insanity of the conflict. Unlike the adolescent mythic battles in *Star Wars,* the terrors of warfare and the dislocation and death of young, innocent civilians and soldiers are depicted as frighteningly real. If Lucas took us on a virtual-reality war adventure into outer space, the drug-induced nightmare of the Vietnam War, ably reconstructed by Stone, Kubrick and Coppola, gave us the terrorizing images of the awesome power and violence that marked this conflict, heightening our perception of what this Asian war was all about.

The Dark Side of the American Dream

Apart from Hollywood directors concentrating on blockbuster hits or realistic interpretations of the Vietnam War, there emerged a group of film directors in the 1980s who began to look at the dark side of the American dream. George Lucas in *The Empire Strikes Back* touched upon this theme when Luke Skywalker found himself battling against his own shadow as he trained to become a Jedi knight. This powerful encounter reinforced the dangers that heroes must overcome. David Lynch follows the same theme in *Elephant Man* (1980), based upon the life of a real person, John Merrick, who was physically deformed by disease. By relating his story, Lynch is able to expose the sexual hypocrisy within 19th century Victorian morality. He continued his interest in the dark side of Victorian industrialization and imperialism with a science-fiction fable, *Dune* (1985), in which sexual rites and mysteries combine with acts of colonization and try to take control of the "spice" trade on a planet. In *Blue Velvet* (1986), Lynch brings the nightmarish qualities that informed his other films into an imaginary small western town. He touches upon child abduction, voyeurism, sexual abuse and drug addiction to expose the dark, sexual deviance and criminal world existing behind the clean facade of this placid town. Lynch carried his aberrant world into a TV series, *Twin Peaks* (1990), that was similar to the corrupt world of *Blue Velvet.* Lynch exploits the fairy-tale myth of the open road in *Wild at Heart* (1990), in which a love story is contrasted with violent encounters with people the lovers meet, including the police. Similar on the road themes are found in a number of films made in the early 1990s. From Oliver Stone's *Natural Born Killers* (1994), depicting how the media manipulate the violent activities of criminal killers, to the Coen Brothers spoof of criminal activities in *Raising Arizona* (1987) and Ridley Scott's *Thelma and Louise* (1991), viewers clearly find evidence of retreading genre forms which display sexual and political dysfunctions leading to cynical breakdowns in the myths of marriage and morality found in the American Dream (Denzin 1988, p. 462).

The Films of Ridley Scott and Adrian Lyne

English director Ridley Scott (b. 1939) uses his film narratives as science-fiction projections on what the future will hold for us, predicting that technology and capitalism will merge into some diabolical union to alter human beings forever. In *Blade Runner* (1982), Scott presumes that "replicants" will serve people as workers on other planets. However, the replicants want to return to Earth, and like earlier humanoids, want to change their built-in life span. The film explores the moral dilemma facing humanity when these powerful working and thinking replicants revolt. Their only flaw is their need to have their memories programmed. The conflict on how to control and reproduce life forms to colonize space becomes one of the themes of this film. Scott began the nightmarish future struggle between human beings and alien life forms in his science-fiction thriller, *Alien* (1979), in which the space voyagers combat an unknown life form that incubates inside their warm human bodies. These disturbing mythic adventures go against the "feel-good" blockbusters Lucas and Spielberg created.

Other English directors who made feature films in Hollywood during the 1980s are Adrian Lyne, Alan Parker and Tony Scott. Lyne directed a series of anti–feminist films that struck a chord with American audiences by defending family values and the Protestant work ethic while seductively exploring the female protagonist's sexual desires. In *Flashdance* (1983), Lyne exploits dance videos to show how a young woman uses her talent to achieve her dream of joining a ballet company. In *9½ Weeks* (1986), he explores a casual meeting of adults that turns into a heterosexual fantasy close to sadomasochism. This story leads into *Fatal Attraction* (1987), with an adulterous seduction becoming a marital nightmare that makes a family tremble in fear of retaliation.

Fatal Attraction is at its root a film about the fear of sex. Made at the dawn of the age of AIDS, the film convinced viewers that the casual sex of the swinging sixties was bad. The film's sex scenes were tinged with horror, reinforcing the view of how terrible sex can be. "Moreover, *Fatal Attraction* had an important effect on Hollywood for it was a successful rearrangement of familiar conventions, as in the feminized male and in the masculinized female character. Since its release, *Fatal Attraction* has been imitated to death and launched a whole cycle of erotic-psychological thrillers" (Levy).

The Independent Films of Spike Lee and John Sayles

African American filmmaker Spike Lee (b. 1956) tackles the racial problems besetting black people living in decaying cities of the 1980s. As a graduate of New York University film school, he gained international acclaim and recognition as an independent filmmaker with three small-budget films that he produced, wrote and directed. In *She's Got to Have It* (1986), Lee designs a comic triangle based upon a woman's prerogative to select the man she desires rather than concede to what is offered. *School Daze* (1988) deals with the split in a black university over who should observe white value systems and who should not. The battle lines are drawn between two groups within the Gamma Ray sorority, the Wannabees and the Jigaboos. The director uses this pretext to discuss a number of issues: the sexist treatment of black women, the causes of discrimination and reasons behind apartheid. Spike Lee's third film, *Do the Right Thing* (1989), explores the deep-seated fears and frustrations within a black community that erupt into racial violence and tragedy. His film technique uses Brechtian episodic structures with a jazzy musical score to reveal a series of basic social and political relationships in which he questions the ideologies and cultural myths that bring about racial violence toward black people. Lee strongly attacks the return of the myths because they become a way of presenting an "already always" given solution to many complex social and political problems. He deplores acts of interracial violence in which the "good" white guy defeats the "bad" black guy.

Lee asserts that such actions are both immoral and impractical because an eye-for-an-eye rationale leaves both blind. In his powerful biographical film *Malcolm X* (1992), Lee claims that violence does not help one gain political power. When violence breaks out, people are more likely to justify its use as self–defense. Lee condemns such social stereotyping and claims that racial hatred is a learned social construct that needs to be seen for what it is. Only through a self–conscious inquiry into the causes of racial intolerance will a solution be found, even when politics divide a black community.

Another well-known American independent filmmaker is John Sayles, a New Englander, whose films of the 1980s concern themes dealing with personal and political relationships. His first low-budget film as a writer-director was *The Return of the Secaucus Seven* (1980), based upon a reunion of a motley group of 1960s activists. They meet ten years after their activist days to recount, among other events, their arrest in New Jersey on their way to a peace demonstration. Reflecting upon their past idealism and romantic liaisons, they ponder the implications of their relationships as they reach age 30. Sayles' film delves deeply into unraveling the American myths that brought them together in the first place. *Lianna* (1983) takes us into the life of a married woman after she discovers her interests in a lesbian relationship. With *The Brother from Another Planet* (1984), Sayles' fantasy takes us into Harlem with a mute, black alien who grapples with the myths behind racial prejudice and drug dealings. In *Matewan* (1987), set in the 1920s, Sayles explores racial tensions arising from attempts to unionize workers in the coal mines of West Virginia. In the late 1990s, Sayles

investigates racial prejudice and politics in two films, *Lone Star* (1996) and *Men with Guns* (1998). Both films are written as murder mysteries, and Sayles focuses on the criminal element that flourishes from racial discrimination. *Lone Star* challenges the myth of American identity by carefully weaving three different histories of interracial marriages in a small town on the U.S.-Mexican border. *Men with Guns* also is a journey in time as a retired Latin American doctor seeks to find the whereabouts of his former medical students, trained to bring new medical discoveries into poverty-stricken areas of his country, only to discover the corruption and hypocrisy of the dictatorial government.

The Myths of the 1980s and 90s

There are a number of films made in the 1980s and 1990s that illustrate beliefs in cultural myths and the collapse of being trapped by that fantasy.

Scorsese's *Goodfellas* (1990) does not spare its audience the violence, hypocrisy and paranoia of organized crime, yet makes it fascinating and funny. Scorsese helps the viewer understand why the characters chose such a dangerous path, by comparing the seductive life of a criminal with the mundanity of an ordinary life. "Scorsese also manages to break viewers' moralistic inhibitions by showing truly revolting material — scenes that depict personal tragedies, broken homes, human depravity, violence, bloodshed and murder — in all their uncompromising reality, but in a manner that would make it amusing and funny to the audience. With the use of an ironic soundtrack, manipulative shots, character's dialogue or narrator's commentary, *Goodfellas* represents the new standards of black humor that would become very popular a few years later during the Tarantino era" (Antulov 2000, "*Goodfellas*").

In 1991, Kevin Costner, with *Dances with Wolves*, won the Best Director Oscar over Scorsese for *Goodfellas*. *Dances with Wolves* was an epic film about Sioux tribal life in the years after the Civil War, when white settlers and sol-

Kevin Costner's *Dances with Wolves* (1990) is a story about the spiritual journey of a disenchanted Civil War officer who decides to become a member of a Sioux tribe when the West is invaded by white soldiers and new settlers.

diers began encroaching on tribal lands. Costner plays the role of a disenchanted Civil War soldier stationed in the West who works hard to become a member of a Great Plains Sioux tribe. Though emotionally moving, the film is merely "a mildly stirring revisionist cinematic portrayal of the West as a place where manifest destiny meant not only modernity's expansion but also ancient cultures' decimation" (Schager 2003).

RoboCop (1987), the story of a police officer resurrected as a cyborg, "gleefully takes on every myth told about the U.S. during the Reagan 80's: Cities are dens of evil and full of constant gunplay, authority has been brought to heel by capitalism, technology has crushed our humanity to atoms, the media destroys the

morals of children." The movie, both comical and violent, illustrates the underlying truths of the Reagan-era myths. *RoboCop* is "one of the best dystopian fantasies about America put on film. What endures, though, is the film's ability to show what makes us human in an inhumane world, for it is a story about how humanity strives to do the right thing" (Athitakis 2003).

Some people consider Quentin Tarantino's *Pulp Fiction* (1994) to be a collection of recycled movie scenes interpolated with scenes of extreme violence and overlaid with 70s music and modern pop culture references. However, the film is much more than that. After all, Tarantino's formula has been copied since, to lackluster results. For one, most of the violence

In Verhoeven's *RoboCop* (1987), starring Peter Weller and Nancy Allen, U.S. cities during the 1980s become "dens of evil" where constant gunplay shows viewers the ways we need to become human in such an inhumane world.

actually takes place off screen. Tarantino, like Hitchcock before him, toys with the audience, letting a scene play out slowly, creating the illusion of experiencing more violence than is actually shown. Instead of showing Butch's fight where he kills his opponent, we see him unhurriedly relating the tale to a cab driver, all while unrealistic black-and-white footage plays in the cab's rear window, yet somehow this works. "Pulp Fiction is a movie about the in-between spaces that Hollywood movies don't show. In a normal movie, every gesture, every prop, every line of dialogue is related somehow to the final outcome of the story. *Pulp Fiction* shows us people sleeping, taking showers, going to the bathroom, the scenes where characters get ready for scenes, and the scenes af-

terwards.... It's a movie that says more about the nature of film and the thrill of making movies than any other film in the 90s" (Anderson 1994).

Unforgiven (1992) can really be called an anti–Western, since the story often strips the mythology from Western heroes and anti-heroes. The character English Bob (Richard Harris) doesn't defend the honor of a lady, he is just a drunk and jealous cold-blooded murderer. Munny (Clint Eastwood) actually did murder innocent people in cold blood. The Schofield Kid is simply an immature and insecure young man. Though the characters in *Unforgiven* are revisionist, the story is not. It follows a time-honored formula by building up the antagonist in the middle of the film in order

Tarantino's *Pulp Fiction* (1994), one of the best films of the 90s, engages the audience with characters who invade common spaces and where violence leads to welcome outcomes for members of the underworld. Hit men Jules (Samuel L. Jackson) and Vincent (John Travolta) call on Winston Wolf (Harvey Keitel), a fixer, to help them clean up a gruesome mess.

to increase the suspense of the final conflict. "English Bob ... is made fearsome by his arrogance. Little Bill (Gene Hackman) is made fearsome by his complete humiliation of English Bob. Little Bill is built up only so that he can be bested by Munny, whose drinking binge has finally led him to fully embrace" his dark side (Koller 1999). Interestingly, the audience is made to feel compelled to root for Munny in the inevitable final conflict that will avenge his friend Ned (Morgan Freeman), even though Ned was in fact a murderer, and his punishment was just by the standards of the frontier.

The Usual Suspects (1995) highlights the myths of good and evil through plots twists and turns that make the viewer unsure of the allegiances of each character. The film has "style to burn, and, initially, that is this crime drama's most mesmerizing aspect. The plot's convolu-

tions and unexpected surprise ending all seem to be extensions of the film's stylistic flourish" (Baumgarten 1995). "Unraveling with the air of a 40's film noir, the crime mystery lulls you into a trance and then sneaks up behind you and knocks you on your backside" (Villarreal 2006).

The perfect crime gone bad has long been an almost irresistible movie theme. "In *Fargo* (1996) iconoclastic filmmakers Joel and Ethan Coen manage the precarious balancing act of respecting genre conventions and simultaneously pushing them to an almost surrealistic extreme." The film is full of dark humor and "is absorbing less for plot machinations than for the people who populate the piece. Once we know the individuals, its their personal interactions that prove striking and emotional." Marge (Frances McDormand) is a pregnant

Ridley Scott's _Blade Runner_ (1982), starring Harrison Ford, captures the fear of sexual relations when casual sex comes into play by a woman who wants it all.

small-town policewoman who, while trying to solve a triple murder, shows concern for her husband's wish to get one of his wildlife paintings on a postage stamp. Jerry (William H. Macy), a failure at almost every aspect of life, must explain to his son about his mother's disappearance, and does not a very good job at it. "_Fargo_ is a strikingly mature, unique entertainment that plays on many levels ... all very satisfying" (Klady 1996).

Philip K. Dick, one of the most influential science-fiction writers of the 20th century, inspired the making of two great science-fiction films, the cult classic _Blade Runner_ (1982) and its overlooked cousin, _Total Recall_ (1990). In his stories and novels, Dick wrote about alternate realities that were created with futuristic supertechnology, and how that technology

caused the loss of identity in humans. The fear of technology and the way it might change the human race found its way into these two movies. The plot of _Total Recall_, which is directed by Paul Verhoeven, is loosely based on Dick's short story "We Can Remember It for You Wholesale." The movie is set in 2084 A.D. and Arnold Schwarzenegger plays Doug Quaid, a man who seems to have everything he needs—a nice home, a beautiful wife, and a steady job. However, he is haunted by nightly dreams involving a woman who is not his wife. He visits a company that offers virtual reality vacations so he can figure out what the dreams are all about, and he is sucked into a world in which he is not sure what is real and what is fantasy. "_Total Recall_ has an original, exciting, intelligent and thought-provoking script.

Opposite: Top— Bryan Singer's _The Usual Suspects_ (1995) follows the conventions of film noir mysteries and generates a criminal unraveling that has a surprising ending. In a police lineup are Dean Keaton (Gabriel Byrne) and Verbal Kint (Kevin Spacey). _Bottom_— The Coen Brothers' _Fargo_ (1996) is a dark yet sophisticated adventure that uses genre conventions to introduce personal interactions between lawmakers and emotionally confused violators, including Carl (Steve Buscemi) and Gaear (Peter Stormare).

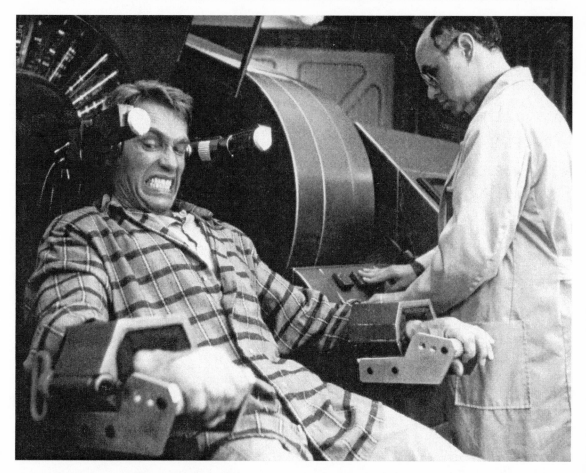

In Verhoven's *Total Recall* (1990), written by Philip K. Dick, viewers are caught in a science fiction film where the central figure (Arnold Schwarzenegger) must travel to Mars to help him solve the mystery of his own identity as well as find the woman of his dreams.

[The] most interesting aspect of the film is the idea that [a] sufficient level of technology can erase any difference between objective reality and subjective perception of the world" (Antulov 2000, "*Total Recall*").

The Spin-Offs from Blockbuster Films

The blockbuster feel-good movies of the 1970s and 1980s found Hollywood directors "offering a wide-screen, color, stereophonic and special effects ride, constructed for speed and thrills rather than contemplation, with a simple, forceful, unthreatening message" (Mast and Kawin 1996, p. 547). Film school graduates like George Lucas utilized a catchy scenario

steeped in pop mythology or modeled after Japanese samurai films. Lucas introduced new marketing strategies to enhance the packaging of his films and his own profits. This licensing practice becomes a standard method of producer-directors for the successful merchandizing of blockbusters. The generic conflict between Good and Evil was played out again with the "good guys" always defeating the "bad guys," bringing back the happy ending to these action-adventure films. What was new was the fast-paced, high tech science-fiction worlds never seen before in the cinema. Other heroes appeared in films in which the Protestant work ethic found fulfillment: Work hard and give it your best shot and things will pan out for you. *Saturday Night Fever*, *Rocky* and *Flashdance* handed back the American Dream to a younger film audience in the form of heroic men and women who achieved their dreams. Further, the blockbuster movie became its own kind of elixir, one that gave viewers an emotional charge. It also brought back a winning experience for viewers in the audience.

Financially, the Hollywood blockbuster films of the 1970s and 1980s provided a new production strategy. When a Hollywood studio produces a blockbuster hit, it can afford to fund off-beat stories that end up, more often than not, doing rather well at the box office. Such "sleepers" cost $20–$30 million and return grosses over $100 million. The best kind of word-of-mouth and excitement over such films gives these pictures the ability to reach across different market audiences and become popular. *The Crying Game*; *Sister Act*; *Rocky* and *Sex, Lies, and Videotape* are examples. From the concentration on blockbuster hits, a general perception arises of a lack of good genre movies being produced in Hollywood during the 1980s. Because of this perceived vacuum, the independent film scene has been encouraging for younger filmmakers and has proven commercially successful. This independent or alternative cinema is probably the most exciting diverse movement that evolved during the 1980s, in a similar vein to that of the French New Wave that overtook the French studio pictures 30 years earlier.

However, there is one striking difference. This development is not an evolution or a displacement of one film culture for another, but rather the integration of various film styles being produced at the same time. This postmodern marketplace is transcending the old Hollywood movies. There is no dominant style or contemporary look. Instead, there seems to be an acceptance of innovative story ideas and film techniques which can be defined as cool, hip or trendy, be it a personal ultra–modern collage or a retrospective parody of early films from the 1950s. With these films a host of "third cinema" productions are now being distributed worldwide through DVDs and other forms of digital media. These films are evidence of the growth of post–colonial countries outside Europe contributing evocative film narratives that are deliberately "framing the framer."

References

Anderson, Jefferey M. 1994. "*Pulp Fiction.*" www.combustiblecelluloid.com

Antulov, Dragan. 2000. "*Goodfellas*: A Film Review." Rec.arts.movies.reviews

Antulov, Dragan. 2000. "*Total Recall*: A Film Review." Rec.arts.movies.reviews

Athitakis, Mark. 2003. "*RoboCop.*" Filmcritic. com

Baumgarten, Marjorie. 1995. "*The Usual Suspects.*" www.austinchronicle.com

Conner, Steven. 1989. *Postmodern Culture: An Introduction to Theories of the Contemporary*. Oxford, England: Basil Blackwell.

Denzin, Norman K. 1988. "*Blue Velvet*: Postmodern Contradictions." *Theory Culture and Society* 5 (2–3): 461–73.

Eco, Umberto. 1986. *Travels in Hyper-Reality*. Translated by William Weaver. New York: Harcourt, Brace, Jovanovich.

Hutcheon, Linda. 1989. *The Politics of Postmodernism*. London and New York: Routledge.

Klady, Leonard. 1996. "*Fargo.*" www.Variety.com

Koller, Brian. 1999. "*Unforgiven.*" www.toptenreviews.com

Levy, Emanuel. "*Fatal Attraction.*" http://emanuel levy.com

Mast, Gerald, and Bruce F. Kawin. 1996. *A Short History of the Movies*. 6th ed. Boston and London: Allyn and Bacon.

Rosenbaum, Jonathan. 1997. "*Touch of Class.*" www.chicagoreader.com

Said, Edward W. 1979. *Orientalism*. New York: Random House.

Schager, Nick. 2003. "*Dances with Wolves.*" www.slantmagazine.com

Villarreal, Phil. 2006. "Infamous Keyser Soze a Most Unusual Suspect." www.azstarnet.com

CHAPTER 25

Third Cinema and Post-Colonial Narratives in Africa, Latin America and Asia

Introduction to Third Cinema

In the Edinburgh Film Festival of 1986, a conference was initiated to debate new practices of cinema within contemporary culture that avoided both the sentimental leftist cultural theory emanating from the UK and the cultural and educational practices in line with corporate cultures and market consumerism that related to variants of postmodernism. In its place the conference focused upon non Anglo-American cinematic practices and their approaches to cultural politics. Therefore, in turning to Third Cinema, the conference was able to draw attention to "questions of Brechtian cinema and cultural identity [which directors] ... now posed in a different context" (Willemen 1994, p. 176). The central concept of Third Cinema (not Third World Cinema) was adopted by the conference "partly to re-pose and [re-examine] the question of the relations between the cultural and the political, and partly to discuss ... a kind of international cinematic tradition which exceeds the limits of both national-industrial cinema (First Cinema) or those of Euro-American as well as English cultural theories (Second Cinema)" (p. 177).

Historically, Third Cinema received its impetus from the success of the French New Wave and its use of Italian neorealism for low-cost, location-based, improvisational cinematic practices. These were inspired by an infusion of neo–Marxist cultural theories ranging from Louis Althusser and Brecht and the Soviet formalists to post-structuralist thinkers like Jacques Lacan, Michel Foucault and Jean-François Lyotard. As these cinematic practices found success within the international scene, the notion of a Third Cinema

> was first advanced as a rallying cry in the late 60s in Latin America (including South America). As an idea, its immediate inspiration was rooted in the Cuban Revolution (1959) and Brazil's *Cinema Novo*, for which Glauber Rocha provided an impetus with the publication of a passionate polemic entitled "The Aesthetics of Hunger" (or "The Aesthetics of Violence") [Willemen 1994, p. 178].

"One of Third Cinema's more readily noticeable characteristics seems to be the adoption of a historically analytic, yet culturally specific, mode of cinematic discourse," states Willemen, which is best exemplified by Theo Angelopoulos, Nelson Pereira dos Santos, Ousmane Sembène, Fernando Solanas and others, "each summing up and reformulating the encounter with diverse cultural traditions into new, politically as well as cinematically illuminating types of filmic discourse, critical of, yet firmly anchored in, their respective social-historical situations" (Willemen 1994, p. 177).

Latin America and the Cine Liberación

In advancing his notion of Third Cinema, the Argentinean filmmaker and essayist Fernando Solanas (b. 1936), with Octavio Getino and members of a pro–Peronist left-wing collective, Cine Liberación, produced a three-part film, *La Hora de los Hornos / The Hour of the Furnaces* (1968). The film was screened secretly to audiences in three parts. As an heuristic device Solanas presented a collage of documentary portraits of pop-art culture icons depicting Argentinian history and politics

Fernando Solanas and Octavio Getino directed *The Hour of the Furnaces* (1968), a three-part documentary film using newsreel footage, still photos and provocative interviews to document Argentinian culture and history. The directors promoted Third Cinema and called for an anti-colonial cinema based upon experiments with documentary techniques.

from a neo-colonialist position. Between each part of the film, he would stop the screening to engage the audiences in spirited debates on the future directions of his country. Solanas regards his work "as a meeting ground of the political and avant-garde engaged in a common task which is enriching to both" (Solanas, cited in Shohat and Stam 1994, p. 260). In Solanas' essay "Toward a Third Cinema," quoted at length by Willemen (1994, p. 182), he argues:

> First Cinema expresses imperialist, capitalist, bourgeois ideas. Big monopoly capital finances big spectacle cinema as well as authorial and informational cinema.... Second Cinema is all that expresses the aspirations of the middle stratum, the petite bourgeoisie. Second cinema is often nihilistic, mystificatory. It runs in circles. It is cut off from reality.... So called author cinema often belongs in the second cinema, but both good and bad authors may be found in first and third cinema. For us, Third Cinema is the expression of a new culture and of social changes. Generally speaking, Third Cinema gives an account of reality and history. It is also linked with national culture. (It) is the way the world is conceptualized and not the genre nor the

explicitly political character of a film which makes it belong to Third Cinema.

> Third Cinema is an open category, unfinished, incomplete. It is a research category. It is a democratic, national, popular cinema. Third Cinema is also an experimental cinema, but it is not practiced in the solitude of one's home or in a laboratory because it conducts research into communication. What is required is to make that Third Cinema gain space, everywhere, in all its forms. But it must be stressed that there are 36 different kinds of Third Cinema.

Solanas as a filmmaker and polemicist is paralleling the educational theories of Paulo Friere, who in *Pedagogy of the Oppressed* (1973) advocates an adult education of illiterates, submerged in a "culture of silence," to move them from the colonialized conformity of their situation into more than a counter-cultural attack, "raising consciousness" of their own social and political situation. "Like the defining characteristic of Third Cinema itself: the aim of rendering a particular social situation intelligible to those engaged in a struggle to change it in a socialist direction" (Edward Said, cited in Willemen 1994, p. 194). Although Solanas refers neither to class struggle in a revolutionary way nor to status, there is room for "an analytic perspective aimed at evoking possible strategies for change" (p. 185). Solanas emphasizes the experimental nature of Third Cinema wherein and economic liberation would be a necessary precondition for the emergence of a popular culture" (p. 193). Therefore the primary task of directors of Third Cinema is to create a cinema of lucidity with the emancipatory power of reason advocated by Brechtian agonistics. The cinematic discourses in which the audience finds its cultural identity relies on an understanding through cinematic representation of the multifarious social-historical processes at work in a given situation" (p. 194).

Two characteristics that keep Third Cinema from being a didactic cinematic endeavor are defined as the following: "One is the insistence on its flexibility, its status as research and experimentation, a cinema forever in need of adaptation to the shifting dynamics at work in social struggles. The second is its attempt to speak a socially pertinent discourse excluded from mainstream and authorial cinemas" (Willeman 1994, p. 185).

When the military junta took over Argentina in 1976, Solanas sought refuge in France. He directed two fictional narratives, *Tangos — El Exilio de Gardel / Tangos — The Exile of Gardel* (1985) and *Sur / South* (1988), that exemplified his continued use of cultural models and myths to advance his political discourse for the overthrow of imperialism.

In Brazil, Glauber Rocha (1938–1981) became the leader of the *Cinema Novo* movement, which adopted Third Cinema techniques to bring awareness of the social and political realities in his country through cinema. He claims in his manifesto, *Esthetic of Hunger* (1965), that "the moment of violence is the moment when the colonizer becomes aware of the existence of the colonized" (Shohat and Stam 1994, p. 256). He adopted the documentary style of Eisenstein with the self-reflexivity of Godard and Brecht to establish his political discourse of cultural resistance against fascist military regimes and popular left-wing reformists. Drawing upon westerns and popular cultural icons, Rocha directed his noted film *Antonio des Mortes* (1969) to demonstrate how a gov-

ernment mercenary can "turn his guns around" and espouse revolutionary guerilla warfare against the real oppressors of the poor. After exile in Spain for eight years, Rocha returned to Brazil to direct an allegorical tale of a hybridization of Brazilian people in *A Idade da Terra / The Age of the Earth* (1980), featuring multiple characters as the Christ figure. Similar in scope to Griffith's *Intolerance*, the film presents a series of mythic narratives from different cultural histories.

Nelson Pereira dos Santos (b. 1928) is another *Cinema Novo* director who established himself with his neorealist rendering of poverty in the barrios of Rio de Janeiro in *Rio, Quarenta Graus / Rio, 40 Degrees* (1954). In *Vidas Secas / Barren Lives* (1961) he portrays the struggle of a homeless family seeking to survive the drought and the poor economic situation in the outlands of Brazil. In both films he relied upon a low-cost documentary style and nonprofessional actors. In the 1970s he moved into a more Buñuelian style of production in directing *Como Era Gostoso o Meu Francês / How Tasty Was My Little Frenchman* (1971), a powerful allegory on colonial exploitation and military repression. The film follows an anthropologist mistaken as a French soldier by cannibal tribesmen of the Tupinamba who capture and sentence him to death for a previous massacre of natives by Europeans. He is invited to partake of marriage and witness tribal ceremonies for one year before he meets his fate. Later, Pereira dos Santos films of the 1970s allowed the director to reflect on themes from the popular culture (Shohat and Stam 1994, p. 76).

The most notable filmmaker in Cuba is Tomás Gutiérrez Alea (1928–1996), who came into prominence soon after the Cuban Revolution in 1959. He was responsible for co-founding the revolutionary film institute, Instituto Cubano del Arte y Industria Cinematográficos, based upon the Italian Centro Sperimentale di Cinematografia in Rome, shortly after Castro came to power. Alea directed his first feature, *Historias de la Revolución / Stories of the Revolution* (1960), using a neorealist style to dramatize the actual armed conflict and defeat of Batista. More than other Third Cinema advo-

Tomás Alea's *Memories of Underdevelopment* (1968) is a thought-provoking drama combining documentary footage about a bourgeois Cuban man confronting the uncertainty of life in a country supporting a revolution.

cates, Alea used satire to produce political commentary on the social chaos caused by the Cuban Revolution. In *Memorias del Subdesarrollo / Memories of Underdevelopment* (1968), he used a combination of Godardian collage techniques, from voice-over narration to still photographs, newspaper headlines and television broadcasts to simulate a documentary style. This technique introduces a wealthy businessman who chooses to live a bourgeois life of uncertainty as a property manager in Cuba after the Revolution. Not only is this person confronted by sexual neuroses, but he finds himself paralyzed by his European business ideas in trying to operate in a Marxist country. Alea's insightful analysis of a common linguistic struggle for many people in his country leads the viewer to reflect on the "underdevelopment" of the title and how difficult it is to get rid of it. The film also attempts a self-criticism

regarding the rigidity of the new government's attempts to replace the obsolete "mental formulas" of Western thought.

For Alea it was necessary to use cinematic discourses as a means of reconstituting an historical past for Cubans. In *Una Pelea Cubana Contra los Demonios / A Cuban Struggle Against the Demons* (1971) and *La Ultima Cena / The Last Supper* (1976), Alea bases his dramas on historical incidents of the 17th and 18th centuries when religious fanaticism dominated Cuba. In *The Last Supper*, Alea reflects upon the current Cuban situation through a retelling of a slave revolt on a sugar plantation during Easter. Although Alea celebrates the Afro-Cuban musical motifs, he also reveals an incident of religious hypocrisy when the owner suppresses an uprising solely for economic interests. Thus, implicitly, Alea subtly critiques the political dogma hidden in the cultural colonization happening in today's Cuba. In *Strawberry and Chocolate* (1993) Alea adapts an Octavio Paz short story, "The Wolf, the Forest, and the New Man," into a film parable about holding fixed beliefs and opinions on sex, politics and friendships in Havana. The film is a romantic comedy about a developing friendship between a young heterosexual male student with an older, educated gay man who introduces the younger man to radical ideas on sexuality and politics. Following a direct cinematic treatment of the narrative, Alea's screenplay also questions Cuba's restrictive and limited political policies on its paranoia and censorship of other world cultures the regime fears will infiltrate and subvert Cuban-Marxist thinking.

Stuart Hall on the Caribbean Experience

The Third Cinema of the Caribbean is related to other black filmmakers emerging from a post-colonial position and also raises questions of cultural identity. Stuart Hall (1990) asks, "Who is this emergent, new subject of the cinema? From where does he/she speak" (p. 222)? Hall explains how "positions of *enunciation*" are problematic, since the person as a subject who speaks from his or her own experience also acts as the object who is spoken of, and that their cultural identity is not the same. In his investigation of the politics of representation within the field of cultural identity, Hall acknowledges how "We all write and speak for a particular place and time, from a history and a culture which is specific. What we say is always 'in context,' *positioned*" (p. 222).

Hall takes his perspective from the "diaspora experience" and "its narratives of displacement." He suggests that cinematic representation as part of the Third Cinema can be thought of as containing both a history of continuity and similarity or "oneness," and a second position of "difference" that relates to what black people have become as a result of white rule and colonization. The first perspective transforms the black subject through a retelling of a past where people learn of a common ancestry and share cultural codes, one that "imposes an imaginary coherence" on the black experience of dispersal and fragmentation in new forms of visual and cinematic representation. These "hidden" histories recount the "lost world of signification. They are the resources of resistance and identity, with which to confront the fragmented and pathological ways in which that experience has been reconstructed within the dominant regimes of cinematic and visual representation of the West" (p. 225).

The second perspective carries narratives of the colonial experience as a continuance of rediscovery of the past, but does not follow a linear descent into a "fixed" cultural identity. These narratives of "difference and rupture" construct identities from a black experience as a break from the past, one that acknowledges the fact of people becoming "different" from their ancestral roots. This translation and hybridity is the play of difference within the cultural histories of black people transported into these foreign locations. These narratives speak of the power that brought about poverty and racism, and the underdevelopment of these people. In cinematic representation the colonial discourse of exploration and adventure, the romance of the primitive, ignores the forgotten tales of expropriation and exclusion of rights. As Hall observes, "The common history — transportation, slavery, colonization — has been profoundly formative." Yet, the "doubleness" Hall describes concerning the black experience as both a history of the past, and a recognition of the present, of a they/we binary, continues repositioning of any signification in the sense Jacques Derrida sets up with the suspension of representation and meaning in his use of the word differance. Here the play of signification and representation is always open to additional or supplemental readings (p. 229) and a new translation of the post-colonialist subject.

French Colonialism in Africa and the Clash of Cultures

In serving its political aims, directors of Third Cinema are engaged in anti-imperialist struggles for cultural as well as economic and political independence. However, they realize in their films how hybridization of ideas occurs in the "double references" to both the national and international aspects of their situation. Thus Hall reasons that a gap or "space of ambiguity" emerges in issues of political power in that the participants represent both "outsiders" or "others" to the dominant social-historical discourses and "in and of" the culture simultaneously. Yet "it is no accident but rather a logical consequence that a sense of non-belonging, non-identity with the culture one inhabits, ethnically or in any other way, [becomes] a precondition for 'the most intense and productive aspects of cultural life'" (p. 201). Willemen stresses that Third Cinema polemicists conceive this otherness as disjointed, "as an in-between position, that the production of social intelligibility thrives, at least as far as socialist cultural practices are concerned" (p. 201). Ambiguities which arise for Third Cinema directors are derived more from the "openness" of the political signification based upon historical passages of a particular culture than from the documentary processes of production (Shohat and Stam 1994, p. 261).

The movement toward anti-colonial rebellion began ten years earlier than the Cuban revolution of 1959 in French Indo-China (Vietnam). The warfare continued until Ho Chi Minh's forces and their guerrilla tactics defeated the entrenched French military forces at Dienbienphu in 1954. In the same year the National Liberation Front (FLN), representing native African Muslims, began their guerrilla warfare against French settlers and officials in Algeria, thus proclaiming a revolution. *Battaglia di Algeri / The Battle of Algiers* (1966) is an exemplary film using documentary techniques to reconstruct the terrorist actions of members of the FLN that took place in 1954 against French colonial forces. Directed by the Italian news correspondent Gillo Pontecorvo (b. 1918), the film presents an anti-imperialist narrative that focuses on different Algerian people bravely using terrorist bombings to offset the presence of French colonists and the French occupational army. In a Brechtian manner, the film is able to "raise the consciousness" of the viewer to the importance of the rebels' struggle for freedom and independence, with a startling reenactment of French military tactics and atrocities against Muslim terrorists.

It remains for Ousmane Sembène (b. 1923), a Senegalese director, writer and producer, to achieve international recognition as an African filmmaker. Trained in Moscow at the VGIK, his first feature film addressed the post-colonial situation of an African country still living under a dominant French culture. In *La Noire de... / Black Girl* (1966) and *La Mandat / The Money Order* (1968), he uses satire to ridicule the new black bourgeoisie who attempt to continue the patriarchic traditions of the French while proving incapable of running their own affairs. Sembène continues this satiric strategy in *Xala / Impotence* (1974) in which he depicts a rich but Westernized Moslem businessman losing his social standing after he takes a third wife and discovers he is impotent. In attempting to revive his manliness, he resorts to tribal customs only to discover public mockery and ridicule.

The experimental films of Trinh T. Minh-Ha, born in Vietnam during French rule, effectively critique the discourse of the other that anthropologists use in representing West Africans and other cultures in their ethnographic films. Trinh T. Minh-Ha traveled through Senegal and other parts of West Africa making provocative films, notably *Reassemblage* (1982), about the Senegalese people. Later, on returning to Vietnam, she directed and produced *Surname Viet, Given Name Nam* (1989). In both films she challenges the objectivity of the positivist paradigm of logic toward comprehending the "identity" of tribal cultures of Africa or elsewhere. For Trinh the concept of plurality, of multiple identities emerging from the differences between the insider and the outsider, shifts the polarity of subject-object into a recognition and respect for the multiple, constantly changing relationships among different selves and others. Thus, in *Reassemblage,* Trinh forgoes the use of a single, observant narrator, who uses voice-over dialogue to define "underdevelopment," or observations on "developing countries" for an ironic discourse

In Ousmane Sembène's *Xala* (1974), a Senegalese filmmaker uses satire to attack the new black bourgeoisie who have Westernized their ways but still return to certain cultural rituals from their native country.

that destabilizes such "given assumptions." Her camera distances the cinematic sign or image away from "framing" an anthropological gaze of women and children and engages the viewer in the daily activities of gathering and preparation of food and clothing. Her cinematic style reassembles multiple images with recorded sound effects and dialogue that take imaginative leaps of discontinuity and uncertainty that challenge and startle the contemplative viewer.

Her explorations into documentary storytelling continued in *Surname Viet, Given Name Nam* as she used interview techniques with a number of Vietnamese women who survived the war to demonstrate how films can alter the perceptions of the viewer as to the truth of the subjects' statements. The initial interview presented a seemingly authentic representation of these women. A second series of "real" interviews are presented to the viewer with the same women but within a different context, challenging the viewer to question the truth or falseness of the initial interview, which the viewer then realizes is a staged reenactment of the women's involvement in the Vietnam War.

Yet historical reenactment is commonplace in many stories represented by the cinema. According to Willemen, "One of Third Cinema's more readily noticeable characteristics seems to be the adoption of a historically analytic, yet culturally specific, mode of cinematic discourse." This narrative style is demonstrated by European directors like Theo Angelopoulos (b. 1935) who, as part of the new wave in modern Greek literature and art, explores the impact of classical heritage on contemporary politics. Following the example of poets like Constantine Cavafy and George Seferis, his films are among the best examples of a cinematic discourse that analyses the political and historical traumas affecting a country torn by its struggle against the hegemonic discourse of postwar dictatorship. Angelopoulos' first trilogy recreates a political and social history of modern Greece during the 1930s. In *Meres Tou '36 / Days of 36* (1972), he reviews political life during the dictatorship of Ioannis Metaxas. *Thiasos / The Traveling Players* (1975) depicts the misfortunes that beset a group of thespians attempting to overcome their own political jealousies. In *E Kenege / The Huntsmen* (1977), Angelopoulos completes his trilogy with an examination of the issues surrounding the Greek Civil War (1945–1949), with history and myth intersecting in the narrative.

Angelopoulos studied in Paris at the Institut des Hautes Études Cinématographiques (IDHEC) with Jean Rouch, where he learned his documentary style of cinema. Under Rouch's tutelage, he began his own film productions based upon this new discourse. Like the other Third Cinema directors, his films "refused to oppose a simplistic notion of national identity or of cultural authenticity to the values of colonial or imperial predators" (Willemen 1994, p. 177). Instead, his cinematic discourses "started from a recognition of the many-layeredness of their own cultural-historical formations, with each layer being shaped by complex connections between intra and international forces and traditions" (p. 177).

What is notable in each film Angelopoulos directs is his ability to build his film narrative on at least four thematic levels. First, it is a play-within-a-play in which a group of traveling players attempt to perform a popular Greek play, helping to signify the role-playing in life. Second is a mythological level where the modern myth reflects and reconstitutes the lessons from the classical myth of the House of Atreus. Third, a political and historical level involves contemporary events finding associations metonymically with the classical themes of power and betrayal. On the fourth level, psychological and personal realities connect the incidents to moral and ethical principles that relate to "a creative understanding" of the situation which the film is addressing (Horton 1986–1987, pp. 84–94).

Angelopoulos interweaves these four themes into his trilogy of the 1980s, which features a central character on an odyssey to discover a missing person or to find his or her own identity. He starts his trilogy with *Taxidi stin Kythera / Voyage to Cythera* (1984).

Voyage to Cythera begins as an old political refugee, Spyros (Manos Katrakis), returns to his Northern Greek village after many years of exile in the Soviet Union. When he gets close to his old home, he begins making a sound like a bird chirping. Soon, this sound is echoed, and an old man joins him. They were friends and collaborators in the Occupation and Civil War in Greece that followed and had used this secret language to communicate. This joyous moment is shortly followed by a scene of Spyros performing a "Pontiko" dance on the grave of another friend.

> This dance on the grave clearly strikes all viewers as a kind of triumph over death, destruction, war, exile and separation. In short, the moment is like a New Orleans "jazz funeral": a celebration of life after death through dance and festivity. And yet if we embrace a larger world of the "comic spirit" as it has existed through centuries of literature, song and culture in Greece and the Balkans, one can surely identify both "comic" and "humorous" as well as ironic moments throughout the many journeys Angelopoulos's protagonists embark upon [Horton, "Greek and Balkan Spirit"].

He follows *Voyage to Cythera* with *O Melissokomos / The Beekeeper* (1986), featuring Marcello Mastroianni as a retired schoolteacher, and concludes with *Topio stin Omichli / Landscape in the Mist* (1988). *Landscape in the Mist* features two children, a young boy and his older sister, trying to go to Germany by train in search of their father. As they travel through the bleak Greek landscape, they encounter different people who aid or impede their quest for identity. Angelopoulos creates a circular pattern in the narrative, like a recurring nightmare, that returns the viewer to a new beginning. Viewers tend to grasp whatever myths or incidents the narrative provides, some which appear to be missing or lost, that would assist in allowing them, like the children, to emerge from overwhelming darkness into the light of knowledge. Angelopoulos assists the viewer in relating to the reality of a situation by using long, continuous camera shots, keeping the camera fixed in one position and panning to capture the carefully composed actions within each scene. This cinematic approach, as Bazin argues, suggests an objective reality which allows viewers to modify their preconceived notions of a planned outcome, and as viewers, "we are always aware that this reality transcends our designs on it."

References

Friere, Paulo. 1973. *Pedagogy of the Oppressed.* New York: Continuum, 1990.

Hall, Stuart. 1990. "Cultural Identity and Diaspora." In *Identity: Community, Culture, Difference.* Edited by J. Rutherford. London: Lawrence & Wishart.

Horton, Andrew. "The Greek and Balkan Spirit of Comedy During the Journeys with the Films of Theo Angelopoulos." http://www.greecetravel.com/film/angelopoulos.htm

Horton, Andrew. "Theodor Angelopoulos and the New Greek Cinema." *Film Criticism,* Fall-Winter 1986–1987, pp. 84–94.

Rosaldo, Renato. 1989. *Culture and Truth: The Remaking of Social Analysis.* Boston: Beacon Press.

Said, Edward W. 1994. *Culture and Imperialism.* New York: Random House.

Shohat, Ella, and Robert Stam. 1994. *Unthinking Eurocentrism.* London and New York: Routledge.

Solanas, Fernando, and Octavio Getino. 1976. "Towards a Third Cinema." In *Movies and Methods.* Edited by Bill Nichols. Berkeley and Los Angeles: University of California Press, pp. 44–64.

Trinh, T. Minh-Ha. 1992. *Framer Framed.* New York and London: Routledge.

Willemen, Paul. 1994. *Looks and Frictions: Essays in Cultural Studies and Film Theory.* Bloomington: Indiana University Press.

CRITICAL ESSAY

"From a Hybrid Place"

by Trinh T. Minh-Ha with Judith Mayne

Mayne: One of the things I admire about your work — your films as well as your book *Woman, Native, Other* — is that it resists any easy categories. Your book is a work of theory, but it is very poetic: the reader has a different relationship to it than is usually the case in theoretical writing. Your films are obviously not documentaries in any classic sense, and it's not accurate to call them "commentaries" on the documentary genre either. Could you talk about this resistance to categorization that seems to be a crucial part of your work?

Trinh: I am always working at the borderlines of several shifting categories, stretching out to the limits of things, learning about my own limits and how to modify them. The book, for example, was completed in 1983. It took me that long to find a publisher. Ironically enough (although not surprisingly), what I went through in submitting it for publication seemed to be sadly consistent with certain repressed realities of women's writing and publishing, which I discussed in its very first chapter. The book was rejected by no less than thirty-three presses. The kind of problems it

repeatedly encountered had precisely to do with marketable categories and disciplinary regulations; in other words, with conformist borders. Not only was the focus on postcolonial positionings and on women of color as a subject and as subjects of little interest to publishers then, but what bothered them most was the writing itself.

For academics, "scholarly" is a normative territory that they own all for themselves, hence theory is no theory if it is not dispensed in a way recognizable to and validated by them. The mixing of different modes of writing; the mutual challenge of theoretical and poetical, discursive and "non-discursive" languages; the strategic use of stereotyped expressions in exposing stereotypical thinking; all these attempts at introducing a break into the fixed norms of the Master's confident prevailing discourses are easily misread, dismissed, or obscured in the name of "good writing," of "theory," or of "scholarly work." I was continually sent back and forth from one publisher to another —commercial, academic, and small presses— each one equally convinced in its kind suggestions that the book would fit better in the other marketing

This interview was conducted by Judith Mayne in May 1990, when *Surname Viet, Given Name Nam* was screened at the Wexner Center for the Arts. First published as "Feminism, Filmmaking and Postcolonialism: An Interview with Trinh T. Minh-Ha," in *Feminisms*, September-October (part I) and November-December (part II) 1990; and in *Afterimage* 18, no. 5, December 1990.

context. What transpired through all the comments I received was mainly that the work never quite corresponded to what these diverse publishers were "looking for." Obviously, as they said, they were very interested in writings "from the Third World," but this one, "would not fit in the series" they had or were in the process of establishing. An editor of a small press specializing in creative writing seriously felt he was being helpful when he decreed "it's not good writing because it's too impure."

It was a depressing experience. But I accept it as part of the struggle that this book is carrying on. I have to find a place for myself since I am at odds with all these categories of writings and modes of theorizing. A straight counterdiscourse is no longer threatening. It ultimately contributes to things remaining in place, because it tends more often than not to block critical thinking; it is unable to do much but repeat itself though the same anti-repressive rhetoric of modernist ideology. Let's take the example of a notion in vogue like "interdisciplinary." This notion is usually carried out in practice as the mere juxtaposition of a number of different disciplines. In such a politics of pluralist exchange and dialogue the concept of "inter-"(trans)formation and growth is typically reduced to a question of proper accumulation and acquisition. The disciplines are simply added, put next to one another with their boundaries kept intact; the participants continue happily to speak within their expertise, from a position of authority. It is rare to see such a notion stretched to the limits, so that the fences between disciplines are pulled down. Borderlines remain then strategic and contingent, as they constantly cancel themselves out. This "new" ground, always in the making, is what interests me most in everything I do. It constitutes the site where the very idea of a discipline, a specialization, and an expertise is challenged. No single field, profession, or creator can "own" it.

I never think of my films as specifically documentary or fictional, except when I send them off to festivals. Then I have to choose my jury. It is with this jury in mind that I place the film in a category. For years, no matter which one I chose, it seemed as if I constantly made the "wrong" selection. When I chose "documentary," I knew the problem would have to do with what people expect from a documentary and the ensuring rigidity of criteria. Most of these specialized jurors not only had difficulty in accepting my films as documentaries but also hardly considered them befitting the social, educational, or ethnographic categories. The same problem occurred when I opted for "film art" or "experimental," because jurors of such a category tend to see "experimental" as a genre on its own rather than as a critical venture working upon "genre" itself. Many still hold on to a mystical concept of "visionary art," and any preoccupation with or attempt at exposing ideology is rejected as "corrupt"—lacking pure vision, hence being no real Art. Now it seems that as my work is getting better known the categories become less important. But these used to be something that completely limited the ground on which the films could circulate.

M: You mention the word "borderline" several times, and the immediate connection that comes to mind is Gloria Anzaldua's *Borderlands / La Frontera*. That notion of a space in between conventional opposing pairs has been very important to the work of many women of color. I wonder how you see your own work in relation to that of other women writers of color?

T: I really like Anzaldua's works, and I often quote her in my own writings. I don't want to collapse all fights into one, however. I do realize the question of borderlines is particularly exigent in the Latina/Latino community because for many it remains physically an acute, everyday experience. This being said, and without forgetting the specificities of each context, I also recognize the commonalities between that border fight and the ones carried out, literally as well as figuratively, by women of color across ethnicities and cultures.

As in all struggles there are divergences among us; mostly in terms of strategy and location, I would say, but sometimes also in terms of objective and direction. What I understand of the struggle of women of color, however, is that our voices and silences across difference are so many attempts at articulating this always-emerging-already-distorted place that remains so difficult, on the one hand, for the First World even to recognize, and on the other, for our own communities to accept to venture into, for fear of losing what has been a costly gain through past struggles. To unlearn the reactive language that promotes separatism and self-enclosure by essentializing a denied identity requires more than willingness and self-criticism. I don't mean simply to reject this language (a reactive front is at times necessary for consciousness to emerge) but rather to displace it and play with it, or to play it out like a musical score.

Many of the younger diasporic generation who come forth today, on the artistic as well as the theoretical scene, have voiced their discomfort with any safeguarding of boundaries on either side of the border. This is precisely because the repressed complexities of the politics of identity have been fully exposed. "Identity" has now become more a point of departure than an end point in the struggle. So although we understand the necessity of acknowledging this notion of identity in politicizing the personal, we also don't want to be limited to it. Dominated and marginalized people have been socialized to see always more than their own point of view. In the complex reality of postcoloniality it is therefore vital to assume one's radical "impurity" and to recognize the necessity of speaking from a hybrid place, hence of saying at least two, three things at a time.

M: What's loosely called "French theory" has obviously influenced you.

T: France colonized Vietnam for a long time. Despite having fiercely resisted the French colonials, someone like Ho Chi Minh would admit that he preferred the French mentality to the American one. Colonialism really has a grip on its people. At a recent conference on African cinema in San Francisco, the Mauritanian filmmaker Med Hondo started out saying a few lines in perfect English, but he immediately ruptured his speech by saying that he was colonized first by the French, and he went on in French for the rest of the session! "French theory" is certainly part of my hybrid reality, although I would say it is only one part among others.

M: At one point in your book, commenting on the work of Helene Cixous, you say, "The One is the All and the All is the One; and yet the One remains the One and the All the All. Not two, not One either. This is what Zen has been repeating for centuries." I think there is something very contemplative about your films and your writing, a meditative quality. So-called "high theorists" never want to talk about a spiritual element in the text, but I sense that element very strongly in your work — specifically in the references to Zen, but more generally in your approach to representation.

T: This is a point hardly ever discussed. Since it took so long to find a publisher for the book, I had to resort to other publishing venues. Hence, some parts excerpted for this purpose had appeared here and there, in different journals. Now people confidently talk about earlier versions that "were later elaborated in the book," but in fact the book was written in its entirety long before any of these "articles" came out. After submitting these "excerpts" to journals, I received detailed comments from academic readers whose advice was sought by the concerned editors. Some of the readers, indeed, had a major problem with the Zen materials included, which they considered to be useless in a theoretical context. They reacted most scornfully, focusing on the " and turning a blind eye to the "how"—the way the materials are used and the inter-links created (as with Cixous's feminism in the example you mentioned).

I can understand such a reaction, especially living in California. I think that Zen—as it has spread in the West, especially in the 60s, with prominent names like John Cage, Alan Watts, Allen Ginsburg—has been mystified in its very demystifying practices. (This despite and *not* because of the works of the individuals mentioned.) Zen was recuperated into a dualistic and compartmentalized worldview. Speaking again of classifications and borders, you are here either "holistic" or "analytical," but you can't possibly be both, because the two are made into absolute antithetical stances. Zen has the gift to frustrate and infuriate the rational mind, which hurriedly dismisses it as simply one more form of mystification. So Zen's tenets are a real problem for a number of academics; but I myself do not operate within such divisions, and I don't see why I have to be bound by them. Spirituality cannot be reified. It's difficult to talk about it, not only because it escapes the principles of logic but also because "spiritual" itself is an impossible term: disinherited and vacated in this society of reification, hence not easy to use without exacting negotiations. The first book I wrote in 1976–77, *Un Art Sans Oeuvre* (*An Art Without Masterpiece*, published in 1981), includes a chapter relating the works of Jacques Derrida and Antonin Artaud to those of Krishnamurti and Zen Buddhism. For me many of Derrida's theories, including the critique of the metaphysics of presence, are forces that have been active in Zen and in other forms of Buddhism for centuries. So what he says is not really "new," but the way he puts them into discourse, the links he makes, are. The weaving of Zen in my text is therefore not a "return to my roots" but a grafting of several cultures onto a single body—an acknowledgment of the heterogeneity of my own cultural background.

M: This connects to one of the issues you discussed at the screening last night, the notion of "negative space."

T: In my films the notion of negative space has always been crucial. The "object-oriented camera"—a camera that focuses only on catching the object and is eager to objectify—obscures the role of negative space. I don't mean the ground behind the filmed subject or the field surrounding it, but rather the space that makes both composition and framing possible, that characterizes the way an image breathes. To see negative space as intensely as the figure and the field, instead of subjecting it to the latter in cinematography, mise-en-scène, and narrativity, implies a whole different way of looking at and of relating to things. This is not far from the notion of the Void in Asian philosophies. People often don't even know what you are talking about when you mention the vitality of the Void in the relationships between object and non-object, or between I and non–I. Again, they may think it's a form of mystification. This is a problem and reifying, binarist thinking: emptiness here is not merely opposed to fullness or objecthood; it is the very site that makes forms and contents possible—that is, also inseparable.

M: I'm curious how you see your most recent film in relationship to your two previous films, both of which depict the women of Africa and your relationship, as an Asian woman, to Africa. I'm thinking here especially of the term "hybridization" that you used last night to describe your approach to filmmaking.

T: The title of the film —*Surname Viet, Given Name Nam*— is taken from recent socialist tradition. When a man encounters a woman, feels drawn to her, and wants to flirt with her, he teasingly asks, "Young woman, are you married yet?" If the answer is negative, instead of saying no, she will reciprocate, "Yes, his surname is Viet and his given name is Nam." In this apparently benign replay the nation-gender relationship immediately raises questions. One of the recurring motifs in the film is the wedding, women being married: to a little boy or to a polygamous husband through family arrangements; to the cause, the fatherland, the state; to a foreigner bowing *à la* Vietnamese; then to a native man in Western outfit. The predicament of married women, which is woven here with the condition of single women insinuated or directly commented upon in poetry, proverbs, and popular stories, is unfolded in contexts of Vietnam that cut across the times before, during and after the revolution, including the periods of Chinese and French dominations, as well as the shift to life in the Vietnamese community in the United States. As one interviewee affirms toward the end of the film, whether a women marries a foreigner or a Vietnamese, her surname will always be "Viet" and her given name "Nam." A slight mutation of meaning occurs in that affirmation as it gets transferred from one context to another.

The question of nation and gender is opened up in a multiply layered way. The inquiry into identity provides another example. The latter can be said to develop in the film through a (re)appropriation of the inappropriate(d) body — the relations indirectly built up between the problematics of translation; the multiple (re)naming of a country; and the plural expropriation (owning, selling, humiliating, burning, exposing, glorifying) of women's bodies. Translation, like identity, is a question of grafting several cultures onto a single body. For example, the name of Trieu Thi Trinh, one of the historical heroines who resisted Chinese domination, has at least five variations (heard and seen on screen); each of these is a different reading, a different emphasis of her attributes — her lineage (by her last name), her gender and age status, her leadership, or merely her simplicity. Similarly, each of the numerous names used to designate Vietnam (also heard and seen on screen) relates to a historical period of the nation, thereby to the diverse

outside and inside influences that have contributed to what is viewed as the Vietnamese culture. So hybridization here refers to a negotiation of the difference not merely between cultures, between First World and Third World, but more importantly within the culture. This plural singularity and the problematization of the insider-outsider position are precisely what I have explored at length in my previous films, although in a way that is hardly comparable since it is so differently contextualized.

M: One of the most striking features of *Surname Viet, Given Name Nam* is your exploration of different modes of story-telling, or what you described last evening as two different kinds of truth.

T: Story-telling is an ongoing field of exploration in all of my works, hence a vast subject to discuss. I'm afraid I can only cover a few aspects of it here. The interviews originally carried out by Mai Thu Van in Vietnam were published in the book *Vietnam: Un Peuple, des Voix* (Paris: Pierre Horay, 1983. *Vietnam: One People, Many Voices*). I ran across this book while browsing in a small bookstore in France some years ago. It was certainly a discovery. I was very moved, both by the stories of the women interviewed and by the personal story of the author herself. Born in New Caledonia, she is a second-generation exile, her mother having been sent there by force to work in nickel mines because her village was among those that rose in rebellion against the French colonials. Mai came to Paris at the age of twenty-three to work and study and went to Vietnam in 1978 to research Vietnamese women, which resulted in the book mentioned. Being a Marxist, she landed in Hanoi with "a plethora of images of liberated women who have disturbed old concepts to meet socialism," and her stay there, as she puts it, "had profoundly shaken [her] preconceived ideas as well as pulverized the stereotypes of [Vietnamese] women made up by the press." It took her tenacity and an almost morbid care for the truth to wait for the ice to melt, to develop trust in an atmosphere of fear and suspicion, to take the blows, and to accept the eye-opening realities of women who refused to let themselves be mystified as heroines in postrevolutionary times. In brief, it took her five years to collect the interviews in question.

So in using some of the interviews in my film, the question for me is: Which truth does one want to offer to the viewer? The truth that Mai spent five years to approach, or the truth that we can easily claim by setting up an interview situation, directing a microphone at a person (like myself right now!), and trying to skim the cream off the answers afterwards? The point at issue is somewhat different here, however, because when an interview is recorded and transcribed for publication you can work on it, and the length of the interviewee's replies is usually respected. But in film the problem of editing is much more acute, because you can't reword to condense, nor can you add to clarify; you can only cut. And you cut what you want people to be saying: you cut only the statement that will help you to make your point. So there are certain kinds of unintended surface truths that may emerge as unique to the filmed interview situation, but there are also other kinds that can never be accessible through this antiquated device of documentary — unless the element of realism is worked on.

Perhaps one can find an example in a film like *Chronique d'un été* (*Chronicle of a Summer*, 1961, by Jean Rouch), where an interviewer just pointed a microphone at people in the street, asking, "Are you happy?" The shallow answers might have been a reaction to such a question, but they also implied the shallowness of such an interview setup. The director must then "work on" this shallowness, that is, deliberately acknowledge it in order to further the film's inquiries. As spectators, our attitude toward interviews often proves to be naive. We tend to forget how tactical

speech always is, no matter how naturally it seems to come out. To assume that testimonies filmed on the site are de jure more truthful than those reconstructed off the site is to forget how films are made. Every representation of truth involves elements of fiction, and the difference between so-called documentary and fiction in their depiction of reality is a question of degrees of fictitiousness. The more one tries to clarify the line dividing the two, the deeper one gets entangled in the artifice of boundaries.

The making of *Surname Viet* allows the practice of interviews to enter into the play of the true and the false, the real and the staged. In the first part of the film, the interviews were selected, cut, and blueprinted for reenactment. A certain length of the speech and the image was deliberately kept to preserve the autonomy of each story as it unfolded and, paradoxically, to render perceptible the play on traditional realism. The latter becomes more and more manifest as the film progresses, until further on the viewer is presented with a series of "real" interviews with the same women as in the first part, but in the explicit context of the U.S. The editing of these last interviews comes closer to the conventions of documentary and the statements are chopped up, redistributed, and woven in the filmic text with footage of the women's "real" life-activities. By using both reenacted interviews and on-site interviews and by demarcating some of their differences (in the duration, mode of address, use of English, camera work), in other words, by presenting them to the viewer together, what is visibly addressed is the invisibility of the politics of interviews and, more generally, the relations of representation.

I am not really interested in judging which truth is better than the other, but rather in working with both together to open a critical space in the viewing of the film. Whether the viewer is knowledgeable enough in cinema to attribute some of the strategies to a questioning of the conventions of documentary authority is also not the point. The viewing situation created is such that it is likely to provoke questions and reactions. By playing with the false and the true at work in the two kinds of truth, what is usually taken for granted in interviews suddenly becomes very prominent. As a bewildered Vietnamese viewer told me: "Your film is different. I can't yet tell exactly how, but I know it's different from the documentary films I am used to seeing." The recognition that the early interviews in the film are reenactments comes at different places and stages for different viewers. This is deliberately planned, as I previously suggested. Of course, as you probably noticed at yesterday's screening, some viewers were furious because they expected to be told about it at the outset of the film (as the norms dictate). But other viewers felt that to reveal the reenactment from the start would be to give away the "plot" of the film; they were uncomfortable with the lingering uncertainty, but retroactively they loved the challenge and the intermittent discomfort. I obviously do not intend to "hide" the reenactment — on the contrary — only to delay or grade its visibility for strategic purposes. Nor do I feel compelled to flatten out the film to facilitate its consumption. Instead of being a mere illustration of a point that is evident from the beginning, a film could be a constant discovery process. Much of filmmaking and story-telling relies on an ability to withhold information as well as to let go of knowledge and intention.

M: The process of "recognition" in the film is very unsettling.

T: The distance between the written texts and the images is necessary. The women are asked both to embody other selves, other voices, and to drift back to their own selves, which are not really their "natural" selves but the selves they want to present or the images they want to project in front of the camera.

M: Another kind of distance is the discrepancy between written text and voice, sometimes

small — suggesting that the text is being performed.

T: If it is unsettling, it's because the line between performance and nonperformance in these interviews is not so evident. You can't tell right away that they are staged — you do ask the question, but you can't tell for sure until you get enough "cues."

M: In conclusion, could you say something about the kind of work that has most influenced you?

T: It's very difficult for me to talk about influence. Even with someone like Ho Xuan Huong, the early nineteenth-century poet quoted in the film: I knew of her, but she was hardly taught in school. I remember how perversely excited we (the students) were whenever a teacher announced that a poem of hers would be read in class. Not only because her poetry is known for its forbidden sexuality and explicit defiance of Confucian (male-chauvinist) mores, but mainly because she is a poet whose work we are never truly exposed to. All this to say that on the side of women you always have to do more; you have to be committed to reach out to non-mainstream works and to the writings of other women. This is one of the constraints that you necessarily assume as a feminist. The writing of *Woman, Native, Other* touches upon this specific issue. For example, the only chapter that deals exclusively with the world of white males is the chapter on anthropology. This chapter is also one, however, in which all the names of the representative famous men are replaced in the text by impersonal, stereotyped appellations ("The Great Master," "The modern anthropologist," "the wise man"). Their proper names, their "true" names, are "buried" in the footnotes.

For me there is no such thing as a one-way influence. In (re)reading women's works — actually any work — I am not sure who influences whom, for I have the feeling that I've contributed as much as I've learned. And if I take the example of a few Western writers with whom I have affinities, such as Roland Barthes, Walter Benjamin, Maurice Blanchot, or Derrida, sure, I find their writings uplifting and penetrating. But our actualities are undeniably different. They have their own house to empty out, their own obsessions to pursue. However, their works do provide tools of resistance that we can use on our terms. Tools that also allow me independently to rediscover, let's say, Zen Buddhism or other Asian philosophies as if I were reading them for the first time; *and* vice versa. What has become more evident to me is that I can't settle down with any single name, any single work. The only times I felt that something could strongly inspire me, and in ways that were both moving and baffling, was when I was staying in the villages in Africa. The richness of the diverse oral traditions is humbling. Again this may seem romantic to many — although in the context of other cultures it is rather "realistic." As a Yoruba song of divination says, "Anybody who meets beauty and does not look at it will soon by poor." Stories, songs, music, proverbs, as well as people's daily interactions, certainly constitute for me the most moving sources of inspiration.

CHAPTER 26

Revisioning History: Contesting Colonialism

Introduction

A new kind of film narrative emerged during the latter part of the 20th century that contested the underlying assumptions about the nature of film as it represents the past in present time. Some historians have already recognized that the cinema, as a visual and aural medium, can construct an historical event in the present as effectively as a written text. Postmodern techniques now avoid evoking a past historic time merely as a setting for romantic adventures but as a filmic space to contest, envision and re-vision historical events and their impact on present-day crises. Through different but complex narrative structures today's filmmakers are motivated by screen narratives that aspire to re-position one's identity and heritage.

Such film narratives use new forms of presentational modes to help the viewer gain an understanding of the past as it reforms, re-shapes and redirects the present (Rosenstone 1995, pp. 8–10).

These historical films locate the actions within the space between the "already given" of a particular metanarrative, or a story about a story in a political perspective, or political perspective on a country and the smaller, intimate historical truths of a family or minority group. In contesting the unspoken assumptions of a culture, such films undercut and critique the historical determinants that have provoked political repression, random violence and the notion of individual heroism.

Postmodern Films from Australia and India

In the English speaking world of Oceania, Australia founded its own postwar cinema with the creation of the Australian Film Development Corporation in 1970. As a funding agency, it sponsored the production of feature films that promoted Australian culture "other than kangaroos and Ned Kellys." Australia's drive to create a feature film industry of its own was designed to overcome Hollywood imports and their own slapstick comedies with Barry Crocker. Despite early distribution problems, the films focused on the contradictions of British political policies and colonialist bigotry that led to personal disasters and death for Australian settlers. The major productions were art films set in a rebellious turn-of-the-century period that exemplified an Australian past. At the end of the 1970s, a number of directors emerged, notably Peter Weir, Fred Schepisi, Bruce Beresford, George Miller and Gillian Armstrong.

Peter Weir (b. 1944) established the characteristics of this new film policy with the haunting *Picnic at Hanging Rock* (1975), in which the natural environment breaks down the repressive sexual values of a group of girls from an English boarding school. In *The Last Wave* (1977), a "civilized" rational man faces the onslaught of otherworldly ritual mysteries. In *Gallipoli* (1981) besides attacking British military protocol, Weir examines the slaughter of innocents in an alien environment. His final film in Australia was *The Year of Living Dangerously*

Peter Weir's *Picnic at Hanging Rock* (1975) is one of the first Australian-made films to herald the arrival of New Wave in that country. Weir uses a picnic scene as a means to contrast repressive colonial cultural values with the hidden forces of the natural elements that liberate a group of boarding school girls, to their delight.

(1982), in which he establishes an atmosphere of political fear and paranoia in Indonesia during a military coup in 1965. Weir was invited to Hollywood to continue his film work, and directed a number of major films that explored themes of displacement and identity as in *Witness* (1985), *The Mosquito Coast* (1986), *Dead Poets Society* (1989) and *Fearless* (1993).

Fred Schepisi (b. 1939) adapted Thomas Keneally's novel, *The Chant of Jimmie Blacksmith*, into a powerful 1978 drama about a half-caste aboriginal who goes to war on white settlers after the British play politics and disinherit him on the eve of Confederation in 1900. Schepisi also moved to Hollywood in the 1980s, and directed *Plenty* (1985), *Roxanne* (1987), *A Cry in the Dark* (1988), about a disturbing murder trial taking place in Australia, and another mystery-thriller, *The Russia House* (1990).

Bruce Beresford (b. 1940) uses a true inci-

dent from the Boer War to make a tense drama of Australian soldiers court-marshaled by British field officers in *Breaker Morant* (1980), which continues the Australian critique of British politics. Dividing his time between Australia and Hollywood, Beresford selected interesting character studies for his Hollywood dramas, including *Crimes of the Heart* (1986), and *Driving Miss Daisy* (1989) about a spirited Jewish woman and her black chauffeur during the changing social and political world of Atlanta in the 1950s.

Gillian Armstrong (b. 1950) brought to her films a series of coming-of-age stories portraying free-thinking young women who desire to succeed in other roles than those decided by a patriarchal society. In her first feature film, *My Brilliant Career* (1978), set in the outback during the 1900s, Armstrong depicts the struggle of a young woman trying to avoid marrying a local landowner by following her dreams of becoming a writer. With the success of this film, Armstrong also traveled to Hollywood to direct *Mrs. Soffel* (1984). As a fine turn-of-the-century period piece, the drama is based upon a true incident that demonstrates the strong will a woman needed to break her marriage vows and help a convicted murderer escape.

Following Armstrong is another graduate of the Australian Film and Television School, Jane Campion, from New Zealand. After directing award-winning short films, she directed three feature films that are part black comedy and social melodrama. Thematically, she explores the hidden, dark, surreal world masking the desires of women caught in suburban life and its superficial rituals. First in *Sweetie* (1989), then in *An Angel at My Table* (1990) and again in *The Piano* (1993), she depicts the thin line between madness and normality as the central character is motivated by desire, not custom. *The Piano* takes place in New Zealand in the 1860s, revealing the surreal beauty of the landscape that envelops the lovers in this dark, erotic drama (Murray 1980, p. 83).

In India, during the late 19th century, English colonization took on a different military and political strategy than it did in Australia. Heavily populated by Hindu, Sikh and Muslim people, with a powerful caste system, India was deemed the jewel in the English crown. Before granting India its independence in August 1947, the British played divide-and-conquer politics that triggered an unprecedented division, splitting the country into two. Thus Pakistan, a new Muslim country, emerged to flank Hindus and Sikhs in India on both the East and West coasts. In East India, the Bengal province was split, to become known as Bangladesh. In Calcutta, on the East Coast of India, Bengali filmmaker Satyajit Ray (1921–1992) grew up as a member of a prominent Bengali family, well established in literature and the fine arts. After India gained its independence, Ray formed Calcutta's first film society, eschewing Bombay's popular dance musicals for a "new cinema" modeled after European art films. Significantly, Ray conceived his cinema on the Italian films of Zavattini and De Sica. These films concerned the everyday problems of survival, and the experi-

ences facing children growing up in poverty. Ray's first film, *Pather Panchali* (1955), is a story of Apu, a young boy in a small family coping with life and death in a poor Bengal village. Ray's next two films, *Aparajito / The Unvanquished* (1956) and *Apur Sansar / The World of Apu* (1959), complete *The Apu Trilogy* that follows the adventures of Apu through schooling and marriage, then the suffering and death of his parents. The films displayed neorealist cinematic techniques, but included long reaction shots to depict human feelings, a technique Ray learned when working with Jean Renoir when Renoir filmed *The River* (1950) in Calcutta.

Ray's importance as a filmmaker of international stature develops from his belief in an alternative cinema that parallels the dominant commercial industry in Bombay. His films are recorded in English and Bengali with Indian artists performing as actors and musicians. They are made for local as well as international audiences. His attention to rendering the humanist writings of Rabindranath Tagore in reconstructing his Bengali heritage characterizes all his films. This humanist literature emphasizes the conflicts between British and Indian cultures and attempts to show the clash of rational, positive thinking with the social and political folklore of the Indian people. Thus Ray's later films of the 1960s and 1970s, especially *Shatranj ke Khilari / The Chess Players* (1977), *Ghare Baire / The Home and the World* (1984) and *Ganashatru / The Enemy of the People* (1989) address these complex themes.

The Home and the World, which Ray started in 1947, is his own screen adaptation of Tagore's novel. Here he examines the effects of caste and custom upon women during the Hindu-Muslim trade wars and riots in 1906–1907. In the film, a love triangle grows as a liberal-minded husband begins to educate his wife into the ways of the modern Western world. His altruism brings a male friend into their home in the form of a Muslim political activist. This man woos the wife, who is given the opportunity to leave her sanctuary and indulge in a new way of life breaking with traditional feminine activities as part of her education. As the outer world draws the man and wife into an economic conflict between political nationalists and Western colonialism, the husband sets out to extinguish the growing rivalry between Hindu and Muslim merchants. His efforts fail, both in facing this uprising on his property and in bringing his wife into a new life. As a social and political tract the film questions the price one has to pay to enter the modernist movement toward enlightenment.

The social and political reflexivity developed by Ray in his films about Indian life during the 1950s encouraged a group of Bengali filmmakers. These directors emerged after recovering from the trauma of the Hindu-Muslim riots and mass migration caused by the partition of Bengal. They learned their political lessons at the Independent Peoples Theatre Association, founded in 1943 to revive Indian folk art and literature from a Marxist viewpoint. This left-wing group was part of a movement to nurture the artistic and theatrical talents of young people who took their didactic plays into the villages and towns of West Bengal. Ritwak Ghatak (b. 1925) with Mrinal Sen (b. 1923) became two of its leading directors when they realized their scripts for revolutionary drama would be more effective using film as a medium to reach a much larger audience. Encouraged by the local reception of Ray's *Pather Panchali*, their early films became part of a "parallel cinema" in contrast to the mainstream Indian film industry and its escapist musical melodramas.

In advancing the cause of this new Indian cinema, Sen and Ghatak wrote screenplays using a variety of cinematic techniques gleaned from the documentary styles of Eisenstein, Pudovkin, and the New Wave films of Godard and Truffaut. Sen's early films, *Bhuvan Shome* (1969) and *Interview* (1971) are political in calling into question middle-class rituals that culturally exploit people caught in their own social-historical experiences. *Genesis* (1986) is a fable about two men who cultivate farmland in a lost village in order to build a new society free of poverty and strife. A chance arrival of a woman refugee brings into play sexual politics and disintegrates their escapist dreams. Among Ghatak films, *Ajantrik / Pathetic Fallacy* (1958) is best known in Europe, but its theme of a symbiotic relationship between a man and his machine appeared novel to Hindi audiences. His last film, *Jukti, Takko aar Gappo / Reason, Argument, Story* (1974), follows attempts by his allegorical hero to find some meaning for the political and cultural turmoil overtaking his country. This narrative pursues a struggle for identity that became paramount to Ghatak in his later days as he watched himself becoming victimized and exiled by the powerful forces of change. Ghatak's importance to film history arises from his short tenure at the Calcutta Film and Television Institute in 1965. His students became new adherents to the tenets of parallel cinema. They included Shyman Benegal, Aparna Sen and Mira Nair, whose *Salaam Bombay!* (1987) testifies to the commercial vitality and compassion of a film community protesting against poverty and exploitation (Banerjee 1985, pp. 107–143).

Revisioning History in Eastern European Films

Other historical films envision history as a recreation and appropriation of past time through a juxtaposition of two kinds of film images, one using documentary footage to gain an "objective perspective" of the event and the other a dramatically staged reenactment of the event which places the actor within the site of the action. In envisioning neo–Marxist critiques against repressive Soviet totalitarian methods within the Soviet Bloc, Polish filmmakers such as Andrzej Wajda, (b. 1926), Roman Polanski (b. 1933), Krzysztof Zanussi (b. 1939), and Krzysztof Kieslowski (b. 1941) revision and reaffirm Polish history as material for political reforms which, in turn, encouraged the rise of the Solidarity movement.

Wajda's most powerful trilogy, *Generation* (1955), *Kanał* (1957) and *Ashes and Diamonds* (1958) traces the actions of young Resistance fighters at the end of World War II. Each film deals with the personal dilemmas war forces upon these men as they strive to find refuge from it. *Generation* takes place in occupied Warsaw and depicts the hopes, fears and disillusionments of young Polish men living under the Nazis. *Kanał* involves the preparations of an underground rebellion against the Germans in 1944. *Ashes and Diamonds* takes place at the beginning of the Civil War between anti-communist Home Forces and communist security agents. A member of the Home Force is ordered to kill an older communist leader. After meeting his victim at a victory party, the assassin begins to harbor doubts about the idealism of his mission. Ironically, once he carries out his mission, he is shot trying to escape. In *Man of Marble* (1977) and its sequel, *Man of Iron* (1981), Wadja uses documentary footage and directed sequences with Lech Wałesa to support the rumblings of the anti-communist Solidarity movement. Yet, the films carry a fatalistic sense of tragic irony that an accord between the union and the government would be binding. When the communist military junta took over in 1981, Wadja emigrated to France. In the following year he made *Danton* (1982), a dark, tragic revisioning of the ideological struggle between the political leaders of the French Revolution that parallels the Polish debate between Jaruzelski and Wałesa.

Roman Polanski's first feature film was *Knife in the Water* (1962), an imaginative rendering of the Oedipal conflict in which a young man takes on an older man with a knife to enjoy the affections of the older man's wife. In a film full of emotional tensions and sexual power games, Polanski's direction exposes the dark, malevolent side of humankind. Polanski advances this theme in *Repulsion* (1965), *Rosemary's Baby* (1968) and *Macbeth* (1971). In Hollywood, Polanski revisioned the corruption, greed and incest in *Chinatown* (1974). The film is set in Los Angeles during the 1930s and is fashioned as a strange film noir detective thriller, starring Faye Dunaway and Jack Nicholson. It succeeds in relating the uncovering of crimes against government officials in the past to the hidden motives behind the 1973 Watergate cover-up.

The main thrust of Krzysztof Zanussi's film narratives revolves around student life within the scientific community. In *The Structure of Crystals* (1969) he explores the reasons why two fellow students choose different career paths. With *Illumination* (1973), Zanussi introduces a philosophical premise to examine the human

condition as a person matures into adulthood. Using a series of brief episodes, he portrays the moral and intellectual conflicts precipitated by his adherence to an objective, scientific orientation to his job (Turaj 1989, pp. 148–149).

The psychological loss of moral imperatives is located in the films of Krzysztof Kieślowski. After making documentaries on the social and economic predicaments confronting Polish workers, his first feature film was the award-winning *Amator / Camera Buff* (1979), which examines the effects censorship has on a filmmaker when the authorities decide his political spin on current events is too revisionist. *Blind Chance* (1981), allows him to introduce a variety of scenarios for the future of the Communist Party, the final one suggesting the overthrow of the party itself as it continues to suppress civil liberties. The role chance plays in a person's ability to make moral decisions is brought to bear in a series of ten one-hour film narratives drawn from the directives of the Ten Commandments. *Decalogue* (1988–90) uses a postwar housing complex in Warsaw to place the interaction of different tenants during the ten episodes, each startling in understating the uncertainty and unpredictability of the forces of life. *A Short Film About Killing* (1988) concerns the justice system in relationship to murder, and *A Short Film About Love* (1988) follows a peeping-tom whose obsession with a next-door neighbor brings about humorous results. Both films are carefully rendered spin-offs from the original *Decalogue*. Kieślowski's last films, *Primary Colors*, including *Blue* (1993), *White* (1994) and *Red* (1994), are a close-knit trilogy on revisioning history. In each film narrative, Kieślowski skillfully brings a history of past events into the present, only to find such events repeating themselves through the strange unfolding of chance encounters among various people (Kieślowski 1993, pp. 212–227).

Hungarian filmmakers developed themes involving an historical analysis of the past when political oppression defined the state of the nation. The foremost Hungarian director to gain international status in the late 1960s was Miklós Jancsó (b. 1921). With a distinctive visual style that used extensive long takes, his films examine a series of social revolutions in which

In *Mephisto* (1981), directed by István Szabó, the white-faced mask of Mephistopheles is worn by Klaus Maria Brandauer as Hendrik Hoefgen in an Academy Award winning film based upon a novel by Klaus Mann. This actor plays many different roles, but his Nazi sponsors show interest in only this beguiling mask which shows his political allegiance to Nazi tactics and outright moral betrayal.

both sides commit various atrocities. In his political parable about the 1956 Hungarian uprising in Budapest, Jancsó's *The Round-Up* (1966) describes the aftermath of the 1848 Hungarian revolution against the Hapsburg rulers who were determined to eliminate all guerrilla bandits hiding among peasant farmers. Without any focus upon a central hero, the camera allows the viewer to witness the slow but inexorable execution of these men. *The Red and the White* (1967) takes place during the Russian Revolution of 1919, when many Hungarian soldiers joined the revolutionary "Reds" against the government "White" forces. In this film, Jancsó places the viewer's attention on a Hungarian soldier's ordeal of being captured and tortured to reveal how political oppression operates. In *Red Psalm* (1972), Jancsó examines the misery of landless agricultural workers who try to alleviate their suffering with an uprising during the early 1900s. Again, Jancsó's long camera takes contrast the beauty of nature with the brutality of human oppression as the director explores the nature of power at different times of social insurrection.

István Szabó (b. 1938) focuses his films on historical dramas in which the ambitions of his central characters fall under the power of ruthless military leaders. In his trilogy, *Mephisto* (1981), *Colonel Redl* (1985) and *Hanussen* (1988), Szabó revisions history to unmask the illusory dreams of professional men who forget the realities of history imbedded in political power. In *Mephisto*, a talented German actor helps legitimize the Nazis' rise to power with his popular star appeal. Ironically, his public support of the Nazi Party in Germany during the 1930s brings about his own imprisonment as a propagandist for them. Paradoxically, while the mask worn by this actor provides him with an opportunity to alight upon many different roles, his sponsors show interest in only one mask, which they fix permanently upon him as part of his political obligation and allegiance to Nazi tactics for spectacle and propaganda. *Colonel Redl* is a man wearing a rigid mask that hides his own Jewishness and homosexuality as he rises within the mighty Hapsburg Empire. Once caught in a counter-spy trap, he arouses the suspicion of his superior officers. His exposure and final humiliation close out his life. In *Hanussen*, Szabo returns to Berlin of the 1920s to follow the extraordinary career of an ex-sergeant turned clairvoyant who can predict the future. His prophecies on Hilter's rise to power incriminate him as a Nazi supporter and he loses his earlier sponsors and his own sense of reality.

Márta Mészáros' own autobiographical trilogy, starting with *Diary for My Children* (1984), takes a feminist view against the repressive tactics of Soviet politics. Mészáros trained as a filmmaker in Moscow during the 1950s. While her earlier short films focused on the emotional deprivation of younger women, her later films concerned her interest in father-daughter relationships, and the political realities behind the bureaucratic conditions under which women are forced to work in Hungary. Her films revision the 1950s, when Stalinist policies brought on the fighting in Hungary. *Diary for My Loves* (1987) examines her frustrations as a filmmaker attempting to make an honest documentary film. *Diary for My Mother and Father* (1990) describes a child growing into adolescence unaware of the brutality and military repression that split her family (Paul 1989, pp. 172–212).

Rituals of the Past in Films from China, Japan and Russia

Filmmakers who revision history in their own film narratives use modes of representation other than neorealism, such as romanticism (Zhang Yimou), postmodern parody (Juzo Itami) and mythic representation (Andrei Tarkovsky). These historical film narratives are mostly set in remote villages of the past, and contain a "politics of representation" which follows a sense of reflective filmmaking in the narrative discourse. Zhang Yimou (b. 1950) favors retelling folktales to reveal the legends associated with the strength and resilience of a peasant culture. In *Red Sorghum* (1987) he subversively entertains the viewer with scenes of sexual passion that haunt a woman seeking liberation from her repressive situation. *Ju Dou* (1990) is set in the 1920s, and involves a plan

Andrei Tarkovsky's *Solaris* (1972) is a space-travel fantasy that explores another planet. It attests to the director's quest to make contact with a regenerating spiritual world. On Solaris a mysterious Ocean reveals and reflects a person's unconscious desires without warning.

by an older, impotent husband that leads to tragic reprisals when he allows his nephew the privilege of taking his young wife as a lover. In *The Story of Qui Ju* (1991), the narrative follows a pregnant woman who seeks redress from a Chinese administrator for inflicting injuries upon her husband. Each film tells a simple story that is enhanced by rich cinematography.

In Japan, Juzo Itami (b. 1933) approaches the conflict between a new technological society coming to grips with traditional rituals in his black comedy, *The Funeral* (1985). This film depicts the episodic adventures of a man making arrangements for his wife's father's funeral. Here the old traditions of Japan are followed blindly without any understanding of their significance or history. While gently satirizing other Japanese filmmakers, Yasujiro Ozu in particular, Itami has fun with television com-

mercials and instructional videotapes that provide whatever the new consumer society desires. *Tampopo* (1986) allows Itami an opportunity to parody the Western genre as he explores various forms of industrial espionage, military operations and Zen lessons on eating to help his heroine marshal her forces and become the finest noodle chef in Tokyo. Throughout the film, Itami playfully connects sex with the enjoyment of eating. In *A Taxing Woman* (1987) and *A Taxing Woman's Return* (1988), Itami develops a helter-skelter comedy that focuses upon a woman tax collector in pursuit of crafty tax dodgers. In his parody of the traditional detective genre, he displays how all the small-time hoods play for the big fish. In *A Taxing Woman's Return*, the tax collector takes on big-time industrialists, politicians and other racketeers who are involved in a game to

In *Tampopo* (1986) director Juzo Itami parodies the Western genre with Japanese cowboys coming to the rescue of a damsel in distress. The director employs forms of industrial espionage, shock military operations and Zen Buddhist techniques on eating to help his heroine become the finest noodle chef in Tokyo.

inflate property values. Although it is difficult to laugh at the seriousness of the offenses, Itami seeks to help Japanese society break away from the restrictions of traditions that hide corruption and graft (Sipe 1989).

Taking a different postmodern approach is Andrei Tarkovsky (1932–1986), a Soviet director whose historical dramas search for a spiritual revitalization of people caught in a dehumanizing scientific modern age. *Solaris* (1972), *Stalker* (1979) and *The Sacrifice* (1986) all attest to a quest for contact with a regenerating spiritual world. *Solaris* is a space-travel fantasy to a planet where a mysterious Ocean reveals a consciousness. In *Stalker,* a "wasteland" becomes a rendezvous for three travelers contemplating life's mysteries. *The Sacrifice* sees the efforts of a family attempting to survive nuclear war.

Preceding all these films was *Andrei Rublev* (1966), a story of an icon painter fleeing from Tartar invasions of Russia and the horrors of that war. As time passes he sheds his vow of silence and attempts to become a believer in his ability to add beauty to his own icon paintings. The moment of epiphany arrives at the unveiling of his new paintings in a church marked by the film moving into color from black and white. Another spiritual moment occurs when he tells a story about a boy being able to cast a bell (Tarkovsky 1996, pp. 37–43).

Revisioning Ourselves

In today's discourse on media culture, the uniqueness of the postmodern condition allows the interfacing of individuals with a broad range of new "high-tech" mass-produced computer products that are essentially reproductions or abstractions of memories, images and copies of original experiences, similar to those implanted in replicants in Ridley Scott's film, *Blade Runner* (1982). This media culture has also spawned a consumer demand for TV instant-cameras and projections, VCRs, computers and other electronic gathering machines that can reproduce subjective emotions and experiences. As the forms of high-density television broadcasts expand cinema into a medium

carrying multi-image projections of environments, they penetrate our daily lives with their "virtual realities." In this manner these machines have inhabited our consciousness and colonized our desires and imaginations.

Forrest Gump (1994) revolutionized modern filmmaking. Special effects, especially those made with CGI technology, were previously reserved for use in science fiction and fantasy films. Robert Zemeckis expanded its use into mainstream films by using the technology to recreate history. "At its time, just as now, Forrest Gump was often criticized for its revisionist version of modern American history and less-than-flattering portrayal of individuals and movements that tried to change [the] status quo of American society." Forrest Gump (Tom Hanks), instead of trying to change the status quo, follows the rules, obeys his parents and the authorities, and in return is rewarded by success in business and family. Jenny (Robin Wright), on the other hand, who rebels against authority, is punished with violence, drug addiction, and AIDS. "Some might find traces of Taoism in philosophy of Forrest Gump, but in the end [the filmmakers] provide an ending closer to Hegelian dialectics—Gump, as embodiment of "proper" America, and Jenny, as the embodiment of counter-culture, reconcile their differences in a bittersweet ending that gives hope for future generations" (Antulov 2003).

An example of the cultural schizophrenia that overwhelmed German survivors after 1945 is represented in the Wim Wenders' film, *Kings of the Road* (1976). The central character is a postmodern hero, an unadaptable man, a wanderer and dreamer caught in an "illusion of reality." The history of his past was created by American motion pictures. As he uncovers this alleged history of Germany through cinematic representations made after the rise of Hitler, he realizes that "the Yankees have colonized our subconscious." The amnesia that befalls this man is visually depicted as a constant disruption between the contemporary social conditions and the film representations of past lives. Here the denial of identity causes a restlessness; the man is continually forced to live in a threatened state of anxiety. Through witnessing this film a spectator realizes that myth-making is an integral part of identity-making. Further, revisioning history helps liberate people caught in memories of a fixed historical context. Yet it will require an educational transfer and reorganization of that past to allow people to re-function as they reform their own imaginations according to the changing needs of their own cultural lives. Then, a contextualist film critique will be able to situate film narratives within an existing social and political conflict that is not just a discourse for a monolithic and dominating ideology, but a space where persons can influence change as they separate their own creative imaginations from the illusions projected about themselves.

In contrast to *Forrest Gump, The Lives of Others* (2006) destroys that which is good. The film takes place in East Berlin in 1984, when the Berlin Wall is still standing. The central character, a member of the Stasi secret police, deliberately teaches students how to defeat the innocent. "Thus the picture opens in a prison, a proper metaphor for the Soviet controlled country, which tortures its citizens with a secret police known as the Stasi. *The Lives of Others* proceeds from there, swiftly moving along and rewarding the mind that grasps what totalitarianism means in theory and practice; how it envelops a nation in fear" (Holleran 2007).

In Woody Allen's *Purple Rose of Cairo* (1985), Allen, as director, reconstructs the period of the Great Depression in the United States of the 1930s. The reconstruction is necessary in order to demonstrate the power of motion pictures to offer people an escape from the harsh realities of beleaguered lives that appear to be somewhat hopeless and futile. In contrast to this drab world, Allen focuses on the bright marquee of the Jewel movie theatre where a romantic adventure story entitled "The Purple Rose of Cairo" is being screened. The audience, filmed in color, is entranced by the brightness of the silver screen, which is, of course, exhibiting a black and white film. Once we see our heroine in the audience, Allen then allows the movie to do a visual trick, having the lead male character (Tom) from the movie walk out of the film and the movie screen into the audience to address a young woman, Cecilia (Mia Farrow), who just happens to be an avid movie fan of this actor.

Tom, the fictional character, then converses with Cecilia as they walk into the streets of this depressing small town in New Jersey. Humor is derived from the juxtaposition of the "fantasy" character, Tom, interacting with a "real" person, Cecilia, and with other real people in the town. In the conversations that follow the courtship of Cecilia, Tom begins to learn that this real world is a very different and indeed a very complex place for a fictional person in which to live. So Tom decides to return as quickly as he can back into the movie in which he plays the lead. But he is surprised when Cecilia returns to the film with him but learns that she must play a different role in this film.

Thus, the device of a "film within a film" helps the audience realize the "dimensions of reality" that can be reached through the cinematic process, one that allows the audience to understand how the cinematic action can be projected by this film. Thus the film attempts to contrast the key turning points of such a revelation into a "film within a film" to create a significant influence on the given film narrative.

"For cinema, the introduction of digital media poses questions about the motion picture screen and our relationship to cinematic space." According to Manovich (1994) the cinema reworks "the classical screen" (Renaissance perspective attempts to represent three-dimensional space on a flat surface), creating "the dynamic screen" where the displayed image changes over time. In watching a film, we focus our full attention on the representation on screen and disregard the physical space outside it. This concentration is enabled by the fact that the image fills the whole screen.

What, then, is the work of theory in the age of digital transformation? Digital theory offers us explanations, interpretations, and predictions which enable us to manage the process of technological change and its impact upon our social, cultural, economic, political, and personal lives. Digital theory provides a point of intersection between the languages and practices of science and engineering on the one hand and the arts and humanities on the other.

Digital theory embraces the utopian imagination not as a way of predicting the future but as a way of envisioning meaningful change and keeping alive the fluidity which digital media has introduced into many aspects of our social and personal lives. Digital theory identifies historical antecedents for contemporary media developments and at the same time, defamiliarizes older media and opens then to re-examination. What is striking about the present moment is not simply that academic theorists have responded quickly to a changing media environment — itself a phenomenon virtually without precedents — but theory production has been embraced by the larger society. Digital cinema refers to the use of digital technology to distribute and project motion pictures. The final movie can be distributed via hard drives, DVDs or satellite and projected using a digital projector instead of a conventional film projector. Digital cinema is distinct from high-definition television and in particular, is not dependent on using television or HDTV standards, aspect ratios, or frame rates. Digital projectors capable of 2K resolution began deploying in 2005, and in 2006, the pace has accelerated. HDTV and pre-recorded HD disks put great pressure on movie theatres to offer something better to compete with the improved home HD experience (Manovich 1994).

George Lucas directed his fifth film in the *Star Wars* series, *Attack of the Clones*, in 2002. He used "a pre-visualization process that allowed him to put scenes together without having to shoot them first. Thus a new process of filmmaking was evolving which felt more believable because there was less cutting to hide visual tricks" (Magrid 2002). This was Lucas's first big-budget film that was shot with digital video cameras, thus was best screened in theaters with digital projectors.

References

Antuluv, Dragan. 2003. "*Forest Gump*: A Film Review." Online Film Critics Society: http://www.ofcs.org

Banerjee, Shampa. 1985. *Profiles: Five Film-makers from India*. New Delhi: Directorate of Film Festivals, National Film Development Corp.

Holleran, Scott. 2007. "*The Lives of Others*." www.boxofficemojo.com

Kieslowski, Krzysztof. 1993. *Kieslowski on Kieslowski*. Translated by Danusia Stok. London and Boston: Faber and Faber.

Magrid, Ron. "Exploring a New Universe." *American Cinematographer*. September 2002.

Manovich, Lev. 1994. "Archeology of the Computer Screen." Wikipedia.

Murray, Scott (ed.). 1980. *The New Australian Cinema*. London: Elm Tree Books.

Paul, David. 1989. "Hungary: The Magyar on the Bridge." In *Post New Wave Cinema in the Soviet Union and Eastern Europe*. Edited by Daniel J. Goulding. Bloomington: Indiana University Press.

Rosenstone, Robert A. (ed.). 1995. *Revisioning History: Film and the Construction of a New Past*. Princeton, N.J.: Princeton University Press.

Sipe, Jeffrey. "Death and Taxes: A Profile of Juzo Itami." In *Sight and Sound*. Summer 1989.

Tarkovsky, Andrei. 1996. *Sculpting in Time: Reflections on the Cinema*. Translated by Kitty Hunter-Blair. Austin: University of Texas Press.

Turaj, Frank. 1989. "Poland: The Cinema of Moral Concern." In *Post New Wave Cinema in the Soviet Union and Eastern Europe*. Edited by Daniel J. Goulding. Bloomington: Indiana University Press.

CHAPTER 27

Contemporary Canadian Filmmakers: 1987–2007

Introduction

In the last decade of the 20st century, Canadian film narratives began demonstrating a new kind of transgressive filmmaking in which adult spectators, like Generation Xers, could pursue different cultural identities through film, video and cybersex activities by following the comings and goings of young and old swingers alike. Despite the ease in finding an imaginary partnership on the screen, the TV monitor or on the internet, each viewer's response to these illusionary tales ignite new expectations for narcissistic pleasures sought by men, women and couples of all ages. The changing sexual dynamics created by most cyberspace fantasies follow the trends set up by a global market economy that includes the illusion of an all too-promising future utopia for everyone and perhaps a dystopia as well.

The breakthrough came in 1987 when Rozema's first feature, *I've Heard the Mermaids Singing,* won the Prix de La Jeunesse at Cannes. The film, and Rozema herself, received tremendous amount of international press attention and *Mermaids* did something almost unheard of for an English-Canadian film — it actually made lots of money at the box office. A number of key films followed in the wake of Rozema's stunning success: Atom Egoyan's *Speaking Parts, The Adjuster* and *Exotica* (which won the International Critic's Prize at Cannes in 1994), Bruce McDonald's *Roadkill* and *Highway 61* and John Greyson's *Zero Patience* (Wise 2004).

But as we enter the 21st century the shifting displacements of human beings have aroused concerns over our own cultural identities and sexual mores. In Canada, many English-speaking citizens appear to define themselves by what they are not — neither British nor American. Their lifestyles in the computer age of simulation also have de-centered their identities, resulting in adoptions of other identities not their own. Most of the confusion arises from models produced by the U.S. film and television industry that continually persuade and inform them as to what identities are deemed "cool" for a person to acquire.

The power of U.S. images to mediate narratives about themselves and others, while advancing new political and economic propaganda, constitute an awareness that Canadian society has entered the postmodern age. Inside this high-tech age people learn to live in an elastic space of multiple forms of identity, ones that are perhaps more personal and even transgressive of traditional models. This movement into other modes of cultural identity clears the way for Canadians to become more narrational, historical and reflexive about their public and personal lives. Moving from the inherited notions of "who I am" into a realization of existing diverse cultural forms require different responses. Thus Canadians recognize the need to make their own connections between the "reality" of the image and the psychological and mythical constructs that are used to represent ourselves to others outside the dominant American culture as promoted by films and television.

In writing about this "postmodern condition," Bill Nichols, a contemporary film critic and art educator, states that poststructural perspectives, "turn away from art, aesthetics, value and man to question texts, codes, effects, and subject positions" (1985, p. 8).

There is an influence of poststructural thought on a variety of contemporary Canadian film narratives which contextualizes a "production of meaning and values, models and standards as aspects of the belief systems that a given social order uses to win the consent of those whose consciousness, identity and desire it regulates" (Nichols 1985, p. 8).

When such poststructural perspectives are applied to film narratives they indicate a series of ruptures in the modernist conception of humanism, its search for ethical models and aesthetic standards, its scientific revolutions, and the Enlightenment which was centered upon the image of rational "man," freed from dogma and intolerance, who was endowed with the mental faculties and capacities to investigate, unravel, and master the mysteries of Nature. The main effect of these varied perspectives has been the de-centering of Cartesian man (Foucault, 1970).

When examining the critical theories of poststructuralism we can discover the relationship between Canadian film narratives and their search for a new cultural identity. I would follow Hollinger (1994) who suggests that the key concepts of politics and community now held by modern Western society "must be re-contextualized in the light of the postmodernist concerns about plurality, otherness and difference" (187). Further, Hollinger states that more inter-disciplinary research would appreciate the insights of literature and the voices of the marginalized by setting aside the assumptions of scientism and modernity found in their dominant discourses.

This approach encourages reflection upon different film narratives whose images convey different ways of depicting cultural identities. Hence, this chapter will focus upon a selection of narrative films made from 1995 to 2001 that reflect the diversity of cultural identities represented within the Canadian landscape. This diversity, in turn, will provide the reader with an interpretative framework to understand "how words, [film] texts and their meanings are constructed to play a pivotal role in race, class, and gender relations as these experiences define what is called the postmodern." In so doing, this study "attempts to connect the worlds of lived experience to the larger textual-cultural systems which create and impose their meanings on everyday life" (Denzin 1993, p. 153).

A new form of radical politics for the 21st Century is emerging from the work of young Canadian film directors. Their film narratives depict a new slant on the traditional forms of filmmaking through a creation of their own "alternative lifestyles" with a gusto and consistency that unites form and content and hence becomes doubly dangerous. It is their conflation of the material world with the "invented" world, between an image and its representation, the real and the imaginary, fact and fiction, language and identity, power and knowledge, self and other, genres and myths that create the new narratives in Canadian films of today. These practices then become the subject matter for many of their films. Canadian filmmakers, working as both writer and director, have developed their own transgressive film narratives in which they dramatize the fragile but volatile human relationships that are being played out within the Canadian landscape.

These Canadian feature films follow a national trend of other film directors in Toronto and Montreal to question or parody the older genres and stereotypes found in Hollywood feature films, ones that set limits or boundaries between socially correct mating rituals and what today's younger generation consider to be boundless and somewhat amoral free-play of characters in search of sexual fulfillment. Many of these films bring into context a sense of contemporary history as the major characters face the trials of growing up in a world where the inherent values of their culture are no longer applicable or are found wanting. Their film narratives avoid the older genre notions of "heroes and victims" to favor aleatory games of chance and accident as each personal narrative questions traditional identities and values founded upon religious ethics, ethnicity, gender and nationality. These forces are put into dramatic conflict within the sexual play of otherness and ambiguity. Themes on cultural identity range from a depiction of contemporary social issues in which men and women revolt against these norms, while women adopt transgressive sexual relations and cross new boundaries, that rupture and split given traditional mores. Young women also seek out fashionable new lifestyles rather than remain attached to traditional or fixed identifications.

The trangressiveness of many new film narratives also capture, in self-reflexive ways, something of "real life" in which social issues are placed in conflict with the politics of a given encounter. Indirectly, the filmmakers focus upon a critique of older cultural concepts that are challenged by the displacement and redefinition of the sexual identities of men and women who desire to explore various sexual games with their mates. Questions of identity continually arise in each film as each character, when encountering new mates or partners, search for a strong and meaningful relationship. They prefer to become more involved in games of chance or risk that have a seriousness of purpose and involve a greater degree of sexual awareness.

Film Theories and Interpretation

Critical theories generated from other fields of cultural study are now finding application in film studies and criticism. From anthropology and linguistics come notions of structuralism and semiotics, tools used critically to analyze the codes and conventions in all film narratives. From political science and psychology, neo–Marxist and neo–Freudian discourses are attempts to explain the ideological content carried within any film discourse. Neo–Marxist inquiries bring out the basic economic determinants in the material exchanges within societies. Feminist critics offer their own discourses on the representation of women in sexual customs, rituals and earlier art forms.

Further, they deconstruct the different kinds of codes and messages produced in film narratives which reinforce the patriarchal system by depicting women as objects of sexual desire for men. Neo–Freudian discourses express the psychological conflicts between gender boundaries, personal identities and cultural conditioning. Lacan's re-reading of Freud in linguistic terms places women and men within language and semiotic readings. It expresses the concept that cinema is a "structured language" system. Films use "regimes of truth," advocated by Foucault, as symbolic representations to reflect historically, the psyche or self, as an imaginary structuring of identities within the social/political realities of a culture.

The Canadian Scene

During the mid–1970s, the most popular English-Canadian film to receive international distribution was Ted Kotcheff's *The Apprenticeship of Duddy Kravitz* (1974), based upon Mordecai Richler's novel. Kotcheff filmed the majority of scenes in Montreal, where he captured the character of the Jewish environment of St. Urbain Street. The story is about a young man who exploits everyone to parlay an investment into a fortune. Unfortunately, his ambitions defeat not only his friends and lovers, but ultimately become his own undoing. Kotcheff continued adaptations of Canadian novels that explored the social conditions of life in Canada. *Why Shoot the Teacher?* (1976), starring Bud Cort, introduced life on the prairies during the harsh Depression days of the 1930s. *First Blood* (1982) brought the Rambo character to the screen as a Vietnam veteran being provoked into acts of revenge.

David Cronenberg (b. 1943) is an English-Canadian director who successfully developed a series of experimental horror films that led to Hollywood feature film productions. *Shivers* (1975), *Rabid* (1977), and *Scanners* (1981) displayed various special effects to illustrate the explosive nature of sexual and emotional frustration. The visual depiction of sadistic-erotic programs that telepathically transmit human sexual fantasies is featured in *Videodrome*

(1983). Genetic programming that biologically transforms an individual is examined in *The Fly* (1986).

These gruesome tales of mutations become the focus of Cronenberg's adaptation of William Burroughs' novel, *Naked Lunch* (1991). In this film, the director transforms the narrative on drug addiction to various forms of sexual dread and madness. Some critics claim these science-fiction fantasies serve as metaphors for patriarchal control of human beings by the medical profession, while others relate them to AIDS or forms of cancerous growths. In *Crash* (1996), based on the J. G. Ballard novel, the director examines the sexual eroticism aroused in relationship to real car crashes. Cronenberg's *eXistenZ* (1999) allows him to use the virtual reality of computer games as an electronic system to stimulate variations in human sexual drives.

Since the beginning of the 21st century, Cronenberg adapted a series of new books about a mental patient trapped by his own acts of schizophrenia in the recollections of past sexual adventures. First, he chose Patrick McGrath's novel *Spider* and used its experimental story line in his film *Spider* (2002). Here the director mixes memory of sexual violence with nightmares of past fantasies.

The adaptation of John Wagner and Vince Locke's graphic novel *A History of Violence* (2005) features a man (Viggo Mortensen) who gains notoriety through his actions to foil a violent robbery attempt in his diner. His actions brings about the recovery of a bloody past that explore questions of his true identity, one that brings about a psycho-sexual drama of a dangerous past.

Cronenberg's third film is the long-awaited gangster thriller *Eastern Promises* (2007). This time he cast again the English actor Viggo Mortensen for the lead role to explore London's criminal underworld.

Atom Egoyan is one of the foremost film directors of the Toronto New Wave of auteur writers and directors who has gained international

Cronenberg's *History of Violence* (2005) revives a diner owner's bloody past and helps him explore questions of his true identity.

attention through the making of two Canadian features films—first *The Sweet Hereafter* (1997) and second, *Felicia's Journey* (1999), based upon William Trevor's novel Both feature films achieved box office success and earned Genie awards in Canada. Egoyan was strongly influenced by Cronenberg's "clinical detachment, expositional minimalism and resolute intellectualism" since they work together at the University of Toronto in the 1980s. What is significant about Egoyan's work is his emphasis on the emotional under-currents that his characters search for during the electronic era. The films both uncover their search for self-fulfillment through final intimacy.

Patricia Rozema is another producer, writer and director who is also a member of the Toronto New Wave. Her first low-budget feature film was *I've Heard the Mermaids Singing* (1987), which displayed her ability to design fairy stories in a sensual visual style which won the Prix de la Jeunesse Award at the Cannes Film Festival. In the next ten years she directed a Canadian production of Jane Austen's *Mansfield Park* (1999) and *Happy Days* (2000), an Irish production based on Samuel Beckett's play about a older woman caught in a mound of dirt. What is unusual about members of the New Wave in Toronto is their avoidance of big money and bigger films to lure them to Hollywood and their choice to stay in Canada and gain international recognition as filmmakers like Cronenberg and Egoyan.

In French-Canadian filmmaking two Montreal directors, Claude Jutra and Denys Arcand, stand out as the most prominent directors of the 1970s. Jutra and Arcand worked as documentary filmmakers for the National Film Board. In the 1970s they initiated a "direct cinema" as a technique to compare two ways of living in Quebec. The political range of their films showed the power relationships that shaped the country. Jutra's *Mon Oncle Antoine* (1971) is an historical reconstruction of life in a small mining village in Quebec during the 1940s. It tells the tale of a young boy's rites of passage with his family. *Kamouraska* (1974) is another historical tale of a young French woman seeking liberty from the demands of her French husband.

Denys Arcand directed *On est au coton* (1970), a documentary on the history of the labor movement in the textile industry and the abuses suffered by the workers. The National Film Board of Canada banned the film from 1971 to 1976 because of the radical political orientation. It details a film crew making a documentary about acts of violence and revenge on a textile worker. Arcand uses this narrative structure in his later films but applied to different topics. *Le Déclin de l'empire américain / The Decline of the American Empire* (1986) and *Jésus de Montréal / Jesus of Montreal* (1989) brought Arcand international acclaim (Pratley 1989, p. 236).

Jesus of Montreal depicts the obstacles a group of young Montreal actors overcome to support themselves. As actors, they are seen easily changing their roles throughout the film. By day, they are hilarious in making soundtracks for pornographic films and beer commercials. At night they transform themselves into biblical figures to enact the Passion of Christ for tourists visiting Mont Royal park. The major conflict in the film involves a reinterpreation of the Passion Play made by the lead actor. He illustrates how present day Church hypocrisy together with modern bureaucracies betray people today in the same way as Christ was betrayed by His own followers.

With *Stardom* (2000), Arcand continued his bitter social satires but this time ventured into the high-stakes arena of the fashion industry and its obsession with the young, the beautiful and the glamorous. When a young girl is given the star treatment and finds herself a celebrity based upon that superstar image, Arcand turns the television cameras and reporters on to her as she indulges herself in this newly acquired allure to marry influential and wealthy men. Soon they regret the media attention as the dark side of her personality begins to affect their own public careers. This is similar to the Robert Altman film on the fashion industry in Paris.

At the beginning of the 21st century, Denis Arcand returned with his portrayal of members of a French-Canadian family caught by the corruption and management of a hospital staff. In *The Barbarian Invasions / Invasions barbares*

In Denys Arcand's *Decline of the American Empire* (1986), in a secluded retreat, four history professors discuss the "sexual revolution" as they pursue carnal pleasures outside their own marriage.

(2003). Arcand focuses on the hospital staff management as members of a family are caught in a sudden life and death situation. Arcand then shows how they can influence the mis-management of this hospital by uncovering the pretensions of the hospital staff as the staff at first refuse to deal with reasons to care for the illnesses of older members of the family. But in a very direct but humorous manner Arcand's film portrays how these characters attempt to escape from some serious politics within this hospital staff. The film won two awards at the Cannes Film Festival in 2003 for best screen-play and for best actor and then an Oscar for Best Foreign Film in 2004, which is an excep-tional achievement of the times.

Another exceptional film writer/director is Deepa Mehta who now resides in Canada where she wrote and directed three films dealing with women who are searching for love and mar-riage in India. Her film *Water* opened the Toronto Film Festival in 2005 after years of

disapproval by religious and political parties against the script in India. Only after finding a location for shooting, a village in Sri Lanka, could she make the film. Thus Mehta was able to complete her trilogy which concerned older women who seek to find love forbidden by their widowhood. *Water* is the third part of her elemental trilogy that starts with *Fire* (1996) and then *Earth* (1998). *Water* is set in pre-in-dependence India and is the powerful story of an eight-year-old child bride who becomes a widow but attempts to remarry after she is sent into a harem, in exile following her husband's death. While the film gained approval in Canada as well as India, Mehta had challenged protests by political Indian members about the problems of being a widow living in India under their strong religious traditions and po-litical codes.

There are other new and important films made during the new century which include films from the following directors: Robert Lep-

Acting out the Passion Play, Lothaire Bluteau plays a Christ figure caught in the evils of modern times, from media hype to the hypocrisy of some Catholic fathers, in Denys Arcand's *Jesus of Montreal* (1989).

age, Zacharias Kunuk, Denis Villeneuve, Gary Burns, and Sylvain Chomet,

Possible Worlds *(2000), directed by Robert Lepage*

This is Lepage's first English-language film that plays upon themes of illusion and reality as they create ambiguity during the unraveling of a murder mystery. In the film, an adaptation of a play by John Mighton, the main character, George, lives simultaneously in a variety of parallel universes. He remains the same, but the universes change as he appears in one and then another and returns to previous ones. The continuity in this strange world is provided by the woman he loves, who herself appears in different roles and identities. This bizarre narrative is framed by an investigation into his murder and the theft of his brain. Part science

fiction, part philosophical treatise, part police drama (the investigating cop is played by Sean McCann), *Possible Worlds* is equally confusing and enthralling.

George's death can be related to a number of existences he lived simultaneously. Thus the crime can be connected to one of these realms, whether it was lived vicariously or not. These parallel universes find George and his wife Joyce living in a small northern town in Quebec. Yet in another world, they are strangers who are having a romantic affair. But then they also exist together in another world where neither knows the another. The examination to determine which world they belonged to becomes a fascinating scientific probe into the meaning of existence and the reflection of this in the daily newspapers. Lepage follows his earlier films that have two or more worlds collide *The Confessional, The Polygraphe* and *No* (Melnyk 2004, p. 207).

Atanarjuat / The Fast Runner (2000), directed by Zacharias Kunuk; script by Paul Angilirq

Based upon an old Inuit legend told to the director by Inuit elders, this film is the first feature film produced in Northern Canada among a remote Aboriginal community. Basically it is a "good versus evil" dramatic rendering of an old folk tale in which Atanarjuat is compelled to defeat his supernatural and natural enemies led by a rival hunter Oki, who vows to win back his promised bride-to-be lost in a ritual fight to Atanarjuat. The film traces the actions of a shaman who put an evil curse on a small group of nomantic Inuit hunters to break their community bonds. Oki's jealousy leads to a war between the two men about who will lead the group and have the rights to the woman. The climax is a thrilling chase between the two hunters as they endure the hardships of a severe Arctic winter (Melnyk 2004, pp. 260 — 261).

Maelstrom (2000), written and directed by Denis Villeneuve

This powerful emotional drama startles the viewer as he witnesses a medical abortion taking place. This is intercut with the decapitation of a huge fish head just as he starts to tell the tale about life and death. The story continues to depict scenes of depression and despair that overcome a woman who accidentally killed a fishmonger with her car. Torn by her own guilt and grief over another death, she is drawn into driving her car into the bay to commit suicide. Fate intervenes to give her another chance. With this in mind, she attempts to right the wrongs she has caused, and ironically falls in love with a person who she saved from another fateful accident (Wise, p. 136).

waydowntown (2000), directed by Gary Burns; screenplay by Gary Burns and James Martin

The city of Calgary lays claim to a downtown cluster of commercial buildings that are interconnected to each other by a maze of glassed-in bridges hanging 15 feet above the street level. This walkway system insures that workers and shoppers alike can escape inclement weather. By imagining what would happen if a person was kept inside this maze for a long period of time, breathing recirculated air, Gary Burns creates a fascinating study of claustrophobia as four young office workers wager a month's salary to the person who can remain inside the longest. After day 24, some of the competitors lose their composure but gain the respect of their co-workers (Melnyk 2004, p. 220).

The Triplets of Belleville (2003), directed by Sylvain Chomet.

Triplets is the first feature-length animation from Sylvain Chomet, who was born in France but now lives in Canada, which may explain his combination of pantomime and whimsy. With only a few lines of dialogue, *Triplets* celebrates the tradition of silent film through animation, the most visual school with the visual medium of cinema. The laconic hero, Champion, is drawn to resemble a cartoon version of Buster Keaton from his movie posters. As a boy Champion never seemed happy until his grandmother, his only family, gave him a tricycle. Now his grandmother trains him constantly for their country's most celebrated national event, the Tour de France (Westhoff 2003).

References

Denzin, Norman K. 1993. *Studies in Symbolic Interaction*. Greenwich,Conn.: Jai Press.

Foucault, Michel. 1970. *The Author Function*. Ithaca, New York: Cornell University Press.

Hollinger, Robert. 1994. *Postmodernism and the Social Sciences*. Thousand Oaks, Calif.: Sage Publications.

Melnyk, George. 2004. *One Hundred Years of Canadian Cinema*. Totonto: University of Toronto Press.

Nichols, Bill. 1985. *Movies And Methods Vol. 2*. Berkeley: University of California Press.

Pratley, Gerald. 1989. "The Eyes of Canada: The National Film Board at Fifty." In *Sight and Sound* 58 (No. 4): 229–236.

Westoff, Jeffrey. 2003. "*Triplets of Belleville* Movie Review." *Northwest Herald* (Crystal Lake, Ill.).

Wise, Wyndham. 2004. *Take One Special Edition* September — November 2004.

CHAPTER 28

Cultural Politics: Contemporary Inquiries into a "War on Terrorism"

As a manifestation of today's information society and its popular culture, film narratives can act as persuasive historical documents to introduce different social and political realities into our educational system. Film narratives also serve us as cultural artifacts, and with other literary and historical texts, are primary sources of learning about the paradoxical conditions of living in a postmodern computerized society. As part of the pedagogical / socializational process in our society, every film narrative lets us play with multiple identities within the imaginative world of cinema. Many areas of our social-political life are continually saturated by such narratives to provide the necessary illusions for the maintenance of a social/political order. There is an analogy, therefore, between film language and identity where meaning arises in the relations of similarities and differences that words and action have with other words and actions within a cultural context.

For this chapter I have chosen Margaretha Von Trotta's film *Marianne and Juliane* (1981), a.k.a. *The German Sisters* as a film narrative to re-enter the spaces between reality and illusion, self and other, and fact and fiction, in an imaginary play of contemporary power politics to reconsider the definition of acts of terrorism. This film narrative is a post-modern translation of Sophocles' play *Antigone* yet is carefully constructed as the fictive life and death of Gundrum Esslin. As a member of the Red Army Faction (RAF), a terrorist group, she was found guilty of committing of "acts of terror" in Germany during the 1970s. The film intermixes the

past and the present to demonstrate the forms of oppressive police tactics necessary to secure a "regime of truth" within a postmodern Western institution. In her film version, von Trotta, as playwright and director, brings into focus three important contemporary discourses relating to the legendary confrontation between civil disobedience and social order. First, she examines the Lacanian formation of identity in the complexities of feminism; then, the impact of such power relations with historical knowledge from a Focaultian viewpoint; and lastly, the concept of empowerment towards a discourse for human rights and a sense of justice as advocated by Paolo Freire and Jacques Derrida.

By targeting the "already always given," this film narrative deconstructs the "regime of truth" existing between the presence/absence of self and Other, between justice and the law.

In entering the spaces of a cinematic world, the viewer is placed within a political struggle between the imaginary and the symbolic. Here the boundaries on identities are firmly set at the beginning of the narrative, but are challenged by a series of metonymic activities that become generative of new possibilities for viewers to locate "the language games" of a repressive logic used by a totalitarian police state. These deconstructions also allow both viewer and educator opportunities to disengage and disrupt the narrative codes, cultural values and ideological goals of rationality.

Introduction

It is a major assumption of this chapter that all film narratives have several basic functions. First, they are a means of symbolizing events that situate the viewer in different space/time perspectives. Second, they also become "experiences of experience," giving expression to different cultural identities or representations of the "Other." However, some film/video narratives provide situational learning experiences in which to develop new ways of seeing the world and new frameworks to understand differences among other cultures in the world. They encourage an open-mindedness toward different value systems other than one's own. Also, they can be interpreted as important ideological weapons for disseminating propaganda by the state for the maintenance and/or subversion of the dominant political order.

Today, the profusion of images produced through film/video/television by a plethora of television channels inform and persuade us about our "imaginary" selves in multiple forms of representation. This new hyper-space world of electronic transmission becomes directly linked to how motion pictures mediate information about the world while advancing discourses about postwar political alliances towards Western globalization. In television, every broadcast makes a connection between the "reality" of the image and the cultural constructs operating within any given society. Therefore, each narrative contains within its illusionistic framework a cultural power to mediate reality based upon actual historical happenings or events. The purpose of this chapter is to analyze one recent film narrative, *Marianne and Juliane*, to study how a Western democracy reacted to the political actions of a terrorist gang taking state officials hostage.

When asked why some people believe in the power of cinema, the producer in Peter Weir's, *The Truman Show* (1998) responded, "We accept the reality of the world as it is presented to us. It is as simple as that." The implication of this cinematic situation hopefully forces the viewer/spectator to realize that illusions are part of our reality. This becomes the political condition of our lives, as Bertolt Brecht, the German playwright and essayist, declared during the 1920s (Wright 1989, p. 21).

Cultural Politics and Representation of Women

As part of the new historicism of today a new mode of cultural politics has emerged which is grounded in the belief that "history" is not a set of fixed and unchangeable objective facts but is, like literature, a text that interacts and re-presents "reality" as "ideological products" or "cultural constructs" of a particular time and place. Thus, contemporary film narratives, based upon historical events, require analytical study both as seeming to be a representation and reflection of a "reality," and as a cinematic construct by filmmakers, in most cases serving as a personalized political text about society consciously re-formed into a powerful narrative discourse.

By gaining an awareness of the cinematic structures and genres used by most filmmakers, educators can gain a new understanding of several key concepts such as culture, ideology, ethics and aesthetics, as filmmakers re-present and re-interpret events and people in their film narratives. Educations then can question why film directors choose particular myths or stories to recount and contest "the already given" in a postmodern society. Moreover, they can interrogate these meta-narratives of the past as representations of "historical truths." Thus, while adhering to a chronology of time, today's postmodern films engage the viewer with a fusion of the past and the present by reconstructing the ways memory and imagination can validate their own narrative films. This revisioning of the past into the present becomes a significant strategy for today's political feminists like Sunera Thobani, a UBC professor of sociology, whose speech to a women's conference on the subject of violence against women generated much public controversy in news reports, including vicious personal attacks upon her. In brief, she said in rebuttal, "In the aftermath of the terrible attacks of September 11 [destroying the World Trade Center towers in New York City], I argued that the U.S. response of launching 'America's new war' would increase violence against women."

Part of the learning process with respect to political speeches and pedagogical practices requires an identification of the social/political discourses in which the formative ideological frameworks are placed to characterize the power/knowledge structures representing both aspects of Western society. This is also applicable to institutions of learning or schools which are structured as one of the major mechanism for the transmission and reproduction of the dominant culture. In the 1980s, schools were challenged as cultural and political sites that disregarded the relation between the knowledge/power nexus and domination. Like film narratives, schools are politically structured as agencies for cultural propagation and reproduction. The reason radical educational critics and feminists as well have sought to raise questions regarding the curriculum was to "unmask" the hidden ideological constructs operating within the schools and to reflect upon the assumption that most "cultural constructs" operate in Western society as a way of assigning meaning to pre-determined social/political discourses over time. As stated by Bill Nichols, "Ideology uses the fabrications of images and the processes of representation to persuade us that how things are is how they ought to be and that the place provided for us is the place we ought to have" (Nichols 1981, p. 1).

Thus, educational critics such as Henry Giroux and Peter McLaren (1989) have struggled on how to deconstruct the logic of traditional pedagogy found in different school sites. As Giroux states, "Far from being neutral, the dominant culture of the school was characterized by a selective ordering and legitimating of privileged language forms, modes of reasoning, social relations and lived experiences. In this view, culture was linked to power and to the imposition of a specific set of ruling-class codes and experiences" (p. 129). But not until these same radical pedagogues were concerned with acting as "transformative intellectuals" were they able "to help students acquire critical knowledge about the basic societal structures, such as the economy, the state, the workplace and mass culture, so that such institutions

could be open to potential transformation" (Giroux and McLaren 1989, pp. 138–139).

This new position, which carried both political and moral authority, was accomplished at the beginning of the 1990s. For some, it indicated that as transformative teachers, they had "to be concerned about issues of social justice and political action" (p. 139). The pedagogical rationale behind this new position was a notion of a "commitment grounded in an affirmative view of liberation which acknowledges that the notion of 'truth' does not reside in abstract definitions of principle, but is, in part, the outcome of particular power struggles that cannot be removed from either history or existing networks of social and political control" (p. 139). Thus the stage was set for them to test their beliefs in a deconstructive analysis, one that recognized how their own perspectives could also be "both challenged and transformed." Their own pedagogical practices thus would be critiqued in a manner similar to judges who are required to re-interpret the law in each situation with respect to the liberating notion of justice, since "justice is the relation to the other" (Derrida, cited in Caputo, 1997, p. 17). Yet would their own recognition of schooling as a form of cultural politics cultivate a "reality" that would be productive of greater knowledge, understanding and life-supporting values? Here, the postmodern condition of our times promotes critiques on modernism, offering alternate definitions on the role of intertextuality in all cultural constructs. In any deconstruction of them, it discloses not only the dominant ideology but also the subversive forces at play in such texts. This dramatic relationship is clearly demonstrated in film narratives that are in conflict with the dominant politics and ideology. These films attempt to uncover the power struggles arising between cultural groups that play a role in molding contemporary society.

In philosophical terms, the key discourses of postmodernism examine concepts on the relationship of knowledge to power (Foucault), interpretations of subjectivity (Lacan) and empowerment towards a liberatory discourse in education (Freire) as well as a rethinking of Marxist models of society (Jameson). In all of these discourses, reason, objectivity and certainty are displaced by a focus on "regimes of truth," a deconstruction of the binary, linear logic of Western rationality (Derrida) and a foregrounding of ambiguity, plurality and contingency.

Further, people diverse as Wittgenstein, Kuhn and Foucault argue that objects of knowledge are locally and historically specific, and that they become available for human understanding only within certain "language games," "paradigm shifts," and "discursive formations." From these different positions, postmodernist texts contain multiple histories that attempt to "distance" and "estrange" the reader from the illusions of a humanistic idealism based upon modern Western thought. In doing so, these texts search for the "discontinuities, breaks, and ruptures" between the past and the present. The sense of repositioning our subjectivities suggests that our identities, beliefs and practices are culturally 'contingent' upon the construction of paradigms or models, subject to revisions or paradigm shifts, but not connected to any historical determinism. Foucault calls these measures part of a "disciplinary society" where all future conflicts appear already won in advance by this Western society since the exercise of power and the forces policing this power are no longer visible. They are now hidden, diversified and strong enough to avoid battle.

Henry Giroux reiterates this argument in his powerful foreword to David Trend's text *Cultural Pedagogy: Art / Education/Politics* (1992). Giroux states that "the new work on pedagogy ... as a form of political and cultural production is deeply implicated in the construction of knowledge, subject-ivities and social relations" (p. vii). While computer information systems enhance electronic transmissions of knowledge and skills, the older concepts of pedagogy are shifting away from the transmission of information to encounter a form of cultural politics. For Giroux, the practice of the new pedagogy begins in the production and representation of meaning through "the link between education and cultural work ... in the light of recent developments in feminism, cultural studies, post colonialism, deconstruction and the new historicism" (p. vii).

Such pedagogical shifts toward a new cultural politics are central to film narratives when they serve as sources of history in relationship to the postmodern reforms in pedagogy. By implicating the cinematic representation of subversive discourses educators can approach contemporary concerns illustrating the relation of the "self" to "other" in the dynamics of Western hegemonic thought. Some film narratives of the late 1970s and 1980s, now broadcast over television, are international in scope, ranging from Coppola's *Apocalypse Now*, (1979), Fassbinder's *Ali: Fear Enters the Soul* (1972), Bertolucci's *The Conformist* (1970), David Lynch's *Elephant Man* (1980), Antonioni's *The Passenger* (1975), von Trotta's *Marianne and Juliane* (1982), and Kurosawa's *The Shadow Warrior / Kagemusha* (1980).

In the 1990s, Hollywood produced a number of films that attempted to deconstruct the power of cinema to "construct a reality" for viewers. First on the scene was Lawrence McTiernan's *Last Action Hero* (1993) starring Arnold Schwarzenegger, playing a superhero who willing deconstructs his own film persona. Then James Cameron's *True Lies* (1994), also starring Arnold, in a Bond-like action-adventure that deconstucts the hero when the narrative doubles as a romantic comedy. *The Truman Show* (1998), directed by Peter Weir, attempts to convince the viewer that a television show can house a real-life community. Director Barry Levinson's *Wag the Dog* (1997) satirizes the powers in the White House who resort to television replays to create a bogus war with Albania to divert media attention from a serious presidential indiscretion with a young woman.

In a more serious framework, von Trotta's *Marianne and Juliane* depicts the personal struggle of two sisters fighting against the actions of the secret police in West Germany as they combat the unknown terrorist actions of bombings and hostage taking. While this film is based upon the real-life terrorist acts of the Baader-Meinhof Group the director only hints at those historical events to construct this personal memoir of two German sisters. Questions arising from the analysis of such a film narrative are as follows: What political power informs such "terrorist actions" both by the state and by the insurgent terrorist agents within this narrative? How believable are the causes of these actions in relationship to the rise of Western democracies? How is justice served by such cultural representations? Further, how do such personal cinematic depictions deconstruct the political justice system and foreshadow future political actions that would implicate education?

Germany in Autumn *(1978)*: *An Omnibus Film*

The political situation in West Germany was severely shaken by the constant rise of urban terrorism during the early 1970s led by the Red Army faction known as the Baader–Meinhof gang. In April of 1975, this group invaded the West German embassy in Stockholm and took a number of German diplomats as hostages. They demanded the release of their leaders, Baader and Meinhof, who were already imprisoned, but they were denied. Two of the hostages were then killed before the German police captured the remaining gang members. After the trial, the two gang leaders were found guilty. The German police claimed they then committed suicide in prison.

In reaction to the violence and political motives of this small group of terrorists, the Federal Republic instituted legislation to place restrictions on the liberties of all citizens. Like the Canadian War Measures Act, they sought to protect the public and to insure that such terrorist acts would be stopped since it posed a serious threat to civil law and order. By claiming that terrorists were jeopardizing the civil liberties of other citizens, the government created a political atmosphere where they curtailed the freedoms of citizens by using military tactics to impose a neo-fascist state.

In response to the cultural politics of this specific situation, a group of leading German filmmakers, including Werner Fassbinder, Volker Schlöndorff, and Alexander Kluge assembled several short documentaries and interwove them with fictional narratives to protest the government's strict laws in reac-

tions to terrorism. Under the leadership of Kluge, who used voice-over narration to tie the film together, the filmmakers compared the government's police state taken to combat terrorism as similar in many ways to the Nazi past and its military mentality.

The final sequence of the film, written by Heinrich Böll and directed by Schlöndorff, concerns the refusal by a West German television programming committee to broadcast a production of Sophocles' *Antigone*. As a satire, the ban reveals their fears of being considered as sympathizers for pro-terrorists. Further, the suicides of Haemon and Antigone in the play are all too similar to the actual suicides of members of the Baader–Meinhof gang whose bombings, killings and kidnappings openly defied the authority of the state. The implications of censorship and political correctness comes to the fore. In its own way, *Germany in Autumn*, with Kluge's ironic commentary on the search for justice in the present based upon the past, achieves its goal by using the Brechtian device of "distanciation" to produce a critical awareness in the audience of the current situation (Sandford 1981, p. 148).

Foucault's Theatre of Discipline and Surveillance.

However, the "great, tragic theater" of the past no longer survives. As Foucault describes in *Discipline and Punish* (1978), the theater of public torture and execution allowed the public to act as participants in the public ritual where the execution could be resisted and possibly reversed. Foucault states that this public theater where power is seen face-to-face has been displaced by the theater of discipline and surveillance. Now, any intervention of the public is neutralized and, like watching the event unfold on the TV screen, the public are only spectators to the interrogations, and are silenced by being kept in their own place. Contact in a public space is now broken. All that remains in the theater of surveillance and discipline are "thousands of tiny theaters of punishment" (Foucault 1977, p. 113) that provide for a regulating form of interrogation to produce "docile bodies." Power and authority remain invisible, masked by various discourses in education, knowledge, humanist ideology, judicial reform, etc., as is the case with different TV programs on law and order. This is "serious theater with its multiple and persuasive scenes" which is more absolute and is all more successful against public outrage.

Foucault addresses the different effects created by discourses on the power/ knowledge nexus. Foucault claims a new type of power and control came into existence in Europe at the end of the 19th century that he designates as "disciplinary power." It is concerned with the regulation and surveillance of the human species and the governance of the individual and the body. It is sited in the new institutions of the modern world, from schools and hospitals to workshops and prisons, infiltrating and shaping what is said and done. Its purpose is to produce human beings as "docile bodies" through the power of administrative regimes and the expertise of the professional (Hall 1994, p. 123).

By employing Foucault's writing of history or "genealogy," von Trotta's film *Marianne and Juliane* illustrates the mixture of the past with the present, from the rise of fascism in Germany in the 1930s, to the wartime atrocities of the Nazis, followed by the postwar terrorism of the 1970s. In this manner, the director carefully demonstrates how a "disciplinary regime ... brought individuality into the field of observation through a vast meticulous documentary apparatus" (Dreyfus and Rabinow 1982, p. 122).

Marianne and Juliane *(1982)*

Von Trotta's *Marianne and Juliane* is a fictional narrative that dramatizes the public and personal rebellion of two German sisters caught in the turmoil of the post-war West German state of the 1970s. The film was inspired by the real life and death story of Gundrun Ensslin, a

In Margarethe von Trotta's **Marianne and Juliane** (1981), two sisters meet with a friend to discuss the uses of terrorist action against the state.

Marianne, the Baader-Meinhof terrorist, confronts her journalist sister on the loss of freedom in prison.

member of the German Baader–Meinhof terrorist group. However, Von Trotta's film articulates the emotional bond experienced by two sisters when one, Marianne, is incarcerated by the police and dies in prison.

Throughout this film, the historical developments are analyzed and understood from the point of view of the older sister, Juliane, who attends to the needs of her younger sister, Marianne. The younger sister is shown learning her newly honed terrorist tactics to provoke her debate on the "regimes of truth." These "truths" mask the totalitarian state as an excuse to destroy terrorism. In her attacks upon the state's surveillance policies, Marianne demonstrates how "rituals of power" are brought into the public space in order to counteract and deconstruct the binary logic of Western rationality. Her terrorist activities thus become symbolic forms of retribution to combat the repressive acts of this neo-conservative post-war German government and their implementation of Draconian laws. In the film, however, these terrorist attacks are not depicted. Paradoxically, what is depicted

throughout this narrative is the way such "disciplinary powers" of a police state operate on the body of the "self," upon Marianne. Here, Von Trotta reveals, in many ways, the disguises worn by the police, whose punitive actions against the sisters are legitimized by the authority of the state and its martial laws.

Most of the film is a reconstruction of the rebellious natures of the two sisters; Juliane, as the older sister, plays the role of journalist/reporter for a small anti-abortionist newspaper. Marianne, as the younger rebel, disowns her marital role as mother and adopts a new identity by becoming a member of the El Fath terrorist group. She learns to place bombs in public places to demonstrate how terrorist tactics can disrupt and destroy Western institutions in the play of power politics.

In particular, Von Trotta's *Marianne and Juliane* is important since it takes a classical Greek tragedy, Sophocles' *Antigone*, and reshapes it into a postmodern film interpretation of this dramatic conflict. Here, however, in her retelling of the story, the central conflict emerges between the political tactics of an "urban terrorist" against the hidden powers of a police state. Unlike the Sophoclean play, in which there are two central characters, Antigone and Creon, caught within a tragic vision, von Trotta's film becomes, in part, a narrative on the knowledge/power nexus in relation to the imposition of the law against the rise of terrorism in Germany. Moreover, the film also presents a powerful feminist critique on the struggle for justice by women caught in a dominant patriarchal society.

More in keeping with Sophoclean tragedy, in which the situation illuminates the tragedy of Creon rather than the passionate death of the heroine, von Trotta's dramatization of a local and historically specific series of events shows the effects of unreasonable power on the body of its female victim in episode after episode, and declines to represent the powerful leaders that inflict such punishment upon her crime. The film narrative doubles then both as a critique on the roles played by women represented in a film narrative and on the surveillance and identification of a subversive group of people in relationship to a growing resistance to the postwar policies of the new West German government and its disciplinary society. The major issue, as in *Antigone*, is the question of justice, with deference and regard towards imposed martial law, in affording the rights of human beings to receive a public burial regardless whether or not they are deemed enemies of the state.

The film is designed in a Brechtian fashion using episodic flashbacks to bring the past into close examination with the present. Most of these flashbacks reveal the psychological traumas experienced by the two sisters when, as high school students, they first learned about past Nazi terror and violence through viewing a Alain Resnais documentary film (*Night and Fog*, 1956) on the Holocaust. Further, their father is a Lutheran pastor whose weekly sermons always portray the wrath of God. His home prominently displays Gruenwald's painting of the bloody crucifixion of Christ, with its stoic images of Mary and John confronting the cruelty of Christ's agony on the cross. These images run through the narrative as a comparison to the horrors faced by Marianne after she is captured by the police. Over a long period of time Marianne undergoes a series of tortures and dehumanizing experiences that end in her death, apparently by suicide.

Within this political situation and the pending trial, von Trotta concentrates the major portion of the film on the ways Juliane attempts to protect and defend her sister, Marianne, against the pervasive influence of the police authorities as well as the public. Throughout the narrative, each sister exchanges their mental identities with the other, and Juliane, who opposes the role of motherhood, adopts Marianne's son, Jan, and serves as his surrogate mother in the end. Yet, ironically, this ending reminds the viewer that Juliane is the narrator of the film. In response to Jan's tearing up his mother's photograph, Juliane decides to tell the young boy about his mother "all that I know, but it is not everything." This ending brings us full circle to the opening sequence when we are introduced to Juliane and Jan.

Thus, the entire film then becomes the personal recollections by Juliane of the events that brought imprisonment, suffering and death to her sister, Marianne, at the hands of German prison officials.

Feminism and the Patriarchal Society

Into this narrative von Trotta's film brings two important approaches to a political movement called Feminism as part in the cultural politics of the time. On the one hand, feminism is regarded mainly as an Anglo–American perspective attempting to recover and reevaluate literary works by women as subjects of a minority culture. Within this critical perspective, the major goal is to seek out the discontinuities within the film narrative that challenge the patriarchal culture of a society that defines "woman" by the maternal roles she should play. On the other hand, a more aggressive French perspective focuses on Lacanian psychoanalysis, the unconscious, and the symbolic role language plays to de-center the sociological subject of woman (Fowler 1973, p. 92). Basing her critiques upon Lacanian psychoanalysis and

Derridean deconstruction, Julia Kristeva provides critiques of the patriarchal society by unmasking the means through which linguistic strategies form and produce the feminine as a gendered subject. One aspect of her feminist readings uncover how cultural politics process the identity and subjectivity of men/women, sons/daughters, and mothers/fathers. The importance of an independent, imagined self is registered as a political challenge in these life histories. Film narratives like *Marianne and Juliane* thus becomes a retelling/telling of self and other as they seek to subvert patriarchal authority. Instead of being reduced to silent acceptance of societal roles, the women depicted in this film seek a place for the "melancholic imagination." The term "melancholic imagination" comes from Kristeva's psychoanalytical exploration of a subject's affective experience of loss or despair. As a disciple of Lacan, she echoes Lacan's point about the signifier-signified as a distinction between the semiotic and the symbolic. Lacan claimed that the signifier preceded all verbal representations. Kristeva uses the term semiotic to understand the mental representations of the senses as they are informed by the primary Freudian processes of unconscious displacement and condensation. To this notion, she identifies the semiotic with the material, maternal body or *khora*: "the psychic receptacle — archaic, mobile, unstable, prior to the One, to the father." Like a "floating signifier" it cannot be defined in the language system since it is a desire proceeding from a need or "lack" within a person. Kristeva equates the symbolic with language formation — or the signifier — and with the paternal hegemony of grammar, syntax, and the law (Kristeva, cited in Silverman and Welton,1991, pp. 22–23). Like Lacan, Kristeva reveals that the "subject" of a discourse becomes a "split subject," a woman (Marianne/Juliane) divided but also a woman belonging both to the semiotic khora as well as to the symbolic order. Thus her reaction to a loss and despair created by this melancholic imagination in which a desire of the "self" attempts to unite with the Other.

I place *Marianne and Juliane* within this French perspective. In many ways, the role of Juliane is both one who seeks justice in terms of deconstructing the law that brought about her sister's death and it is Juliane who acts as a seeker for the place of the khora as she gathers information on the death of her sister to illustrate the repressive patriarchic system and its effects upon women. In both instances the call for justice and the khora gives Juliane "the impulse, the drive and the movement to improve the law, that is, to deconstruct the law" (Derrida, cited in Caputo 1997, p. 16). Juliane becomes the storyteller for von Trotta as she attempts to expose the audience to the conditions that brings about revolution, ethics, and morality into a cultural politics, and that deconstructs the identity and subjectivity of women. Von Trotta's film serves as a cultural text of a postmodern society to show that the "condition of possibility of deconstruction is a call for justice" (p. 16). Thus, as part of a historical and pedagogical discourse, the film illustrates the tragic, political struggles of women caught within an oppressive patriarchal system.

References

Buñuel, L. " Cinema: An Instrument of Poetry." *Theatre Arts*, July 1962.

Caputo, J. H. 1997. *Deconstruction in a Nutshell: A Conversation with Jacques Derrida*. New York: Fordham University Press

Dreyfus, H. and Rabinow, P. 1982. *Michel Foucault: Beyond Structuralism and Hermeneutics*. Brighton, Sussex: The

Harvester Press.

Foucault, M. 1977. *Discipline and Punish: The Birth of the Prison*. Translated by Alan Sheridan. New York: Pantheon.

Fowler, R., Ed. 1973. *A Dictionary of Modern Critical Terms*. London: Routledge & Kegan Paul. Revised 1990, 1991.

Giroux, H.A., and McLaren, P., Eds. 1989. *Critical Pedagogy, the State, and Cultural struggle*. Albany: State University of New York Press.

Hall, S. 1994. "The question of cultural identity." In J. Rutherford, Ed., *Identity: Community, Culture Difference*. London: Lawrence & Wishart.

Nichols, B. 1981. *Ideology and the Image*. Bloomington: Indiana University Press.

Sandford, J. 1980. *The New German Cinema*. New York: DaCapo Press.

Silverman, H. and Welton, D., Eds. 1988. *Post-Modernism and Continental Philosophy*. Albany: State University of New York Press.

Trend, D. 1992. *Cultural Pedagogy: Art/Education/Politics*. New York, London: Bergin & Co.

Wright, Garvey E. 1989. *Postmodern Brecht*. London: Routledge.

Index

355